PUBLIC CITIZEN

THE SENTINEL
OF DEMOCRACY

PUBLIC**CITIZEN**

CONTENTS

Preface: The Biggest Get 7

Introduction..11

1 Nader's Raiders for the Lost Democracy 15

2 Tools for Attack on All Fronts....................................29

3 Creating a Healthy Democracy....................................43

4 Seeking Justice, Setting Precedents............................... 61

5 The Race for Auto Safety 89

6 Money and Politics: Making Government Accountable..............113

7 Citizen Safeguards Under Siege: Regulatory Backlash 155

8 The Phony "Lawsuit Crisis" 173

9 Saving Your Energy 197

10 Going Global 231

11 The Fifth Branch of Government................................. 261

Appendix..271

Acknowledgments..289

THE BIGGEST GET

NINETEEN SIXTY-EIGHT WAS the first full year of my television talk show, a visually dull hour-long interview program featuring a guest who had something important to say and was willing to confront the often-surprising questions from faceless telephone callers and the uncensored commentary of a studio audience. We were competing with game shows. Our local TV experiment in Dayton, Ohio, featured the not very animated video of two talking heads, while on the other channel, "Let's Make A Deal" was giving away $5,000 to a very animated woman dressed like a chicken salad sandwich. What chance, in the late sixties, did this ho-hum TV show have?

The "Phil Donahue Show" featured no band, no announcer who laughed at all my jokes, no famous movie stars; this was Dayton after all. All WLWD (our station) had to offer was a young team of ambitious producers filled with the passion of revolutionaries and too inexperienced to understand the size of the challenge.

With an absence of fear owing to our youth, we charged forward with the only thing we had: issues. This was 1967; the women's movement was brewing. The nation, already reeling from the killing of the president, was about to witness the assassinations of Martin Luther King, Jr. and Robert Kennedy. In August 1968, the whole world was watching as the cops beat up kids outside the Democratic Party convention in Chicago.

Guests I coveted were not breathless to fly to Dayton to appear on a local talk show. One of my earliest longed-for guests was a young lawyer from Washington, D.C., who had swept onto America's front pages less like a storm than a tsunami. His well-researched, detailed book condemning General Motor's Corvair as "Unsafe At Any Speed" had so angered the largest manufacturing company in the world that the wounded corporation committed its lawyers and a bottomless public relations budget to the task of destroying the young crusader whose book was destroying sales of their beloved rear-engine car.

By 1968, Ralph Nader was appearing on coast-to-coast TV, but not the "Phil Donahue Show." I can still hear the phone voice of Ralph's secretary, "Phil who?"

I was totally awed by Ralph's no-notes grasp of detail and no-pause answers to every question that came his way from cynical reporters. He knew the math of the Corvair's high center of gravity and the car's differential, the physics of the rear-engine placement as well as the thermal dynamics of the car's gas tank. This was the guest I wanted to have.

Then I learned that Ralph was appearing in Cincinnati. I drove the 60 miles to the city's airport, located across the Ohio River in northern Kentucky. This being prehistoric times, I left my car unattended at the curb (no Transportation Security Administration) and walked directly to the arrival gate and through the exit door out onto the tarmac as the aircraft came to a stop near the rollaway stairs. I positioned myself at the bottom step, clinging to my no-proof faith that he would say, "You came all the way from Dayton to meet me? How can I say *no*?"

The plane's passenger door opened and down the stairs came my gangly hero, schlepping a bulging briefcase and adorned in an ill-fitting dark blue suit, a skinny tie and shoes he'd been wearing since his junior year in high school.

With my hand extended, I said, "Hi Ralph, I'm Phil Donahue." He looked surprised. "You came all the way from Dayton to meet me? How can I say *no*?"

I drove to the Dayton Inn Hotel with my prized passenger in the right-front seat of my 1959 Chevy. When I finally got to sleep that night over my excitement, I dreamed I had killed Ralph Nader. I had an accident and my car had no seat belts.

The next day, March 27, 1968, Ralph Nader made his first appearance on my television show. He spoke of the danger of the second collision. The collision of unbuckled bodies rattling around the inside of the car like eggs in a crate bouncing off a steering column that did not collapse, protruding knobs on an unpadded dashboard and doors that fly open, ejecting passengers to almost certain death. A small audience of housewives never took their eyes off the young lawyer. A friendship was born between the local Dayton TV host and the single most important consumer advocate in the history of consumption.

Throughout the 29-year history of my program, we produced almost 5,000 shows. Public Citizen became a major resource for the young show producers outside my office door. Public Citizen experts are the GET people. A GET is the sought-after guest that all the shows wanted. Ralph was my best GET, followed by more great GETS from the busy organizations founded by Ralph. Dr. Sidney Wolfe, who headed Public Citizen's Health Research Group, came to our program and cautioned women against allowing their ob-gyn to pat them on the head, patronize them and thrust an illegible prescription in their hand. "You have a right to know the side effects of drugs, the ingredients and how they work." It wasn't long before women all over America were asking their doctors questions and demanding information.

Dr. Wolfe's health group published a book titled *Worst Pill, Best Pills,* a detailed alphabetized reference of hundreds of pharmaceutical products that help, hurt or do nothing at all. I held the book up and displayed the address at which viewers could order this valuable assembly of important information for $10. The resulting orders turned Public Citizen and the office of the "Donahue" show upside down. About half a million dollars flooded in for the next several weeks and from subsequent programs. The money enabled Public Citizen to buy a building near Dupont Circle in Washington, D.C., which has served as its headquarters for 22 years.

Joan Claybrook served Public Citizen as the most tenacious nonprofit CEO I have ever known. She is as fearless as Ralph and has stiff-armed her share of white-collar grandees from the government, the insurance industry, Wall Street, the law and many One Percenters. Joan has also been a valuable resource in helping our show producers get the GETS that kept us on the air for so many years. Open this fabulous book to any page and you will find a "Donahue" show.

And now Robert Weissman, the new president of Public Citizen, is at the helm of this singular organization. Long before the U.S. Supreme Court decision in *Citizens United,* Public Citizen was the modern-day version of the little Dutch boy who saved Holland with his finger in the dyke. It remains to be seen how much help Naderites get as they struggle to hold the constitutional dam against the rising tide of money surging toward Congress. Robert is leading the charge on this and many other important fights.

It has been 47 years since I stood in an unguarded area of the Cincinnati airport greeting Ralph Nader. For me, that moment began a lifelong tutorial on justice, power, democracy and the never-ending need for vigilant oversight of all three. I read this book and learned all over again why oversight can come only from a populace informed by a free press beholden to no corporate interests and aided by the Freedom of Information Act.

For me, this book is another reminder of how the handshake I made with Ralph in 1968 in a no-trespassing zone of the Cincinnati airport led to countless "Donahue" programs that made our Constitution come alive for millions of Americans. A handshake that led to the biggest GET of my life — and the biggest GET for the American public.

—*Phil Donahue*

INTRODUCTION

——

GLANCING AT HIS WATCH, the young attorney strode through Washington, D.C.'s National Airport, a man in a hurry. He had 10 minutes to spare before flying to Hartford, Connecticut, where more than a thousand people were waiting in the square to hear him speak at a noon civic rally.

Standing in line at the Allegheny Airlines desk, he recognized the person in front of him as a senior aide to a U.S. senator. He overheard the aide being told the flight was full, that no more passengers could board, that the only way to make it to Hartford that day was to take another flight via Philadelphia.

The aide, John Koskinen (later President Barack Obama's head of the Internal Revenue Service) shrugged and accepted the alternative arrangement. The attorney did not. He told the airline official he had not paid for a ticket only to take a long detour that would make him miss the rally.

"Go speak to the guy in the purple coat," said the airline official, pointing to a man standing a few yards away. The man in the purple coat said the same thing, that all the seats were taken, that the alternative flight was the only option.

"This is going to take a lot of your time and a lot of your company's time," warned the attorney. "You're going to regret this."

"Sorry," the man said. "We're full. Door's closed."

The attorney headed straight for a pay phone and called a colleague, Reuben Robinson. "I can't believe what's just happened," he shouted angrily into the receiver. "A contract doesn't mean a thing anymore."

Unfortunately for Allegheny Airlines, the attorney was Ralph Nader.

A year earlier, in 1971, Nader had established the consumer advocacy group Public Citizen to fight for consumers whose rights were being trampled by powerful corporations and government agencies. The Allegheny policy was just one example among thousands of the corporate arrogance and indifference toward consumers that were then ingrained in the American marketplace.

The bumping policy became the first of many battlegrounds for Public Citizen. Its lawyers ended up taking a lawsuit against Allegheny all the way to the U.S. Supreme Court — and winning, unanimously.

———

A modern prophet of the consumer movement, Ralph Nader has always regarded an active, politically informed public as the key to guarding democracy. He has brandished a standard that was first held aloft by such citizen leaders as Thomas Jefferson, who warned against the rise of "banking institutions and moneyed incorporations" that threatened to destroy the freedoms won in the American Revolution. These special interests, warned Jefferson, would establish a "single and splendid government of an aristocracy." From its first days, Public Citizen followed that standard to achieve landmark changes in the American way of doing business.

Nader's boyhood heroes were muckrakers such as Lincoln Steffens, Upton Sinclair and George Seldes. "I would read them trembling with excitement, literally," he recalled. "It was so natural to me."

Like millions of other adolescent boys, Nader enjoyed reading the Hardy Boys mysteries. He listened to the New York Yankees on the radio and played sandlot baseball with his friends. But what gripped him the most were the exposés. "They were like detective books."

Although energized by tales of fights against corruption, the young Nader didn't want to be another writer. Even as a young boy growing up in the small town of Winsted, Connecticut, this son of Lebanese immigrants saw himself as a crusading lawyer. The county courthouse was a block from his father's restaurant, and the young Nader would listen to jurors and attorneys when they came in to eat lunch. Other times, he would go to the courthouse to watch the action. "I grew up identifying lawyers as fighters against injustice."

By the time Nader reached his 30s, he had become a lawyer working to shield citizens from the ravages of unbridled — and largely unregulated — corporate power. Degrees from Princeton University and Harvard Law School, a short spell as an Army cook, and several years of practicing law and traveling the world as a freelance journalist had afforded Nader a rich combination of academic and real-world experience. When he took on Allegheny, he had been in Washington, D.C., for eight years and was already a formidable policy lobbyist and a nationally celebrated consumer champion.

The airlines' practice of bumping people from flights was just one small way that large companies abused their customers. Allegheny was not the only airline that routinely overbooked its planes on the assumption that some people wouldn't show up for their flights. Every year, tens of thousands of travelers were bumped from flights because of what the airlines called "space planning" — 82,000 in 1972 alone.[1] During a deposition for Nader's case against the airline, Allegheny's chief executive admitted that his company deliberately bumped people and routinely overbooked planes.

Eventually, the Supreme Court ruled in Nader's favor. The court wrote in its June 7, 1976, decision that a passenger who had bought a ticket but was denied a seat could go to court to get damages for fraudulent misrepresentation by an airline that failed to give notice of its overbooking practices. The case led to the current system where airline passengers are compensated for staying behind. "Now it works beautifully," Nader explained. "They ask people to give up their seats. And for that, you get compensation. Now those who need to get on the flight can do so."

The case also demonstrated a fundamental belief of Nader's. "I proved that one rebuffed passenger can make a difference," he said.

The idea that one person can make a difference had resonance in the early 1970s. Challenging established authority was nothing new for young and politically active people in those days. Campuses and communities bristled with activists campaigning against the Vietnam War and for civil rights, women's rights and environmental preservation. But winning was relatively novel. And the summons to struggle for consumer rights was a different kind of clarion call.

Robert Fellmeth was in his early 20s when he went to work in Washington, D.C. "At the time, people were kind of divided into two groups—the hippies who wanted to drop out, and the activists," he said. "But the activists were very revolutionary. They thought capitalism was essentially corrupt, and they had a Walter Mitty view of revolution." Nader had a deep critique of the corporate-dominated economy but had in mind practical measures to make it work better for everyday people.

Fellmeth, like others, found an outlet for his political energy in Nader's consumer movement. "The reason some of us were so angry was because we were lied to. We'd been given ninth-grade civics. We were given the democratic model as something to respect, and we did respect it. We bought it, but we found out it was a lie. We found out what money was doing. And we got angry. Some responded by wanting to tear it down, but we said, *'Damn it, we want what we were promised. We want that democratic system!'"*

For nearly two generations now, Public Citizen's mission has been to make that system—our economic system and our democratic institutions—work for all Americans, not just for corporate or government elites. Public Citizen has battled for patients who are prescribed dangerous drugs, workers exposed to toxic chemicals, motorists with unsafe and defective vehicles, voters with corrupt representatives, citizens exploited by colluding energy companies, consumers injured by unsafe products and journalists trying to unearth government secrets, incompetence and malfeasance.

Through the awakening of the consumer movement and the struggle for health, safety and environmental safeguards in the 1960s and 1970s, through the corporate backlash of the 1980s and 1990s, and into the fights against abuses of globalization in the new millennium, Public Citizen has served in the halls of power as the eyes, ears and voice of citizens. The organization worked then and now to protect and enhance democratic processes, to serve as a check on corporate greed and to champion government accountability. It always has refused to accept funding from the government or from any corporation, so its ability to challenge power remains uncompromised.

Author and activist Noam Chomsky paid tribute in 2006 to the organization's steadfast advocacy: "It is hard to exaggerate the importance of the role that Public Citizen has played for many years in helping those who care about this country become public citizens in the best sense of the word: informed, focused on critical issues, in a position to act constructively. It is a remarkable contribution to making the world a better place."[2]

But Public Citizen's accomplishments are not celebrated in song and story as fully as they have changed American life. "We really don't toot our horn enough," Nader observed ruefully at the organization's 40th anniversary dinner in 2011. "It's just not our personality."

This book is a first attempt at correcting that oversight. It is the story of Public Citizen's first 38 years — from its founding by Ralph Nader in 1971 to the retirement of Joan Claybrook as president in January 2009. Her departure marked no change in Public Citizen's operations, only a handing forward of the task from most of the founding generation of organizers to the next generation of activists, who are now writing their own history.

This book also makes no attempt to tell the complete saga of Public Citizen's work during that time. The group took on too many legislative campaigns, lawsuits and advocacy efforts to recount fully in this one volume.[3] Nor is it a warts-and-all backstage look at the individual foibles and quirks of the many strong personalities at Public Citizen, or at their legendary clashes. As Nader admitted dryly in his 40th anniversary speech, "You can always tell a Public Citizen project director, but you can't tell him much."

Rather, this history is a sketch of the most salient accomplishments and innovations in citizen activism by the first generation of Public Citizen leaders — achievements that have altered the American marketplace, government and political culture in ways that reverberate today. We hope it will both instruct and inspire.

Endnotes

1   U.S. Supreme Court, *Ralph Nader v. Allegheny Airlines,* 426 U.S. 290 (96 S. Ct. 1978, 48 L.Ed.2d 643), Washington, D.C., June 7, 1976.
2   Noam Chomsky, *Public Citizen Special Anniversary Issue,* March 2006.
3   For a timeline and list of major Public Citizen achievements, see Appendix.

1

NADER'S RAIDERS FOR THE LOST DEMOCRACY

WHEN RALPH NADER WAS at Harvard Law School in the 1950s, pursuing his childhood dream of being a crusading lawyer, he became disillusioned with the way attorneys were trained. "When I went to law school I realized it was like a high-priced tool factory," he said in an interview. "They were basically grooming lawyers to service and broker and ease corporate power into being."

The corporate path was not for Nader. But neither was arguing in a courtroom against particular cases of injustice. He wanted a broader and more direct role.

While at Harvard, Nader took a look at the engineering design of automobiles and was appalled at what he found. In 1959 he wrote a piece for *The Nation* magazine called "The Safe Car You Can't Buy." The article accused the Detroit auto industry of sacrificing the safety of drivers and passengers for the sake of style.

Further investigating the subject, in 1965 he wrote a groundbreaking book on the same theme, *Unsafe at Any Speed*. It exposed the reckless rear suspension design of the 1960–63 Chevrolet Corvair by General Motors (GM). Nader's work was well reported, but the book initially failed to attract much public attention.

It spooked GM, however. Apparently fearful that lawyers might use the book's exposé of its poor design practices to bolster product liability lawsuits against the company, the automaker decided to try to discredit Nader. It sought ways to unearth any unsavory personal details of Nader's life.

Suddenly, Nader recalled, attractive women approached him while he was shopping — an apparent attempt to "honey trap" him into compromising situations. The company also hired a private detective, former FBI agent Vincent Gillen, to snoop around Nader's friends and associates and to tail him wherever he went.

"Our job," Gillen told his team of sleuths, "is to check his life and current activities to determine what makes him tick, such as his real interest in safety, his supporters if any, his politics, his marital status, his friends, his women, his boys, and so forth, drinking, dope, jobs — in fact all facets of his life."[1]

In early 1966, several months after GM's probe began, police at the U.S. Capitol noticed that Nader was being followed. They let him know. He told others, and the story soon made its way into *The Washington Post*. That was followed by a larger story on the surveillance in *The New Republic*. The publicity forced GM officials to admit to *Detroit News* reporter Bob Irvin that they had ordered the investigation.

Politicians sympathetic to the young activist were outraged. Nader's home-state senator, Democrat Abraham Ribicoff of Connecticut, summoned GM President James Roche to a congressional hearing to grill him about the harassment.

On March 22, 1966, the Senate's largest hearing room was jammed with TV cameras and reporters. "There is too much snooping going on in this country," Ribicoff told Roche at the highly charged hearing. "Before you know it, you have a man who has led a private and honorable life having reflections cast upon his entire character, and that of his family, because of these questions that detectives, who basically aren't very sensitive, ask ... and this must be happening all over America with many other Ralph Naders."[2]

In a rare and dramatic moment of corporate contrition, amid massive media coverage, Roche publicly apologized to Nader. Nader immediately became a house-hold name, anointed in that hearing as the tireless crusader for the "little guy." Without the ham-fisted attempt to discredit the young lawyer, *Unsafe at Any Speed* might have languished in obscurity. But GM inadvertently made Nader a star.

The Early Nader's Raiders

Armed with his newfound celebrity, Nader helped forge the first federal law regulating the safety of automobiles. Then he quickly turned his attention, and the attention of the media, to other corporate abuses and government ineptitude. It didn't hurt that he was a compelling media personality: articulate, sardonic, accessible and at ease with journalists.

In the years immediately after the GM incident, he and his growing cadre of colleagues tackled unsanitary practices in meat and poultry factories; the hazards of natural gas pipelines; radiation risks from X-rays; smoking on airlines, trains and buses; and dangerous working conditions in coal mines.

These early forays into corporate practices were characterized by painstaking research and scrupulous attention to detail. The resulting exposés not only received massive media coverage, but they also encouraged mainstream journalists to go beyond the mere reporting of daily news and launch major investigations themselves. More important, they electrified a whole generation of activists.

Bright young students like Robert Fellmeth flocked to work for the new consumer movement. They were assigned projects as fast as Nader could dream them up. "I had read an article in *Newsweek* magazine [in the spring of 1968] about Ralph, and I wrote and told him I wanted to join him in his 'judicious jihad,' which I thought was very clever at the time," Fellmeth recalled. "He said, 'Why don't you come to Washington to talk about what to do this summer?'" So Fellmeth and fellow Nader follower Andy Egendorf flew to the capital that summer to be interviewed.

Fellmeth and Egendorf showed up at O'Donnell's, a restaurant in downtown Washington, D.C. Wearing a trench coat, Nader sat down. Dispensing with pleasantries, he went straight to the business at hand.

"There's an agency that's been pulling the wool over folks' eyes in this town for a long time," Nader said. "You know which one I'm talking about, of course."

"Oh, you mean the Securities and Exchange Commission," Fellmeth answered.

"No."

"The Federal Power Commission?"

"No."

"Federal Communications Commission?"

"No."

They guessed on and on. Finally, Nader looked mysteriously at the two recruits and said, "The Federal Trade Commission."

"Gee, I'd never think of them," Fellmeth said.

"Precisely the point."

Fellmeth and six other law students — including William Howard Taft IV, great-grandson of the 27th president — spent the summer investigating the Federal Trade Commission (FTC). The FTC was supposed to be a watchdog protecting the public from deceptive advertising and fraudulent business practices, but the young students instead found offices full of lethargic bureaucrats resentful of public scrutiny.

Nader's team put in long hours of investigative legwork. One of the student researchers, Edward Cox (who later married President Richard Nixon's daughter Tricia), once walked into an FTC office and found a senior official lying asleep on a couch with the sports page draped over his face.

The energetic team wrote it all up and distributed copies of the report to the news media and the public. "It was hard work," Fellmeth said. "We didn't have automatic machines, and we were sitting there and just collating this 238-page report all night long."

The students' findings made a huge national splash in January 1969. *The Nader Report on the Federal Trade Commission*, a book written by Fellmeth, Cox and young law professor John E. Schulz, found that the FTC routinely failed to enforce various laws designed to protect consumers in the marketplace. It resulted in a major overhaul of the commission.

The investigation succeeded, said Fellmeth, because "people who worked for Nader were people who were willing to work. They had the Calvinist ethic and said, 'OK, I want to get the facts right, I want to be right.' Ralph did his homework. He was the model, and we learned just by watching him."

More and more young activists sought the opportunity to participate in Nader's projects and to see how he worked. The day after the FTC report was published, reporter William Greider of *The Washington Post* dubbed Fellmeth and the others "Nader's Raiders." The moniker stuck.

Inventing a New Citizen Advocacy

Nader decided he needed a permanent institutional base from which to coordinate his activist-oriented research. In that year, 1969, he founded the first of dozens of citizen-based organizations, the Center for Study of Responsive Law. Attracted by the success of the FTC investigation, 30,000 applicants wrote to Nader asking to be part of his team the following summer. From that roster, 200 new Raiders were selected. Many were to be unpaid volunteers.

Those who were paid, however, were not paid much. Starting salaries for fresh law school graduates at major firms then were about $10,000 a year; Nader paid $5,000. "He said, 'You know people really want to work for you if they're willing to make a bit of a sacrifice,'" recalled Joan Claybrook. "All the best and brightest young lawyers wanted to come and work for him, so the law firms had to raise their pay, first to $15,000 and then to $20,000. Ralph went to $8,000." Raiders who won raises after several years' experience would throw parties when their salaries hit five digits.

The new crop of dedicated recruits would investigate and uncover more examples of ineffective government regulation and enforcement. In their first three years, the Raiders produced dozens of shocking books and reports about a host of government agencies and serious social problems.

A short list of the early targets: the Food and Drug Administration's lax oversight of the food industry (*The Chemical Feast*, James Turner, 1971); incompetence and corruption at the now-defunct Interstate Commerce Commission (*The Interstate Commerce Omission*, Robert C. Fellmeth, 1970); the health hazards of air pollution (*Vanishing Air*, John C. Esposito, 1970); chemical contamination in food (*Sowing the Wind*, Harrison Wellford, 1972); water pollution (*Water Wasteland*, David Zwick and Marcie Benstock, 1972); government failure to enforce antitrust laws (*The Closed Enterprise System*, Mark J. Green, 1972); and workplace health hazards (*Bitter Wages*, Joseph H. Page and Mary-Win O'Brien, 1973).

By 1970, Nader had expanded the scope of his citizen movement with three additional groups—the Center for Auto Safety, a joint effort with Consumers Union to push for strong auto safety standards and spot auto defects and trends; the Project on Corporate Responsibility, headed by Mark Green, to analyze and critique corporate responsibility and push for a larger voice for consumers in corporate policymaking; and the Public Interest Research Group, known as PIRG, to agitate at the state as well as the national level for reforms through research and analysis, petitions to the government and grassroots organizing. All three became independent organizations.

Nader believed citizens needed a broad countervailing force to check the power of large corporations and to lobby for reforms. "Only a decentralized, loosely affiliated corps of 'public citizens' with their own institutional resources and expertise, could have the staying power," wrote author David Bollier in a 1989 history of the consumer movement.[3] "And so Nader set out to found one advocacy group after another, a Johnny Appleseed planting different seeds in novel locations, hoping they would sprout and bear fruit."

Joan Claybrook and The Congress Project

Of the scores of young activists Nader hired in these early years, few would rise to greater heights in the consumer movement than Joan Claybrook. She first met Nader in 1966 when she was an American Political Science Association fellow working with Representative James Mackay, a Georgia Democrat. She later worked for Senator Walter Mondale, a Minnesota Democrat, on auto safety legislation that was enacted in the wake of Nader's exposé of the auto industry. She then became a special assistant to the first director of the National Highway Traffic Safety Administration, Dr. William Haddon Jr.

Claybrook took a pay cut from $24,000 at that job to $8,000 a year to be one of Nader's dozen workers at the PIRG, which Nader funded in 1970 with the money awarded to him from a lawsuit against GM for invasion of privacy. Claybrook, who had graduated from college a decade earlier, was attending night school at Georgetown University Law Center.

"All of us knew we were part of a new movement," Claybrook said in an interview. What Nader's childhood heroes Upton Sinclair and Lincoln Steffens had done was impressive, but publicizing social problems and political corruption wasn't enough. "They were muckrakers, and we were doers. They wrote and we acted. We saw it as taking information and using the same government processes that corporations used to change the rules. We wanted to change the rules to benefit consumers. We were a new phenomenon."

Claybrook's political initiation had come at an early age. As a 10-year-old, she had been a walking billboard in Baltimore streets to help her father's successful campaign for the City Council. Her exposure to the realities of politics followed when she accompanied her dad to council meetings. "I'd see people saying the dumbest things. There was one guy who used to set an alarm clock at the start of the meeting to go off at eight o'clock, at which point he would move to adjourn the meeting."

Claybrook was joined at the PIRG by Clarence Ditlow, a chemical engineer who had earned a law degree from Georgetown University and a master's degree in law from Harvard Law School. He later directed the Center for Auto Safety. "Ralph was very visible as an individual, and some people who went to work for him liked identifying with him as an individual," Claybrook said. "One of the strengths of all the Nader groups was that they attracted incredibly smart and dedicated people."

After successfully exposing several government agencies as lazy, fraudulent or worse, Nader turned his sights on Congress. This would be his most ambitious undertaking so far—The Congress Project.

At the time, press coverage of Congress was minimal. Few people bothered to understand its arcane procedures, and autocratic committee chairmen regularly used secrecy and subterfuge to get their way, often betraying the public interest. Nader's ambition was to expose all this to the American people. The project would produce reports on the secretive operations of congressional committees and in-depth profiles of every member of Congress who was running for re-election. It was designed to allow voters to more easily hold their representatives accountable for their performance by providing information about them prior to the 1972 elections.

Fellmeth was chosen to head the mammoth task. "I was too stupid not to know it was impossible," he recalled jokingly.

About a thousand people worked on the project at some level. It was an experience few of them would ever forget. During the torrid summer of 1972, many of the students stayed in dorm rooms at George Washington University with no air conditioning. Fellmeth earned $400 for a full summer of work. "It was hot. It was crowded. We had manual typewriters. We had carbon paper. We were just beginning to use copiers. We were on the phone all the time, and we gathered a huge amount of information on the politicians."

The research included hundreds of personal interviews, a 633-question survey and investigations in each congressional district. Catholic nun Jackie Jelly organized the field operation for a year, using her church network to try to find reliable researchers in 435 districts throughout the country. The field researchers pored over campaign contributions and interviewed local labor and community leaders, reporters, former election opponents and campaign officials. Nader's band of recruits in Washington, D.C., then compiled and analyzed the information.

The importance of what they were doing and the promise of public recognition for their work kept the young people going through the long, hot summer. "I thought, 'Here I am, in a position to have an impact on public policy at the age of 25,'" Fellmeth said. "'I'd better take advantage of this; it might not come again.' I knew I was in a very special place."

But the task was too big. In 1972, as the elections approached, the project was faltering under the weight of its own ambition. There simply weren't enough hours in the day for the available bodies to get the job done. Nader gave Claybrook the task of overseeing the writing of hundreds of individual profiles. She decided the only way to finish was to bring in reinforcements. She recruited a cadre of young journalists and journalism students, paying them $50 for each footnoted, magazine article-length profile. Even at the time, that was chicken feed.

Some among that group would go on to become distinguished journalists, including James Fallows (writer and editor for the *Atlantic Monthly* who also served as President Jimmy Carter's chief speechwriter), Evan Thomas (assistant managing editor of *Newsweek* magazine), E.J. Dionne (syndicated columnist for *The Washington Post*), David Ignatius (columnist and editor for the *Post*), Frank Rich (syndicated columnist with *The New York Times*), Margaret Carlson (columnist for *Time* magazine) and Walter Shapiro (political columnist for *USA Today*). "It was investigative," Claybrook said. "We were investigators before Watergate."

On October 22, 1972, two weeks before Election Day, Nader released 484 profiles — all the representatives and the incumbent senators who were seeking re-election. The studies garnered revelatory media coverage in virtually every congressional district. The project also resulted in a hugely popular book, *Who Runs Congress?*, written by Mark Green, James Fallows and David Zwick. The book topped *The New York Times* best-seller list in November 1972, eventually going through four editions and print runs of more than a million copies.

The impossible project became a stunning success. Not only did it expose the machinations of Congress to the electorate as no other publication ever had, but it helped pave the way for major reforms of the congressional system. Those included new limits on the power of once-omnipotent committee chairs and "sunshine in government" rules that opened closed committee mark-up meetings to public scrutiny. The project enlisted hundreds of new activists to Nader's crusade and validated Nader's brand of citizen activism as a national force to be reckoned with.

"Ralph was exciting to work with, and he made the work of public policy — challenging the economically and politically powerful — stimulating," Claybrook said. "It was a cause. The work was structural, it was preventive and it had a long-term impact."

Public Citizen — The Founding Generation

As Nader was launching The Congress Project, he began another ambitious project — a new organization called Public Citizen. On March 29, 1971, he purchased advertisements in 13 publications and sent out letters asking for financial support.

The response was phenomenal. By the end of May 1971, more than 62,000 people had donated a total of more than $1.1 million to start Public Citizen. Some contributors sent a dollar. Most sent the suggested $15, and others mailed in as much as $5,000.[4] Nader became the first president of Public Citizen.

He soon was joined by three exceptionally able colleagues. In 1969, Nader had met a young physician named Sidney M. Wolfe, a veteran of the anti-war movement and a researcher at the National Institutes of Health. Nader suspected that Wolfe, with his inquisitive mind and passion for social justice, was the right choice to investigate public health threats. By January 1972, Wolfe was working full-time for Public Citizen as director of a division called the Health Research Group. At 34, he told Nader, "This is the last job I'll ever have." He was right. Wolfe headed Public Citizen's Health Research Group for more than four decades, until June 2013, and stayed with the group after that as senior adviser.

A few months after Wolfe came on board, a lawyer named Alan Morrison joined to direct the organization's new Litigation Group. Morrison, like Wolfe, was in his early 30s and a seasoned lawyer. Like many of Nader's young disciples, he was a product of Harvard Law School. He had served in the Navy during the 1960s and spent two years working with a Wall Street law firm, then litigated for the U.S. Attorney's Office in the Southern District of New York. He remained at Public Citizen until 2003, and 10 years later he was still doing public interest work. "I still say 'we' when I talk about Public Citizen," he said.

After the 1972 elections, at the conclusion of The Congress Project, Nader persuaded Claybrook to join too. She urged Nader to establish a division to lobby Congress, a specialty job that she argued was just as technical and complicated and vital to the organization's success as litigation. He agreed and asked her to become the first director of the new division, which they named Congress Watch. She stayed until 1977 when she departed to run the National Highway Traffic Safety Administration for Carter. In 1982, she returned to take over as president of Public Citizen for the next 27 years.

With Nader as founder, Wolfe, Morrison and Claybrook were the nucleus of Public Citizen's leadership for nearly four decades. They headed the founding generation of activists whose achievements this book seeks to document.

The Radical Alternative

The new movement had attracted top-drawer talent with a generally clean-cut appearance. This made the Raiders look deceptively unthreatening to many in the establishment. "We were the alternative to the radicals," said Fellmeth, who would later chair Public Citizen's board of directors. "They made us possible because their irrational posturing made us look—relatively speaking—like someone you could deal with. We were the alternative to people who wanted to blow things up."

Initially, many government and business people dismissed Nader's movement as ephemeral, likely to fall out of fashion as fast as bell-bottoms. In 1966, W.R. Murphy, president of Campbell Soup Co., reassured his colleagues that the movement would fade. "It's of the same order of the hula hoop—a fad. Six months from now, we'll probably be on another kick."[5]

But the movement in fact had durable, long-range goals—a fair shake in the marketplace for consumers, systemic reforms in government for citizens, and greater democratic accountability for the country's most powerful institutions. Four decades later, those remained the guiding objectives.

In the early days, many people in positions of influence appeared confused about the aims of the consumer movement and struggled to grasp the Nader phenomenon. In 1971, for example, Nader was invited to the White House for the wedding of his friend Edward Cox and Nixon's daughter Tricia. "I entered the White House and all of these Republicans were everywhere," Nader remembered. "They were almost stereotypical in gesture, behavior and appearance. So there was a receiving line for Richard and Pat Nixon, and I proceeded down the line. I approached Nixon and shook his hand."

The exchange, as Nader recalled in an interview, went like this:

"Ralph Nader, Mr. President."

"Ah yes," Nixon said. "Raider's Nader. We were just discussing you last evening because we had a defective toaster."

Nader later said: "I was about to say, 'Well, Nixon's Richard, you should have called me and I might have gotten it recalled.' But I smiled and proceeded on."

American Business Fights Back

Elements of the business community, however, began to understand the implications of the consumer movement all too well. It threatened cozy cartels, reckless manufacturing practices and contempt for fair dealing in the marketplace. This was no hippie, flash-in-the-pan project that could be ridiculed into retreat, but a serious social movement that was increasingly popular, respected and covered favorably by national news media and talk shows.

Leading corporate executives pondered how to respond. On August 23, 1971, Lewis F. Powell, then general counsel of the U.S. Chamber of Commerce and a future justice of the U.S. Supreme Court, submitted a confidential memo to the chairman of the organization's education committee. His memo was titled "Attack on American Free Enterprise System."[6]

"What now concerns us is quite new in the history of America," Powell wrote. "We are not dealing with sporadic or isolated attacks from a relatively few extremists or even from the minority socialist cadre. Rather, the assault on the enterprise system is broadly based and consistently pursued. It is gaining momentum and converts."

Revealingly, Powell suggested that it was the freshly scrubbed face of reform that posed the greatest menace to the old order: "Although New Leftist spokesmen are succeeding in radicalizing thousands of the young, the greater cause for concern is the hostility of respectable liberals and social reformers."

And who was the greatest cause for concern? "Perhaps the single most effective antagonist of American business is Ralph Nader, who — thanks largely to the media — has become a legend in his own time and an idol to millions of Americans."

Powell's memo wrongly accused the new consumer movement of trying to dismantle American capitalism. The movement was actually aiming only to level the playing field between corporations and consumers and workers, to keep what worked for the public benefit and to fix what didn't. But defenders of corporate America would continue to repeat this false charge over the following years.

Powell's memo suggested a multifaceted corporate campaign that would both combat calls for reform and push the political agenda further to the right. "There should be no hesitation to attack the Naders ... and others who openly seek destruction of the system," Powell advised.

Powell's memo urged corporations each to appoint an executive vice president "to counter — on the broadest front — the attack on the free enterprise system" and suggested that the U.S. Chamber of Commerce and its local branches undertake long-range planning and implementation "over an indefinite period of years."

Powell's plan called on the Chamber to commit to that long-term political and social defense against the reform movement. "The national television networks should be monitored in the same way that textbooks should be kept under constant surveillance," he wrote. Big business should learn that "political power is necessary; that such power must be assiduously cultivated and that when necessary, it must be used aggressively and with determination — without the reluctance which has been so characteristic of American business."

Powell's strategy, which now seems commonplace, was innovative at the time. It became reality during the 1970s, 1980s and 1990s, cost billions of dollars and had significant impact, with ramifications that continue to this day.

Powell himself was appointed to the Supreme Court a few months after the memo was written. He remained there until 1987. He was considered a centrist on the court — especially when measured against justices appointed in later years. Ironically, Powell was on the Supreme Court when it heard Nader's suit demanding compensation for being bumped by Allegheny Airlines. In the end, the court's verdict in Nader's favor was unanimous — and Powell wrote the opinion.[7]

Taking it to the Agencies

Nader and Public Citizen tried throughout the 1970s to get Congress to establish a Consumer Protection Agency, a government arm that would be an advocate for consumers before Congress and agencies within the government and authorized to take those agencies to court. It was a novel idea, not to say revolutionary. It alarmed corporate interests that already regarded the Consumer Product Safety Commission (CPSC), established in 1972 with Public Citizen pressure, as a radical threat. They were jolted into defensive action.

"There was a huge coalition of companies against us; it was the first time the big companies all started working together," Claybrook said. "They were scared to death of an agency that would have had access to all the inside information and would represent the consumer. It galvanized the business community." The Consumer Protection Bureau was set up within the Federal Trade Commission as a stopgap measure in 1970, but with limited powers, and Public Citizen persisted in seeking an independent advocacy agency. After intense business lobbying, the legislation to establish the bureau was narrowly defeated in 1975 by a series of filibusters — a procedure in which senators stop legislative action by talking for an extended period of time. At that time, it took 67 votes to defeat the filibuster but only 66 votes were secured. The Senate majority leader changed the filibuster rule as a result to require only 60 senators, rather than 67, to vote to stop the filibuster and proceed with a vote.

Despite that loss— and another loss on the same issue in 1978— Public Citizen has fulfilled many of the functions that Nader envisioned for the lost advocacy agency and has continued to expand the scope of this work over the years. Each of its current and former divisions works on regulatory matters: the Health Research Group on drugs, medical devices and workplace safety and health; the Energy Program on nuclear energy, electric utilities, oil and gas policy, and related matters; the Auto Safety Group on vehicle and passenger safety, fuel economy, highway speed, truck driver work rules and licensing; Global Trade Watch on international agreements that pre-empt consumer, labor and environmental protections; Congress Watch on consumer products, consumer finance and the regulatory process itself; Global Access to Medicines on drug prices in developing countries and Democracy Is For People on advancing a constitutional amendment to curb the influence of money in politics. Meanwhile the Litigation Group brings suits in all these regulatory areas as well as to enforce the Freedom of Information Act.

With Nader's Raiders often in the spotlight, the consumer and environmental movements succeeded in creating numerous new public health and safety agencies in the late 1960s and early 1970s. In addition to the CPSC, they included the National Highway Traffic Safety Administration, the Environmental Protection Agency, the Occupational Safety and Health Administration, and the Mine Safety and Health Administration, among others.

These agencies were charged with administering a host of new laws aimed at ameliorating many of the threats the activists had exposed. These laws included (in order of their enactment) the National Traffic and Motor Vehicle Safety Act, the Child Protection and Toy Safety Act, the Occupational Safety and Health Act, the Clean Air Act, the Clean Water Act, the Consumer Product Safety Act, the Safe Drinking Water Act, the Resource Conservation and Recovery Act, and the Toxic Control Substances Act. An impressive list that transformed American life over the next decades, but Public Citizen was just getting started.

As these agencies worked to bring corporate practices into line with new standards, the business community turned to Nixon's White House for help.

Claybrook traced the beginning of this corporate recoil to Roy Ash, head of the Bureau of the Budget under Nixon. "In 1972, he put forward the idea that there should be more control over these new health and safety regulatory agencies by his office. It never came to fruition under Nixon, but it was the first of a number of attempts to quash the interests of consumer groups, because [the White House] could see their growing power." Another way the Nixon administration sought to keep the new regulatory bodies in line was to appoint business-minded people to head them.

Evidence on the Floor

In Public Citizen's first year, Sidney Wolfe began investigating working conditions at a chemical plant in Moundsville, West Virginia, where the local union suspected that workers were being poisoned by mercury. Wolfe visited the plant and found the volatile substance all over the floor.

"If you see mercury, then by definition the air levels are above the allowable level," he said in an interview. "The workers were breathing in dangerously high levels. One had been hospitalized with mercury poisoning, and there was evidence that a number of other workers were getting mercury poisoning."

Wolfe went to see the newly installed head of the Occupational Safety and Health Administration (OSHA) to ask for an inspection at the plant, the first such request made of the agency. "Nixon had picked a cigar-chomping former textile executive to run OSHA," Wolfe said. "We asked him to order the inspection and he said, 'I sure wish the first request for an imminent-danger inspection under the new law had been an exploding boiler rather than mercury poisoning' — meaning he'd prefer to deal with simpler things rather than chronic hazards." Despite this initial resistance, Wolfe secured the inspection, and the company was cited for serious violations involving mercury contamination.

During the mid-1970s, corporate America began to exert increasing political influence, as Powell had urged. He had suggested that effective resistance to reform depended on a "scale of financing available only through joint effort" of companies, and an army of business lobbyists duly began to flow into Washington, D.C.

In 1968, only 100 corporations had registered lobbying offices in the nation's capital. By 1978, that number had grown to 500. By 1986, the city was home to 3,500 corporate trade associations — more than triple the 1960 number.[8] They stayed busy tracking developments, creating fact sheets and thick reports advocating or opposing new laws and regulatory changes, writing newspaper opinion pieces and policy recommendations. By 2007, registered lobbyists considered personally active at buttonholing decision-makers on Capitol Hill and at regulatory agencies numbered 14,842 — about 28 lobbyists for each of the 535 House and Senate members.[9]

In short, consumer advocates found themselves increasingly outmanned and outgunned. Corporations even used their money to try to influence or neuter the advocacy of public interest groups by offering them financial support. Public Citizen refused — and has always refused — to accept money from government or businesses, and so has enjoyed the luxury of independence from corporate and government influence. But having to send back checks from well-intentioned companies has meant that Public Citizen has relied heavily on its citizen membership for support, and on its staff to accept low salaries.

Direct mail membership solicitations were from the beginning the bedrock source of Public Citizen funding, and they still are, with assistance from professional advisers. Other income is from foundation grants for particular projects; proceeds from sales of books and other publications, especially Health Research Group reports; so-called "cy pres" awards of funds remaining after proceeds of class-action lawsuits have been distributed to available claimants; rent from its previous headquarters building; and some large donations.

Very few nonprofit organizations have so successfully resisted the lure of the business dollar, which is a gift that opens a group to charges of being influenced by its financial backers. "Businesses that give you money want to control you," said Claybrook. "It's very seductive. What happens is that they give you a little bit, and then they give you a little bit more, and then all of a sudden you're dependent on it, and then they say, 'We want you to do X.' If you won't, they say 'No money,' and then your organization is in dire straits. It's inevitable and it's happened to other organizations. But Public Citizen has always been fiercely independent."

When Claybrook served as the top government official regulating the automobile industry at the National Highway Traffic Safety Administration in the Carter administration, she got a taste of how some in business view money and power. It came during an appointment with General Motors President Pete Estes in his executive suite on the 14th floor.

"We were talking generally about the poverty in Detroit," she said. "He took me to the window and pointed to a local neighborhood. He said one of the things that worried him was that secretaries who worked late had to travel through that area to get home, and he mentioned they had a plan for it. He said, 'See that community across the street? We're buying it house by house really cheap because no one knows it's us. House by house and we'll have the whole community.'

"It's the mentality of big corporations: total control," Claybrook said. "Even if they have to step on people."

Obligatory frugality had its merits. In Congress Watch's early days, "we had no copiers so we had to make copies on purple mimeograph machines," Claybrook recalled. "So we whittled down every letter and fact sheet to fit on one page, to minimize the mess. Then I saw that members of Congress would take our fact sheet, fold it up and put it in their pocket, which meant that later they had to take it out and look at it again. That was much more effective than the big binders that industry lobbyists handed out — those got left on the members' office shelves."

At the group's 40th anniversary celebration in 2011, Nader suggested half-seriously that Public Citizen could win more attention by describing its achievements in cost-benefit terms. "I estimate that Public Citizen has spent in 40 years ... about $200 million" exclusive of fundraising expenses, he said. "That's about the cost of one F-22 [jet] fighter, before cost overruns." He then named a few achievements, many detailed in this book (see Appendix for an extensive list), that have saved taxpayers many billions of dollars and preserved tens of thousands of lives.

"You would think in a rational society that someone would have looked at that and said 'Hmmm — that's a pretty good investment! Let's double it ... quintuple it!'" he said. But no one has. Yet.

Endnotes

1   Charles McCarry, "Citizen Nader," *Saturday Review Press*, 1972, p. 13.

2   McCarry, p. 24.

3   David Bollier, *Citizen Action and Other Big Ideas: A History of Ralph Nader and the Consumer Movement*, Center for Study of Responsive Law, 1991, p. 6.

4   Public Citizen Annual Report, Issue No. 1, 1971–72.

5   David Bollier, *Citizen Action and other Big ideas*, p. 1.

6   Lewis F. Powell Jr., Confidential Memorandum, "Attack on American Free Enterprise System," to Eugene B. Snydor Jr., Chairman, Education Committee, U.S. Chamber of Commerce; Aug. 23, 1971.

7   *Public Citizen News*, Anniversary 1997 edition, p. 5.

8   Hedrick Smith, *The Power Game* (Collins, 1988), p. 31.

9   For the number of registered lobbyists: U.S. Senate Office of Public Records, Feb. 6, 2007. For number of lobbying firms: Center for Responsive Politics, April 5, 2007. www.opensecrets.org/lobby/index.php. Accessed Sept. 25, 2013.

2
TOOLS FOR ATTACK ON ALL FRONTS

RALPH NADER ORGANIZED PUBLIC CITIZEN in a way that would enable it to challenge corporate power on multiple fronts. "If corporations can lobby Congress, Public Citizen can lobby Congress," he said. "If they can attack the safety regulatory agencies, Public Citizen can challenge those attacks. If they can use the courts, Public Citizen can use the courts. If they're going to use the media or if they control the media, Public Citizen will use the media. If you don't do that, you can be outflanked," he warned in a 1997 article in *Public Citizen News,* the organization's newsletter.

"For example, environmentalists blocked the Alaska pipeline in court, and so the oil and gas industry went to Congress and got the decision overridden. You always have to go after all fronts."

Joan Claybrook said having many paths to success was critical to maintaining both momentum and morale. "Ralph set it up to be able to deal with all the pressure points — the agencies, lobbying in Congress, litigation, publicity. If you lose in one forum you go to another forum if you can." Losing is just part of the day's work, she said, which didn't seem to discourage her or anyone else at Public Citizen. "There are so many opportunities to win, is the way I look at it. You pick your battles but mostly you just keep pushing."

The new organization shared many of the traits that had made Nader's Raiders so successful, including a lean administrative structure. "The second concept of Public Citizen was to organize it in a way that minimized the possibility of bureaucracy, which I defined as starting with two people," Nader said.

Public Citizen's staff was tiny during its first year, 1971. Its first annual report shows a Tax Reform Research Group made up of three lawyers and a research assistant; a Litigation Group with Alan Morrison and two other lawyers; and a Health Research Group with Sidney Wolfe and a handful of lawyers, doctors and other medical professionals. There also were a Retired Professionals Action Group and a Citizen Action Group. Volunteers handled the mountains of mail. That was it. The total spent on general administration that year: $10,236.64.

"Unlike many conventional fundraising organizations, the administrative expenses of Public Citizen have been kept deliberately minimal," the annual report proudly announced to its members in 1972.

Nader explained the reasoning for such a spartan setup. "There are different sub-segments of Public Citizen. You don't want people to go to work and say, 'Well, I'm going to pass the buck to my superior,' or, 'It's my manager's fault.' You want them to go to work thinking that if they succeed, it's to their credit, and if they fail, it's their responsibility."

Nader was famously hard-working day in and day out, and he expected — and usually got — the same from his employees. When one staffer asked for a two-week vacation to go to the beach, Nader was reportedly baffled. "After one day, what do you do?" he asked. Another staffer, slaving to meet a critical deadline, told Nader that if he didn't take a day off soon his wife would divorce him. "Is that a good thing or a bad thing?" Nader replied. He later said he was joking in both cases, but the stories resonated. The work was important.

What distinguished Public Citizen from the dozens of other public interest groups springing up in the early 1970s was not only such stamina but the ability on such a meager funding diet to be active in multiple battles at the same time. By sharing central administrative and fundraising departments, bare-bones as they were, each of Public Citizen's policy groups was largely free to focus on its own substantive issues. Public Citizen was to be "like a supermarket," Nader said. "It had lobbying, litigation, regulatory oversight, research and so on." Staffers in one group could be readily helped by expertise in another group. The lack of bureaucracy made the divisions nimble, once their chiefs managed to agree on a joint target. That wasn't always easy.

"Ralph hired people he thought had the strength to take on the challenges of facing corporate America," Claybrook said. "They're not going to be all that flexible if they're already working at three other jobs."

Early on, Nader and Claybrook agreed that Public Citizen should own its own turf in Washington, D.C., a cost-effective decision, as it turned out. Nader began in 1979 with a three-story former car dealership on Capitol Hill that also had been an FBI listening post. In 1994, Public Citizen purchased a former mansion in Dupont Circle that had been converted to offices for an architecture firm that had gone bankrupt, buying it from the Resolution Trust Corporation for half its book value.

Accountability and Openness

Far greater than the sum of its small parts, Public Citizen soon showed how effective its multi-punch method of attack could be. In its first years, the Litigation Group tried and failed to gain access to government documents by using the 1966

Freedom of Information Act (FOIA). This landmark measure had been shepherded into law by Democratic Representative John Moss of California after congressional hearings revealed how easily the government could keep its supposedly public information secret. Moss and other members of Congress wanted a law that would let them not only provide government information to the public but also get their own hands on documents that the executive branch agencies routinely withheld.

Although valuable, the existing FOIA did not go far enough in allowing the public to scrutinize government operations, and Public Citizen believed the courts were too narrow in their interpretations of the documents the law required to be made public. After a series of U.S. Supreme Court defeats in the early 1970s, it became clear to Morrison that the law itself would have to be changed.

"Sometimes you can't get Congress to fix something until you've gone to court and litigated and lost," Morrison said in an interview. "Otherwise they won't believe things are as bad as you say, and there's always inertia anyway."

Public Citizen's Congress Watch division, formed in early 1973 to specialize in legislative matters on Capitol Hill, took up the documents issue under Joan Claybrook's guidance.

One key concern was whether, during the course of an investigation of a company, a government agency should have to release information to the public that was already known to the company under investigation, or whether the probe had to be completed and the files closed before the public could see the paperwork.

This issue arose after Clarence Ditlow spent the summer of 1971 wading through every auto defect investigation file to which the National Highway Traffic Safety Administration (NHTSA) would grant him access. With information gleaned from letters that consumers had written to Nader, his research unearthed a number of defect investigations that had been improperly closed, including one concerning Chevrolet engine mounts.

"The mounts became unglued, and the defective design allowed them to separate, jamming the throttle open, and off you went out of control down the road," Ditlow said. Nader's Public Interest Research Group eventually got the defective engine mounts recalled, thanks to Ditlow's careful scouring of the government files.

But the larger problem remained: What about potential defects that were still being investigated? These were of obvious interest to the public, because government investigations could drag on for months or years while drivers remained unaware of possibly deadly defects. "At that time, you could get access only to files where the investigation had been closed."

At Nader's urging, Ditlow filed a request under FOIA for access to all pending investigative files. "We said there's no harm to the investigatory process," Ditlow said. "All we want is the correspondence back and forth between NHTSA and the auto companies, because the only people who don't know what's going on or what's being investigated are the people who are riding in cars that might be under investigation and who might be at risk."

NHTSA refused to release the information. Public Citizen sued through its Litigation Group and won the case at trial in federal court. Then the court of appeals reversed the decision. That was when Public Citizen took the battle to Congress. It was 1974, as the Watergate scandal climaxed with the resignation of President Richard Nixon, and issues of accountability were high on the public agenda.

"It was definitely a big fight because the industry didn't want the law amended," Claybrook recalled. It was a key issue for other consumer groups, too, because they knew a more expansive FOIA would make a crucial difference in their ability to hold corporations and the government accountable to the public.

Democratic Senator Ted Kennedy of Massachusetts took charge of piloting the amendments through the Senate. Public Citizen's small team of lobbyists in its Congress Watch division, aided by the legal experts in its Litigation Group, pushed hard for the reforms. "We pored over every bit of language in the bill, talked to every member of the Senate Judiciary Committee, every member of the subcommittee — we knew when they sneezed," Claybrook said.

Their work was rewarded when an impressive bill passed the Senate. But the House counterpart was weak, and the future of the reforms depended on the House-Senate conference committee that would produce the final version.

"Kennedy was the strength," Claybrook said. "He'd had a lot of heavy hits in one decade — his brothers' assassinations, Chappaquiddick and losing the majority leader race to Senator Robert Byrd. This was the first real fight he took on after all that, and he was just wonderful. He rammed this through the Senate, and he really took charge in the conference committee."

President Gerald Ford, who moved into the White House upon Nixon's resignation in August 1974, had been in office only two weeks when he vetoed the new bill. Undeterred, Public Citizen, Kennedy and others mustered enough congressional votes to override the veto. This was an amazing feat, because presidential veto overrides require two-thirds majority votes in both the House and Senate. The amendments became law.

Agencies now are supposed to respond to public information requests within 20 working days; search and copying fees can be waived if the disclosures are judged to be "primarily benefiting the general public"; requesters can recover legal fees when they successfully sue agencies to force compliance; and the definition of "investigatory" records (which can be withheld) is substantially narrowed.

"It was a great victory," recalled Ditlow. "Today the government has to make public every investigatory file made known or available to the defendant. It doesn't matter what agency; it could be an FBI file. The impact of those amendments is just truly astounding." In the wake of the 9/11 attacks, the Patriot Act narrowed these openings, but the FOIA law remained essential in the areas of corporate and regulatory information where Public Citizen concentrates.

The organization has wielded the act with vigor ever since its enactment, to the benefit of countless consumers. Suits using FOIA obtained government meat inspection reports that showed unhealthy conditions in meat-packing facilities and the failure of inspectors to report the hazards. Another branch of Public Citizen—the Critical Mass Energy Project—used the law repeatedly to compile lists of safety lapses at the country's nuclear power plants. It was used in the late 1970s to expose the dangers of the Firestone 500 steel-belted radial tire and the Ford Pinto's exploding gas tank. Likewise, it was used to confirm that the FBI mounted the notorious COINTELPRO scheme in the early 1970s to spy on and harass political dissidents.

"Some FOIA cases are easy—the agencies send the stuff right away," Morrison said. "Other cases last seven or eight years with filings and appeals and so on, and they set precedents at every turn. It's hard to keep count because of that."

Nowhere has Public Citizen wielded the anti-secrecy law more beneficially for consumers than in the area of health care. Public Citizen lawyers used it to discover that the Eli Lilly pharmaceutical company suppressed data on adverse reactions to various drugs, including the arthritis medicine Oraflex, which had caused the deaths of dozens of elderly patients. The finding resulted in the criminal prosecution of several company officials.

Public Citizen also used FOIA to press for information about Tagamet, a breakthrough drug for treatment of ulcers. The Health Research Group suspected that clinical trials indicated a significant risk of sterility to male patients taking Tagamet, and Public Citizen wanted the data from animal studies about any adverse effects. As Public Citizen lawyers prepared to go to trial to force release of the information, the manufacturer, SmithKline Beecham, released data confirming the suspicions.

Public Citizen had not asked that the drug be withdrawn from pharmacy shelves—it merely had wanted attention paid to the risk of adverse effects. Indeed, successor drugs were developed without these side effects.

Exposing Tagamet side effects and the Oraflex scandal were classic examples of collaboration between Public Citizen's various parts—in this case, the Litigation Group and Health Research Group—that resulted in major victories for the public. Countless other examples were spread across a wide spectrum of health issues, notably in the field of workplace health and safety.

"Many of the cases that we bring simply would not be brought were there not a Litigation Group," said David Vladeck, a longtime Public Citizen lawyer and director of the Litigation Group from 1992 to 2002. "The level of expertise, of legal sophistication, and our ability to draw on expertise from people in the Health Research Group and other public interest groups, is unparalleled anywhere."

Dangerous Drugs and Hazardous Workplaces

During the 1970s, Public Citizen, through its Litigation Group and Health Research Group, opened a new front in the battle to improve public health: workplace exposure to toxins. The organization filed groundbreaking suits against the Occupational Safety and Health Administration (OSHA), created by Congress in

1970, arguing that the agency was neglecting its statutory duty to protect the health and safety of hundreds of thousands of U.S. workers.

"Most of the cases involved exposure to toxic substances," Vladeck said. "To fight the agency's lethargy, Litigation Group lawyers had to become experts not only in administrative law but also, with the help of the Health Research Group, in aspects of epidemiological science."

Labor unions often didn't have the in-house capacity to pursue the complex litigation, so it was left to Public Citizen to advocate in the courts for safer workplaces. "The reason we could do these cases is that we had the Health Research Group to help us translate very difficult scientific arguments into language that lawyers and judges could understand," Vladeck said.

One of the most important cases Public Citizen initiated concerned ethylene oxide, an extremely potent, heavy gas used to sterilize an assortment of products, including rare books and heat-sensitive medical equipment. About 200,000 U.S. workers came in contact with the substance daily. Most of them were women who toiled in the bowels of hospitals, working with large sterilizing units.

Sidney Wolfe had noticed that studies appearing in medical journals were linking the substance to cancer. Delving further into the literature, Wolfe found that the gas had been linked to certain types of leukemia and stomach cancers as well as to a high incidence of miscarriage.

At the time, many hospitals paid little attention to whether their sterilization machines leaked, and some even allowed them to be vented near air conditioning units. Some leaked so badly the workers could smell the gas, an indication that they were getting an extremely high dose of ethylene oxide.

Because OSHA had done nothing to address the hazards of this toxic substance, Public Citizen, working with labor unions, sued the agency, representing some hospital workers exposed to the gas. It took eight years of litigation and three trips to the U.S. Court of Appeals before OSHA finally imposed restrictions on worker exposure to the chemical in 1988. "Ultimately, because of our work, OSHA now has in place a very tight standard for ethylene oxide," Vladeck said. "The data show that exposure levels of American workers to ethylene oxide is down to almost zero."

Taking on Big Tobacco

Public Citizen's ability to coordinate the talents of its independent-minded employees is one of its legendary strengths. The division heads meet every other Friday morning with the president to discuss developments in their areas and ways they might cooperate on next steps. Such organization-wide cooperation was critical in 1998, when Public Citizen joined an ongoing battle against tobacco companies that hoped to buy themselves immunity from lawsuits.

At the time, state attorneys general across the country were trying to recover billions of dollars from the industry to help pay for the staggering public health costs of smoking. Lawyers had uncovered thousands of secret internal company documents that showed the firms had lied to the public for decades about tobacco's dangers (see Chapter 4). They had manipulated nicotine levels in cigarettes and callously marketed their products to teenagers with the intention of hooking them into being lifelong smokers.

Even though at that point the industry had never lost a jury verdict, the tobacco companies offered to settle the state suits. The settlement would apply Food and Drug Administration regulatory controls to tobacco products for the first time, and the industry would pay $368 billion to the states over 25 years to reimburse them for health costs incurred by smokers. But in exchange, the tobacco companies wanted protection from future lawsuits that might be filed by consumers or other government entities. That's where the big congressional debate focused, because legal immunity could be granted only by an act of Congress — which meant the settlement needed congressional approval.

Some public health groups backed the deal as a way to get clear authority for the FDA to regulate tobacco, limit industry advertising and secure money for state programs to educate teens about the dangers of smoking. But Public Citizen was unimpressed by the industry's bait.

Led by lobbyist Joan Mulhern, Public Citizen joined a coalition of health and consumer groups that opposed trading away the future rights of citizens to seek justice against tobacco companies. Public Citizen believed that being able to hold the industry liable in court — what the industry most feared — would be the greatest deterrent to future malfeasance.

It was a hard fight. "The tobacco companies had one lobbyist for every three members of Congress. The public interest community had about one for every 25 members," said Frank Clemente, director of Public Citizen's Congress Watch division from 1996 to 2006. Even in the high-priced world of Washington influence-peddling, the amount of tobacco cash spent on lobbying was staggering at the time — an average of $81,000 for each member of Congress.[1]

Public Citizen's typical response to floods of industry money in electoral and legislative campaigns is to publicize who is giving how much to whom, in the belief that embarrassment can be a potent weapon. The organization pointed out that the 12 senators who voted most often for the tobacco industry had received an average of about $32,000 in industry contributions between 1991 and 1996, the period of the most recent campaign for each senator. That was more than 15 times the average of $2,031 received by the 16 senators who consistently opposed Big Tobacco.[2]

While Congress Watch was delving into tobacco industry spending for lobbying and campaign contributions, the Health Research Group was further documenting tobacco's health hazards, and the Litigation Group's lawyers were advising congressional staffers about the legal ramifications of the deal — a three-front attack. Morrison also testified before a House subcommittee in opposition to legislation that sought to limit the fees of attorneys representing the public in tobacco cases.

Morrison told the subcommittee that not only would such a price control on fees violate the Constitution, it also was bad public policy. Plaintiffs' attorneys, he said, needed strong financial incentives to prosecute product liability lawsuits against wealthy corporations, because in virtually all cases, the lawyers paid their own expenses of preparing and trying the cases and were compensated only if they won in court. If consumer attorneys couldn't recoup what could be enormous costs, most cases would not be brought. Public Citizen prevailed; that legislation was defeated.

Meanwhile, Public Citizen's Health Research Group released the first systematic study of health warning labels on packets of American cigarettes sold in foreign countries. The study found that health warnings in developing countries were inferior to those in the United States. Although U.S. tobacco companies generally complied with local laws in other countries, they did not go beyond the often-inadequate requirements, doing only the bare minimum to pass legal muster, usually far less than required in the United States.[3]

By helping to organize more than 350 health, religious and neighborhood groups around the country, Public Citizen fought the tobacco industry toe to toe for more than a year. Focusing on key members of Congress and their districts, especially conservatives, Public Citizen used decades of lobbying experience to defeat the one provision the tobacco companies coveted the most: legal immunity for their past wrongdoing. When that provision was stripped from the bill, industry support for the legislation evaporated, and the deal was dead.

The states eventually settled their suits against Big Tobacco, which paid them hundreds of millions of dollars, but the industry got no special legal immunity. And indeed, tobacco firms have been forced into court many times since then by lawsuits that would have been stopped if not for the defeat of the 1998 tobacco bill.

As is typical when facing wealthy corporate interests, Public Citizen was vastly outspent during the tobacco debate. The industry put well over $40 million into television and other advertising, while Public Citizen relied on regular news coverage, its website and networking with its allies to communicate its positions to the public.

"It's enormously challenging intellectually to put yourself up against people with such huge resources," Morrison said. "It couldn't be any more professionally rewarding."

Working With the Media

The news media have always been a key to Public Citizen's success. The media helped launch Nader's consumer crusade in the 1960s, and without exposure in newspapers, television and radio, the early Public Citizen could never have flourished. Public Citizen's experts continue to appear regularly on television and radio news programs, and in news stories and opinion pieces in national, local and online outlets. Lacking the corporate millions of dollars to spend on advertising campaigns, the organization still relies on the media to publicize its research and policy positions.

"Our voice in the media both educates the public and lays down markers for members of Congress and federal agency officials," Claybrook said. "They know they're going to get into a public spat if we disagree."

The news media have changed dramatically since the exposés by Nader's Raiders in the 1960s and 1970s created pressure for reform by making front pages nationwide and being featured on the must-watch evening news shows of the three television networks that existed at the time. Competition for public attention is far keener today. Much of the broadcast media, particularly on the talk show circuit, focus on "infotainment," celebrity gossip, crime, fashion or sports, rather than stories about problems in government policy. As cable TV networks have fragmented the national audience and the Internet has flourished, people increasingly get their news in snippets from free websites, videos, friends, humorists or social media, often reading little more than a headline before surfing to another site.

"Now the media are into the superficial coverage of street crime, sports, weather, chitchat, animal stories," Nader said. "It's a huge negative for the citizen movement."

People also use the Web to trade goods and find jobs that used to be posted in advertisements that financed newspapers and brought in readers. With ad revenue and circulation plummeting in the early 2000s, many newspapers merged or closed, reducing the number of outlets that might be approached with a story. Those that survived laid off thousands of reporters, cutting the numbers of "beat" reporters who follow an issue area. Most publications, print and online both, now require their journalists not only to do basic reporting but also to write blog posts, produce videos and update the website several times every day. Media have trimmed the size of their Washington bureaus, leaving fewer already-overworked reporters available to cover newsworthy information from organizations like Public Citizen.

But Public Citizen is still cited or quoted half a dozen to a dozen times a day worldwide, and often more—a testament to its compelling information and relentless attention to the details of legislation and regulations, and to the processes that create them.

Because it is harder today for a younger generation of public interest leaders to grab the fleeting public attention span long enough for reform pressure to build, Public Citizen's work with journalists often goes hand-in-hand with its lobbying on Capitol Hill.

As a matter of routine, Public Citizen's research and legislative analyses provide reporters with the pro-consumer side of a congressional debate, and they in turn routinely call on Public Citizen for that information. Sometimes Public Citizen researchers uncover little-known facets of legislation that can tilt votes one way or another. The media are critical at that point.

In July 1998, for example, after years of intense lobbying and campaign spending by corporate interests, the Senate was preparing to vote on a bill that would have severely limited the rights of consumers to hold corporations accountable in court for making dangerous products. Public Citizen staffers conducted a legal analysis of the legislation, suggested amendments to congressional allies and organized state groups to oppose it. But what probably made the final difference was a front-page story in *The New York Times*.

Sparked by Public Citizen, the story exposed a last-minute amendment inserted by Senate Majority Leader Trent Lott, a Republican, to benefit a company in Mississippi, his home state.[4] The story broke the morning of the vote, and Democratic Senator Ernest "Fritz" Hollings of South Carolina, the bill's chief opponent, laid copies of the *Times* article on each senator's desk. Lott was then unable to muster the 60 votes he needed to end a filibuster and bring the bill up for a final tally, so the measure failed.

Despite such successes, Public Citizen lobbyists are competing with business interests that can spend millions on ad campaigns as well as trips, fundraisers and other perks for legislators and regulators. In the 1950s and 1960s, a favorite method of corporate lobbyists was simply to stuff an envelope bulging with cash into a lawmaker's pocket. But now, says Claybrook, permissive campaign contribution rules mean that's no longer necessary. "Campaign money is much more pervasive. When you go to lobby somebody, you have to look up ahead of time who their campaign contributors are, whether or not they've already been rented out on that issue."

The public interest, offering legislators only the satisfaction of doing the right thing, is often the loser in these engagements, but Claybrook spent 27 years seeing each loss as an opportunity to try something else. "Look who we're battling," she exclaimed. "It's amazing that we win anything at all!"

Rob Sanders saw just how effective Public Citizen's tactics could be. Sanders, of Baltimore, Maryland, lost his seven-year-old daughter Alison in October 1995 when a poorly designed air bag in his Chrysler minivan opened with too much force during a minor fender-bender, killing her almost instantly. He helped establish a group — Parents for Safer Air Bags — for families whose children had been killed or injured in similar circumstances. In the years following Alison's death, he joined Claybrook in pressing Congress to require improvements in air bag safety standards.

"We walked the halls of Congress together on numerous occasions trying to get this better statute, and it was a marvel to watch her lobbying skills," Sanders said in an interview. "She would directly engage the member either in a formal meeting in their office, or more typically in the hallway. She would approach them, introduce herself and immediately get to the core of the issue in a non-confrontational way. Then depending on the member and the member's reaction, she would either use political arguments or arguments to the heart, saying how necessary it was for the public well-being." The new air bag safety law was enacted with the help of Arizona Republican Senator John McCain and a coalition of health and insurance groups.

In response to the success of organizations like Public Citizen in buttonholing members of Congress to remind them of the public interest, then-Representative Newt Gingrich, a Georgia Republican, moved in 1995 shortly after becoming House Speaker to cut off public access to lawmakers.

"It's harder to actually get to see members in the House now," Claybrook said. "We used to stand in the lobby of the House either on the Republican or Democratic side, and we would catch representatives all the time, ask them if they'd decided how to vote on such-and-such a bill, give them our fact sheet and say we'd be back in touch. Then they knew we were working on an issue and they had our information.

"Gingrich abolished all that. You cannot stand in the lobby like that any more. We then decided to catch them in the Capitol subway, but then that was closed to outsiders as well. Now we have to stand outside, and it's much harder. It's easier for people with money to get office appointments, and they have enough lobbyists to do that, so these rules work disproportionately against us." Many corporate lobbyists are hired simply because of their ability to gain access to just one influential lawmaker.

The tobacco industry's bipartisan army of lobbyists in the 1990s included seven former members of Congress and at least 18 former congressional staff members. Among them were several big-name politicians, including former Texas Governor Ann Richards and former Senate Majority Leader George Mitchell, both Democrats; and Haley Barbour, the former chairman of the Republican National Committee who was elected governor of Mississippi in 2003.

When Barbour was a lobbyist, he exemplified insider influence-peddling. "He was from Mississippi and a bosom buddy of Trent Lott," Claybrook recalled. "Whenever anyone wanted something done with Trent Lott, they hired Haley Barbour, because he could pick up the phone and immediately talk to Lott. He could charge a corporation thousands of dollars and then just make a phone call. That's how things worked."

A New Consumer Front: Global Trade

Jostling for access, finding documents and presenting the pros and cons of legislation aren't the only ways Public Citizen has influenced the political landscape. Spotting a rising abuse of consumer rights is critical, as is mobilizing against it, but getting such an issue onto the public policy agenda can be the hardest part.

Ralph Nader identified international trade agreements as a key consumer concern as early as 1990, when he urged Public Citizen to organize opposition to the North American Free Trade Agreement (NAFTA) and the Uruguay Round amendments to the General Agreement on Tariffs and Trade (GATT). At the time, few people knew much about the impact of such pacts. But by reading the fine print, Nader could see that the agreements privileged investor interests over democratic processes and the health and safety of ordinary citizens.

Public Citizen jumped into opposing both pacts. But with strong support from President Bill Clinton and business groups, both were approved.

It was clear to Claybrook and other Public Citizen leaders that these so-called "free trade" pacts posed a very serious threat to fundamental American democratic values and procedures — as serious as the influence of corporate money on legislation that led Ralph Nader to create Congress Watch; the threats to public health that drove creation of the Health Research Group; the nuclear and utility deregulation issues that had sparked creation of the Energy Program; and the need for legal firepower that led to the Litigation Group. In 1995, Global Trade Watch was created as Public Citizen's fifth division to specialize in trade issues. Another Harvard-trained lawyer, Lori Wallach, became its first director (see Chapter 10).

The Global Trade Watch staff spent much time during its early years trying to educate journalists and lawmakers, arguing that the new trade agreements were not just the same old boring rules about tariffs and quotas but a new power grab by global corporations, an effort to trump domestic policymaking as never before. At a 1996 meeting in Singapore, Renato Ruggerio, then-director general of the World Trade Organization (WTO), was frank about the corporate goal: "We are writing the constitution of a single global economy."[5] Public Citizen mobilized to try to preserve U.S. consumer and citizen protections under that new economy.

Under Wallach, Global Trade Watch held media and congressional briefings, published books and reports, and helped forge a powerful coalition of religious, labor, environmental, farmer, human rights and other groups to challenge the pacts' pro-industry bias. The briefings for congressional staffers revealed that very few understood the impact of the WTO. Only one—Hank Brown, a Colorado Republican—bothered to read the full text, and he became an opponent as a result.

"It was a real eye-opener for many congressional staff," said Mary Bottari, who worked at Global Trade Watch from 1999 to 2009. "We were telling them about the WTO's implications for public health, food safety, the environment and so on, and the staffs just went, 'Wow!' Many of them really hadn't thought through the implications."

Twice during the 1990s, Global Trade Watch organized coalitions that defeated "fast track" legislation that would have granted the Clinton administration authority to negotiate new trade agreements with no input or amendments from Congress—only limited debate and up-or-down votes. By December 1999, when the WTO met in Seattle with hopes of launching a new round of talks to expand its jurisdiction, Public Citizen's years of spade work paid off: Some 50,000 people showed up there to protest the WTO and its anti-democratic, corporate-managed trade agenda.

That round of expansions has stalled ever since, and new agreements have faced much greater public scrutiny, in large part because of Public Citizen's work. The term "globalization" has become a loaded word in policy debates. However, trade deal proposals have continued to proliferate under corporate pressure for a so-called "level playing field" worldwide. The struggle to protect citizens' rights in the emerging global economy was one of Public Citizen's top agenda items as Claybrook left office.

It remained, however, just one of the many fronts on which Public Citizen works for the public good, as each program group uses an array of inventive approaches and legislative tools like FOIA that they were key to creating. Public Citizen's resulting achievements have been far greater than are commonly acknowledged, perhaps because so many were at the critical but less visible nuts-and-bolts level of government functioning.

However, the founding generation was always less interested in fame than in winning. Their *modus operandi* is perhaps expressed best by the Washington truism that you can get a lot done in this town if you don't care who gets the credit.

Endnotes

1   *Blowing Smoke*, Public Citizen's Congress Watch division, Oct. 29, 1998.

2   *Sweethearts of Big Tobacco*, Public Citizen's Congress Watch division, Feb. 13, 1998.

3   *Smokescreen: Tobacco Label Double Standards*, Public Citizen's Health Research Group, Sept. 9, 1998.

4   Neil A. Lewis, "The Fine Print: Helping a Home-State Company; Lott Tries to Avert Amendments to Bill; Then He Adds One," *The New York Times*, July 9, 1998.

5   Public Citizen fact sheets, found at www.citizen.org/Page.aspx?pid=1328.

3

CREATING A HEALTHY DEMOCRACY

O N OCTOBER 21, 1971, *The New England Journal of Medicine* printed a letter from Ralph Nader and Dr. Sidney Wolfe announcing the formation of "a new Health Research Group, a Washington-based organization that will conduct consumer-oriented studies in three major areas: occupational health and safety; drugs and product safety; and the health care delivery system." The group would be an arm of Public Citizen, which Nader had founded earlier that year.

The Health Research Group proposed to look into such things as industrial mercury poisoning, the hazards of blood transfusions and "the non-accountability of the current health care system."

Three weeks later, the new group launched its first offensive. In a letter to the Food and Drug Administration (FDA), it urged the agency to remove Red Dye No. 2, a food, drug and cosmetic color additive, from the market. It was the first of hundreds of such letters and petitions that Wolfe and his staff would fire off to the FDA during the next four decades.

In this case, Russian studies had shown a relationship between the food dye and cancer. The FDA's own advisory committee and others had cited concerns about birth defects and fetal deaths related to the additive, and urged its prompt removal from the marketplace.[1] But nothing had happened.

Public Citizen's Health Research Group repeatedly presented the government agency with more and more evidence about the food dye's dangers, and the battle raged on. Five years later, Public Citizen won: The dye was banned.

The victory was high-profile, emblematic of the fledgling consumer health and safety movement of that politically volatile era. The Health Research Group's meticulous research and persistence helped establish its credentials in the medical and scientific communities, government agencies and the news media.

With only five staff members and an annual budget of $125,000, the Health Research Group quickly mounted many new campaigns. In its first year alone, it educated chemical workers about symptoms to look for in occupational diseases, made site visits to meet and discuss with workers the Occupational Safety and Health Act and their rights under it, developed scientific data on possible product hazards for presentation to the FDA and the public, formulated tests local activists could perform to measure rates of surgery and their necessity, and surveyed the use and misuse of various drugs in hospitals — while developing ways to change these practices.

Wolfe came to Public Citizen from the National Institutes of Health (NIH), where he had conducted medical research on blood. In March 1971, a doctor from the Centers for Disease Control (later renamed the Centers for Disease Control and Prevention) in Atlanta had called Wolfe to complain about the government's failure to ban contaminated intravenous fluids. Hundreds of patients who received fluids from Abbott Laboratories had developed severe bacterial infections, and dozens had died. Instead of ordering a product recall, the government merely warned doctors to keep watch for infections and to stop using the fluids if they spotted any. Wolfe called Nader, who suggested they write to the FDA and, more importantly, release the letter to the press.

The letter hit the news media. Within a few days, Abbott recalled the contaminated fluids. "I was very surprised that we'd won," Wolfe said. "I'd never tried to do anything like that before. It was very satisfying to see that if you did your homework and had the facts on your side, you could succeed."

Electrified by the possibilities he saw, Wolfe teamed up with Nader in the fall of 1971. It didn't take long for the gravity of the public interest work and his heavy workload (he was still employed at the NIH) to persuade him to devote his energy full time to Public Citizen.

"Initially I was a little skittish about giving up 10 years of research, and I thought I would work at Public Citizen part-time, but that only lasted for about a month and a half, because I thought it was much more enjoyable and satisfying than NIH," he said. In January 1972, he became director of the Health Research Group.

Under Wolfe's guidance, Public Citizen's Health Research Group not only conducted new research but also gathered and analyzed existing scientific data with an eye toward exposing health hazards in the marketplace and challenging anti-consumer behavior among health providers.

"There were a large number of serious medical problems where studies had been done or could be done, but where the public health issue had not been addressed," Wolfe said. "If there is a drug that's uniquely dangerous but not uniquely beneficial, why is it still on the market? What was missing was someone doing something about it, partly because the people who traditionally did this research weren't trained or aware of how to change things. I wanted to start this group to change things, including to translate into common language other people's research, but also to do our own research."

One thing Wolfe understood immediately was the importance of attracting media attention. Wolfe's early activist experience included taking over a meeting of the American Medical Association (AMA) in the late 1960s with a dozen other progressive physicians and grabbing the microphone to declare that health care was a right, not a privilege, as the AMA was then asserting. He has been grabbing both literal and metaphorical microphones ever since to speak out for public health.

As one result, the pharmaceutical industry and many in the medical community became arch-adversaries. "Sidney Wolfe? We will have nothing good to say about Sidney Wolfe," an unidentified spokesman for the Pharmaceutical Manufacturers Association told *The Wall Street Journal* for a 1992 profile of Wolfe.[2] In January 2009, the same newspaper wrote about the industry's reaction to Wolfe's appointment to the FDA Drug Safety and Risk Management Committee. "Happy Halloween," headlined an industry blog reporting his appointment. An industry lobbyist was quoted as saying, "I don't see an upside to this."[3]

"Scorning gentlemanly critiques, he attacks the medical establishment with blunt and bruising rhetoric rarely found in the physician-researcher," wrote *Wall Street Journal* reporter Marilyn Chase. "Is there unnecessary surgery? It is a 'blood bath,' he says. Has a popular drug failed? It is a 'fraud,' he asserts. No polite medical euphemisms soften his language. Where politicians may fear to indict, Dr. Wolfe doesn't flinch from calling a company a liar."[4]

Wolfe's famously undiplomatic style proved popular with journalists, and his press conferences tended to draw large crowds of reporters and camera crews to capture his fist-pounding outrage. His personal energy and sense of mission transformed the otherwise routine release of information into urgent national news.

"His level of outrage is about twice everyone else's," an unidentified government scientist told *The Washington Post* in 1989.[5]

But Wolfe is also a classical pianist and former college sprinter, and Nader offered a more sophisticated analysis of Wolfe's consumer activism: "He's thought this through. He sees this as an important role for doctors. He doesn't have this hidden guilt that doctors have who work in public policy, that they should get back to patients where they belong. He thinks doctors belong in arenas that prevent patients from *becoming* patients."

Wolfe's sense of moral outrage came from his early days growing up in the Cleveland suburb of Shaker Heights. His mother taught in some of Cleveland's most financially deprived public schools, and his father was a Labor Department inspector who enforced child labor laws and was full of tales of dangerous workplaces. Wolfe's grandmother also lived with the family. She was a seamstress and shop steward in the International Ladies' Garment Workers' Union, "and she would come home telling me about struggles with bad working conditions and bosses," Wolfe said.

He first chose to study chemical engineering at college, but changed his mind after a summer stint at a chemical plant. The work was "too dangerous ... I was leaving work every day with first-degree burns on my body from hydrofluoric acid. But I was passionately interested in chemistry and chemicals, and when I decided to go to medical school, it was clear I wanted to do research. I spent all the time I could in medical school doing research on drug toxicity."

Wolfe even took a year off from school to investigate the toxicity of an anti-biotic, chloramphenicol. At Case Western Reserve University medical school, he studied under the legendary Dr. Benjamin Spock, who "made it very clear that it is not possible to understand people's health problems without understanding the circumstances from which they come."[6] One summer prior to medical school, he worked for the Cleveland coroner and investigated several deaths related to pre-scription drugs, getting an early education on the hazards of adverse drug reactions.

In July 1966, after medical school and his first year of residency, Wolfe went to Washington, D.C., to take the NIH job as a clinical and biochemical researcher. During his spare time, he plunged into activities that involved both medicine and politics, coordinating programs that gave free physical exams to inner-city children and medical care to anti-war demonstrators.

And then he met Ralph Nader.

A New Politics of Health

Since its founding, Public Citizen has been a tenacious watchdog of the FDA, sounding the alarm when dangerous medicines are being approved for sale or when later evidence mandates a ban or strong warning. When the FDA acts promptly on a problem highlighted by Public Citizen, hundreds of thousands of patients can benefit. But the government often is fatally slow to respond to the warning signs. That is when Public Citizen's Health Research Group steps in.

Wolfe defines the Health Research Group's role with characteristic specificity: "There is a selection process that determines what we work on and don't work on. The criteria haven't changed since 1971."

First, good data must be available to document a problem. Second, it has to be an important problem, which is defined by how many people are affected and the severity of the problem (cancer, for example, rather than a skin rash). Third, it must be something that other people do not appear to be successfully working on, and fourth, there must be a high likelihood of changing the situation. "We don't work on something just because it makes an interesting study or paper. We wind up doing projects that are doable, exciting and will make a difference."

Wolfe had been racking up victories on behalf of consumers for 13 years by 1984, when medical student Peter Lurie joined the Health Research Group for a year. Lurie was put to work on the group's effort to get the FDA to require that aspirin bottles carry labels warning that the pain reliever could cause a disease called Reye's Syndrome in children who were suffering from chicken pox or the flu. The disease was severe, often causing brain damage or death.

The research group had been warning the public about the dangers for several years when the government finally responded, announcing that it would ask manu-facturers to place a warning on the bottles and expand a public education campaign about the risks. But Wolfe and Lurie believed the labeling should be mandatory.

Experience had shown that voluntary guidelines were too easily disregarded. So they kept up the pressure.

First, they pursued congressional action. Then with the help of lawyers in the Litigation Group, the Health Research Group also sued the FDA in federal court. Finally, pressed from all sides, the FDA issued a final rule in March 1986 that made the warning labels mandatory, giving aspirin makers no choice in the matter.

Publicity from the fierce legal and political battle and the labeling changes that ensued have virtually eliminated Reye's Syndrome among children in the United States. Previously, as many as 5,000 cases occurred each year.

"The case taught me there were ways you could actually be an activist and be successful," recalled Lurie. "You could pinch off pieces of this bigger social problem, identify them, bring data to bear on them, and then you could win. Once you know you can win once, it's completely addictive, and all you want to do is keep on winning." Lurie later became deputy director of the Health Research Group.

Tackling Workplace Safety

One area where the Health Research Group's tenacity was particularly successful was in improving workplace health and safety. The Occupational Safety and Health Administration (OSHA) was established in 1970 to mitigate health and safety hazards in America's workplaces. But Wolfe found the agency slow to act on a number of toxic chemicals to which millions of workers were chronically exposed. He began petitioning OSHA to set exposure standards for these chemicals.

The Health Research Group often teamed with lawyers from the Public Citizen Litigation Group to sue OSHA when it delayed enactment of new regulations — as it usually did. Typically, such litigation took years to complete. But the combination proved formidable even in the face of massive resistance from chemical and other manufacturing industries. Wolfe and Public Citizen's lawyers eventually forced OSHA to limit workplace exposure to a group of common carcinogens (1974); then to the powerful industrial chemical benzene (1978); the carcinogenic pesticide DBCP, a major hazard to farm workers (1978); lead (1978); cotton dust (1978); asbestos (1985); and grain dust in the air of grain elevators or mills, which can explode when ignited by sparks or hot metal (1987).[7]

The cotton dust battle was typically groundbreaking. Wheezing and shortness of breath from a lung disease called byssinosis, caused by cotton dust in the air, had long been common among textile mill workers. Nader is credited with nicknaming the illness "brown lung disease" in a 1971 article in *The Nation*, a reference to the "black lung" disease of coal miners.

In December 1976, Public Citizen criticized OSHA for proposing inadequate standards for cotton dust at textile plants, for delaying the standards for five years and for failing to require the industry to warn its 250,000 workers of the danger of breathing the dust. The textile industry fought hard, and the debate put the term into the national lexicon. In 1978, responding to Public Citizen's pressure, OSHA revised and sped up its rule— and the incidence of brown lung disease was down by 97 percent by 1983.[8]

In 1988, Public Citizen won new limits for worker exposure to ethylene oxide, a highly carcinogenic gas used to sterilize hospital equipment (see Chapter 2). It later forced OSHA to lower the allowable exposure to cadmium (1992) and to hexavalent chromium (2006), both of which, like ethylene oxide, are known human carcinogens. New struggles over exposure limits for other substances continue to this day.

The FDA and Drug Safety

Georgia grandmother Lola Trippe Jones was one of more than 30 million Americans suffering from arthritis in the summer of 1982. The disease had crippled her so badly that she was in a nursing home. She was devoutly religious, but her joints were so gnarled and painful that she couldn't even turn the pages of her Bible. Then her doctor read about a new wonder drug, Oraflex (benoxaprofen), for treating the pain of arthritis. He prescribed the drug for her.

Within a month, Jones began to notice blood in her stool. She was sent to the hospital, where an alert physician suspected her problem might be related to the drug, and she stopped taking it. It was too late. Ten days after she was admitted to the hospital, she died from the liver damage Oraflex had caused.

Oraflex had burst onto the U.S. market in May 1982 and was vigorously promoted by its manufacturer, Eli Lilly. Almost every physician in the country received two promotional "Dear Doctor" letters weeks before it went on sale. More than 6,000 press kits were sent to the media in a then-unprecedented drug marketing campaign. An advertisement in the "Annals of Internal Medicine" in June 1982 suggested that Oraflex inhibited the underlying pathology of arthritis, an assertion for which there was no support from human studies.

In the first six weeks that it was marketed in the United States, the drug was prescribed to 500,000 people. But unbeknownst to consumers, problems had arisen with the wonder drug even before the FDA approved it. Eli Lilly had tried to have the drug approved in the 1970s, but the FDA had said the company had failed to show the drug's safety. Undeterred, Eli Lilly sold the drug in Britain through Lilly's wholly owned subsidiary, Dista, beginning in October 1980.

By May 1981, British medical authorities were receiving reports that some users of the drug had died from liver or kidney failure, gastrointestinal bleeding or perforated ulcers. Three months later, without telling the FDA about the suspicious deaths overseas, Lilly resubmitted Oraflex for U.S. approval. The FDA gave the drug a green light in April 1982.

Meanwhile, Wolfe and his researchers were burrowing through the scientific research, scouring national and foreign medical journals for information about Oraflex. They discovered alarming data in the British medical press. Studies described the deaths of 12 patients between the ages of 57 and 88. A month after

Oraflex went on sale, on June 17, 1982, Public Citizen fired off a petition to the FDA asking the agency to declare Oraflex an "imminent hazard" and to ban its use. The group said there was no evidence that the drug was any more effective than inexpensive aspirin or other non-steroidal anti-inflammatory drugs.

A month later, when the government had taken no action, Public Citizen sent it more evidence of the drug's dangers and threatened to file suit if it delayed any longer. By now, reports of American deaths related to Oraflex had surfaced, and Wolfe appeared on the Public Broadcasting System's "MacNeil-Lehrer NewsHour" to warn the public not to use the drug.

Edgar David, Eli Lilly's vice president for corporate affairs, accused Public Citizen of making "sensational accusations." He urged the public not to be alarmed and continued to push the merits of the drug to company stockholders. "Oraflex has a unique mechanism of action that differentiates it from other drugs in its class," trumpeted the company's "Six Months Report" in July 1982. The company denounced the FDA petition submitted by a "Ralph Nader-sponsored consumer activist group" as "irresponsible and without scientific merit."

On August 2 — a day before the U.S. House of Representatives opened hearings on the drug — Public Citizen filed suit in federal court to have Oraflex withdrawn from the market. On the second day of the hearings, Britain announced a 90-day suspension of the drug, and officials from the FDA and Eli Lilly met for four hours. At the end of the meeting, Lilly agreed "voluntarily" to suspend the sales of Oraflex worldwide.

Public Citizen vigilance had helped save arthritis patients from any more harm from Oraflex. But the consumer group believed that justice demanded more. In September, Public Citizen asked the FDA to direct the Justice Department to criminally prosecute Eli Lilly for withholding safety information from the FDA.

Although the company's 1983 annual report dismissed the Oraflex tragedy as "an unfortunate event in which the company believes it acted responsibly," Eli Lilly faced a host of civil lawsuits. In a settlement with the family of Lola Trippe Jones, the grandmother in Georgia, company chairman Richard Wood acknowledged "shortcomings" in Lilly's failure to report to the FDA 32 Oraflex-related deaths in Great Britain prior to U.S. approval. The drug also was implicated in the deaths of at least 49 Americans and injuries to almost 1,000 others.

The U.S. government prosecuted the company, as Public Citizen had suggested. Lilly pleaded guilty to several criminal misdemeanors and was fined $25,000, and its chief medical officer was fined $15,000. But $40,000 was a pittance compared to the $30 million the company had netted in sales from Oraflex during the 14 weeks it was on the market. And no company officers went to jail.

The FDA Doesn't Test Drugs

Although Oraflex was pulled from pharmacies, the incident raised questions about how the government could have approved such a dangerous drug in the first place. "A lot of people, including physicians, think the FDA tests drugs," Wolfe said. "It doesn't. It is totally at the mercy of the data submitted by industry, which is often analyzed to accentuate the positive."[9]

In the latter half of the 1990s, Public Citizen's health researchers had documented that the FDA approval process not only was inadequate, but was getting worse — partly because Congress had eased the standards for drug approvals and was not overseeing the FDA from a consumer protection viewpoint.

"There were drugs approved in 1996, 1997 and 1998 that wouldn't have been approved in the late 1980s," said Larry Sasich, a pharmacist who was on Public Citizen's Health Research Group staff for more than 10 years. "We are worse off than at any time since Public Citizen was started," he said in 1999. "The law now requires only a single clinical trial to measure a drug's efficacy before it can be approved. It used to require two. The safety standards for pharmacy compounding — where pharmacists can mix and match drug 'cocktails' — have been put back to pre-1938 standards."

Sasich's observation has continued to prove prescient. In 2012, a severe meningitis outbreak in Massachusetts that sickened 751 patients in 20 states and killed 64 patients in nine states was traced to the New England Compounding Center in Framingham. "There's almost no penalty for pharmacies that break the rules," reported *USA Today*, "and the people who run them simply continue with business as usual, sometimes with tragic results."[10] Under pressure from Public Citizen and others, Congress stepped in to improve the regulations and grant more regulatory authority to the FDA.

In 1996 and 1997, the FDA had approved 92 new drugs for the U.S. market, almost double the number approved during 1994 and 1995 and most other two-year periods. Drugs were increasingly winning FDA go-ahead despite warning signs. In a 15-month period in 1998 and 1999, the government had to withdraw three drugs it had recently approved; it allowed three others to remain on the market despite their withdrawal in other countries. "The FDA used to be the worldwide gold standard; now we are dangerously behind Europe on pharmaceutical safety," Sasich said.

In 1992, the pharmaceutical industry formally complained that the government was taking too long to review new drugs. The FDA cited a lack of resources as a reason for the delays. In response, Congress passed the Prescription Drug User Fee Act (PDUFA) to make the industry contribute to the cost of the reviews, allowing more FDA staffers to be added to speed up the process.

Five years later, this new arrangement came up for renewal. The drug industry launched a lobbying campaign to widen the scope of the original deal and cut back key elements of the drug safety and efficacy reviews. In the end, Congress passed the misnamed FDA Modernization Act of 1997, which weakened some safety and effectiveness standards, pushing some of them back to pre-1962 levels.

For example, it allowed companies to promote their drugs to doctors for "off-label" uses under certain conditions. This meant that if a company's drug is approved by the FDA for the treatment of, say, athlete's foot, the company is free to encourage doctors to use the drug for combating something else — eye infections, perhaps, or anything else it wants, even though the manufacturer may not have adequately researched the safety and efficacy of other uses. The law did limit promotional material for such off-label uses to peer-reviewed medical journal articles that were submitted to the FDA for review and approved by the agency for company distribution to doctors, and the FDA has acted to curb some off-label uses.

Some of the FDA's own medical officers — physicians responsible for studying the safety data submitted by drug companies — were aghast at the agency's falling standards. The Health Research Group did a survey of FDA medical officers, promising them anonymity, and revealed in 1998 that many believed the standards for approving new drugs had been dangerously lowered, to the point that many ineffective or dangerous drugs were being approved.[11]

In the survey, 19 medical officers identified 27 drugs they had recommended not be approved in the previous three years, but that the FDA had approved anyway. Seventeen medical officers described the 1998 standards of FDA review for safety and efficacy as "lower" or "much lower" than pre-1995 standards.

"In the last two years, I recommended that two drugs not be approved," recalled one officer. "They were both approved without consulting me. This never happened before. In one case, the drug did not meet the standards set up by the division, so they nullified the *standards*." Others complained that industry pressure had diluted safety criteria.

In one case, an FDA doctor reviewing a new painkiller called Duract (generic name bromfenac sodium) recommended that the drug carry a prominent label warning patients that it could damage the liver. He was overruled. In July 1997, the FDA approved Duract for use for 10 days or less, but without the recommended strong warning. The following February, after receiving complaints about adverse effects that included one death, the FDA told the manufacturer, Wyeth-Ayerst Laboratories, to strengthen the warning label and to reiterate that Duract should not be used for more than 10 days. Even after that warning, some 15 percent of patients were taking it for longer than that.

Finally, in June 1998 — just 11 months after approval — the FDA banned the drug. But by that time, four patients had been killed and eight others had to undergo liver transplants.

Duract was not an isolated case. A distinct pattern was emerging. By August 2001, the FDA had banned 11 drugs it had approved since the beginning of 1992, all but three in 1996 or after. These included some widely used medications, such as the diet drug Redux (dexfenfluramine), the diabetes drug Rezulin (troglitazone) and the heartburn medicine Propulsid (cisapride).

Public Citizen has repeatedly pressed the FDA to ban dangerous drugs. By the end of 2008, Wolfe and his staff had petitioned the agency to remove 31 prescription drugs from the market, and the FDA had complied in 19 cases. These included the painkillers Suprol and Tandearil, the diabetes drug Rezulin, the diet drug Redux and the irritable bowel medication Lotronex. In late 2003, the FDA banned the dietary supplement ephedra after a two-year campaign by Public Citizen. The supplement was blamed for 155 deaths, including that of Baltimore Orioles pitcher Steve Bechler.

In July 2008, a Public Citizen lawsuit forced the agency to require its most serious "black box" warning for packages of fluoroquinolone antibiotics such as Cipro, Avelox and Levaquin, which can cause tendinitis and tendon rupture. And in 2009, the FDA granted Public Citizen's 2008 petition to require strong warnings to doctors and patients about dangers of botulinum toxin (Botox, Myobloc and Dysport).

"The Prescription Drug User Fee Act really let the companies in the door," Sasich said. "The FDA culture now is to treat the industry as a customer, someone it has to please to keep its business. More drugs are being approved, including drugs no better and sometimes worse than what's already out there." And in September 2007, Congress voted to reauthorize PDUFA for another five years.

The industry continues to develop more "me-too" drugs, a practice related more to marketing than medicine, and this helps drive up the prices of prescription drugs. Duract, for example, hardly represented a medical breakthrough: it was the 20th compound in a family of medicines called nonsteroidal anti-inflammatory drugs, or NSAIDs. Ibuprofin, Advil, naproxen — all had similar physiological effects, but the newer ones shared a common trait: They were more profitable for the manufacturers.

"Instead of doctors prescribing older generic drugs with longer safety records, the new ones are promoted," Sasich said. "It cost California pharmacists 85 cents a pill to buy Duract, but it was no better for pain relief than ibuprofen at 7 cents. And unlike Duract, ibuprofen has no liver toxicity problem."

The costs of promoting the newer, expensive medicines — often in TV advertisements — are passed on to American consumers, resulting in rapidly increasing prescription drug prices as well as soaring costs for health insurance. Another Health Research Group survey in 1998 revealed that American patients were paying as much as six times the price Europeans paid for some prescription drugs used to treat mental illness. The U.S. price for a month's supply of the anti-psychotic drug clozapine (brand name Clozaril, made by Novartis), for example, was $317.03, compared to $51.94 in Spain. For fluoxetine (Prozac, manufactured by Lilly), the U.S. price was $72.16 for a month's supply, almost three times the $25.93 charged in Spain.[12]

Other governments negotiate drug prices through their national health insurance systems, while U.S. consumers are left at the mercy of pharmaceutical companies, which often have monopoly patents on drugs they popularize and can charge whatever they want.

"Drug prices and patients' out-of-pocket payments began soaring in the late 1980s and have continued to do so," Sasich said. "The HMOs' fastest-growing costs are prescription drugs. These price rises literally force some senior citizens who do not have prescription drug coverage to make decisions about buying drugs or food."

Advocacy for Patient Information

If being able to afford prescription drugs is the first obstacle for many patients, dealing with inadequate warning labels and misleading literature is often the second. Wolfe and his team hammered away at these problems. Getting warning labels about Reye's Syndrome on aspirin bottles was just one of many successes. In 1989, Public Citizen scored another victory for consumers when it obtained a court order forcing the FDA to require labels on tampon boxes to warn women that high-absorbency tampons were more likely to cause life-threatening toxic shock syndrome than less-absorbent ones.

In 1998, Public Citizen petitioned the FDA to attack the problem of inaccurate drug information leaflets that pharmacists hand out. Many people are killed or injured because of inaccurate or misleading information contained in these leaflets, which are commercially produced and completely unregulated.

One victim of these leaflets was Cory Christen of Houston, Texas, who died at age seven in September 1996. He had an adverse reaction to imipramine, which had been prescribed to treat his attention deficiency-hyperactivity disorder. The patient information leaflet given to Cory's parents failed to provide information about possible drug-induced hallucinations and tremors, which Cory experienced, or about the potentially deadly adverse effects of the drug, such as cardiac arrhythmias, from which he died. Instead, it warned only of minor reactions, giving the Christens a false sense of security.

"We found out the hard way that you cannot rely on your doctor or pharmacist," Cory's father said at a press conference Public Citizen held in June 1998. "These take-home sheets were our only hope, and there was no section on the most severe toxic side effects. We learned after Cory died that the serious toxic effects were well known to doctors and pharmacists and were published in the medical literature. But nobody told us."

To demonstrate the inadequacy of patient information leaflets, Public Citizen researchers examined the leaflets distributed by pharmacists for 15 NSAIDs to see whether they contained sufficient information about the severe gastrointestinal problems often associated with the drugs. Only 15 of 59 leaflets advised patients to stop taking the drug if symptoms of problems such as abdominal pain or gastric bleeding occurred.

The FDA eventually denied Public Citizen's petition for better pamphlet requirements, so the organization's attorneys filed suit in February 2003. That resulted in the agency's agreement to hold public hearings to determine if its rules covering leaflets needed to be strengthened.

The hearings were held, but the FDA still did not act. Wolfe continued to prod the agency, and in 2008, he was appointed to a four-year term on an FDA drug safety and risk management advisory committee. The following year, the committee voted unanimously that the FDA should begin regulating the content of all of these leaflets and requiring their distribution to patients.

Consumer Knowledge Is Consumer Power

Public Citizen's petition about patient leaflets was aimed at empowering people by giving them the information they need to protect themselves. This principle has always been a Public Citizen hallmark.

In 1974, Wolfe published a directory of doctors in Prince George's County, Maryland, the first of its kind in the country. The report listed the physicians' fees, office hours, credentials and hospital privileges. Another guide Wolfe released that year evaluated a community hospital in the Washington, D.C., area by investigating nursing, medical equipment and governing procedures.

Because consumers had virtually no ready access to information about the competency of their doctors, Wolfe decided in the late 1980s to publish a national compendium of physicians who had been disciplined by their state medical boards or federal agencies. Much of this information was publicly available from state medical boards but often took weeks or months for consumers to obtain, if they knew where to look. Plus, some bad doctors moved across state lines, making it even more difficult for consumers to check their disciplinary records.

"Patients have a right to know about their doctors — if they have been disciplined for sex offenses, or substance abuse, or incompetence or anything else," Wolfe said.

Public Citizen published the first edition of the book on doctors in June 1990 and called it 6,892 Questionable Doctors. The book, eventually available in national and regional editions, listed physicians who had run afoul of criminal and ethical rules for offenses such as misprescribing drugs, having improper sexual relations with patients, negligence and incompetence. It proved so popular that Wolfe began to update it periodically as the number of disciplined doctors grew.

In 1990, in part as a result, the federal government began operating its own database of disciplinary actions and additional information about malpractice lawsuits and hospital disciplinary actions. However, privacy provisions in the authorizing legislation kept much of it — including identifying information — from patient view.

In August 2000, Public Citizen published the sixth edition of its doctors' book: 20,125 Questionable Doctors. It included the astonishing examples of a South Carolina doctor who used an amputated human foot to bait a crab trap, and a Virginia doctor who used HIV-positive semen to artificially inseminate a woman — and then did it again to another woman. Public Citizen moved the information to the Internet beginning in 2002, ending the print edition, and within 18 months, people had searched more than 400,000 times on the website for reports on their doctors.

Not only did Questionable Doctors serve as an invaluable guide for patients, it pressured the medical profession to do a better job of policing itself. It also prompted state governments to find better ways of disseminating doctors' disciplinary actions and other information. State medical boards began posting more information on the Web, due in part to pressure from Public Citizen surveys that compared such sites — enough disclosure so that Public Citizen deemed the publication no longer necessary and discontinued it.

Demystifying Health Care

Questionable Doctors was just one example of the many publications Public Citizen's Health Research Group has produced to demystify the health care system and put patients on a more confident footing when dealing with doctors.

The organization's first best-seller came in 1980. *Pills That Don't Work: A Consumers' and Doctors' Guide to Over 600 Prescription Drugs That Lack Evidence of Effectiveness* included information about more than 600 prescription drugs, representing one in eight prescriptions. It was followed in 1982 by *Over the Counter Pills That Don't Work*, and in 1988 by the best-seller *Worst Pills, Best Pills*, which, in its first four editions, sold more than two million copies — and financed not just raises for most Public Citizen staff but also, eventually, the purchase of the organization's current Dupont Circle office building in downtown Washington, D.C.

A newsletter version, *Worst Pills, Best Pills News*, was first published in March 1995 and grew quickly, attaining 160,000 subscribers. An Internet version (www.worstpills.org) began in 2003 and now offers its 6,800 subscribers a searchable database and access to monograph drug reviews. The fourth print edition of the book, published in 2005, included profiles of the 538 most commonly prescribed medicines and warned consumers of particularly hazardous medications and potentially dangerous interactions. The website now includes all information in the latest edition of the book with regular updates and warnings about new prescription drug dangers.

"We are a consumer organization primarily, and our effort is to reach out in various ways to consumers," Wolfe said. "Our research is not aimed primarily at physicians, although sometimes we publish letters and articles in medical journals to exert influence on certain issues, like human experimentation."

Clinical Testing Ethics

Protecting people — often those in the most vulnerable socioeconomic groups — from unethical medical experiments has also been a cornerstone of the health group's work. In 1996, Wolfe and Lurie triggered a controversy over a needle-exchange study in Alaska by charging that the proposed study, which the NIH had approved for funding, was immoral and unethical. "The study violated Principle One of the Nuremberg Code (informed consent) and Principle Five (prior knowledge of potential harm)," said Lurie.

Under the study, some injection drug users, randomly selected, were to receive clean syringes from a needle exchange program, and their HIV and hepatitis infection rates would be compared to those of other users who would be prevented from using the program. After Public Citizen's protests, the study was put on hold and partially redesigned to expand efforts to give all participants hepatitis vaccinations.

The following year, Public Citizen stepped in against a series of HIV experiments in some of the world's poorest countries. At a medical conference in West

Africa, Lurie heard about a planned experiment that involved giving thousands of HIV-positive pregnant women a placebo instead of AZT, a drug already shown to reduce mother-to-infant HIV transmission by two-thirds. The idea was to compare low-dose AZT treatments to a placebo, but about a thousand babies were expected to die needlessly because their mothers would get the placebo. Most of a dozen such studies in developing countries were to be funded by American taxpayers through the Centers for Disease Control and Prevention (CDC) or the NIH.

Lurie's outrage spread worldwide. In September 1997, Public Citizen wrote an article for *The New England Journal of Medicine* charging that the experiments violated basic ethical guidelines that require researchers to provide study patients with the best-proven therapy. The journal also ran an editorial in support of Public Citizen's position, triggering a worldwide debate on the morality of the studies.[13]

Public Citizen recommended that the studies be redesigned so that researchers were comparing patients given shorter regimens of AZT to those who received longer regimens, rather than comparing the effects of shorter regimens to those of placebos. Eventually, when a CDC-funded study in Thailand confirmed that a four-week course of AZT did work better than a placebo in reducing maternal-infant HIV transmission (as Public Citizen had predicted), the government announced that all women in placebo groups of the various studies would be offered AZT.[14]

"When we knew nothing, they brought the matter to public attention," said Nigerian virologist Oyewale Tomori, who first became acquainted with Public Citizen during this ethical debate. "They stood fierce in support of the vulnerable, the poor, the uneducated, the ignorant and the helpless. They fought for justice, fair play and ethics. They gave us courage to fight at our own end."[15]

Improving the Health Care System

Wolfe and the Health Research Group have long been concerned with the overall inadequacies of the health care system and its harmful effects, especially when people fall through the cracks.

For years, controversy raged over whether cesarean sections represented a gross and excessive danger to mothers or a new and more convenient way of delivering normal babies. Are C-sections the guarantee of a perfect baby and the root of the decline in infant deaths, or knee-jerk and often unwarranted acts by physicians? Are they a reaction to problems of malpractice, or perhaps motivated by the additional income they generate for doctors and hospitals?

In 1987, the Health Research Group published a pathbreaking report on this issue. For the first time, it made data on hospital and physician cesarean rates widely available. In a 1994 update, the group expanded its database to cover nearly 4 million births occurring in U.S. hospitals in 1992. The 1994 report was at the time the most comprehensive source of information available on the rates of hospital and state caesarean section and vaginal birth after previous cesareans.

It concluded that C-sections, while at times a life-saving intervention for both mother and child, can cause significant harm to mothers without providing additional benefits to infants if performed outside of certain well-defined medical situations.[16]

Looking at other health care issues, the Health Research Group released a report in 1996 on "hospital merger mania," describing "an unprecedented wave of buyouts, mergers and acquisitions." It found that in 1995, about one in 12 hospitals was involved in merger and acquisition activity, accelerating a trend toward hospitals run primarily for profit, often at patients' expense.[17] A few years later, Wolfe's researchers looked into "patient dumping" — hospitals' deliberate shirking of care to the needy. They found it had reached alarming levels. Another report found that very few hospitals were fined for this abuse, even after they were found to have violated laws prohibiting such dumping.

Wolfe and the Health Research Group argued for years that the real, most enduring solutions to these problems would be comprehensive reform of the American health care system in the form of universal health coverage, also known as a "single-payer" system. The government would be the sole source of pay to doctors for care given to patients, and health insurance companies and the costly bureaucracy they create would be eliminated. With the savings, the U.S. health care system could afford to provide care to everyone.

Wolfe has always been passionate about this, arguing that health care is a right, not a privilege. When President Bill Clinton tried to reform health care in 1994, Public Citizen dived in, with Congress Watch in the lead, enlisting nearly 100 co-sponsors for a single-payer health care bill. The reform effort crumbled, however, and throughout the late 1990s and 2000s, more and more people became uninsured — from 40 million in 1997 to 47 million in 2009. Health care costs began not only to break small businesses but drag down the economy. Even large companies began to call for change.

As Joan Claybrook departed Public Citizen in January 2009, President Barack Obama was taking office. He had pledged dramatic reform of the health care system, but it was clear that neither the White House nor congressional lawmakers were going to fight for any single-payer solutions. They faced overwhelming pressure from an army of lobbyists for the drug, insurance and hospital industries, among others, who demanded — and got — what Wolfe regarded as only incremental reforms. The Affordable Care Act, requiring Americans to obtain health coverage but basing it on the private insurance industry, became law in 2010. The need to replace the private insurance system with a single-payer approach — an expanded and improved Medicare-for-all — remains.

Advocacy Is Preventive Medicine

Wolfe knew when he started working for Public Citizen that he wanted to remain with the organization and devote his life to health advocacy. And he did. On stepping aside to become a senior adviser to the group in June 2013, he said, "I am as — or more—enthused now as I was at the beginning."

He wasn't the only one to spend his career at Public Citizen. Phyllis McCarthy joined Public Citizen's health team in 1978 and made it her life's work. She went from doing clerical tasks, answering consumer calls and typing to editing the group's many publications. In 2001, a year before she died, she said she got enormous satisfaction from the work because she was reminded continually of the group's impact on the lives and health of thousands of people.

"You really feel like you're a health agency," she said. "Sid has said on occasion that it's like we're in an operating room. If you get the information out there quicker, that one day might save that one person who is taking something and might have an adverse reaction to it."

Lurie assesses the Health Research Group's work this way: "If you go out to your average physician in Kentucky, the chances are overwhelming that they won't have any idea who Sid is, but there's probably not a day that goes by that they do — or don't do — something that Sid has had an impact on."

Public Citizen is working to create more Sid Wolfes by supporting medical school courses that promote research-based health activism. By 2009, such courses were offered at Boston University, the University of Pennsylvania, Tulane Medical School in New Orleans, and Montefiore Hospital and Medical Center in New York.

Dr. Michael Carome, who succeeded Wolfe as Health Research Group director in 2013, said that under Wolfe, the group had set the global standard for research-based health advocacy work. "The group has never backed down in the face of enormous industry and government pressure, and as a result, citizens in our country are safer and healthier," he said.

Nader also sees Wolfe's contribution on a macro level. "His role is preventive medicine, and not many doctors spend full time doing that. Sidney's one of the best vaccines around."[18]

Endnotes

1   Health Research Group letter to FDA Commissioner Charles C. Edwards, November 12, 1971.
2   Marilyn Chase, "A Consumer Crusader with an M.D. is a Pain to the Health Industry: Sidney Wolfe Wins Bitter Fights Against Breast Implants, Risky Drugs and Practices," *The Wall Street Journal*, April 2, 1992.
3   Alicia Mundy, "A Wolfe in Regulator's Clothing: Drug Industry Critic Joins the FDA," *The Wall Street Journal*, Jan. 9, 2009.
4   Marilyn Chase, *The Wall Street Journal*, April 2, 1992.
5   Susan Okie, "Running on Outrage," *Washington Post Health Section*, Dec. 5, 1989, p. 14.
6   David Bollier, *Citizen Action and Other Big Ideas: A History of Ralph Nader and the Consumer Movement*, Center for Study of Responsive Law, 1991, p. 98 and Sidney Wolfe, interview.
7   David Bollier, *Citizen Action and Other Big Ideas*, p. 63.
8   Justin Feldman, "Regulations at Work: Five Rules that Save Workers' Lives and Protect Their Health," *Reality Check: The Forgotten Lessons of Deregulation and Unsung Successes of Regulation*, Public Citizen, Washington, D.C., 2013, p. 135–137.
9   Alicia Ault, "Health Care Watchdog," *Health Watch*, July/August 1991, p. 51.
10 Peter Elsler, "Harsh Punishments Rare for Drug Compounding Mistakes," *USA Today*, March 22, 2013.

11 *FDA Medical Officers Report Lower Standards Permit Dangerous Drug Approvals,* Public Citizen's Health Research Group, Dec. 2, 1998.
12 *International Comparison of Prices for Antidepressant and Antipsychotic Drugs,* Public Citizen's Health Research Group, July 15, 1998.
13 Peter Lurie and Sidney M. Wolfe, "Unethical Trials of Interventions to Reduce Perinatal Transmission of the Human Immunodeficiency Virus in Developing Countries," *New England Journal of Medicine,* Vol. 337, No. 12, Sept. 18, 1997.
14 "NIH Experiments on HIV-positive Women in Developing Countries," Public Citizen press release, March 18, 1998.
15 Oyewale Tomori, e-mail correspondence.
16 *Unnecessary Cesarean Sections: Curing a National Epidemic,* Public Citizen's Health Research Group, May 1994.
17 M. Gabay and Sidney Wolfe, *Who Controls the Local Hospital? The Current Hospital Merger and Acquisition Craze and the Disturbing Trend of Not-For-Profit Hospital Conversions to For-Profit Status,* Public Citizen's Health Research Group, June 1996.
18 John W. Kole, "Leaning on the Medical Establishment," *The Milwaukee Journal,* June 9, 1986.

4

SEEKING JUSTICE,
SETTING PRECEDENTS

——

IN SEPTEMBER 1966, Jagdish Chadha arrived in the United States from Kenya to attend Bowling Green University in Ohio. He studied hard and played on the varsity tennis team, and by 1972 he had earned bachelor's and master's degrees. With his student visa expiring, Chadha prepared to go home. But things had changed in his native land. Chadha was of Indian heritage, and the newly independent government had launched a policy of "Africanization" that kept him from being recognized as a Kenyan citizen. In Kenya he would have no rights, no job prospects, no future.

Chadha tried to go to Britain instead because he had a British nationality certificate (Kenya was a British colony until 1963). But Britain at that time was inundated with immigration requests. Britain told Chadha that it could take years for them to decide his case. With his student visa expiration date looming, Chadha was trapped in legal limbo.

After a series of stressful hearings, the U.S. Immigration and Naturalization Service (INS) announced that Chadha could remain in the United States. He thought his troubles were over. Then, without explanation, the U.S. House of Representatives singled out Chadha and four other recent immigrants and overturned the INS decision to let them stay. The House, for reasons unspecified to this day, had chosen to target them with its "legislative veto." This device allowed Congress — often acting through only one chamber or even one committee, as in this case — to overturn individual rules or other decisions of the executive branch, for any reason whatsoever.

To Chadha this meant disaster: he would be deported to Kenya. To Public Citizen's Alan Morrison, it was a perfect example of why the legislative veto was wrong. Not only was it bad public policy, he reasoned, but it violated the U.S. Constitution because it gave power to Congress that rightfully belonged in the executive branch.

"The subcommittee didn't have much power so it chose to use this one, just to show the INS who's the boss," he said.

Morrison decided to challenge the Chadha decision. He saw that Congress had become enamored of the legislative veto because it allowed members to vote for a popular measure and bask in public approval, then quietly sabotage implementation at the behest of industry lobbyists. For federal agencies, the legislative veto's existence meant that no decision was really binding because Congress could always step in.

"The case became bigger than Chadha," Chadha said. "I became a legal footnote."

Chadha's story would turn into one of the most significant constitutional arguments the U.S. Supreme Court had ever heard. For six years, from 1977 to 1983, Morrison made a complex legal case, but the principle behind the argument was relatively simple. As Chadha put it, "You can't write the law and execute it too."

It was a classic separation of powers issue. Congress writes the laws, but it is the responsibility of the executive branch, in this case the INS, to carry them out — with no interference from Congress.

In June 1983, the Supreme Court invalidated the legislative veto. The ruling in *Immigration and Naturalization Service v. Chadha* that the veto provision was unconstitutional was one of the most dramatic high court decisions ever, affecting more than 200 federal statutes — at the time, more than all other Supreme Court cases overturning statutes in history combined.

It strengthened the power of executive branch agencies to craft and enforce standards to protect the environment and to ensure the safety of food, automobiles, prescription drugs and other consumer products. It also meant Chadha could stay in the United States.

"Public Citizen called me," Chadha said. "I didn't know them. But if Public Citizen had not taken the case, I'm sure I would have been deported."[1] In his own way, he said, he had "tested the pillars of democracy" and "done a service to the Republic."

A New Form of Citizenship — Public Interest Litigation

Clarifying the constitutional separation of powers was far from the minds of Ralph Nader and Alan Morrison when they founded the Public Citizen Litigation Group on February 5, 1972. After starting Public Citizen a year earlier, Nader knew he needed legal firepower. Writing investigative reports and exposing consumer threats through the media were important tools, but sometimes litigation was clearly going to be the only way to force change.

At the time, few lawyers were working in the public interest. Law schools were producing too many lawyers eager to serve big business, Nader had complained in 1969: "Lawyers labored for polluters — not anti-polluters; for sellers — not consumers; for corporations — not citizens; for labor leaders — not rank and file; for — not against — rate increases or weak standards before government agencies; for — not against — judicial and administrative delay; for preferential business access to government and against equal citizen access to the same government."

Thanks in large part to the popularity of Nader's consumer movement, this picture changed dramatically over the next few years. Before 1969, an estimated 23 public interest law centers existed in the United States, employing fewer than 50 full-time attorneys. Fifteen years later this number had mushroomed to 158 groups nationwide with 906 lawyers,[2] and by the time Joan Claybrook left Public Citizen in 2009, Harvard Law School listed nearly 500 firms in its guide to private law firms doing public interest work.[3]

From the beginning, the Public Citizen Litigation Group chose its cases for their potential to improve public policy and set precedents for advancing the public interest, based on a few guiding principles. First and foremost, its attorneys would serve the lawyering needs of Public Citizen, as well as the independent spin-offs Nader had started — the Center for Auto Safety, the Corporate Accountability Research Group, the Public Interest Research Group, the Center for Study of Responsive Law, and the Aviation Consumer Action Project — and, of course, Nader himself.

Second, the lawyers would pursue important cases in areas where none of Nader's groups were then working. Morrison and Nader foresaw many opportunities to use the courts to bring about change by applying existing legal principles to new situations.

Third, the group knew it could not take on every worthy cause, not to mention every person with a worthy claim but no lawyer. It therefore adopted the general principle that it would not take a case if some other public interest group was already working on the issue. This meant that it usually declined cases in civil rights, education, employment and housing, as well as environmental cases, except when the specific issue, such as nuclear power, related to the work of Public Citizen. (However, because Public Citizen over the years acquired considerable expertise in litigating before the U.S. Supreme Court, it has often assisted other groups in bringing high court cases in civil rights, open government and administrative law.)

Fourth, the lawyers provided non-litigation legal advice and assistance to other parts of Public Citizen: drafting petitions to federal agencies, writing and delivering congressional testimony, reviewing reports for libel and scrutinizing legislation for constitutional flaws.

You Can Fight City Hall

No formal search occurred for a director to start the Litigation Group. Alan Morrison's name arrived through the U.S. mail.

In the summer of 1971, Morrison was assistant chief of the civil division in the office of the U.S. Attorney for the Southern District of New York. One day at lunch, an employee named Jerry Neugarten, then between his second and third years at Harvard Law School, asked Morrison what he was going to do next. Morrison said he was thinking about starting a public interest law firm. Neugarten had worked the previous summer for Nader and he immediately suggested writing to Nader. Morrison demurred. But several weeks later, when Morrison returned from a vacation, he found a phone message: "Call Ralph Nader's office." Neugarten had written the letter for him.

When Morrison arrived at Public Citizen, he was flush with ideas for using the law to help the public. "I began to keep a list on a piece of yellow folded paper in my wallet for ideas for cases," he recalled. The crumpled legal-pad list included ideas for making the legal profession more accessible to the public, taking on the power of the presidency, protecting the free speech rights of nonprofit groups and bringing antitrust actions. It was so ambitious that it was laughable — except that many of its goals were achieved.

"At the time, federal agencies often didn't pay attention to what the law was, because no one except industry had ever called them on it before," Morrison said. That would soon change. Neither Morrison nor the other lawyers at Public Citizen believed in the old adage that "you can't fight city hall."

In the ensuing years, Morrison's ambitious young lawyers filed petitions and lawsuits one after another. They demanded investigations and disclosure of campaign contributions by corporations and unions alike. They demanded that the Food and Drug Administration release data on the safety of birth control pills. They challenged the use of carcinogenic food additives in cured meats. They questioned government authority to give corporations exclusive patents to products developed with public money. They attacked the failure to hold public hearings on auto price increases during the wage and price freeze of the early 1970s. And that was just for starters.

"Choosing cases was an art rather than a science," Morrison said. "We weren't always true to [the guidelines] because sometimes we just couldn't let something go by."

This initial legal maelstrom was so intense that within a few months, the Department of Justice issued an internal memo: "If any attorney receives a call from the staff of Ralph Nader, he is not to give out any information whatsoever, but should refer the call to the Office of Public Information."[4]

The beauty of working in the courtroom, as opposed to the legislative chambers, Morrison said, was that if you had the law on your side, you could prevail over money and politics. "If we file a lawsuit, the system requires that it be adjudicated," said Brian Wolfman, a longtime lawyer in the Litigation Group who served as its director from 2004 to 2009. "In the other arenas, it's entirely political — they can lie, they can ignore you or they just raise more money than you. But not in litigation."

In its first 38 years, the Public Citizen Litigation Group represented all the Nader-related organizations, individual citizens, civic groups, workers, journalists and members of Congress. It took on major corporations, bar associations, state and local governments, labor unions and many federal agencies. Its lawyers argued hundreds of cases in all 12 regional circuits of the U.S. appellate courts, as well as the Federal Circuit, a specialized national appellate court. And by the end of Claybrook's tenure in early 2009, the Litigation Group had argued 55 times in the Supreme Court, winning 32 times.

This was and is an incredible record, given that the adversaries were almost invariably large corporations or the government, with their nearly unlimited legal resources.

"You lose a lot, but mostly you bring cases where something bad is going on and there's always a chance to stop it. And if you lose you're just back where you started," Morrison said. "You aren't going to make it any worse."

In addition to its own Supreme Court work, Public Citizen helps lawyers around the country prepare public interest cases as part of its Alan Morrison Supreme Court Assistance Project, named in 2004 in Morrison's honor. Many of these cases pit the meager resources of small groups — with little or no funding for lawsuits and no clerks or legal aides — against high-powered Washington, D.C. law firms or the Justice Department. "It requires a certain childlike optimism to continue in this job, a naïve belief that you can actually make a difference," said Morrison. "If you start losing that, then you might as well not be here. Our message is: You can fight city hall."

Challenging the Executive Branch

During the Litigation Group's first year, when the Chadha case was still several years away, Morrison found himself defending the balance of powers among the three government branches. President Richard Nixon had refused to spend money that Congress had appropriated for a specific purpose, an act called "impoundment." In this case, money was intended for highway construction, and while Public Citizen might have preferred that it be used for something else, that was beside the point. A vital principle was at stake: When Congress enacts a law, the president cannot simply refuse to comply with it.

The case, *State Highway Commission of Missouri v. Volpe*, was between the Missouri Highway Commission and the U.S. Department of Transportation. It was pending in the federal court of appeals in St. Louis, and the Litigation Group wanted to file an *amicus* (friend of the court) brief to support Missouri's position: The funds had to go toward the roads. Because Congress had a major stake in the controversy, the Litigation Group recruited some formidable allies to join its brief: the chairman of every standing Senate committee, the Senate majority leadership and a group of prominent senators and representatives, including Senator Sam Ervin, a North Carolina Democrat, who was leading the fight against impoundment.

Then, just days before the court of appeals was to hear oral argument, a telephone call came from the court clerk, inviting Public Citizen to present the *amicus* at oral argument — an extremely rare invitation. With the Litigation Group voicing the claim, the appellate court ruled that Nixon's action was unlawful and that he had a duty to faithfully execute the law as Congress had written it.

Several years later, Nixon again withheld money that Congress had appropriated, this time for sewage treatment plants as part of an effort to clean up the nation's waterways. Public Citizen again filed suit, this time in Virginia, and the suit was combined with another and sent to the Supreme Court. In *Train v. City of New York* (1975), the high court agreed with Public Citizen and ruled that the president had no authority to refuse to spend appropriated funds. Congress solidified the verdict with hearings where Morrison and Nader testified, and the two then helped write the Impoundment Control Act of 1974, which formally outlawed the practice.

"The separation of powers is one of the remarkable virtues of the Constitution," Morrison told *The New York Times* in a 1988 interview. "There are temporary ebbs and flows due to the political climate, but basically each branch has the power to do what it needs to do, and not so much that it can keep the others from doing what they need to do. I regard the separation of powers as a fundamental part of our system that we shouldn't tinker with."[5]

The Watergate Case

Public Citizen's legal battles with the Nixon administration were many. In May 1973, Attorney General Elliot Richardson appointed a special prosecutor, Archibald Cox, to investigate the myriad allegations about abuse of power by the Nixon White House, charges that grew out of the bungled burglary of the Democratic National Committee headquarters at the Watergate hotel and apartment complex on June 17, 1972.

A few months after Cox's appointment, with the Watergate scandal in full bloom, a Nixon staffer revealed to Congress that the president had secretly tape-recorded conversations and telephone calls in his office. Nixon resisted the special prosecutor's demands to turn over the tapes, and Cox refused to accept a White House compromise offer to release summarized material. Nixon ordered that Cox be fired.

On October 20, 1973, in what became known as the Saturday Night Massacre, both Richardson and his deputy William Ruckelshaus resigned rather than follow Nixon's order to fire Cox. Nixon then turned to Solicitor General Robert Bork, who carried out the order.

But the rule establishing the special prosecutor's office said that Cox could be fired only for "extraordinary improprieties." Nixon's lawyers did not accuse Cox of such improprieties. Instead, they argued that the president had the authority to fire members of the executive branch at his discretion, and that any attempt by Congress to impose conditions was unconstitutional. Ralph Nader, joined by Utah Democratic Senator Frank Moss and two members of the House of Representatives, filed a lawsuit claiming that the firing was unlawful.

Public Citizen won the case, *Nader v. Bork*, in the U.S. District Court for the District of Columbia in November 1973. Although Cox decided not to reclaim his position, the victory won considerable legal and moral protection for future special prosecutors. More critically at the time, it was the underpinning for the pivotal July

1974 ruling in which the Supreme Court ordered the tapes of 64 White House conversations turned over to Cox's successor, Leon Jaworski. Facing impeachment, Nixon resigned on August 8, 1974.

Rebalancing the Powers

A decade after Watergate and two years after the Chadha victory, Public Citizen's lawyers returned to the Supreme Court to argue another case involving the separation of powers between the executive and legislative branches. In 1985, Congress approved the Gramm-Rudman-Hollings Act, legislation giving civil servants and bureaucrats in the General Accounting Office the power to make automatic cuts to agency budgets. With this law, Congress in effect pre-empted the executive branch's authority to determine how much money would be spent on what.

Public Citizen challenged the law on behalf of Representative Mike Synar, an Oklahoma Democrat, arguing that it breached the lines of authority separating the branches of government. Once again, the Supreme Court agreed, declaring in *Bowsher v. Synar* (1986) that the law's key provision was unconstitutional.

The work continued into the 1990s struggle over the line-item veto. President Ronald Reagan had campaigned in the previous decade for this power so he could strike individual appropriations from massive congressional spending bills, rather than having to veto entire bills. Most states have some form of line-item veto in their constitutions, but the U.S. Constitution contains no such authorization. In 1996, after Republicans took control of Congress, lawmakers passed a federal version.

The law not only allowed the president to zero out an appropriation Congress had approved, it also authorized him to simply reduce the amount if he desired. "This was an astonishing gift of authority, a transfer of power from Congress — which always has had primacy over budgetary matters — to the president," said David Vladeck, who joined the Litigation Group in 1977 and succeeded Morrison as director in 1993.

Soon after the line-item veto act went into effect, Public Citizen attorneys joined a small group of other Washington, D.C. lawyers to challenge it. On behalf of four senators and two representatives, they argued that the measure interfered with constitutional lawmaking powers. The act specifically authorized members of Congress to bring such a suit.

Public Citizen persuaded a trial court to strike down the law, but in 1997, the Supreme Court reversed the decision. It ruled that members of Congress had no legal "standing" to bring the suit because they had no personal stake in the outcome. The following year, the same issue returned to the high court in a different case, involving the city of New York, and this time the justices ruled 6 to 3 that the line-item veto could not stand, relying largely on the same arguments that Morrison had made in the earlier case.

Assuring Freedom of Information

Public Citizen's pioneering role in preserving the separation of powers is widely known in Washington, D.C., but its Litigation Group may be even better known for ensuring the public's right to obtain government information. From its inception, as described in Chapter 2, the Litigation Group has actively represented (and informally advised and assisted) a wide variety of public interest organizations, journalists, authors and others in using the Freedom of Information Act (FOIA) to get information from the federal government, and in some cases from state governments as well.

This work is driven by the conviction that meaningful citizen participation in democracy depends on access to information — in particular about what the government is actually doing or not doing, rather than what it says it is doing or not doing. For many years, the Center for Study of Responsive Law funded the work through what Public Citizen called its Freedom of Information Clearinghouse.

To this day, Public Citizen helps individuals, nonprofit groups and others obtain statistics, reports, policy statements, or other records that they need to further their work.

Public Citizen attorneys have successfully opened up grand jury records of great historical significance. They have required federal agencies to preserve papers and data, and forced compliance with the Federal Advisory Committee Act, which controls the way the executive branch gets advice from outside advisory groups. Overall, the Litigation Group has handled "many hundreds, possibly thousands" of open government cases since its founding, far more than any U.S. law firm, nonprofit or private; an exact count is difficult because of refilings, addenda and appeals. These cases not only shape the way laws are carried out, but they also update the very meaning of the law as technology and circumstances change.

"They're also a wonderful educational tool for the public," Morrison said. "They force the defendants to explain what they're doing and why they're doing it. Agencies change when they have to explain things. The cases also open lots of avenues you can pursue in other forums."

A case in point involved government electronic records. On January 20, 1989, Ronald Reagan was about to leave office and George H.W. Bush was about to be sworn in. As one of his final acts, Reagan ordered the destruction of all electronic records in the White House, arguing that paper records had been created for anything worth saving. Two researchers and the National Security Archive filed suit to preserve the electronic records, and because of the complexity of the issues, asked Public Citizen to handle the case. A key issue was whether FOIA and related laws on records preservation and disclosure applied to electronic records as well as paper records.

Public Citizen lawyer Mike Tankersley, who took the laboring oar after Public Citizen defeated most of the government's early attempts to get the case thrown out, strongly believed that these records should not be destroyed. "The parts of history that really give it substance and humanity are not official documents but the private correspondence and individual reflections," said Tankersley, a former history major. "Historians have a great wealth of that from the 19th and early 20th centuries because people were much better at writing letters. The currency for that today is not the post office letter, but electronic mail, and if you strip that away, all you have is the official record, and history loses a lot."

Tankersley almost single-handedly led the long fight against an army of high-level Justice Department and agency lawyers. After years of litigation, the U.S. Court of Appeals for the District of Columbia affirmed its prior ruling that the law did indeed require electronic records to be preserved and made public under FOIA, just like paper records, and that most of the records that plaintiffs sought were available under FOIA.[6]

This was an historic achievement that greatly expanded the public's right to have access to government decision-making, research and data. Among other things, it preserved electronic documents that President George H. W. Bush and Col. Oliver North, a prominent figure in the Iran-Contra scandal, had likely hoped would disappear. North had deleted incriminating e-mails concerning the U.S. sale of missiles to Iran to fund rebels fighting against (or "contra") the government of Nicaragua. But North did not realize that the National Security Council computer had saved backup copies on tape.

Reagan's order would have destroyed even the backup tapes not already turned over to Iran-Contra prosecutors, and at the end of the elder Bush's administration in 1993, Bush directed the erasure of *all* records from White House computers and backup tapes. But because of the litigation, electronic messages concerning Iran-Contra and other initiatives of Reagan's National Security Council are now in the National Archives.

"There's every manner of stuff in the files, from the announcement of the schedule for a softball game to high-level correspondence between Colin Powell and an official on the National Security staff about how they should respond to an emerging international crisis," Tankersley said. "A large amount covers the correspondence between Oliver North and [John] Poindexter about the Iran-Contra affair, and how they had arranged to set up a private foreign policy."

Researchers discovered that the tapes contained important revelations about the exploits of North and his associates that prosecutors had overlooked. Other messages covered developments in the Soviet Union and the Middle East and terrorism in Libya. As a result of the litigation, the government released more than 3,000 White House and National Security Council e-mails from the Reagan administration. Much of that record was later published by the National Security Archive in the book *White House E-mail*. Further Public Citizen litigation ensured the preservation of electronic records from all subsequent administrations.[7]

For Tankersley, the opportunity to pursue such cases and shape the law was a major attraction of working for Public Citizen. "It's a unique opportunity to work on a regular basis on issues of public importance where you can advocate the views you believe in, rather than merely respond to the desires of a client," he said. "We're not passively waiting to respond to a legal issue that clients we serve have encountered. We're very actively trying to identify problems before they arise or move the law in a particular direction."

Another major open government case involving the presidency sprang from the Watergate crisis. When Nixon resigned in 1974, Congress passed a law requiring the White House to turn over and make public all materials involving Nixon's abuse of power. It was Public Citizen that went to court repeatedly to make sure this law was obeyed, while the disgraced former president fought to keep secret as much as possible.

In April 1996, after more than 15 years of exhaustive litigation and Nixon's death, Public Citizen won an agreement with the former president's estate to release thousands of hours of White House audio tapes. In the years since, patient scholars listening to and studying these tapes have found important new information about the Nixon era. The tapes can now be heard and copied at the National Archives.

The Truth About Alger Hiss

In the late 1990s, Public Citizen got involved in another case of historical significance — a re-examination of the Alger Hiss espionage case of the 1940s. The Hiss indictment, trial and ultimate conviction were among the defining political and legal events of the early Cold War.

Hiss was seen as among the best of the New Dealers. He was educated at Johns Hopkins University and Harvard Law School, was a law clerk for Justice Oliver Wendell Holmes, became a senior State Department official and, at the time of his indictment, was president of the Carnegie Endowment for International Peace. His accusers were Whittaker Chambers, a self-confessed ex-courier for the Soviet underground in the 1930s, and Richard Nixon, then an obscure junior congressman from California. They accused Hiss of being involved in a Soviet underground "apparatus" while he was serving in the State Department during the 1930s.

In 1948, Hiss was indicted and convicted on two counts of perjury, and served nearly four years in prison. He maintained his innocence until his death in 1996. Questions have persisted ever since about his guilt, about possible grand jury improprieties and about possible political interference from Nixon with the legal process.

The American Historical Association and a group of historians asked Public Citizen in 1998 to help them gain access to the grand jury records that led to Hiss' indictment. With cooperation from people on both sides of the Hiss controversy, David Vladeck and another Litigation Group lawyer, Lucinda Sikes, asked U.S. District Judge Peter K. Leisure of New York to order the release of 4,250 pages of grand jury records. In 1999, Leisure ordered the release, citing the documents' value to historians and the lack of any serious privacy concerns 50 years after the events. He also noted that disclosure would not interfere with any legitimate government law enforcement purpose.

The released documents included the testimony of Chambers and Elizabeth Bentley, the principal witness against dozens of alleged Soviet spies, and 80 other witnesses, many of whom were key Cold War figures. Since the release, combatants on both sides of the Hiss debate have cited the grand jury records in their ongoing argument about Hiss' guilt or innocence.

One was Hiss' son Tony, who finally got to see the grand jury testimony that helped send his father to jail. "Alger had been trying to get the records since 1949," Tony Hiss said in an interview. "In early 1949, he asked the judge to release the testimony because it would help him prepare his defense. Clearly there is a great deal of material here that, had it been known, would have been a great help to the defense. There are points that raise new questions about the intervention by Congressman Nixon, who seems clearly to have presented misleading information to the grand jury."

Apart from illuminating the history of the Hiss case, Judge Leisure's decision set an important precedent. It was the first time that grand jury records had been released to the public on the principle of their historical importance. Subsequent releases included those related to spying charges against Ethel and Julius Rosenberg and to President Richard Nixon's Watergate testimony.

"I know my dad would have been extraordinarily proud to have served as a test case that is extending the reach of the Constitution and establishing the principle that there are cases of such historic importance that the public has a need to know that outweighs the traditional importance of grand jury secrecy," Tony Hiss said. "It's not just about the Hiss case. There are potentially many cases in the federal vaults that ought to be examined by the public in the interests of a free and open society and an informed citizenry."

Protecting Public Health and Safety

Many of Public Citizen's open government cases attract little public attention but are critical to public safety. In the late 1990s, for example, the Food and Drug Administration (FDA) was increasingly approving the marketing of new prescription drugs even when safety concerns lingered, provided that the drug company agreed to conduct post-approval safety studies. Those studies were supposed to be available to the public. But too often, at the industry's urging, the FDA refused to disclose information about a study's design (called protocol), making it difficult to assess the data's validity.

The Litigation Group filed a series of FOIA cases that succeeded in forcing the agency to make these protocols public. This means that Public Citizen's Health Research Group and others interested in drug safety can now monitor both the design and the results of drug safety studies to see whether the public is being protected.

The FDA was the Litigation Group's most frequent FOIA defendant in its first 38 years, but the group took on virtually every federal agency and the Executive Office of the President. The organization then and now has seen FOIA cases as essential to fulfilling one of its primary missions: making sure that federal health, safety, law enforcement and environmental regulators do their job to protect the public. Under relentless pressure from lobbyists and sometimes from legislators feeling that pressure themselves, federal agencies often have withheld information and acted to protect the interests of businesses they were supposed to regulate.

Some administrations were more persistent lawbreakers in this sense than others, but none has had anything close to an unblemished record. From its inception, the Public Citizen Litigation Group brought lawsuits to require agencies to comply with the laws and ensure that their decisions are based on relevant criteria; that their factual premises are sound; that the reasons they give for their actions are not arbitrary; and that whistleblowers—both at corporations and at government agencies—are protected from retaliation. The Litigation Group also has been active in the fields of occupational safety and health, nuclear power, auto safety and consumer product safety (see Chapters 3, 5 and 9).

Such suits are hard to win because courts afford the agencies great deference. But knowing that watchdogs like Public Citizen are out there and willing to resort to litigation tends to make agencies more attentive and rigorous in their work. "Agencies know we can sue and that changes their behavior," Morrison said. "Even in the cases we didn't win, they often gave us a bunch of documents anyway to show the judge how reasonable they were."

Fighting Toxic Toys and Chemicals

Beginning with the Reagan administration, Public Citizen often went to court to force laggard agencies to act on requests for rulemaking. The toxic toys case was a good example.

In 2008, reports had begun to surface that many children's toys were laden with dangerous chemicals, including harmful chemicals called phthalates. Animal studies had linked phthalates with reproductive abnormalities and decreased production of sperm and testosterone. When the widespread use of phthalates in toys became known, Congress by an overwhelming majority banned their continued use after February 10, 2009.

Before the ban went into effect, however, a law firm wrote to the Consumer Product Safety Commission (CPSC) on behalf of unidentified companies, requesting that the agency block only the production—and not the sale—of toys with phthalates. This would be a huge loophole, allowing manufacturers to stockpile toys with the banned phthalates right up to the date of the ban, and then sell them to consumers long after the ban was supposed to go into effect. Just two days later, the CPSC, under Bush appointee Nancy Nord, granted this anonymous request.

Public Citizen sued to enforce the law as Congress had written it. Just days before the effective date of the ban, a federal court agreed with Public Citizen, finding that the rule was unlawful and that all toys with phthalates must come off the shelves.

In 2008, another Public Citizen lawsuit forced the government to implement a law it had ignored for 16 years. In 1992, Congress voted to require the government to create a national database to help car buyers determine whether a vehicle had been stolen or rebuilt after a wreck. It allowed consumers to instantly check the validity of the car's title and mileage, and learn whether it had been stolen, junked or salvaged. Public Citizen argued that the government's 16-year neglect of the law was putting consumers at risk of buying dangerous cars. A federal court agreed and ordered the government to implement the database immediately.

Battling Big Tobacco

For all its opposition to federal foot-dragging, Public Citizen often supports agencies when they try to do the right thing. Starting in the mid-1990s, for example, Public Citizen helped the FDA as it tried to curtail tobacco industry marketing and make it harder for minors to obtain cigarettes. The proposed FDA regulations would have restricted the industry's use of outdoor advertising and limited distribution of promotional items such as T-shirts and tote bags. It also would have banned tobacco industry sponsorship of concerts, tennis matches and auto races, and placement of ads in magazines with significant youth readership.

Representing a consortium of the nation's best-known public health groups — including the American Medical Association, American Lung Association, American Cancer Society and American Heart Association — Public Citizen backed the FDA effort by filing 160 pages of highly technical legal comments to buttress its case.[8]

"The point of the rule was that smoking is fundamentally a pediatric disease," Vladeck said. "Virtually everyone who smokes is addicted by the time they are 16 or 17. So if you can shield children and young adults from the sales messages and the promotional activities of the industry, which are largely targeted at them — if you can get a kid through adolescence without becoming a smoker — the chances are good that he or she will not become a smoker."

The multibillion-dollar tobacco industry found itself at a crossroads. Hooking teenagers on cigarettes was critical to its future, and internal industry documents showed that the companies carefully plotted ways to appeal to children, such as running marketing campaigns around the cartoon mascot Joe Camel. In addition, tobacco companies feared that if the FDA's legal authority to regulate tobacco was established, the agency might be emboldened to take further actions — perhaps regulating the level of nicotine or other ingredients in cigarettes. Some figured the FDA might even ban cigarettes altogether, although few believed it would go that far.

Few if any public health issues had higher stakes. During 1995–1999, smoking-related illnesses killed more than 440,000 Americans each year — more than alcohol, AIDS, car crashes, illegal drugs, murders and suicides *combined*. Annual health care economic losses related to tobacco were estimated at $157 billion.[9]

Everyone knew that such a huge industry would throw enormous resources into a legal fight to overturn any meaningful regulations. And sure enough, after the final FDA regulations were issued, on August 28, 1996, the industry filed suit in federal court in North Carolina, the heart of tobacco country.

At issue was whether the FDA had the statutory authority to regulate the industry at all. Public Citizen's argument was that cigarettes were in effect devices to deliver a dose of nicotine to smokers, and that nicotine was therefore a drug subject to the FDA's jurisdiction. Important First Amendment issues also were at stake, and while Public Citizen had always been a staunch defender of free speech, its lawyers saw ample legal precedent and certainly a moral imperative for restricting tobacco advertising aimed at children. After all, it was illegal for children to smoke. Shouldn't it be illegal to lure them into smoking?

For four years, Public Citizen was in the thick of the battle, with Public Citizen's Allison Zieve taking the lead in filing friend-of-the-court briefs on behalf of dozens of public health groups. The effort first bore fruit in April 1997 when U.S. District Judge William Osteen ruled against the industry, upholding the FDA regulations. But the victory wouldn't last. The 4th U.S. Circuit Court of Appeals overturned that ruling, holding that Congress had intentionally blocked the agency from overseeing tobacco products, so that the FDA had overstepped its bounds. The Supreme Court agreed to hear the case, but in 2000, it upheld the lower court ruling in a 5 to 4 vote.

It was a bitter defeat for the FDA, Public Citizen and the rest of the public health community. Other Litigation Group cases involved the issue of limits to state and local government authority to restrict tobacco advertising, but as in the FDA case, the Supreme Court in 2001 ruled in favor of the tobacco companies. It was not until 2009 that Congress at last approved the Family Smoking Prevention and Tobacco Control Act that gave the FDA authority to regulate tobacco products.

Protecting the Whistleblowers

In 1994, Representative Henry Waxman, a California Democrat, opened investigative hearings into tobacco's health effects. At one of those hearings, on April 14, the chief executives of the top seven tobacco companies stood in solidarity and testified under oath that nicotine was not addictive. They were lying to Congress, and soon Waxman would have internal industry documents to prove it.

Waxman came to obtain those documents in a story worthy of a paperback thriller. Several years earlier, a man named Merrell Williams was working as a paralegal at a Kentucky law firm that defended the industry. Part of his job involved sifting through the files of Brown & Williamson Tobacco Co. and cataloging each document that could possibly aid sick smokers in lawsuits against the company. "The whole point of the exercise was to cover it up," Williams later told a Louisville newspaper.[10]

As he absorbed the contents of the documents, Williams grew angry: the documents directly contradicted what the companies were saying publicly about tobacco. He secretly photocopied more than 4,000 pages that showed the industry knew nicotine was an addictive drug. The papers also suggested that the industry had known since at least 1963 that smoking carried serious health risks, but had denied these facts even in the face of government reports showing otherwise. The documents were, in fact, the proverbial smoking gun — but Williams kept them to himself at first.

After his temporary paralegal job ended, Williams suffered a heart attack that he was convinced was caused by years of smoking. After a heart bypass, he sued Brown & Williamson to recover the costs of his illness. He also sent the company copies of the documents he had smuggled out of the law firm. The company obtained a court order forbidding him from showing the documents to anyone else. But after failing to reach a settlement in his suit, Williams decided to risk disclosure. He met with Mississippi lawyers who were preparing to sue the industry to recover the state's cost of treating sick smokers through its Medicaid program. They took the papers to Mississippi Attorney General Michael Moore, who was directing the litigation.

The tobacco companies had faced product liability lawsuits from sick smokers before, as far back as the 1950s, and the industry's record in those cases was perfect: It had never lost a case. Williams' action would turn the tables. In a 1998 interview with the PBS show "Frontline," Moore described the papers Williams had as "the most damning documents ever produced against the industry."

Moore recalled Williams this way: "The fellow I met that day was a guy who was scared to death. ... remember, I've had all kinds of witnesses turn state's evidence. I have never met anybody that was more afraid of losing their life in some accident. This guy was sweating. ... you could almost see his heart pounding in his chest. He spoke, you know, a few words and backed off a few words. ... You had to pull the information out of him.....When he handed me the now-famous Addison Yeaman memo [Yeaman was general counsel for Brown & Williamson] that says 'We are in the business of selling nicotine, an addictive drug,'... I knew we had the goods on the industry. Having just seen them testify before Congress that...'We swear that nicotine is not an addictive drug,' I knew why he was sweating. I knew why he was scared to death."

Moore turned the purloined papers over to Waxman's subcommittee, the Justice Department and the FDA. Soon thereafter, *The New York Times* published an account of the revelations. Then Stanton Glantz, an anti-tobacco professor at the University of California, received a package from a mysterious "Mr. Butts." Inside were copies of the Brown & Williamson papers. Despite a lawsuit filed by the company against the university, Glantz posted the material on the Internet, making it available for the world to see. Glantz and his colleagues later wrote a book about the documents.

On May 23, 1994, Moore filed a lawsuit against the tobacco industry on behalf of the state of Mississippi. (Dozens of other states followed, and in June 1997 the state attorneys general announced a $368 billion settlement. But because it restricted the authority to sue tobacco companies, Public Citizen opposed the agreement. After vigorous lobbying and coalition building by Claybrook and Congress Watch lobbyist Joan Mulhern, Congress refused to ratify it. (See Chapter 2.)

Minnesota Attorney General Hubert Humphrey III also helped bring the tobacco companies to justice by securing the release of more than 20 million pages of industry documents. Humphrey's lawsuit against seven tobacco companies and two trade associations was the first to use the novel approach of alleging consumer fraud and antitrust violations. He eventually settled for $6 billion and agreements by the industry to curtail its marketing.

The industry, meanwhile, turned its legal guns on Williams. Industry lawyers sued him in Kentucky and tried to have him jailed for violating the old court order barring the documents' release. He was suddenly at serious risk of losing everything he had, and possibly even going to jail, just as he had feared. That's when Public Citizen's Morrison took the case.

Working with a local lawyer in Louisville, Morrison said Williams' decision to blow the whistle on Brown & Williamson was a key factor in unmasking tobacco industry practices. "It was absolutely clear that the company for years knew that nicotine was a drug that kept people addicted," Morrison said. "And they were using all the same words that the FDA was using about nicotine and addictiveness. They manipulated levels of nicotine to keep people hooked. The second thing was, it was absolutely clear they had manipulated the science on this and they had used law firms — the attorney-client privilege — to hide it."

Brown & Williamson spent millions to pursue Merrell Williams in court, even keeping him under secret surveillance. But Morrison and Louisville attorney J. Fox Demoisey managed to get Williams off the hook and keep him out of jail. Under the 1997 settlement between state attorneys general and the tobacco industry, the company agreed to drop its civil and criminal charges against him.

Public Citizen also represented other tobacco whistleblowers who either leaked damaging documents or testified before Congress. These included two high-ranking industry insiders whose identities remain secret, as well as Drs. Paul Mele and Victor DeNoble, scientists who worked for Philip Morris in a lab responsible for studying the addictive properties of nicotine.

In that case, Vladeck represented the researchers at the request of committee staffers in the House of Representatives. "Their testimony was pivotal," Vladeck said. "The key was to make certain the industry would not penalize the witnesses for testifying. And we were successful at that. We represented our share of whistleblowers, probably more than anybody else. Some did not end up testifying even though they provided very interesting and substantial information."

Because of Williams and the other whistleblowers, priceless internal documents were made public and used by state attorneys general and other plaintiffs to hold the industry accountable. The picture they painted was of callous businesses that lied to the public for decades, manipulated nicotine levels in order to hook smokers, abused the legal system and blatantly geared marketing efforts toward young children to guarantee a future market for their products. The result was that thousands of children every year became addicted to tobacco — and for many it was a death sentence. Outrage over these revelations helped lead to the 2009 legislation that finally gave the FDA authority to regulate tobacco products.

Reforming the Legal Profession

When the Litigation Group was formed, few public interest organizations were trying to make legal services more available and affordable for the general public. Public Citizen's lawyers began a series of cases against the legal profession itself, suing to remove the blanket barriers on lawyer advertising and to outlaw minimum fee schedules for lawyers that raised prices and eliminated competition. The Litigation Group also eliminated residence requirements for bar admission, which had limited out-of-state practitioners and thus were a barrier to consumer choice. And it fought rules against the so-called unauthorized practice of law, which mostly prevented non-lawyer advocates from assisting consumers in handling routine legal matters such as uncontested divorces, adoptions and name changes, or in speaking for parents before school boards.

One of the first unauthorized-practice cases began in March 1977 when Morrison opened a letter that started, "Re: HELP." It came from Rosemary Furman, a former legal secretary from Jacksonville, Florida. As part of her involvement with a home for battered women, she had begun helping abused and sometimes illiterate women prepare legal papers so they could get divorces and temporary restraining orders.

"All I'm doing for clients is what a lawyer's secretary does for her boss after he collects a fat fee in non-adversarial cases and hands her the papers to fill out," Furman told *The New York Times* in 1984. For helping women at a fraction of the cost of hiring a lawyer, she was sued by the Florida Bar for the unauthorized practice of law.

Morrison was sympathetic. "At that time, the local police refused to do anything about spouse abuse unless there was a court order," Morrison said. "The wife typically had no access to money to hire a lawyer and hence could not get the court order necessary to protect herself."

Public Citizen fought for Furman in Florida and finally lost before the Florida Supreme Court. When Morrison tried to bring it before the U.S. Supreme Court in 1980, it was dismissed for want of a substantial federal question. Furman continued to provide services to the poor while limiting her activities to comply, she thought, with the Florida court order, but in 1982, the Florida Bar came after her again. She was eventually sentenced to serve four months in jail. Despite Morrison's pleadings, the U.S. Supreme Court again refused to rule.

But Furman did not go to jail, because Florida Governor Bob Graham and the state Cabinet voted to commute her sentence. Although Furman was put out of business, the case exposed the self-serving tactics of Florida's legal elite and cemented Public Citizen's reputation for taking on the most powerful adversaries.

Like Furman, Marilyn Arons was a non-lawyer providing legal services to the vulnerable — and she couldn't get paid. She was "the only person in the U.S. who wasn't an attorney who was litigating cases for handicapped kids" in the 1980s, she said. Herself the mother of a disabled daughter, Arons argued — and won — case after case on behalf of other parents against New Jersey school boards that were trying to get out of their legal duty to offer special — and often very expensive — provisions for children with disabilities. But because Arons was not a lawyer, state law barred her from collecting legal fees.

Exhausted from working for free out of her home, Arons asked a federal court to lift the payment ban in 1987. She lost, although the judge said the law should be changed. She turned to Public Citizen's Vladeck just in time for the Litigation Group to help defeat an attempt by the New Jersey legal establishment to ban her from even representing handicapped clients in court.

By the early 1990s, Arons had won thousands of cases against school boards and was a hero to disabled children and their parents nationwide. Delaware parents called for help in 1994, and she and a colleague won so many cases there that the state sued her in 1997. Again Public Citizen defended her, but in 2000, the state Supreme Court ruled for the state.

In a separate case, though, a federal court in 1999 ordered a New York school district to pay her fees, giving all non-lawyers hope it would be a precedent for them to be paid for their work of this kind. "It's all because of Public Citizen," Arons said. "I couldn't have done anything I did unless they had been there to help me." But the school board appealed, and in 2006, the U.S. Supreme Court ruled 6–3 against Arons.

"We raised awareness and we pressed hard, but the lawyer monopoly is very deeply entrenched," Vladeck said in an interview. "We haven't driven down the cost of legal services enough so that the un-rich can afford them, but putting a spotlight on the problem of access to justice made the effort worthwhile."

The legal profession's unfair and exclusionary practices had been on Morrison's yellow-pad to-do list from the start, and within months of the Litigation Group launch, an ideal test case surfaced. The Goldfarbs, a married couple living in Reston, Virginia, had just bought a house, and on reading the mortgage small print, they found they had to pay a $537.50 fee to a lawyer who would ensure that all documents were in order at the loan closing. They were perplexed by the charge, because they had already paid nearly $200 in title insurance for essentially the same service. They wrote to 36 other lawyers in the area to see if anyone would do it for less than $537.50. All the lawyers said $537.50 was the going rate, and some even claimed it would be unethical to charge anything less.

To Morrison, this was "a clear case of price-fixing that might well bring criminal charges if anyone else had done it." Consumers were being fleeced by a cozy arrangement dressed up in legal jargon. Public Citizen represented the Goldfarbs and other Virginia homebuyers who had joined the case through the class-action mechanism, and steered the case through the lower courts. Despite fierce opposition by the Virginia legal establishment, the case continued, and Public Citizen eventually presented its argument to the U.S. Supreme Court.

"This was precisely at the time that all the Watergate trials were starting, and many of the defendants in Watergate were lawyers," recalled Morrison. "We tried throughout to pitch the case as one in which lawyers were trying to be exempt from the laws that applied to everyone else. While Watergate was never mentioned, the connection between it and lawyers trying to be outside or above the law through an antitrust exemption was one of our themes." It worked, and the Supreme Court agreed with Public Citizen that lawyers were not above the law.

According to one study, the ruling resulted in reduced legal fees for consumers doing house closings in northern Virginia by one-third. More important, the decision prohibited other state bars from setting minimum fees. The case was an enormous victory for consumers because the precedent also applied to doctors and other professionals. It meant that professional associations could no longer operate as cartels to fix prices.

Encouraged by the victory, Morrison set about challenging another legal profession subterfuge for propping up lawyers' fees — the ban on advertising. Ethics rules strictly prohibited lawyer ads, calling them unseemly and damaging to the profession's reputation. Public Citizen wanted to end the ban, arguing that advertising could bring greater competition and lower prices.

Rather than tackling the issue directly, however, the Litigation Group first took a case involving the degree of First Amendment protection for pharmacists' commercial speech. At the time, a Virginia law barred pharmacists from advertising their prices for prescription drugs. Virtually all other states had similar laws. Representing consumers, the Litigation Group won at trial, and the case ultimately went to the Supreme Court. In 1976, the high court reversed a century of precedent and ruled that the First Amendment did apply to commercial speech, and that indeed, pharmacists could advertise their prices.

The following year, the first case involving lawyer advertising came before the Supreme Court, and the court applied the principle established in the Virginia pharmacy case, ruling that lawyers could advertise their services. The decision was fairly narrow, however, and Litigation Group lawyers had to make another trip to the Supreme Court to expand it.

A lawyer in Ohio named Philip Zauderer had run an advertisement seeking plaintiffs injured by a defective intrauterine contraceptive device, the Dalkon Shield. While the Supreme Court had earlier authorized lawyers to advertise their services, this was different. Here was a lawyer seeking plaintiffs to sue a particular defendant. And to top it off, his advertisements scandalously included a picture of the device in question. When the Ohio Bar sued Zauderer, Morrison and Vladeck took the case. Once again, the Supreme Court ruled in 1985 in Public Citizen's favor, saying lawyers could advertise for specific kinds of product liability cases.

No longer able to restrict lawyers' advertising outright, states started trying to keep the ads from being effective. Rules began prohibiting everyday advertising techniques, including client testimonials, dramatizations and slogans—that is, anything interesting. In 2007, New York pushed the trend to a new extreme by prohibiting any "techniques to obtain attention" in lawyer advertising—as if ads had any other purpose. This ensured that even if a lawyer's ad was technically permissible, it would be boring and unlikely to appeal to consumers. Public Citizen filed suit on behalf of a New York attorney, and a court declared the new rules unconstitutional. Other suits struck down similar rules in Florida and Louisiana.

The cases involving lawyer advertising and price-fixing have been extremely beneficial for consumers. "We're certainly better off today in terms of price competition among lawyers than we were in 1974, when lawyers conspired to set fees, and we're certainly a lot better off than we were prior to 1976, when lawyers could not advertise no matter what," Vladeck said.

Another way the Litigation Group sought to foster competition among lawyers—and expand consumer choice—was to challenge rules that restricted lawyers' ability to practice in multiple states, or to open a practice in a new state. In one of the worst cases, the bar in the Virgin Islands—which had fewer than 200 lawyers—required that a lawyer live there for two consecutive years before being admitted to practice. Public Citizen took that case to the Supreme Court and won, affecting rules in other states that had restrictive residency requirements.

Fighting for Union Democracy

In its quest to expand access to the legal system, Public Citizen has consciously sought to help a variety of people who suffer from dangerous or unfair conditions and have few political or legal remedies. The breadth of this advocacy shows in the diversity of Public Citizen clients over the years: truck drivers, mortgage consumers, borrowers fighting debt collectors, Internet users and more.

In 1970, Nader Raider Robert Fellmeth (who later became chair of the Public Citizen Foundation's board of directors) published "The Interstate Commerce Omission," an investigative report that exposed a fatal lack of regulatory enforcement by the federal Interstate Commerce Commission (ICC), which at the time was in charge of truck rates and safety. Fellmeth found that drivers were being forced to drive long hours without sleep, often in trucks they believed to be dangerous. In an astonishing finding, 40 percent of truck drivers who answered a survey Fellmeth placed in trucking magazines reported that their rigs were unsafe.[11]

A year later, however, nobody was doing anything about that abysmal fact—not the ICC and not the leadership of the International Brotherhood of Teamsters, which didn't even have a division or office devoted to its members' safety.

Nader figured that the only way to force change was to begin organizing truck drivers. These were men with families to support and for whom safety was paramount. He asked Joan Claybrook, who then worked for his Public Interest Research Group, to organize a Washington, D.C. conference of truck drivers that would shine a public spotlight on the utter failure of federal regulators to enforce truck safety standards.

The October 1971 conference — the first ever for truck drivers — attracted hundreds of truckers to Washington, D.C. who surrounded the Capitol with their big rigs for an entire day. The event sparked hearings in Congress, but no legislation resulted. However, the meeting did launch a new group nicknamed PROD — Professional Drivers Council for Safety and Health. The organization was guided first by Claybrook and then in 1973 by Arthur Fox, a lawyer in the Public Citizen Litigation Group.

PROD began pressing the Department of Transportation (which took over trucking regulation from the ICC) to upgrade safety standards. Claybrook and Fox quickly found that in those early days, the Teamsters union itself ignored drivers who complained about shoddy brakes, bald tires or engine problems, even those whose complaints got them fired by their employers. Eventually, because of PROD's prodding, the Teamsters created a new health and safety program. But the campaign for truck safety revealed that the larger problem was with union governance itself.

Rank-and-file members had little say about how the union was run, how elections were held and how collective bargaining contracts were ratified. With union corruption rife, Public Citizen realized that democracy within the Teamsters would be critical for any effective safety or wage advocacy. So what had begun as a project on truck safety in 1971 evolved into a legal campaign to ensure that union leaders couldn't trample on the rights of their own members.

Paul Alan Levy, a young lawyer who had been active in the anti-war movement, joined the Litigation Group in 1977 specifically to work on labor issues. He teamed with Fox to file lawsuits on behalf of union dissidents. Although most of the suits were about union democracy, one involved an action against a Teamsters boss in Baltimore named Leo Dalesio. He had set up a lucrative retirement account for himself, enjoyed an unlimited expense account on which he billed near-daily meals at fine restaurants, drove a luxury car, had memberships in local clubs and spent summers at a fancy beach condominium provided by an associate. And he had named that associate to be administrator of the union's pension and welfare funds.

All Dalesio's perks, union members believed, resulted from his access to money from those pension funds. In January 1978, Levy and Fox sued Dalesio on behalf of a long-hauler named Donald Brink, who was president of the Baltimore PROD chapter and who was outraged at Dalesio's handling of the money that belonged to rank-and-file members. Nine years later, after countless hours spent writing briefs, arguing in court and tracing the money trail, Levy and Fox prevailed. It was a significant victory for Brink and other union members because $1.5 million was returned to the Local's coffers.

In 1979, the Litigation Group took on another truck safety case that had broad ramifications in other fields. Drivers who belonged to the Teamsters and worked for a major trucking company called Arkansas-Best Freight System Inc. were performing federally required safety inspections of their vehicles before taking them on the road—but were not getting paid for the time spent on these inspections. An arbitrator ruled against the truckers and their union, saying the union's contract with the company did not require it to pay.

The drivers sued both the union and the company, claiming the union could not give away their right to be paid by requiring them to be bound by the arbitrator. They lost at trial and on appeal. But Vladeck persuaded the Supreme Court to hear *Barrentine v. Arkansas-Best Freight System*, and in 1981, the high court ruled in favor of the drivers. "The Supreme Court said that as a matter of federal law, the union cannot contract away the individual employee's right to be compensated at least minimum wage for the time he spends performing safety inspections," Vladeck said. "It's a very widely cited standard and is still the most useful precedent in our work against mandatory arbitration."

PROD eventually merged with another group of union activists called Teamsters for a Democratic Union (TDU). Levy and Fox continued to represent TDU and dissidents in other labor unions, filing dozens of lawsuits to force unions to be more responsive to their members. Among others, they represented workers disciplined for criticizing union leadership, and they successfully sued in several cases where a union attempted to adopt a new or modified contract with the employer without going through the membership ratification process spelled out in the union's constitution.

Many of these lawsuits brought to light the autocratic way in which the Teamsters union was being run, providing further impetus and evidence for a wide-ranging Justice Department corruption probe. The department's suit against the Teamsters resulted in a 1989 consent decree that set out guidelines reforming the union's election process. It also established an enforcement mechanism to clean up rampant corruption and infiltration by organized crime. Levy and the Litigation Group, representing the TDU and individual union members, played a key role in ensuring enforcement of the consent decree's democracy provisions.

"We were the most important litigation outfit on union democracy issues from 1975 through the late 1990s, when we reduced emphasis on the issue," Levy said. "I think it improved unions—not only in the Teamsters but in a lot of other unions where we've been involved. We helped members hold their leadership more accountable. There's really no substitute for effective, gritty democracy for keeping folks focused on whom they represent."

Seeking Consumer Justice

In 1979, David and Maria Caplan's home outside New York City was about to be taken from them. They were in a dispute with their bank over how much money it required them to set aside each month for local property taxes. In their community, the taxes were to be paid to various taxing entities five times during the year, and the bank took the position that a separate tax account for each bill had to exist and had to contain enough to pay the bill when it came due, without reference to any sum in the other tax accounts.

As a result, the couple had to keep about $2,000 more with the bank than they believed their mortgage required. The bank then was able to lend out this extra $2,000 to others at interest rates at least 4 percent higher than it was paying the Caplans (and much more during the inflation of the early 1980s). Of course the bank was doing this not just to the Caplans but to all its mortgage borrowers, as were many other banks.

Public Citizen took the case after the Caplans' first loss at trial. The Litigation Group obtained a reversal on appeal, and the case eventually was settled favorably for the Caplans. It took several more years and other lawsuits — as well as investigations by the New York attorney general, the federal Department of Housing and Urban Development, and Congress — but eventually, thanks to Public Citizen's intervention, the practice was outlawed across the country.

To broaden the impact of this kind of work, the Litigation Group in 2005 launched a Consumer Justice Project to litigate cases that might establish key precedents on behalf of consumers. Working with private attorneys and other nonprofit organizations, Public Citizen attorneys tackled predatory lending to poorer homeowners, fraud by auto dealers, excessive fees for reverse mortgage foreclosures, and more.

Some early successes involved so-called "check-diversion" companies. These private, for-profit debt collectors arranged with local prosecutors to collect fees on returned checks. Using the letterhead of the local district attorney's office, the companies sent letters threatening consumers with criminal prosecution and jail unless they paid not only the check amount but also high collection fees, which were then split with the prosecutors' office.

Most consumers targeted by these check-diversion schemes had bounced checks accidentally, usually for small amounts. Under state criminal laws, bouncing a check is not a crime unless the check writer intended to defraud someone. But these companies ignored that requirement, treating anyone who wrote a bad check as a criminal. They demanded fees up to $220, even on bad checks for $10 or less. The companies claimed that the fees covered the cost of financial management classes for consumers, but once the fee was paid, the companies did little to compel class attendance, and some companies rarely held classes at all.

The scam had hit people hard. Maryland resident Simona Pickett, a professional at the federal Department of Justice, received an official-looking notice from her local district attorney's "Bad Check Restitution Program," saying that a $21.66 check she had written to a local supermarket had bounced. It demanded that she pay not only the check amount, but $185 in collection fees, and ordered her to attend a class on financial management. It said she would be criminally prosecuted if she didn't pay. Fearing jail, she paid. Hundreds of people were victimized by such practices across the country.

Attorney Paul Arons, who practices law in Friday Harbor, a quiet seaport on San Juan Island off the coast of Washington state, decided to go after these deceptive debt collection practices, which he called an enormous scam. "It is not against the law to make a mistake in balancing your checkbook, yet those are the people these companies go after," he said. Charging that the debt collectors were essentially "impersonating a law enforcement officer," he added, "You shouldn't be threatened with jail and have to pay $170 in fees just because you forgot to write down an ATM withdrawal."

In 2001, Arons and attorney Rand Bragg filed a case against a debt collection company, American Corrective Counseling Services. Among other claims, the case involved a constitutional question about due process because it alleged that the government was participating in theft from its citizens. The case was still wending its way through court in 2005, when Arons met Litigation Group Director Brian Wolfman at a conference. Arons' expertise was in general civil litigation, and he realized that he could use the help of the constitutional law experts at Public Citizen.

Wolfman and his staff joined forces with Arons, and won victories in Florida (2007) and California (2008) that allowed cases against abusive debt collectors to proceed. Meanwhile, a collection agency in Anchorage, Alaska, had tried to sue Robin Pepper, a mentally disabled woman, for refusing to pay its bill collection charges. It sent papers to a nonexistent address, misrepresented to the court that she was competent and tried to get a default judgment against her. When Alaska Legal Services stepped in on Pepper's behalf, the agency asserted that its outrageous conduct was protected by the First Amendment's "petition clause," which guarantees public access to the courts.

In a decision with potentially dangerous implications for consumer law, a District Court agreed. Alaska Legal Services asked Public Citizen to handle the appeal. In late 2009, the Alaska Supreme Court overturned the decision, the first appellate ruling on the issue by any court nationwide. Public Citizen attorney Deepak Gupta, who argued the case, said the decision "sends the message that debt collection companies can't get away with abusive tactics simply by hiring lawyers," and that "the petition clause does not extend to conduct that was unfair, deceptive, and in violation of the Unfair Trade Practices Act."[12] Debt collection companies could no longer hide their unfair practices behind the First Amendment.

Internet Users and the First Amendment

Always eager to develop new case law to protect consumers in new circumstances, Public Citizen in 1999 began to help people whose First Amendment rights were being threatened by big corporations on the Internet.

Carla Virga, a resident of Yuba City, California, lost thousands of dollars because of a shoddy home inspection by pest control company Terminix Corporation. Wanting to share her experiences and warn other consumers, Virga launched a website that included information about Terminix complaints in 50 states. Terminix and its corporate parent ServiceMaster sued Virga to force her to remove all references to Terminix and ServiceMaster from her website. The companies alleged that Virga's use of their names violated their trademark.

Intrigued, Litigation Group attorney Paul Levy took the case, arguing that the suit should be dismissed because Virga had a First Amendment right to post her gripes. At the same time as Public Citizen filed its opposition, it sent a copy to *The Wall Street Journal*, which ran a major story on the case. Terminix quickly dropped its suit.

Shortly thereafter, another case added a nuance to the issue. Virga had a right to make public her complaint about Terminix, but what if she hadn't wanted to use her name? Do people have the right to criticize companies online anonymously?

In December 1999, Northwest Airlines was in the midst of contentious contract negotiations with its flight attendants. To provide a hub of information about the talks, senior Northwest Airlines flight attendants Kevin Griffin and Ted Reeve each created websites. Griffin's site included a message board where people could post comments, and some postings encouraged attendants to participate in a sickout.

On New Year's Eve, a rash of flight attendants called in sick. Angry airline officials went to court and successfully sought a restraining order against Griffin and Reeve, forbidding them from approving of or permitting a sickout — effectively preventing them from engaging in free speech on their own websites. What's more, the court issued the restraining order without notifying them, so they couldn't even challenge it. (Ironically, neither man participated in the sickout, and Reeve had not called in sick once during his 10 years with the airline.)

The airline didn't stop there. It persuaded a judge to allow the accounting firm Ernst & Young to copy the hard drives of the attendants' home computers and search for any documents that might have some relationship to the case — an unprecedented invasion of privacy. Public Citizen leapt in, asking the judge to reverse the search order, require the firm to destroy the records it had seized and release the flight attendants from the restraining order.

"It was extremely high-pressure litigation," Levy recalled. "The airline had two law firms that were throwing associates at the case, making it all but impossible for individual lawyers like Barbara Harvey [another attorney in the case] and me to provide effective representation."

To make the task even more challenging, little case law existed for the two to follow. "We had to construct an argument" about why the computer shouldn't be turned over to the company," Levy said. Once again, Public Citizen made that argument to the news media, and the airline received a flood of negative publicity. Levy and Harvey managed to get the restraining order against Griffin and Reeve lifted. Shortly after, Northwest Airlines dropped the case.

The two cases convinced Levy that First Amendment rights on the Internet deserved greater attention. He began focusing on corporations that were intimidating critics with two common tactics: lawsuits alleging trademark violations against "gripe site" operators, and subpoenas of Internet providers' records. Companies wanted to examine the records to learn the names of angry customers who had aired their views anonymously on Internet chat sites, and sue them for defamation.

Levy began to look for cases to try in courts that hadn't yet ruled on the issues, in order to set precedents. He racked up success after success, carving out a new area of case law that established the First Amendment rights of corporate critics to post their complaints on the Internet. Those he successfully defended against trademark claims included an irate Alitalia passenger whose luggage was lost en route to India for a wedding; a dissatisfied California hair restoration customer; a Dallas man who used the Web to denounce a shopping mall owner; and an Ohio graduate student who had a dispute with an auto dealership over the terms of a warranty. Levy also filed lawsuits on behalf of eBay vendors against companies that wanted to suppress competition from the online sale of lower-priced, secondhand or generic products.

In 2006, a Conyers, Georgia, man named Charles Smith launched two web-sites satirizing Wal-Mart, comparing the mega-corporation's destructive effects on local communities to the Holocaust and to al-Qaeda terrorism. Wal-Mart sued, claiming trademark infringement, in part on the parody's use of a yellow smiley face clutched in an eagle's claws. Public Citizen joined the American Civil Liberties Union of Georgia in defending Smith, and in 2008, the U.S. District Court found that the satires were protected speech. "This ruling shows that even the biggest company in America is subject to parody, and that trademark rights must yield to free speech," Levy said. It was a major victory for online freedom.

In Public Citizen's first 38 years, the Litigation Group carved out a distinctive platform for itself in the world of public interest advocacy, federal regulation to protect health and safety, and U.S. Supreme Court litigation. It became — and is still — versatile enough to represent lone individuals with compelling claims for justice while also litigating landmark cases with sweeping constitutional implications.

Between 1972 and 2015, Public Citizen argued 63 cases before the Supreme Court and won a significant number of them. It also argued hundreds of cases in the federal courts of appeal. When Alan Morrison left Public Citizen in 2004, the organization created the Alan Morrison Supreme Court Assistance Program, under which Public Citizen lawyers have helped hundreds of lawyers keep their public interest victories out of the U.S. Supreme Court by drafting or advising them on their briefs opposing petitions for certiorari.

With an eye on establishing new precedents that can secure citizen and consumer rights, Public Citizen never shied away from taking on the biggest imaginable adversaries, from the tobacco industry to the White House, Congress and federal agencies. When coordinated with Public Citizen's other arms — for lobbying, health care and energy advocacy, and more — the first generation of Litigation Group activists demonstrated just how much transformational change can be achieved through targeted, determined and steady effort.

Endnotes

1 For more on the Chadha case, see Barbara Hinkson Craig, *Chadha: The Story of an Epic Constitutional Struggle* (Oxford University Press, 1988).

2 David Bollier, *Citizen Action and Other Big Ideas: A History of Ralph Nader and the Consumer Movement*, Center for Study of Responsive Law, 1991, p. 96, and Michael Schudson, *The Good Citizen: A History of American Civic Life* (Free Press, New York 1998) p. 256.

3 President and Fellows of Harvard College, *Private Public Interest and Plaintiff's Firm Guide*, Bernard Koteen Office of Public Interest Advising at Harvard Law School (OPIA) and the Center for Public Interest Law at Columbia Law School, Cambridge MA, 2010.

4 Jesse H. Queen, Director, Office of Institutions and Facilities, Department of Justice memo, June 22, 1972.

5 Linda Greenhouse, "Keeping Government's 3 Arms Minding Their Own Business," *The New York Times*, Dec. 26, 1988.

6 Alan Morrison noted that the Supreme Court had said records solely available through the NSC were not subject to FOIA because they were presidential records. But they had to be preserved, so now they are available to the public as part of Reagan's presidential papers.

7 For more on these electronic freedom of information cases (*Armstrong v. Executive Office of the President* and *Public Citizen v. Carlin*) and Public Citizen's other FOIA work, see www.citizen.org.

8 David Vladeck and John Cary Sims, "Why the Supreme Court Will Uphold Strict Control on Tobacco Advertising," *Southern Illinois University Law Journal*, Volume 22, Spring 1998.

9 "Annual Smoking-Attributable Mortality, Years of Potential Life Lost, and Economic Costs — United States, 1995–1999." MMWR Weekly, April 12, 2002, 51(14);300–3. Centers for Disease Control, Atlanta GA. www.cdc.gov/mmwr/preview/mmwrhtml/mm5114a2.htm.

10 Hunt Helm, "Blowing the Whistle on Big Tobacco: Wigand, Williams Lifted Secrecy's Veil," *The (Louisville) Courier-Journal*, May 25, 1997.

11 David Bollier, *Citizen Action and Other Big Ideas: A History of Ralph Nader and the Consumer Movement*, Center for Study of Responsive Law, 1991.

12 Deepak Gupta, "Alaska Supreme Court Rejects Debt Collectors' First Amendment Defense," *Consumer Law and Policy Blog*, Public Citizen, November 24, 2009.

5

THE RACE FOR AUTO SAFETY

THREE DAYS BEFORE THANKSGIVING 1999, Christine Sagrista sat in the back seat of a late-model Ford Explorer as it moved north along the Florida Turnpike. The South Florida night was typically muggy, but the temperature was mild and pleasant and the skies mostly clear. The road ahead was flat and straight. Beside the 23-year-old woman, strapped into child safety seats, were her twin two-year-old sons. Her fiancé, Luar Gutierrez, was driving, and his brother Robert sat beside him in the passenger seat.[1]

The Gutierrez brothers and Sagrista were eager to get home to Apopka, a small town on the outskirts of Orlando, and planned to drive through the night. At about 2 a.m. they heard a loud noise, like a "boom," Christine later recalled. Luar hit the brakes, desperately trying to maintain control, but the right rear tire had literally come apart. The Explorer rolled over three times on the asphalt and then hit the shoulder, where it rolled three more times.

By the time it came to rest along a line of trees and shrubs, the sport utility vehicle was a mangled heap of metal and shattered glass. The roof was crushed and buckled. Remarkably, the Gutierrez brothers, both wearing seat belts, walked away with only minor injuries.

However, Sagrista, who also was buckled in, remembered nothing that happened after the Explorer began to roll. Several days later, she awoke in intensive care in St. Mary's Hospital in West Palm Beach. "The nurses and doctors told me that I had been severely injured, and that they had to remove my spleen," she told reporters at a 2001 news conference. "I also had to have several surgeries in which they put rods and pins in me to fix my broken bones."

Her injuries were nothing compared to what the doctors then told her—that Alex, one of her sons, had died during the rollover. Her other son, Christopher, was only slightly hurt. Christine's injuries were so severe that she could not attend Alex's funeral.

In its investigation of the crash, the Florida Highway Patrol found no evidence of driver error and determined that Luar had not been drinking. Its final report blamed the crash on the blown tire.

Christine had no way to know it, but her tragic experience was not an isolated incident. Almost two years earlier, in January 1998, Matthew Hendricks, 18, was driving to pick up his girlfriend to go bowling in Corpus Christi, Texas, when his left rear tire blew. Like Luar Gutierrez, Matthew could not control his Explorer. It rolled over three times, and he was ejected through the passenger window. Matthew died just five months shy of his high school graduation.[2] Four months earlier, a young man from Houston named Tim Lockwood was driving his brand-new Explorer to a business meeting when his left rear tire shredded, causing the vehicle to roll. The roof crushed in, breaking his neck and causing him to suffocate.

There were others—hundreds of others. And they, too, did not know. None of those involved had any reason to suspect that such a sudden catastrophe could occur.

Then, a few months after Alex Sagrista's death, an enterprising Texas television reporter named Anna Werner began to put the pieces together. Beyond the fact that all the crashes involved Ford Explorers, she noticed another common denominator: Firestone tires.

An investigative reporter for KHOU-TV in Houston, Werner then uncovered a disturbing pattern of lawsuits filed against Ford Motor Co. and Bridgestone/Firestone Inc., the maker of Firestone tires. One by one, she learned of at least 30 people who had died when their Ford Explorers careened out of control and rolled over after a Firestone tire had suddenly, inexplicably, lost its tread on the highway.

In the beginning, Werner had little to go on because the companies had persuaded trial judges presiding over those lawsuits to issue gag orders that kept crucial documents sealed. The National Highway Traffic Safety Administration (NHTSA), the federal agency that investigates automobile defects, told Werner that while it had received a few complaints about Firestone tires mounted on Explorers, the agency saw no pattern that would suggest something out of the ordinary.

Werner then contacted Ralph Nader. He referred her to Joan Claybrook, who had served as head of NHTSA under President Jimmy Carter. She immediately realized the magnitude of the problem. Having presided over the recall of the defective Firestone 500 tire in 1979, Claybrook knew that reported fatalities and injuries were just the tip of the iceberg.

On the night of February 7, 2000, with 164,000 households tuned to KHOU, Werner told the tragic stories of a woman who had lost her husband and both legs in an Explorer rollover crash, and of a couple whose teenage daughter had been killed. The next day, Werner's phone lit up as consumers called to report similar problems with Firestone tires. Three days later, the station aired a follow-up story in which Claybrook urged that the tires be recalled.

For weeks, NHTSA remained silent, but it finally opened a preliminary investigation in March. Ford and Firestone both claimed nothing was wrong with the tire or the Explorer, which was a cash cow for Ford as the top-selling sport utility vehicle in the country. In fact, Bridgestone/Firestone sent a lengthy letter to KHOU and its parent company complaining of "falsehoods and misrepresentations," and saying it "proudly stands behind" its ATX tires. KHOU took the letter as a warning of possible legal action against the station.

On July 31, Werner went on the air again with another shocking story: Ford was replacing Firestone tires on Explorers in Saudi Arabia and some other foreign markets but was continuing to ignore the defect in the United States. The next day, *USA Today* carried a similar article. Other national news media pounced on the story.

After a nationwide uproar over the foreign recalls, Ford realized its precarious situation. It forced Bridgestone/Firestone to announce on August 9 the U.S. recall of 14.4 million Firestone tires. It included the company's ATX and ATXII models and some Wilderness AT tires, but Firestone still refused to acknowledge any design defect in the tire. At that point, 46 deaths had been attributed to what Claybrook called a "lethal combination" of the rollover-prone Ford Explorer and the ready-to-blow Firestone tires. The companies faced more than 100 lawsuits for deaths and serious injuries.

"The shame of this situation is that both Ford and Bridgestone/Firestone have known about this problem for eight years," Claybrook said in a statement to the media. "But because the companies have settled a number of lawsuits under gag orders, which prohibited the lawyers or victims in the cases from talking about them, safety officials and the public have been kept in the dark."

The recall was dramatic, but the story was just beginning. Five days later, Claybrook held a press conference to call on the government to broaden the recall to *all* Wilderness tires. Firestone had at various times blamed the problem on hot weather, driver error and quality control problems—which they implied were related to a labor dispute—at a single tire plant in Decatur, Illinois.

Joined by Tab Turner, a Little Rock, Arkansas, attorney who had brought lawsuits on behalf of plaintiffs injured in a number of Ford/Firestone rollover crashes, and auto safety consultant Ralph Hoar, Claybrook insisted the tire had a serious design defect. She also charged that the Ford Explorer itself was defective because its pickup-truck suspension system and its frame—with a narrow track width and high center of gravity—made it extremely vulnerable to rollovers in the event of a tire failure or emergency maneuver.

Turner revealed that to reduce the propensity of the Explorer to roll over, Ford had recommended lowering the air pressure in the vehicle's tires from the standard 35 pounds per square inch to 26. That action, Bridgestone/Firestone later said, contributed to tread separation in the tires by causing a build-up of heat.

Claybrook and Public Citizen pressed hard to get to the bottom of the problem. They urged members of Congress to authorize NHTSA to upgrade safety standards and toughen penalties for companies and executives who covered up known defects. Working with lawyers who had handled Ford/Firestone cases, Claybrook gathered evidence showing that the companies knowingly withheld life-saving information from the public and the government.

Public Citizen held repeated news conferences in which victims told journalists about their harrowing rollover crashes. Public Citizen also set up a special Internet site to post internal company documents released by congressional committees so that the public and journalists could easily obtain them.

Not satisfied by the tepid response by Ford and Firestone, Claybrook appeared on every major television news show and was quoted in dozens of national and regional newspapers and magazines, becoming the leading public interest spokesperson agitating for reform. Her advocacy culminated in dramatic testimony before the U.S. Senate Committee on Commerce, Science and Transportation about the need for stronger safety standards.

Only two months after Claybrook's first press conference, on October 11, 2000, Congress approved the Transportation Recall Enhancement, Accountability and Documentation (TREAD) Act. The legislation contained a host of provisions sought by Public Citizen and its allies, including requirements for NHTSA to update its tire safety standard; for companies to submit to NHTSA "early warning" information about possible safety defects; and for dynamic testing of new vehicles for their propensity to roll over, using NHTSA's New Car Assessment Program. But relentless follow-up was essential because NHTSA fought release of those reports, in violation of the law. In 2008, after Public Citizen sued, the government began making public some of this information — deaths, injuries, damage claims and possible defects.

The law also provided substantially higher civil penalties for regulatory violations. But auto and tire company lobbyists succeeded in deleting one of the most important measures — meaningful criminal penalties for companies and executives who knowingly fail to recall dangerous products.

Ending the Stonewalling

With a known death toll of 271 and more than 700 injuries, the flawed Firestone tires stand as one of the worst automotive defects in the nation's history. In December 2000, a Firestone report at last acknowledged design flaws in its millions of recalled tires, and blamed both itself and Ford for the consequences. Ford also blamed the design defects and manufacturing problems at Firestone's Decatur plant but refused to accept any responsibility for the flawed Explorer, claiming it was perfectly safe. And despite these developments, the companies steadfastly refused to recall the remaining 5.6 million Wilderness AT tires still on the road.

Public Citizen kept up the pressure by releasing a definitive engineering study of the tire problem in April 2001 — some 14 months after Werner first aired her story in Houston. Public Citizen joined Hoar's SafetyForum, a consulting firm specializing in faulty products, and attorney Tab Turner in releasing a report, "The Real Root Cause of the Ford-Firestone Tragedy: Why the Public is Still at Risk." The report was based on extensive engineering investigations of the Firestone tires as well as internal company documents compiled as part of Turner's lawsuits against the companies. It concluded:

> Although both Ford and Firestone are to blame for the multitude of deaths associated with the lethal combination of this tire and vehicle, the real problem begins and ends with Ford Motor Company. Many of the key decisions were made by Ford: Ford created the original and con-tinuing performance specifications for Firestone's tires; Ford chose to let air out of the tires to cosmetically fix a serious problem that caused the Explorer's wheels to lift off the ground in turns; Ford's request triggered an effort to take weight out of the tire after their reduction in the tire's inflation pressure harmed the Explorer's fuel economy; and Ford ignored every opportunity to fix the rollover and stability problems that plague their Explorer vehicle, despite many loud and continuous signals that such changes were needed to protect vehicle occupants.

The report also explained why the original recall of particular tires made at Firestone's Decatur plant had been too limited, and demonstrated that the 5.6 million non-recalled Wilderness AT tires from other plants were no better, and were possibly worse, than the ones recalled.

"These tires fail because they are poorly designed, and the situation was made worse by poor manufacturing processes," Claybrook said. "It's criminal for executives to sit idly by as more people are unnecessarily killed in the lethal combination with the rollover-prone Explorer just because the top brass wants to save a few dollars."

Christine Sagrista, still mourning the loss of her son, traveled to Washington, D.C., for a news conference convened by Public Citizen. "I know other families are still driving around with these tires believing they are safe," she told the media. "I am here to tell those families that they should have those tires replaced to protect themselves and their loved ones. My life has been destroyed, and if I can get this message across to those who have dangerous tires on their vehicles, I have made a difference."

The response by Ford and Firestone: extensive advertising campaigns that attempted to restore the confidence of shaken consumers.

Pointing Fingers

Ford and Firestone — two of the biggest household names in U.S. business — had enjoyed a relationship that dated to the earliest days of the auto industry. But on May 21, 2001, less than a month after the release of Public Citizen's latest report, Bridgestone/Firestone announced it would stop selling tires to Ford. In a letter to Ford chief executive Jacques Nasser, Bridgestone/Firestone Chairman John T. Lampe cited a lack of trust: "We believe you [Ford] are attempting to divert scrutiny of your vehicle by casting doubt on the quality of Firestone tires. These tires are safe, and as we have said before, when we have a problem, we will acknowledge that problem and fix it. We expect you to do the same."[3]

Ford responded by announcing that, based on its statistical analysis of the failure rate of Firestone tires on Ford Explorers relative to other tires, it would spend up to $3 billion ($2 billion after taxes) to replace all 13 million Firestone ATX tires on Ford vehicles.[4] Firestone refused to take part in the recall, terminated its relationship with Ford and released data showing that the Explorer was twice as likely to roll over in a tire-related accident as other SUVs.[5] In the following days, the feud between the companies escalated into open warfare. Each sent reams of documents to Congress to demonstrate that the other company was at fault.

As the battle intensified, sales of the once-popular Explorer began to slip. Although Ford had already redesigned the four-door version of the 2001 Explorer to eliminate some of its stability problems, millions of older, rollover-prone vehicles were still on the road, and the two-door model remained unaltered. But no recall of the Explorer was ever initiated. As for Firestone, it agreed to pay $240 million to Ford in October 2005 to settle their dispute.

At this point, NHTSA had linked 271 deaths to crashes involving Firestone tires, most of them mounted on Explorers. Bridgestone Corp. had settled or otherwise resolved more than 2,000 lawsuits arising from the controversy, and had spent about $440 million on the recall, not counting undisclosed legal costs. Ford faced hundreds of lawsuits related to issues involving rollovers, weak roofs, inadequate occupant protection and stability.[6]

Anna Werner, the journalist who broke the story, credited Public Citizen and Claybrook in particular with "keeping the pressure on the government and the companies to take this problem seriously, and try to discover what caused the problem and what should be done about it." She noted that Claybrook's experience as a former NHTSA administrator had given her an intimate understanding of the auto industry's behavior toward government and was key to Public Citizen's success.

While Claybrook and her allies were gratified that Congress had reacted swiftly by passing the TREAD Act, they remained concerned that no rollover crash safety standard existed. The assembly lines in Detroit were still churning out SUVs that were prone to roll over, and most had such flimsy roofs that occupants stood little chance of avoiding serious injury or death if the car flipped. Rollover crashes killed more than 10,000 people every year during the early 2000s, representing about a third of all vehicle fatalities. Many thousands more people each year were being paralyzed or otherwise injured.[7]

NHTSA had the authority to establish new, stronger safety standards to stem this carnage, but it had failed to act for years. The agency had not even upgraded its ridiculously weak roof strength standard since 1971 — long before SUVs began to crowd the highways. And the agency did not have any performance standard to prevent rollovers in the first place.

Relief finally came in the summer of 2005. Despite intense partisanship and a decidedly anti-regulatory spirit in Congress, Claybrook and safety lobbyist Jackie Gillan of Advocates for Highway and Auto Safety, along with some manufacturers of automobile safety equipment, persuaded a bipartisan group of senators to support requirements for NHTSA to issue rollover protection standards. Under the leadership of Republican Senators Ted Stevens of Alaska and Trent Lott of Mississippi, the provisions survived debate and President George W. Bush signed them into law on August 10, 2005, as part of a highway bill.

The measure set deadlines for NHTSA to enact new standards to prevent rollovers, strengthen vehicle roofs, prevent occupant ejections, improve side-impact protection and upgrade power window switches to prevent children from accidentally activating them and being choked. It also called for new safety requirements for 15-seat passenger vans, and research into ways to prevent children and others from being backed over. "This is legislation that benefits consumers immensely," Claybrook said in a media statement, "and could produce the most significant safety enhancement since air bags were required in all vehicles in the 1991 highway legislation."

However, the auto industry and NHTSA both dragged their feet during the last years of the second Bush administration. NHTSA did propose upgrading roof crush protection in 2005. But it was a weak standard, requiring only a static test, like the 1971 standard, albeit with more pressure on vehicles' mid-roofs. Rollovers continued to contribute to about a third of all crash fatalities. The final rule issued in 2009 required slightly more pressure on the roof, but resisted a comprehensive dynamic standard to test the roof, belts and ejection. Once again, the auto industry had evaded major safety fixes.

Afterward, however, extensive publicity about the Ford Explorer case and pending legislation forced manufacturers to begin redesigning their SUVs to lower the center of gravity, substantially reducing the likelihood of rollovers. Rollover prevention standards arising from the 2005 legislation eventually forced even reluctant companies to redesign their vehicles.

Nader and the Corvair

To Claybrook, the Ford/Firestone imbroglio was just one more episode in a 40-year history of working to improve the safety of automobiles, often in furious battle with the automakers. Her interest in auto safety began in January 1966, when she was working for Representative James Mackay of Georgia. Prompted by accounts of fatal car crashes and Nader's publication of *Unsafe at Any Speed* six weeks earlier, Mackay asked Claybrook, who was on a fellowship with the American Political Science Association, to look into auto safety.

She found that from 1899, the year of the first fatal auto crash, until the first federal law on auto safety was passed in 1966, motor vehicle crashes had killed about two million people — more than the combat losses sustained by the United States in all its wars.[8] (In the four decades following 1966, crashes killed another 1.5 million.)

Car safety had generally been left to the good will and public spirit of the manufacturers. But Nader exposed their priority: profits over everything else. His book showed that General Motors' design of the Chevrolet Corvair gave it a tendency to overturn or skid out of control without warning. In many cars, drivers had been impaled on ornamental steering wheel spokes as the steering column rammed into their chests. The instrument panels in some autos were perfectly situated to gouge out the eyes of any passengers thrown against them in a crash.[9]

But car manufacturers refused to incorporate available safety technology into their vehicles despite knowing the damage their designs could cause. They knew how to design safer cars. They simply hadn't done it.

Seat belts were a case in point. Nader's book documented that seat belt technology had been around since the early 1900s, when airplanes used them prior to World War I. By the late 1920s, the government required that seat belts be worn on all civilian passenger flights. But lap belts were not available in U.S. cars until 1955, when Ford began to offer them as options — that were desirable and cost extra.

"GM played a central role in this delay," charged Nader. GM vehicle safety engineer Howard Gandelot said in 1954 that he found it "difficult to believe that the seat belt can afford the driver any great amount of protection over and above that which is available to him through the medium of the safety-type steering wheel, if he has his hands on the wheel and grips the rim sufficiently tight to take advantage of its energy shock-absorption properties and also takes advantage of the shock-absorbing action which can be achieved by correct positioning of the feet and legs."[10]

Crash tests, of course, showed that Gandelot's assertion was ludicrous. It is impossible in any significant crash for the driver, much less other occupants, to be protected by holding on to the steering wheel.

These revelations shocked the public and led to calls for laws mandating minimum safety performance standards. Capitalizing on the outrage, Nader pushed hard for legislation to regulate the auto industry for the first time.

The Johnson administration submitted a bill for auto safety regulations, but Nader thought it needed improvements: criminal penalties, a deadline for issuing the first standards and crash-worthiness requirements.

"Ralph went around to members asking if they would introduce various amendments to the bill, but no one volunteered, even though he was by now a somewhat prominent person," said Claybrook. "He finally called me, and I was interested." She first saw Nader in action in February 1966 when he testified before a congressional committee, telling members that the Ford Mustang had "raced off the drawing board" in two and a half years — more than enough time to meet new safety standards. The auto companies had claimed it would take many years.

"I watched him spar with the members of Congress, something few witnesses ever did," Claybrook said. "I was fascinated. People didn't argue with members in those days."

Claybrook immersed herself in the issue and new safety provisions that Nader suggested. "Working with a law professor who was helping Ralph, I typed up 30 pages of his proposed amendments, then gave them to Mr. Mackay, and to [Indiana] Senator Vance Hartke, who introduced them," Claybrook recalled. "The auto industry lobbyists were furious."

After five months of working in the House of Representatives, Claybrook moved in May 1966 to the Senate to complete her fellowship, working for Minnesota Democrat Walter Mondale. There she continued to push the National Traffic and Motor Vehicle Safety Act and the Highway Safety Act. With GM's pursuit of Nader in the news, the bills were hot and moved through Congress with record speed. President Lyndon Johnson signed them into law on September 9, 1966, bringing the safety performance of motor vehicles under federal regulation in a new government agency for the first time.

The laws established a new agency (named the National Highway Traffic Safety Administration [NHTSA] in 1970) and directed it to set minimum uniform safety standards for all motor vehicles. In 1975, Congress required NHTSA to issue the first-ever fuel economy standards within the next five years. It was an historic shift in power from corporate executives to government agencies accountable to the public. It meant that auto companies could no longer design vehicles with reckless disregard for safety or fuel efficiency.

Despite intense opposition from automakers, the first two dozen federal motor vehicle safety standards were issued in January 1967 for 1968 models. Tire standards were introduced in 1968, and lap belts and shoulder harnesses became standard in January 1969, followed later that year by head restraints to prevent whiplash. GM had tried to stop the shoulder harnesses, claiming they were unsafe and could injure occupants. But Volvo produced research on the shoulder systems it had installed since 1959 that showed their safety value. The rule finally took effect.

Another crucial safety advance was the new agency's authority to order automakers to recall defective vehicles. Before 1966, automakers had sometimes initiated secret recalls, asking owners to bring their cars in for a "free checkup." When owners showed up, the dealers would repair the problem without ever telling the customer. The new legislation gave NHTSA the power to order companies to notify owners of potential safety defects, and in 1974, a new law obligated companies to recall the vehicle if a safety defect was found. Rejecting the industry's protests, the agency made all recall information public.

Claybrook Takes Charge

In 1977, following the Watergate scandal and the brief presidency of Gerald Ford, President Jimmy Carter chose Claybrook to head the still-young auto safety agency, NHTSA.

Claybrook was an excellent choice on two counts: She had spent five years directing Public Citizen's lobbying arm, Congress Watch, so she was intimately familiar with the complexities and folkways of the legislative process. She also was an expert on auto safety, having worked on passage of the auto safety legislation in 1966 that created NHTSA, and served for four years as an assistant to its first administrator, Dr. William Haddon Jr. At Public Citizen, she also lobbied for legislation enacted in 1974 that required recalls, authorized subpoena power, mandated standards for school buses and required a congressional veto opportunity for any air bag standard.

At NHTSA, Claybrook pursued an expansive safety agenda. One of her most innovative projects was the New Car Assessment Program, a crash testing process for new models that eventually was adopted by governments worldwide. Under this approach, new models are crashed in tightly controlled tests to see how the vehicle performs in front, rear and side impacts, at speeds five miles per hour faster than minimum safety standards require the vehicle to sustain without harm to the occupants. The results are then made public.

Claybrook also issued the nation's first fuel economy standards, which required that 1976 models' fuel mileage average be doubled to 27.5 miles per gallon on a fleet-wide basis by 1985. She upgraded the agency's defects investigation and recall programs and recalled tens of millions of vehicles and tires. And she helped generate new consumer information rules, such as tire performance ratings. She published *The Car Book,* which reached millions of motorists, allowing them to compare vehicle safety crash test and other data. In 2005, at Public Citizen's urging, Congress passed legislation requiring that the crash test results be included on the price stickers of new cars. For the first time, consumers could see this vital safety information as they were considering their choices.

But perhaps Claybrook's most important initiative was a regulation requiring that all new vehicles include a new form of crash protection for occupants — either automatic seat belts or air bags.

By the late 1970s, the auto industry was staunchly resisting government requirements to incorporate new safety features into its products. It lobbied Congress, called on the White House and sued in the courts. It reflexively opposed every new safety regulation. Just as it had fought for a decade against seat belts, it also used every conceivable tactic to obstruct the introduction of the latest life-saving innovations. Claybrook's effort to require automatic protection restraints started during her first stint at NHTSA in 1969. It triggered a ferocious 20-year battle involving the manufacturers, the government, Congress and safety advocates.

In many ways, the struggle was more than another clash over the introduction of a new safety device. It went to the core of corporate America's anger over the federal government's expanding role in protecting consumers from unsafe products. In the business world, the air bag debate seemed to symbolize all government-imposed limits on its power to generate profits. Safety advocates, on the other hand, considered air bags a necessary "technological vaccine" to prevent death, injury and trauma.

In fact, the debate over air bags had begun long before Claybrook was appointed to head NHTSA. Nader had urged the introduction of air bags in *Unsafe at Any Speed* in 1965. "Protection like this could be achieved by a kind of inflatable air bag restraint which would be actuated to envelop a passenger before a crash," he wrote. "Both General Motors and Ford did work on a system like this about 1958 but dropped the inquiry and now even refuse to communicate with outside scientists and engineers interested in this approach to injury prevention."

For a while, under the leadership of President Ed Cole, GM changed its mind. The company experimented very successfully with air bags in the late 1960s, and in 1970, Cole promised to install them in every new GM car by 1975. These air bags opened relatively softly and slowly in low-speed crashes and more powerfully and rapidly in high-speed collisions. It seemed that at last the auto companies were responding to public concerns over safety.

But Cole's promise never materialized. The Arab oil embargo hit the United States in late 1973, sending gasoline prices soaring and severely reducing new car sales. Cole retired in 1974, and between then and 1976, the company sold only 10,000 vehicles with air bags. This was in part because they were never advertised and because the devices were put only into large vehicles that did not sell well during the oil shortage. Despite the excellent safety record of air bags in the GM cars that had them, the company halted the program in 1976.

In 1977, Transportation Secretary Brock Adams issued a rule developed by NHTSA, the "frontal impact safety standard." It required air bags or automatic seat belts to be phased in for all cars — but not, under Adams' instructions, until between 1982 and 1984. In late 1979, GM told NHTSA that the air bag program would have to be delayed because of a risk to children; their small size made them more likely to be injured by the device's rapid inflation. But two months after that warning, GM President Pete Estes declared that the company had "worked out the child restraint problems" and would begin offering air bags in some 1982 model cars.

Despite GM's assurances, Claybrook designated a special team of engineers, medical experts and accident data analysts to review all relevant data from auto companies and "to immediately carry out whatever studies are required to resolve any outstanding issues" on air bag safety. After exhaustive analysis, the expert panel made specific recommendations for improved air bag designs. The specialists recommended a number of alternatives: dual-stage air bags of the kind GM had sold in the mid-1970s; bags mounted on top of the dashboard so the full force of the inflation hits the windshield first, not the occupants; and air bags with a series of pockets to control air flow and tethers to limit their horizontal deployment.

In 1980, Claybrook provided these options to the presidents of every auto company, which had great latitude to design air bag systems under NHTSA's frontal impact safety performance standard. Their decisions to go with the cheaper, less child-friendly options would have serious ramifications later — especially for Claybrook herself.

When President Ronald Reagan came to the White House in 1981, Claybrook left NHTSA. A year later, she returned to Public Citizen as its president, where she remained for the next 27 years. Meanwhile, Reagan appointees at the Department of Transportation (DOT) revoked the air bag standard, to thunderous applause from the auto companies.

That year, GM canceled its air bag program on grounds of cost, not because it didn't believe that air bags were lifesavers. "We can demonstrate that we can produce a highly effective device," boasted GM Vice President Betsy Ancher-Johnson at a congressional hearing. "[But] ... our decision to terminate the program and not offer air bags is a purely business decision."[11]

Alarmed at this reversal on safety, consumer groups rallied behind the State Farm insurance company, which had filed suit to overturn the cancellation of the air bag rule. In 1983, the U.S. Supreme Court issued a unanimous decision in State Farm's favor. Apparently awed by the ferocity of the battle, the Supreme Court momentarily lost its customary detachment and described the industry's struggle against air bags as "the regulatory equivalent of war."

As *The New York Times* explained, "American auto makers, always ready to under-estimate consumer sophistication and ever resentful of interference by Government, oppose air bags because they would give regulation a good name."[12]

The Supreme Court victory for consumers meant that Reagan's new transportation secretary, Elizabeth Dole, was forced to revive the air bag standard in 1984. Under her rules, air bags were to be phased in from 1987 to 1990. But later, at the industry's request, Dole delayed the requirement for passenger-side air bags until the 1994 model year. She also ruled that the standard would be revoked if, by April 1989, mandatory seat belt laws covered two-thirds of the U.S. population. This gave the industry an incentive — for the first time — to work for passage of laws requiring seat belt use. Every state but New Hampshire eventually passed such laws, but it came too late to meet Dole's 1989 deadline. The standard began phasing in with 1989 models for the driver's side and went fully into effect for 1994 models.

In 1989, the auto insurance industry entered a period of reflection. It had spent around $80 million fighting California legislation to regulate auto insurance premiums and lost after Nader and consumer groups spent $2 million promoting the initiative. Suddenly the executives were willing to talk to Nader's consumer allies. The result, which Nader had suggested, was Advocates for Highway and Auto Safety, a lobbying organization that united the industry with consumer groups. Claybrook and Jerry Maatman of Kemper Insurance were co-chairs and Judie Stone was its first president. Over the years, the organization became a powerhouse in lobbying for advances in safety legislation and standards. Jackie Gillan became its president in 2011.

In 1991, to resolve the ongoing debate, Claybrook and Gillan led consumer groups in pushing for legislation to require air bags in all passenger vehicles. This would eliminate the option, which some manufacturers chose, of installing passive belts rather than air bags. Passive belts, attached to vehicle doors, were not as effective in preventing injury. For one thing, the door might open in a crash, leaving the occupant unsecured. Plus the belts could be easily unhooked, like a regular belt system. In a stunning victory, the air bag-only provision was enacted in the 1991 highway bill.

Consumers had won an important triumph for safety. Not only had advocates finally obtained state laws requiring seat belt use, but they also had ensured that air bags would be installed in all passenger motor vehicles. But the political war over air bags was far from finished.

Claybrook Becomes the Target

In April 1995, Diana Zhang, age 7, was killed by the force of an inflating air bag in a Volvo after a fender-bender in Ohio. More children were killed in the years after that in a pattern that could not be ignored. By late 1995, the news media had documented the deaths of 14 children by air bags inflating in low-speed crashes.[13]

One Sunday in October 1995, 7-year-old Alison Sanders was riding in the front passenger seat of her father's Chrysler minivan in Maryland when the van collided with another car at an intersection. They were going only nine miles per hour. But Rob Sanders turned in horror to see Alison slumped in the seat beside him. Her air bag had deployed so powerfully that she had been instantly rendered brain-dead from the impact.

"I was in a state of quiet, private grief over it for a long time, and then I started to learn about the other [air bag-related] deaths," Sanders said in an interview several years later. "I started doing some research on my own and started to learn, to my horror, about designs the auto companies had rejected, that there were better ways to make an air bag. But for cost reasons, they hadn't used those."

Despite his own traumatic experience, Sanders realized air bags themselves were not the problem. "There is nothing wrong with air bags. They save many lives," he said. "The bodyguard in the Mercedes with Princess Diana in Paris was saved in that horrific collision by the passenger air bag [in 1997]. It just shows that a well-designed air bag has tremendous benefits."

The media began to publicize the child tragedies, and in 1996, *USA Today* traced the development of a nationwide crisis. The industry, afraid that its cost-cutting, life-threatening practices were about to be exposed, searched for a scapegoat. Claybrook, who had been a thorn in the side of auto companies for two decades, was the perfect target.

While in government, Claybrook had publicly championed air bags despite company hostility, and as Public Citizen president, she was no less vigorous in urging that the safety devices be adopted. Just as GM had tried to smear Nader 30 years before, so the companies now turned on Claybrook.

Their news releases and public statements portrayed her as the personification of meddlesome government, as an overzealous regulator more concerned with the principle of regulating the industry than the reality of saving children's lives. *It was all her fault,* cried the auto manufacturers. *She forced us to install air bags before they were ready. We warned her in 1979 about problems with air bags and children.*

In 1996, some reporters from major media outlets received black briefing books from the auto industry that provided a severely distorted account of the air bag history. They had the effect of shifting blame for tragic child deaths from badly designed bags onto Claybrook. The industry's PR machine provided a highly selective version of events to the news media, and for a while, some of the mud stuck. By mid-November 1996, *The Wall Street Journal* and *The Washington Post* carried articles questioning Claybrook's role in pressing so hard for air bags. The gruesome death of baby Alexandra Greer in Boise, Idaho, over Thanksgiving weekend further fueled the industry's propaganda campaign.

Rob Sanders realized something was wrong with the news media's version of events. "I was aware before I met Joan that she was taking the fall in the media ... principally because the industry was putting out press packages laying the problem at the feet of Joan, and a lot of the press articles bought that theory. I remember reading those and thinking, 'This isn't right,' " he said. "They were just groping to find a fall person and they chose Joan, which I thought was absurd. She'd left government in 1981 ... and for [the companies] to reach back two decades to the administrator who promulgated a rule that never went into effect — the absurdity made it laughable if it wasn't so pathetic."

Public Citizen fought back, showing that the companies were trying to cover their own tracks by twisting the record. The organization issued new analyses and the real story eventually became clear. The truth was that, taking advantage of the rule that gave them flexibility, many automakers knowingly had chosen to install cheaper, poorly designed air bags in their vehicles.

Government regulations required only that air bags protect an average-size male crash test dummy in a 30 MPH frontal crash into a rigid barrier. Some companies, given great latitude to design air bag systems, made their air bags comply with the bare technical minimum, even if it meant the designs were dangerous for children or small women. Others, like Honda, heeded the recommendations made by Claybrook's team of experts in the late 1970s and designed systems that were far less likely to harm occupants. As a result, there were no reports of child deaths or life-threatening injuries in Honda-made vehicles. But other auto companies were sued for injuries resulting from their aggressive and badly designed air bags.

By December 1996, the air bag issue had become so hot that Representative Frank Wolf, a Virginia Democrat, and Arizona Republican Senator John McCain held hearings. Claybrook and Sanders, as well as industry representatives, were invited to testify. The manufacturers used the hearings to rehash their three decades of attack on the safety standard.

"Joan and I were of the same opinion," Sanders said, "that the standard should not be watered down as the companies requested, but that it needed to be strengthened and that it had to be expanded beyond the average-size male to protect a 'family' of dummies of various sizes in crashes of different speeds."

For Sanders, the Senate hearings were an emotional experience. "We were fighting the industry hacks who were there en masse. Joan, as always, was very gracious in her testimony, but I was the last one to speak and I completely lost all composure. I was *so* exasperated after hearing all the spin doctors from the industry."

Sanders channeled his anger into finding and organizing other parents whose children had been killed or injured by air bags. He formed a group, Parents for Safer Air Bags, which joined Public Citizen to educate the media and lobby Congress to upgrade the safety standard. Parents from all over the country converged on Washington, D.C., to talk to their members of Congress about improving the standard.

Claybrook's advice for those angry parents was simple. "I tell them you're as important as the senator is."

Alan Greer, whose baby had been killed in the Thanksgiving 1996 crash, flew in from Idaho because his senator, Republican Dirk Kempthorne, was pushing the industry's proposal to get rid of the most important crash test for measuring air bag performance—the test in which a car is driven into a rigid barrier.

"Joan coached Alan and me on how to approach the members and keep it short," said Sanders. "She told us to make the point very simple and to state what the problem is and what the solution is, and to point out the havoc, anguish and misery that has been caused by a poor standard."

The combination of the parents' determination and Public Citizen's expertise paid off. Senator John McCain steered through Congress legislation upgrading the standard to protect the whole family of test dummies—including children and adults of small stature. The industry fought the new safety measures, but at the end agreed to language negotiated with Claybrook, Sanders and other safety and insurance groups.

In September 1998, NHTSA began to implement the new law by proposing new rules to require the introduction of advanced air bags over the next several years—the sort of "advanced" technology the industry had known about 25 years earlier and that Claybrook's team of experts had recommended. But once again, automakers threw their lobbying muscle into weakening the standard. They did not want to redesign their SUVs and pickup trucks to make them capable of absorbing more energy so as to be able to pass the 30 MPH "high-speed" crash test.

In May 2000, the DOT issued its new final rule, and the industry prevailed, winning the less protective 25 MPH crash test requirement. But the overall rule did improve safety because it forced automakers to use a family of dummies in the tests and retained the barrier crash test that the industry had fought. In addition, the companies had to run low-speed tests to simulate the type of crash in which so many children had been killed and injured when air bags inflated with too much force.

The auto industry fought long and hard against air bags, but Public Citizen and its allies prevailed overall. The result: Air bags now save about 2,500 lives every year and reduce the severity of countless injuries.[14]

Taking on the Big Rigs

Improving the safety of automobiles was only one way Public Citizen worked to make the highways less hazardous. In 1981, the organization took an important truck safety case to the U.S. Supreme Court.

"We represented a bunch of truck drivers who wanted to get paid for the time they spent inspecting their trucks before they took them out on the road," said Public Citizen attorney David Vladeck, who argued the case. "Under federal law, before a truck is taken out on the highway, a driver is required to undertake a fairly exhaustive safety inspection of about 15 or 20 minutes. The employer said it wasn't its requirement, it was the government's, so it wasn't going to pay for it."

The issue for Public Citizen was this: If the employer refused to pay drivers for the time they spent inspecting company trucks, then it stood to reason that some drivers would be less inclined to conduct thorough inspections as often as needed. The Supreme Court ruled in favor of Public Citizen, and the truck drivers and the public won an important safety victory.

It was just the beginning of decades of grueling work on truck safety.

One dark night in September 1983, a man named James William Mooney, 55, was killed when his car slammed into the side of a truck that was backing across a quiet country road in North Carolina. "The truck driver had brought the truck home with him and was backing it into a field across from his house on a very rural road," said Mooney's daughter, Jennifer Tierney. "There were cows on either side of the road. He was in a jack-knifed position and had no lights on the side of the trailer."

After years of working on her own "to try to get someone to listen" about making trucks more visible in the dark, Tierney heard about a new truck safety organization called Citizens for Reliable and Safe Highways, or CRASH. In 1991, she agreed to tell her story at a press conference in Washington, D.C.

"It was my first press conference and I was scared to death," Tierney recalled. "You take somebody who has grown up their entire life in a small town in North Carolina, who has never had anything tragic happen to them before and has never been an activist of any sort on any issue, and suddenly because of circumstances you're in front of microphones in the nation's capital. The issue was so important I didn't want to back out. I wanted to make people understand how you feel when something like this happens to you."

Claybrook helped Tierney prepare her statement. It was the start of a long and effective collaboration between CRASH and Claybrook, who became chair of the group's board. Tierney became a savvy, influential spokesperson for truck crash victims and their families and, with Public Citizen's help, grew confident in walking the halls of the U.S. Capitol to lobby members of Congress and secretaries of the Department of Transportation.

"Joan taught me how to confront decision-makers," she said. "At the start it was very intimidating, but you begin to feel you have as much right to access to politicians as corporations do. You feel out of your element when you're there [on Capitol Hill]. You're walking around and seeing these men in business suits and briefcases and they know their way around and they know everybody, and they've had a lot of time and access to these people that you've never even met before."

Truck crashes had become a major cause of highway mortality but had received little attention on a national scale — and little or nothing was being done about them. (According to NHTSA, 4,808 people died in 442,000 crashes involving large trucks in 2007 and another 101,000 were injured.)[15] Many members of CRASH were relatives of those killed or injured in truck crashes and wanted to spare other families the grief they had suffered.

CRASH's first battle involved the 1991 highway bill, called the Intermodal Surface Transportation Efficiency Act, or ISTEA. Public Citizen and CRASH were joined by another new group called Advocates for Highway and Auto Safety.

The ISTEA debate centered on the proliferation of double- and triple-trailer trucks. The industry had persuaded 20 states to allow the operation of these dangerously cumbersome rigs. But some states, including California, had resisted, and the industry wanted the trucks to be able to travel nationwide. "They would go out to the legislatures and get states to pass laws allowing bigger and longer trucks, and then go to Congress and say 'We need uniformity,'" recalled Jackie Gillan, who had worked as a lobbyist with Claybrook at NHTSA and was then vice president of Advocates for Highway and Auto Safety.

Together, Public Citizen, Advocates for Highway and Auto Safety and CRASH worked to persuade Congress to stop the spread of the biggest rigs on the highway. With CRASH's executive director, Anthony Garrett, who helped organize CRASH in 1990, they met one by one with journalists to educate them about the highway hazards of big trucks. "We did that for six months, and we started lobbying members of Congress one by one, visiting their staffs and so on," Claybrook said. "We found organizers in key congressional districts and took out billboards near their district offices so they would see CRASH was in their district."

Invited to testify at Senate hearings about the legislation, Claybrook found herself on a panel of witnesses with the most high-profile industry executive, the abrasive and outspoken chief of the American Trucking Associations, Tom Donohue. "CRASH had this wonderful brochure that opened up wider and wider into a picture of a triple-trailer truck," Claybrook said. "I was sitting next to Donohue at the table in front of the senators, and I pulled out this brochure and held it up right in front of his face, which totally irritated him, and when you get someone like that irritated, they make mistakes and say things they regret. So he became a bulldog, and [New Jersey] Senator Frank Lautenberg jumped all over him. He lost that debate, and they put our provision in the Senate bill."

The consumers had taken on the formidable power of the trucking industry and, in a stunning upset, won legislation limiting these dangerously long vehicles to only the highways where they were already allowed by state law as of June 1991. This amounted to general access in 12 states and on selected highways in eight more. The big rigs generally could not travel on highways east of the Mississippi River except the New York State Thruway. "That was a tremendous victory," Gillan said. "The trucking industry was totally in shock that we won that battle. They were caught off guard, because they had had carte blanche to go to Congress and get whatever they wanted. They were very, very close to a number of the committee chairs."

Despite the industry's political muscle, Public Citizen, CRASH and Advocates for Highway and Auto Safety continued to rack up wins, making the highways safer for motorists. In the 1990s, they defeated attempts in several states to increase the size and weight of trucks and the hours that truckers could log in a week. In 1992, the first Bush administration proposed an "hours-of-service rule" that would have allowed truckers to drive for 100 hours in a week, an increase of 30 hours. The groups mounted a grassroots campaign to defeat the proposal, generating the largest number of public responses to a proposed rule that the Department of Transportation had ever seen.

The rule was withdrawn under the Clinton administration, but the battle over fatigue-related truck crashes was far from over. In 1999, in response to a 1995 directive from Congress, the Clinton administration proposed new hours-of-service rules, but Congress stopped the DOT from issuing them before Clinton left office. The Bush administration did nothing. Then Public Citizen sued successfully to force the issue. As a result of that lawsuit, the Bush administration issued a regulation in 2003 that allowed truckers to drive longer hours, both daily and weekly.

The new rule increased daily limits by 10 percent, allowing truckers to drive for 11 hours instead of 10 hours. The regulation increased weekly driving hours by more than 25 percent, raising maximums from 60 hours to 77 hours over seven days, and from 70 hours to 88 hours over eight days.

This time, CRASH, Parents Against Tired Truckers and Advocates for Highway and Auto Safety, led by Public Citizen lawyers, fought the proposal in court. In 2004, they won a resounding victory when a federal appellate court struck down the new rule, saying it violated the law by not taking driver health into consideration.

The Bush administration produced a new version the following year, but it was nearly identical to the previous proposal. A third rule came out in 2008 and Public Citizen sued a third time. Shortly after Claybrook departed, the new Obama administration issued its own still-inadequate rule, and Public Citizen sued once more to retain the 10-hour limit and a 48-hour rest period. After the DOT issued some further key improvements, the courts let the rule take effect.

Cost Is Not the Issue

Safety improvements often are relatively inexpensive, but the auto and truck industries often resist any government regulations despite their low cost. That's what happened when the consumer groups' truck safety alliance persuaded NHTSA in 1992 to require that all new tractor-trailers be marked with highly reflective materials to increase their visibility. It also pushed the Office of Motor Carriers (OMC) to require uniform reflective tape or reflectors on big rigs that were already on the highway when that 1992 NHTSA rule was enacted. The rule affecting trucks in use was finally issued in 1999.

If the side of the truck that Tierney's father struck on that dark night in North Carolina had been equipped with reflective tape, the crash likely would not have happened. NHTSA estimated in early 2001, before the new rule was fully in place, that putting reflective tape on all big trucks would prevent 7,800 crashes, save as many as 350 lives and prevent 500 injuries each year, at minimal cost.[16]

While reformers were winning numerous legislative battles, they had one intractable problem: The Office of Motor Carriers, which regulated the trucking industry from deep within the Federal Highway Administration. Both had a cozy relationship with the industry and were loath to require strong safety improvements. Industry leaders, by giving large contributions to key congressional committee members for their re-election campaigns, had ensured that the OMC was kept feeble.

A Public Citizen study showed that between 1993 and 1998, the trucking industry gave almost $14 million in political action committee donations, individual contributions and unregulated "soft money" to the national political parties. In addition, it spent more than $15 million to lobby the government. Bud Shuster, a Pennsylvania Republican who had long been chair of the powerful House Transportation and Infrastructure Committee, took $145,400 from the trucking industry during those six years, making him the largest single recipient of the industry's money.[17]

"The more money they give, the less they're regulated," Claybrook said. "It's congressional protection money. You pay them to leave you alone. There are so many deaths and injuries because the trucking industry has used its influence to secure legislative exemptions from existing safety requirements and to block legislation to improve truck safety."

The years covered in the Public Citizen study coincided with marked congressional inaction on truck safety standards as well as a virtual abdication by the Office of Motor Carriers of its regulatory duties. The OMC had even contracted with representatives of the trucking industry itself to conduct studies. "This is an agency that employs 'partnering' and education efforts in lieu of effective enforcement and regulatory efforts," Claybrook said in 1999.

She wanted the OMC moved from the Federal Highway Administration to NHTSA, where at least some regulatory culture existed. The OMC, she said, "completely ignores new technologies — like black boxes that could collect crash data and ensure that truck drivers don't log too many hours in a day. This is an agency that has refused to issue training standards for drivers of larger, combination vehicles or entry-level truck driver training, eight years after being told to by Congress."

Claybrook wasn't alone in calling for reforms. In the later 1990s, the OMC had been criticized in searing reports by the Transportation Department's inspector general, the General Accounting Office, the National Transportation Safety Board and lawmakers at four congressional hearings.[18]

When Jennifer Tierney and other safety advocates were invited to a meeting with U.S. Transportation Secretary Rodney Slater in 1999 to listen to his plans for a series of workshops to discuss truck safety, Tierney got straight to the point. "I thought the workshops were a waste of time, so I just looked at him and I said, 'Mr. Secretary, with all respect, if over 100 people a week were dying in plane crashes in this country, would you respond by organizing workshops?' I don't think he'll ever forget me saying that. He reached over and actually took my hand and he looked at me for several seconds before responding. He said, 'No.' "

In November 1999, after a yearlong campaign by thousands of CRASH members and intense lobbying by Public Citizen and Advocates for Highway and Auto Safety, Congress passed the Motor Carrier Safety Improvement Act. The law specifically states that safety is the agency's "highest priority." It moved the OMC out of the highly bureaucratic Federal Highway Administration to a new independent agency within the Department of Transportation, and mandated that it report directly to the DOT secretary. U.S. Reps. Frank Wolfe, a Virginia Republican, and Democrat James Oberstar of Minnesota were instrumental in pushing for a new agency. It was named the Federal Motor Carrier Safety Administration.

The law also allowed the transportation secretary to delegate authority to NHTSA to develop safety standards for trucks already on the road. NHTSA already had authority over new truck and car performance standards. "The fact that victim survivors could make something so major occur is phenomenal," said Tierney.

The Legacy of Activism: Safer Autos, Lives Saved

Overcoming industry objections to regulations is always difficult for consumer organizations. In 1966, Henry Ford II reacted to NHTSA's first proposed auto safety standards spawned by *Unsafe at Any Speed* by complaining that they were "unreasonable, arbitrary and technically unfeasible ... if we can't meet them when they are published we'll have to close down." Instead, the company prospered. In 1977, Ford admitted this on NBC's "Meet the Press": "We wouldn't have the kinds of safety built into automobiles that we have had unless there had been a federal law."

Despite that admission, Clarence Ditlow, director of the Center for Auto Safety and Claybrook's close ally, sees little change in the corporate attitude toward consumer concerns. "Look at the sport utility vehicle craze [of the early 2000s]," Ditlow said. "That's the epitome of the old mentality. They make the manufacturers $15,000 per vehicle in profit. They're absolute cash cows, and they're not taking the money and building safety into them. They have rollover problems, they're too stiff, too aggressive, too gas-guzzling. It's the same old problem all over again."

Rob Sanders' painful journey from distraught father to investigative consumer activist damaged his trust in corporate good will. "In 1995, I operated under the naïve assumption that in areas of safety and the environment, the government was effectively looking after the public interest and was not controlled by the auto industry, or other industries," he said. "I've now come to the opposite conclusion. I think the regulators are highly captive to regulated industries whether you're talking about environmental issues or auto safety. The agencies really don't zealously regulate or oversee their designated areas of responsibility; they tend to react to problems as they arise; and their response is often dictated by what the industry wants them to do."

Too often that is to do nothing. In 2008, represented by Public Citizen, Ditlow and the Center for Auto Safety filed suit under the Freedom of Information Act to obtain NHTSA records on accident deaths and injuries related to drivers' use of cell phones. Initial public debate had led many states and localities to mandate that drivers use cell phones only with hands-free devices so they could keep both hands on the steering wheel. Automakers knew people didn't want to stop using their phones while driving, and NHTSA wasn't going to make them stop. But in 2009, NHTSA was forced to release documents showing it had known since 2003 about studies showing that the real problem was not fumbling with the device or driving with one hand, but the phone conversation itself: Drivers talking on the phone paid inadequate attention to the road.

The documents sparked headlines and a national debate. "People died in crashes because the government withheld this information," Ditlow said.

Despite foot-dragging by automakers and regulators, U.S. highways were far safer at the end of Claybrook's tenure at Public Citizen than when the first auto safety law passed in 1966. Total traffic fatalities dropped from 50,894 in 1966 to 37,261 in 2008, the lowest level since 1961, despite a doubling of the number of licensed drivers. In 1966, 5.5 fatalities occurred for every 100 million miles driven by the American public. By 2008, that rate had dropped to 1.27 — an historic low and a remarkable shift.[19] The estimated number of people injured in traffic accidents had dropped to its lowest point since NHTSA started collecting data. In all, the standards have saved more than 600,000 lives since the 1960s, making them one of the most important public health successes in American history.

This overall success is attributable at least in part to the oversight of federal regulators and the relentless vigilance of Nader, Claybrook, Ditlow, Gillan, Sanders, Tierney and many others. Since 1991, Claybrook and Gillan led the enactment of nine pieces of major legislation mandating auto and truck safety improvements.[20]

"Persistence is one of our greatest strengths," Claybrook said. "Air bags took us 20 years." Together, these citizen activists took on some of the most powerful industries in America and, working through democratic institutions, changed history, saving untold American families from the lasting grief and sorrow that accompanies the loss of a loved one.

Claybrook's dedication to auto safety, which dated from 1966, ran so deep that when she left Public Citizen in 2009, "I took this issue with me." She was chair of CRASH and became board co-chair and strategic adviser at Advocates for Highway and Auto Safety. She continued to speak out at media events and testify on consumers' behalf before regulatory agencies and at congressional hearings, such as those on the high-profile 2010 Toyota accelerator hazard and the GM ignition switch defects.

The Future of the Auto Industry

Once a major force in the world, the American auto industry had become a shadow of its former self by second decade of the new millennium. Regulation is the industry's favorite whipping boy, but in reality, automobile companies lost their way because they lost touch with their customers. In the 1980s and 1990s, they hired lobbyists to work with friendly members of Congress to stop new safety and environmental initiatives that would have forced the industry to modernize production lines and produce safer vehicles with higher fuel economy. The companies acquired too much speculative debt and sales of their vehicles dropped, so that when the global economy went into a tailspin in 2008, all three major U.S. companies were in deep trouble.

Chrysler and General Motors declared bankruptcy and sought about $100 billion in taxpayer bailout funds in 2009 to survive. Long the champions of free market competition unfettered by regulations, these two companies brought down others with them. They ruined many of their loyal dealers and suppliers, dismissed tens of thousands of workers, left communities bankrupt and refused to pay liability claims to people injured by their products. What's more, the life savings of many retired and nearly retired workers vanished.

In 2009, Public Citizen and its allies successfully pressured the Chrysler Group to assume responsibility for product liability claims brought by people injured in crashes that occurred after the company's bankruptcy but that involved cars sold before the bankruptcy. The organization was gratified that the Obama administration that year issued a stronger single national standard for fuel economy and emissions and was certain to upgrade some safety rules.

The auto bailout finally sent $49.5 billion in taxpayer dollars to GM and $12.5 billion to Chrysler, saving thousands of American jobs, and both companies eventually paid most of it back — all but $11 billion in GM's case and all but $1.3 billion from Chrysler. But what Obama's regulators did not do was use the government's position as majority shareholder to impose significantly improved safety rules and controls on climate change-causing emissions as a trade-off for rescuing the two giant corporations. This was a huge lost opportunity that could have transformed the industry at a moment when it was desperate for rescue by taxpayers.

Endnotes

1 Traffic Homicide Investigation Report, Case #FHP799-42-15, Florida Highway Patrol, Jan. 4, 2000.
2 Statement of Vickie Hendricks, delivered at Public Citizen press conference, Washington, D.C.,

Sept. 26, 2000.

3   John T. Lampe, "Text of Letter to Ford from Bridgestone," *The New York Times*, May 22, 2001.

4   Terril Yue Jones, "Ford's Tire Recall Will Cost $3 Billion," *Los Angeles Times*, May 23, 2001.

5   Caroline E. Mayer and Frank Swoboda, "Ford, Firestone Escalate Feud," *The Washington Post*, May 24, 2001.

6   Karen Lundegaard and Timothy Aeppel, "Bridgestone, Ford Reach Recall Deal," *The Wall Street Journal*, Oct. 13, 2005.

7   National Highway Traffic Safety Administration, *Rollover Data Special Study Final Report*, U.S. Department of Transportation, US DOT H11 435, Washington, D.C., January 2011, p. ii.

8   David Bollier, *Citizen Action and Other Big Ideas: A History of Ralph Nader and the Consumer Movement*, Center for Study of Responsive Law, 1991, p. 64.

9   Ralph Nader, *Unsafe at Any Speed*, 1973 Bantam edition, pp. 3–10 and pp. 85–87.

10 Ralph Nader, *Unsafe at Any Speed*, pp. 100–101.

11 Ancher-Johnson, quoted in Parents for Safer Air Bags, *The Air Bag Crisis: Causes and Solutions*, Oct. 1997, pp. 16–17.

12 David Bollier, *Citizen Action and Other Big Ideas*, p. 66.

13 Parents for Safer Air Bags, *The Air Bag Crisis: Causes and Solutions*, Oct. 1997, p. 37.

14 National Highway Traffic Safety Administration, *Traffic Safety Facts*, U.S. Department of Transportation, US DOT HS 811 580, Washington, D.C., February 2012, p. 1

15 National Highway Traffic Safety Administration, *Traffic Safety Facts 2007: A Compilation of Motor Vehicle Crash Data from the Fatality Analysis Reporting System and the General Estimates System*.

16 National Highway Traffic Safety Administration, *The Effectiveness of Retroreflective Tape on Heavy Trailers*, NHTSA Technical Report DOT HS 809 222, 2001.

17 *Truckloads of Money*, Public Citizen, Dec. 9, 1999.

18 See *Motor Carrier Safety Program, FHWA, Report No. AS-FH-7-006*, Office of Inspector General, U.S. Department of Transportation (DOT), March 26, 1997; Statement of the Hon. Kenneth M. Mead, Inspector General, U.S. DOT, before the Subcommittee on Transportation, Committee on Appropriations, U.S. House of Representatives; *Motor Carrier Safety Program*, Report No. TR-1999-091, Office of Inspector General, U.S. DOT, April 26, 1999; *Motor Carriers Office Hampered by Limited Information on Causes of Crashes and Other Data Problems*, U.S. General Accounting Office, GAO-RCED-99-182, June 1999.

19 National Highway Traffic Safety Administration, *2008 Traffic Safety Annual Assessment — Highlights*. DOT HS 811 172. June 2009.

20 The nine were: Intermodal Surface Transportation Efficiency Act, requiring front-seat air bags as standard equipment, Dec. 18, 1991; Federal Anti-Car Theft Act, Oct. 25, 1992; National Highway System Designation Act, funding biomechanics research, Nov. 28, 1995; Transportation Equity Act, requiring advanced air bags, June 9, 1998; Motor Carrier Safety Improvement Act, Dec. 9, 1999; Transportation Recall Enhancement Accountability and Documentation Act, requiring industry reports, Aug. 10, 2000; Safe, Accountable, Flexible, Efficient Transportation Equity Act: A Legacy for Users (SAFETEA-LU), upgrading roof strength, rollover prevention and side-safety standards, Aug. 10, 2005; Cameron Gulbransen Kids Transportation Safety Act, Feb. 28, 2008; and Moving Ahead for Progress in the 21st Century Act, requiring rule for rear-view cameras and inter-city bus standards, July 6, 2012.

6

MONEY AND POLITICS:
MAKING GOVERNMENT ACCOUNTABLE

———

AS THE NEW MILLENNIUM DAWNED, Jack Abramoff had it all. He enjoyed easy access to the most powerful politicians in the nation's capital and was a welcome guest in George W. Bush's White House. His hands rested on the spigot through which flowed tens of millions of dollars that won friends and purchased influence in high places. He owned a posh restaurant where he hosted the political elite. He treated congressional staffers and their bosses to professional basketball games at his arena skybox and took them on lavish vacations to golf, dine, gamble and relax at ritzy resorts around the world.

Having sharpened his political skills and cemented relationships with future party strategists since being chairman of the College Republicans in 1981, the partisan lobbyist found himself solidly lodged at the nexus of GOP money and influence. His millions, derived from business clients who believed he could pull the right levers in Washington, D.C., kept Abramoff living in high style and aided Republicans in their quest to maintain majority status in both chambers of Congress.

Republicans had dominated Congress almost continuously since they swept aside 40 years of Democratic rule in the House of Representatives in 1994. But the House that Jack built would come crashing down in 2006, and his name would become synonymous with one of the biggest congressional scandals in U.S. history—thanks in part to Public Citizen.

Abramoff's machinations were the stuff of instant political legend. *Newsweek* magazine reported that he had "liberated" $82 million from various Indian tribes in lobbying fees and political contributions, all the while referring to these clients in e-mails as "troglodytes." In one particularly cynical maneuver, he represented the Coushatta Indians in Louisiana in their effort to shut down a rival gambling casino run by the Tigua tribe in Texas. He hired Ralph Reed, a Republican lobbyist who had earlier been the public face of the Christian Coalition, to wage a religion-based grass-roots campaign that succeeded in shutting down the Tiguas. Then, in an audacious move, Abramoff persuaded the Tiguas to pay him $4.2 million to lobby Congress to reopen their casino. The Tiguas lost, but Abramoff and Reed profited handsomely.

On behalf of U.S. business interests, Abramoff persuaded Congress to block federal labor regulations limiting sweatshops in the U.S.-run Northern Mariana Islands. Part of his strategy involved taking congressional delegations on "fact-finding" missions to the Western Pacific. "There were charter fishing boat trips, lavish dinners, massages," an unidentified former congressional leadership aide told *Newsweek*. "Nobody ever reported any of that stuff."[1] From 1999 to 2005, Abramoff directed some $4.4 million, mostly from clients, to candidates and campaign committees. About two-thirds of that went to Republicans.

Abramoff also led several international junkets, including a notorious 10-day golfing trip to Scotland in 2000 for politicos, including House Majority Leader Tom DeLay, a Texas Republican known as "The Hammer" for his ruthless legislative tactics. *The Washington Post* later discovered that, in clear violation of House ethics rules limiting gifts to $50, DeLay's airfares to London and Scotland were charged to Abramoff's credit card. Food, phone calls and other expenses at a golf hotel were charged to another lobbyist who had been DeLay's chief of staff and now worked with Abramoff. The tab for the whole trip exceeded $120,000.[2]

In January 2006, newspapers and TV screens nationwide featured the image of Abramoff leaving a federal courthouse in Washington, D.C., after pleading guilty to fraud and bribery, dressed as the consummate villain in a black fedora and trench coat. Around the same time, DeLay was forced to step down from his House post after being indicted in a separate political money-laundering case in Texas.

Abramoff then began naming names to prosecutors. The news sent shivers through members of Congress who had done him favors. The fact that he was closely associated with Republicans — particularly DeLay, who had called Abramoff "one of my closest and dearest friends"[3] — provoked fears in the GOP that the scandal could cost the party its majority in the upcoming 2006 elections.

Public Citizen, a veteran watchdog of campaign finance and lobbying abuses, was on top of this unfolding drama. In 2004, it had launched a "DeThrone DeLay" campaign to highlight his unethical and autocratic leadership and rally the public to demand that he step down as majority leader. The campaign also promoted lobbying reform legislation. Public Citizen's government affairs lobbyist Craig Holman helped craft the measure with Democratic Representative Marty Meehan of Massachusetts and Senator Russell Feingold, a Wisconsin Democrat. But Republicans were used to ignoring reform proposals, and neither bill mustered enough support in Congress to even earn a public hearing.

However, these particular travel abuses were not so easily swept under the rug. Although large gifts from lobbyists were prohibited, DeLay and others took advantage of a loophole that allowed nonprofit groups to pay for trip expenses, ostensibly for educational purposes. With the Scotland trip, DeLay insisted he knew nothing of Abramoff's involvement in picking up the tab, saying he believed the trip was paid for by the nonprofit National Center for Public Policy Research — on whose board Abramoff sat.

Public Citizen released a report in early 2006, just before Congress began debating reform, that exposed ways like this in which lobbyists easily circumvented the limits on travel gifts to members. The researchers found that nonprofit groups called the Ripon Educational Fund and the Ripon Society — overseen by a board made up almost entirely of lobbyists for wealthy corporations and trade associations — had spent at least $4.6 million taking lawmakers to European capitals and U.S. resorts. Funding for the travel had been funneled through the organization by business interests. Some members of Congress had accepted tens of thousands of dollars in free travel. Representative Michael Oxley, an Ohio Republican who chaired the powerful House Financial Services Committee, for example, took five trips courtesy of the Ripon groups, costing almost $52,000.

Fighting travel abuse was only one part of Public Citizen's larger objective — a goal dating from its founding — to sever the money link between politicians and lobbyists. Lobbyists often serve as campaign treasurers for politicians. They give money to politicians' charities, which are sometimes fronts for cash gifts otherwise prohibited. They put congressional staffers, spouses, friends or relatives on their payrolls. They host fundraising events. Congress rarely shows any inclination to address these abuses.

Even as DeLay surrendered his post as majority leader and resigned from Congress, and as Abramoff pleaded guilty to federal felony charges of defrauding clients, evading taxes and conspiring to bribe public officials, the corporate lobbying machine remained largely intact. DeLay and his political confederates attempted to dominate Congress when, several years earlier, they kicked off the K Street Project, named for the downtown Washington, D.C., corridor garlanded with high-powered lobbying firms. The project was a brazen scheme to force business groups to hire only Republican lobbyists in exchange for access to DeLay and other GOP leaders. Some of these lobbyists in turn served as political strategists and fundraisers for members of Congress.

The project took political back-scratching and corruption to new depths. Instead of merely selling their votes for passage of particular bills or provisions, members of Congress now offered business lobbyists the opportunity to shape virtually the entire congressional agenda. Bills were written by lobbyists and negotiated among GOP leaders, with little input from Democrats. The flow of money from corporate America, in return, became a tidal wave. In some cases, whole measures were quietly inserted into House-Senate conference reports (the last version of a bill before final passage) even though the provisions had never been passed by either chamber or reviewed at hearings.

As a Public Citizen report detailed, business lobbyists managed to secure an almost complete limitation on liability for producers and handlers of any drug, vaccine or medical device that might be used in a government-declared health emergency. The provision was slipped into a defense appropriations bill just before the Christmas 2005 recess — after the Democrats on the conference committee had already signed the conference report. President George W. Bush signed the bill after Congress left town.

Between 1998 and 2004, the lobbying industry nearly doubled its annual spending — from $1.45 billion to $2.18 billion. Public Citizen researchers found in a study released in July 2005 that 43 percent of the 198 members who had left Congress since 1998 and were eligible to lobby had become registered lobbyists. By 2007, according to the Center for Responsive Politics, 2,245 lobbying firms were listed as operating in Washington, D.C., along with 14,842 active registered lobbyists — about 28 for each of the 535 members of Congress.[4] Many of these lobbyists were former members and key staffers who had traded government jobs for lucrative influence-peddling positions.

This investment paid off in spades. Congress acted repeatedly to carry out the business agenda of tax cuts, corporate subsidies, energy deregulation, privatization of government services, pork-barrel earmarks, liability shields for corporate defendants and weaker health and safety standards. The Abramoff affair and related scandals were, in many ways, simply another chapter in the same old story: big money calling the shots in the halls of power.

It is a system that Public Citizen has battled since its founding, through cycles of scandal and reform. The organization believes elected officials should represent the broad interests of the people, not the privileged few. The abiding challenge is still how to make Congress and the White House more responsive to the people they were elected to serve.

In March 2006, Abramoff was sentenced to five years and 10 months in prison for fraud charges related to the purchase of a casino cruise ship in Florida. Because of his cooperation with authorities in the lobbying and ethics scandals, he received a reduced sentence for his crimes relating to political corruption.

The Congress Watch Crusade

Before Ralph Nader launched his consumer revolution in the 1960s, citizens had little direct involvement in Congress. It was an insular institution dominated by corporate interests, and of little interest to the media of the day. Members of Congress took military airplanes to exotic locations across the globe, their expenses paid by the government. They received subsidized health care, cut-rate haircuts and health club privileges, free airport parking, upgrades to first class, subsidized meals and other perks.

Members were entitled to send their constituents free mail, which was usually self-promotional and which helped solidify their grip on office. Corporations and trade associations routinely treated legislators and their friends and staffs to free vacations, or paid them thousands of dollars for speaking at corporate meetings and other gatherings. In return, lawmakers frequently did the bidding of their well-heeled patrons, often at the expense of the people they were supposed to represent.

In 1972, Nader's Congress Project published *Who Runs Congress?* It was a stunning portrait of a legislature in thrall to corporate America and sorely out of touch with the concerns of average citizens. The book was a sensation, exposing corruption and offering some advice for reclaiming democracy. "The rest is up to you — your sense of justice, your faith in people, your energy and imagination," Nader wrote to his readers. "It is your only Congress. If you want to do something about it, you start now."

Nader was optimistic. "It is the mark of our nation's fingertip potential, unprecedented in world history, that we are a generation of Americans who have to give up so little in order to achieve so much of lasting endurance for the earth's people," he wrote. "Two centuries of delegation have worn their course. It is time to grasp the labors of daily citizenship and assume more closely the responsibility of government."[5] This, really, was the whole idea behind Public Citizen — assuming the responsibility, as "public citizens," of participating in democracy and government.

Public Citizen created its Congress Watch division in 1973 to serve as the people's eyes and ears in Congress — to be a watchdog, sound the alarm about abusive practices and mobilize citizens to make the legislative body more responsive and accountable to the public. Congress Watch would be Public Citizen's lobbying arm to counter the growing army of corporate lobbyists swarming the Capitol. Its first director was Joan Claybrook, who under Robert Fellmeth's leadership had guided Nader's two-year Congress Project to completion and had urged Nader to launch Congress Watch. She remained until President Jimmy Carter named her administrator of the National Highway Traffic Safety Administration in 1977.

Public Citizen's reform strategy does not, and never did, rely upon campaign contributions or free vacations or hiring former legislators. Instead, the organization has confidence that the surest way to reform is to shine a bright spotlight on wrongdoing, educate lawmakers and mobilize citizens to demand action.

Public Citizen has always believed that public service should be a high calling, not a ticket to the high life. Yet members of Congress enjoy so many perks that they often lose sight of the concerns of regular people who struggle to make ends meet — people who worry about paying for health care, about clean air and water, about crime in their neighborhoods, about making sure their children receive a good education, about affordable housing, about putting food on the table and about having a pension for their retirement.

For Congress to be more responsive to these concerns and less beholden to corporate interests, and for citizens to regain faith in their elected officials, the corporate domination of Congress must end, Claybrook and Nader believed. They started by exposing routine congressional practices.

Through the Freedom of Information Act — whose strengthening was one of Congress Watch's first triumphs — researchers were able to document clear abuses by members of Congress who had used jets from the Air Force's 89th Military Airwing to hop around the globe at taxpayer expense, sometimes for dubious reasons. Even lame-duck members took trips under the auspices of official government business.

Someone perusing the records might get the impression that Congress had a particularly heavy agenda in France, as it was the most popular destination for House and Senate members in 1981. Rather than flying aboard commercial airliners with the citizens they represented, members traveled on C-135s and C-137s — military planes the size of a Boeing 707.

Congress Watch's first groundbreaking report on congressional travel listed every trip taken by members of Congress in 1981, 1982 and the first half of 1983. It documented numerous junkets, including separate trips by Republican Senators Barry Goldwater of Arizona and John Tower of Texas to the Farnborough Air Show in London in September 1982. As delegation head, Goldwater brought along six staff members and his son, Representative Barry M. Goldwater Jr., who had lost a bid for a state Senate seat in California three months earlier. The army supplied a C-137 aircraft at a cost of $124,122 for the round trip. The army escort to the delegation cost another $3,142.[6]

Three years later, Congress Watch repeated the study and found that little had changed. Congress had spent $93 million on travel in 1984 and the first nine months of 1985. These trips included one led by Democratic Representative Tip O'Neill of Massachusetts to Ireland for St. Patrick's Day festivities, at a taxpayer-paid cost of $118,331. "Travel abroad has increased, as have the costs to the taxpayer," according to the report, "Flights of Fancy, Foreign Travel by the U.S. Congress." "And senators and representatives still flock to southern climes during winter recess and Europe whenever they can."[7]

When Congress refused to reform the travel system, Congress Watch kept up the pressure, and the reports became a staple source of stories for the media.

In 1989, Congress Watch also spotlighted a more insidious perk: travel funded by corporations and other entities. Typically, corporations or trade associations invited senators who sat on powerful committees that controlled legislation affecting their businesses. Senators had taken more than a thousand privately funded trips during 1987 and 1988, most within the United States. Senators often were shuttled to fancy resorts where lobbyists wined and dined them — sometimes paying the lawmakers $2,000 each in "honoraria" for their appearances.

Sometimes foreign travel was included. Louisiana Democratic Senator Bennett Johnston, for example, visited Sweden courtesy of the Swedish Nuclear Fuel and Waste Management Co., while Iowa Republican Senator Charles Grassley traveled to Greece, Turkey, Switzerland and Portugal in a single trip bankrolled by the American Conservative Union.[8]

In part because of the negative publicity from Public Citizen's reports, Congress banned honoraria in 1989 as part of the Government Ethics Reform Act, which also included new rules for congressional travel and pay. The law was a major step forward.

The Endless Cycle of Congressional Pay Raises

Congress in 1989 addressed another contentious issue: congressional pay raises. Under a system established in 1975, the president could recommend a raise for Congress, and lawmakers could reject or modify it, but if they did nothing, it would take effect automatically. As his second term wound down, President Ronald Reagan recommended that members receive a 50 percent pay raise — from $89,500 to $135,000. At the time, the average American income was about $30,000.

Nader and Claybrook were incensed, but they found few members of Congress who wanted to cancel their own pay hike. Other major public interest groups declined to anger the lawmakers by supporting the idea. Claybrook urged mainstream news media to cover the issue, but they showed little interest in something with so little chance of passing. Despite this apathy among the political intelligentsia, Claybrook and Nader were sure the public would not be so indifferent. They began contacting radio talk show hosts around the country and soon found an audience. "The talk show guys went crazy over this," Claybrook recalled. "They reported every detail and constantly called the Speaker."

As public opposition grew, Claybrook asked Congress Watch staff to poll every member of Congress to put them on record as either supporting or opposing the raise. If any member refused to respond, Nader would contact a talk radio show in their district. The constant pressure angered many in Congress, but Speaker Jim Wright finally decided he had to call a vote before the raise was to take effect.

The raise was defeated in February 1989. But that was not the end of it. The following November, just before lawmakers headed home for the holidays, they held another vote. This time, a compromise was in the works, and the bill passed.

The final bill was a mixed bag. The pay raise was trimmed, but only by $10,000. But the law changed the way congressional pay was set, tying raises to the cost of living and making small percentage changes take effect automatically unless Congress specifically voted them down. Honoraria, which often amounted to as much as $26,000 annually for some members, was finally banned after December 31, 1990.

The privately funded travel that Public Citizen had exposed was at last restricted. Under the legislation, House members still could accept gifts of travel as long as they didn't exceed four days for domestic trips and seven days for international trips. The Senate adopted similar guidelines, curtailing the free trips but not eliminating them.

Public Citizen continued to monitor congressional travel for abuses, and in 1991, Congress Watch produced a new report called "They Love To Fly ... And It Shows." It found that House members had taken nearly 4,000 free trips during 1989 and 1990. Corporations or corporate trade associations such as the Tobacco Institute had sponsored 66 percent of the trips.

The most astonishing finding was that corporations had doled out almost $3.6 million to the representatives, sometimes just for showing up at ritzy resorts for golf, tennis, swimming and other pleasures. Representative Dan Rostenkowski, an Illinois Democrat who chaired the powerful House Ways and Means Committee, was second on the list with 48 trips during the two-year period, but he far outpaced his colleagues in honoraria, taking in $207,000. (Rostenkowski was indicted in 1994 on corruption charges stemming from a congressional check kiting scandal and was voted out of office later that year. He eventually pleaded guilty to mail fraud and served 17 months in prison.)

Fortunately for voters, that was the final year for these unseemly payments.[9] But Congress failed to ban travel funded by independent nonprofit organizations and corporate interests, so it was only a matter of time before more scandals erupted—including the one involving Jack Abramoff.

Pork-Barrel Politics

For decades, pork-barrel politics was a way of life in Congress. Bringing federal dollars to constituents and communities—in the form of new federal buildings, highways, ports, canal projects, aid programs and other federal largesse—helped senators and representatives cling to power. The projects created jobs and sent money back to districts, regardless of whether they were really needed.

Those pieces of pork often were slipped into legislation, but members boasted about their successes so voters would become aware of them. Another less noticed form of pork, however, were intricate tax exemptions and credits written quietly into the federal code, some just for one beneficiary, as well as subsidies, contracts, price supports, research grants, mineral and timber rights, and other giveaways.

Prior to the 1970s, very few, if any, attempts were made to quantify the extent of this "corporate welfare" — government handouts that pad corporate profits. When President Ronald Reagan came to power in 1981, he extolled "the magic of the market" and railed against "big government," slashing the budgets of federal regulatory agencies. He inveighed against public welfare programs, creating in the public psyche an enduring image of a fictional "welfare queen" who lives off the dole. But when it came to taxpayer subsidies for large corporations that supported him, Reagan was silent.

Public Citizen challenged this glaring hypocrisy. Congress Watch conducted a study of the federal budget for fiscal 1984 and found that it included $83 billion in market-distorting welfare for corporations.[10] The report was titled "Aid for Dependent Corporations: A Study of the Fiscal 1984 Corporate Welfare Budget"– a name that parodied the Aid for Dependent Children income-support program that Reagan's supporters had attacked so vociferously.

The report showed that squirreled away in the budgetary fine print were corporate handouts masquerading as government investment in private industry; grants ostensibly for research and development to promote commercial activity; government lending at below-market rates; government backing for private loans; government-imposed liability limits on private risk; guaranteed minimum prices; and a bewildering array of giveaways, tax exemptions, deductions and credits. Congress could have cut the budget deficit (then the largest in U.S. history) drastically simply by eliminating these subsidies to corporate America.

Not included in these calculations was the cost of government research that corporations used to develop new products such as pharmaceuticals without paying any royalties to the government. Nor did the $83 billion include the savings to corporate income from weakening regulations designed to protect workers and the public.

The report noted that while Reagan's budget slashed home heating assistance for the poor by one-third, it handed over $19 billion in assistance to big energy companies. While three million children were cut from the school lunch program, billions of dollars were wasted on such boondoggles as the barge canal known as the Tennessee-Tombigbee Waterway, which even today is sparsely used.

The report spotlighted the insidious nature of corporate subsidies. "Instead of being listed as line items in the budget, like the Food Stamp program, corporate welfare resides between the lines — in tax revenue not collected and loans not repaid," the report said. "This means that when politicians ask for across-the-board budget cuts, most corporate subsidies go untouched."

In 1986, two years later, Public Citizen revealed in a new report that little had changed — except that the corporate welfare budget had ballooned to $107 billion. Most of that came in the form of tax giveaways. Among them was the Accelerated Cost Recovery System, which allowed new plants and equipment to depreciate at a faster rate than their actual market value. In effect, it allowed many large, capital-intensive companies to pay little or no taxes. For example, during the previous three years, General Electric had earned profits of $6.5 billion, yet the company paid no federal income tax and claimed $238 million in tax refunds.

In addition to noting the patent unfairness of corporate welfare at a time of cuts to programs benefiting children, the blind and disabled, the report noted that corporate welfare distorted the "free economy" that corporations claim to defend. Corporate welfare directs investment away from businesses that are the most productive and efficient, and toward those that are able to secure subsidies or low-interest loans by lobbying the government. "The result is a less efficient and less productive economy than would exist if the free market determined where investment went," the report noted.

Meanwhile, Reagan was busy eviscerating federal regulatory agencies, laying the groundwork for one of the biggest financial swindles in history. The administration's hostility to the regulating business came home to roost in the late 1980s, when savings and loan institutions across the country began going belly up.

The Savings and Loan Swindle

Immortalized in the famous holiday film "It's a Wonderful Life," savings and loan banks, also known as S&Ls or "thrifts," have been a fixture in American culture since the 1830s. They began typically as small-scale, local institutions that relied for capital almost entirely on savings deposits, which they would in turn lend back to community residents in the form of home mortgages. They were, in fact, owned by their depositors.

After the bank and S&L failures of the Great Depression, the federal government stepped in to insure the savings of S&L depositors up to a certain level. S&Ls were required to contribute to fund the program and follow regulations designed to ensure their solvency—limits on the interest they could pay, for example. For decades, S&Ls operated successfully as low-key affairs, helping millions of middle-class families achieve the American dream of home ownership.

But after the 1960s and 1970s, when important consumer laws were enacted, free market ideologues swept into office, determined to dismantle the regulatory apparatus.

In 1980, Congress phased out the limits on interest rates that S&Ls could pay depositors. It also raised the federal insurance cap from $40,000 per deposit to $100,000, more than doubling the amount that account holders could be reimbursed—at taxpayers' expense—if their S&L failed. Then on October 15, 1982, President Reagan signed a massive bill that further deregulated the S&Ls. They could now offer checking accounts and credit cards, and could make commercial and non-residential housing loans, just like commercial banks. "All in all, I think we've hit the jackpot," Reagan declared.[11] It was indeed a jackpot—for swindlers. For taxpayers, it would be a multibillion-dollar loss.

Deregulation ushered in a period of reckless investment, fraud and corruption that would leave the industry in shambles less than a decade later. The S&Ls virtually stopped courting individual savings accounts and investing in safe and predictable but low-yield 30-year home mortgage loans. Instead they raised billions of dollars in new capital by offering high interest rates for short-term deposits—in accounts insured by the government. To pay investors those higher rates, S&L executives often invested in higher-risk ventures, such as new skyscrapers and shopping malls, betting that tenants and buyers would materialize. Meanwhile, inflation was raising the banks' immediate capital needs far beyond their income from the old, long-term, low-interest mortgage loans that were still on their books.

Executives desperate to cope with the shortfall turned to fraud and criminal insider deals. Some used company treasuries as their own private bank accounts, living as kings to create an illusion of good times and cooking the books to cover up mounting losses. These new white-collar bank robbers were financially savvy, opening the S&L vaults to loot billions from them—and therefore from the federal treasury—in a spree that both Reagan's federal regulators and a complicit Congress virtually ignored. And then in the late 1980s, the real estate market collapsed.

"The sums of money boggle the mind, and defy the imagination," Nader wrote later. "The corruption at work is epic. A program designed to safeguard the savings of the middle class and poor was used to subsidize an unprecedented frenzy of speculation and business criminality."[12]

By 1988, the financial carnage was inescapable. The new George H.W. Bush administration rammed a bailout plan through Congress, establishing the Resolution Trust Corporation (RTC) to handle the task of selling off some $500 billion worth of assets owned by the insolvent S&Ls. Taxpayers would have to make up the difference between the recovered money and the S&L losses.

Michael Waldman, then director of Congress Watch, set his staff to examining the government plan. At a time when the public was still trying to grasp the extent of the debacle, Public Citizen began documenting serious shortcomings in the bailout. Of paramount concern was that the RTC, which was directed to dispose of S&L assets as quickly as possible at the best price, was to conduct its work in secret, with little accountability to the public, and would rely heavily on outside contractors and real estate speculators.

Public Citizen warned that the bailout scheme invited "fraud and abuse on an unprecedented scale."[13] At the time, the General Accounting Office (renamed the Government Accountability Office in 2004) estimated that taxpayers would end up paying out a staggering $285 billion. Shining a light on the shortcomings of the rescue plan, Public Citizen lobbied for several amendments that succeeded in reducing the damage. By 1996, the government had shut 1,043 S&Ls with total assets of more than $519 billion, at direct and indirect costs to taxpayers of about $124 billion.[14]

One of the most stunning S&L failures was that of the Lincoln Savings and Loan in Arizona, run by Charles Keating, a flamboyant Phoenix real estate developer. Through Lincoln, Keating had engaged in a frenzy of speculative investment — in junk bonds, land and construction of a lavish hotel in the Arizona desert. When federal investigators began to scrutinize Lincoln, Keating played his trump card — five U.S. senators to whom he had donated $1.4 million (Democrats Alan Cranston of California, Donald Riegle of Michigan and John Glenn of Ohio, and from Arizona, both Democrat Dennis DeConcini and Republican John McCain). The senators told regulators to back off their probe.

The senators' warnings managed to stave off the feds for a while, but the government eventually seized the S&L. Keating was frank at a 1989 press conference: "One question ... had to do with whether my financial support in any way influenced several political figures to take up my cause. I want to say in the most forceful way I can: I certainly hope so."[15] Rarely has the quid pro quo of corporate influence been admitted so openly.

The debacle's sordid story was laid out in detail in *Who Robbed America? A Citizen's Guide to the Savings and Loan Scandal* by Waldman and his Congress Watch staff. The 1990 book explained how Americans were stuck with the tab for bailing out the bankrupt S&Ls, how businesses influenced congressional decision-making by pouring millions of dollars into campaign coffers and why federal prosecutors recovered just a fraction of the S&L losses.

As Nader wrote in 1990, "The bottom line is this: Those we selected to lead our democracy let it happen, turned their back on us, made us pay for it, and astonishingly, were re-elected."[16]

Public Citizen, through its Congress Watch program, also documented the George H. W. Bush administration's abysmal record of catching and prosecuting S&L crooks. Bush, whose son Neil was implicated but never prosecuted in the failure of the Silverado S&L in Texas, had promised to pursue the S&L criminals vigorously. But a 1992 Congress Watch report, "Take the Money and Run: How the Bush Administration is Letting S&L Crooks off the Hook,"[17] showed an anemic administration effort. It made headlines and was cited in congressional hearings.

The Justice Department had received more than 7,000 referrals for prosecutions but had ignored most of them. By 1996, only 1,098 people had been indicted on S&L crimes since 1988. A total of 839 were convicted and 580 were sentenced, 451 of them to prison terms. The median term, however, was less than two years (22 months), compared to almost eight years for ordinary convicted robbers.[18]

Worse yet, the Justice Department estimated that more than $11 billion had been stolen outright from the S&Ls — not to mention the hundreds of billions executives had frittered away in questionable deals. But the courts had ordered just $335 million in fines and restitution from those convicted. And only $26 million of that had been paid by 1996 when the Resolution Trust Corporation dissolved.[19]

Once again, corporate money trumped the public interest. But Public Citizen had provided an invaluable service by documenting the complicity of the Reagan and Bush administrations in the deregulatory scheme that produced the disaster, their failure to clean up the mess and the willful inattention of a Congress soaked in S&L money, as well as by helping to reduce the ultimate cost to taxpayers.

Corporate Campaign Contributions

Corporate welfare comes in all shapes and sizes, but campaign contributions are usually a key driver. Public Citizen has been dogged in researching, cataloging and publicizing campaign spending abuses, many of which have fleeced the public of billions of dollars or exposed regular Americans to danger.

In 1999, for example, Public Citizen released a study showing that Mississippi Senator Trent Lott, Republican majority leader, aided gambling moguls by helping to eliminate the power of the proposed National Gambling Impact Study Commission to subpoena casino executives and grill them on their aggressive marketing practices.[20] The report found that Lott played a major role in the passage of a 10-year, $316 million tax break for the casino industry and in overturning a decision by the Army Corps of Engineers and the Environmental Protection Agency to assess the environmental impact of rapid casino development along the marshy Mississippi Gulf Coast.

Lott was then the highest elected official in a party that perennially campaigned on "family values," and he represented a state with a large population of religious conservatives. Why would he go out of his way to help casino owners? The most plausible answer was "soft money," the unlimited cash gifts that corporations, unions and wealthy individuals could give to political parties. Strict ceilings limited the "hard money" that could go directly to candidates, but soft money had no such limits. Soft money gave party leaders great power.

During the 1996 and 1998 election cycles, the casino gambling industry gave the Republican Party's national committees $4.2 million in soft money, while bestowing $2.3 million on the Democratic committees. Further, the industry's soft money investment in the National Republican Senatorial Campaign Committee — where Lott was a top fundraiser — soared from $7,800 in the 1994 election cycle to $1.3 million in the 1998 cycle.

When political parties and elected officials take hundreds of thousands of dollars from a friendly contributor, they understand that they will be expected to give something in return. Campaign checks often arrive at strategic times, just before or after big votes, for example. Safe in the knowledge that he was about to retire, Missouri Democratic Senator Thomas Eagleton explained in 1988 how the system worked:

> I've never had — and perhaps other senators have — a guy come into this office or over the phone say, 'Tom, such-and-such vote's coming up next week. You remember I gave X in your last campaign, and I'm certainly expecting you to vote that way.' I've never had anything that direct, blunt or obscene. However, let's change the phraseology to this: 'Tom, this is so-and-so. You know next week an important vote's coming up on such-and-such. I just want to remind you, Tom, I feel very strongly about this issue.' 'Okay, my friend, good to hear from you.' Now, a senator receives gentle calls of that sort.[21]

Another way corporations gain access and influence is to employ lobbyists who have worked as, or with, members of Congress. Capitol Hill is flooded with former members now working as lobbyists. They know their way around, and they have easy access and can drop by their former colleagues' offices for casual chats. Until a 2006 rules change, they could work out in the congressional gym alongside current members.

Frank Clemente, who directed Congress Watch from 1996 to 2006, put it this way: There is a "cozy working relationship between well-heeled special interests and their powerful allies in Congress who determine whether a hearing on legislation occurs, whether a bill gets put on the floor for debate, or whether a special deal gets quietly inserted into legislation without public discussion."

Exposing these ties between campaign contributions, lobbying and legislative results was, and remains, a bedrock Public Citizen strategy. While sunlight does not always stop harmful legislation, it deters some of it, helps voters understand how interest groups shape legislation and motivates citizens to hold members of Congress accountable.

Big Pharma's Big Influence

In the late 1990s, soaring prices for prescription drugs gave Public Citizen another vehicle to show how big money drives public policy. Drug costs were rising by 15 to 20 percent per year, driving up health insurance premiums and leaving many consumers, particularly those without insurance, unable to afford their prescriptions. Many seniors told journalists that they were having to choose between buying groceries or buying the drugs they needed to stave off pain and illness. Medicare did not cover prescription drugs, and at least a third of Medicare recipients — about 14 million seniors and people with disabilities — had to pay drug costs out of their own pockets because they lacked additional coverage.

Joan Cronin was an elderly woman who lived in federally subsidized housing in New York City.[22] She spoke out at a Public Citizen news conference, telling reporters that she paid about $215 each month — more than 25 percent of her income — for medications prescribed after her heart bypass surgery. The drugs were so costly that she routinely took fewer doses than her doctor prescribed. Sometimes, she said, her pharmacist gave her credit until her next Social Security check arrived. Ruth Pitts, 78, a retired home health care worker with diabetes, said one medication alone used up more than a quarter of her $245 monthly Social Security check.

At the time, the pharmaceutical industry was outpacing every other major industry in profits. In the 1970s, the profitability of drug companies on the Fortune 500 was twice the median for all companies on the index. Drug industry profitability grew to three times that of the other Fortune 500 companies in the 1980s and then four times in the 1990s. In 2000, when the nation weathered a steep economic downtown, the 11 drug companies in the Fortune 500 enjoyed a robust 19 percent return on revenue. From 1982 through 2002, the drug industry ranked as the nation's most profitable enterprise, according to *Fortune* magazine.[23]

One way these firms kept prices artificially high was by persuading Congress to extend their monopoly patents. When companies brought new drugs to the market, the government granted them patents lasting 20 years, a period that began when the patent application was filed. A portion of that period was used up during clinical testing, so the effective patent life — measured from when the drug was first sold to the public to the time its patent expired — typically ran 14 to 15 years.

This arrangement was designed to give companies an incentive to develop new and innovative drugs. The company was allowed sell the drug for whatever price it could get. But when the patent expired, other drug makers could begin making generic versions. While generics did not have the brand name, they were required to be chemically identical and typically sold for half the cost — or even much less.

The struggle over a patent extension for one of the most heavily advertised drugs in the United States — the allergy fighter Claritin — was a case study in how far a company would go to get a special favor from Congress — and how Public Citizen works to block it.

Claritin, a powerful antihistamine, became a huge moneymaker for manufacturer Schering-Plough in the mid-1990s. As the Food and Drug Administration (FDA) eased restrictions on TV advertising for prescription drugs, ads for Claritin flooded the airwaves, and millions of Americans asked their doctors for it. At about $3 per pill, it was so expensive that some insurance plans refused to pay for it. In 2000, Claritin generated $3 billion in sales, representing about a third of the company's total revenue.[24] The patent was due to expire in 2002, and Schering-Plough made plans long before that to get an extension to preserve its profits. The company's behind-the-scenes legislative campaign to add another three years to the patent began in 1996. The drive ended up costing consumers $7.3 billion.

Schering-Plough executives knew exactly how Washington, D.C. works. To play the game, you had to put up cash, and it had to go to the right people. The company began pouring millions into lobbyists and political campaigns. Former Senate Majority Leader Howard Baker, a Tennessee Republican, and former Senator Dennis DeConcini, an Arizona Democrat, came on board to press the Claritin case. These men had ready access to key lawmakers.[25]

Schering-Plough also enlisted the help of former Surgeon General C. Everett Koop, who wrote a letter to all members of the House of Representatives on April 29, 1999, urging them to back the patent extension. He also appeared at a press conference in the Capitol six weeks later to support it. Ten days after the press conference, the *Star-Ledger* of New Jersey reported that Schering-Plough had made a $1 million donation to the Koop Foundation and was running advertisements on Koop's website.[26]

The legislation Schering-Plough wanted also would have granted patent extensions to the manufacturers of six other drugs, at an estimated cost to consumers of $11 billion. Alarmed at the company's ease in lining up support for this anti-consumer measure, Clemente and his Congress Watch team began working to expose it.

First, they pointed out that the chief Senate sponsor of the bill for the New Jersey-based company — Democratic Senator Robert Torricelli of New Jersey — had received $31,050 from the company for his campaign during the three election cycles prior to 1999. This made him the leading recipient of money from Schering-Plough's executives and political action committees during that period.

Public Citizen also revealed that the seven senators on the Judiciary Committee who had co-sponsored the patent extension collectively received $75,000 in campaign contributions from the company over the same period — compared to only $4,300 given to the other 16 committee members combined. Within days of speaking out in favor of the special extension, Judiciary Committee Chair Orrin Hatch, a Utah Republican, was jetting around on Schering-Plough's company plane as he pursued the Republican presidential nomination.[27]

By researching and publicizing the perks and money specific members of Congress had taken from the company, organizing dozens of other consumer groups and timing press releases shortly before crucial committee votes, Public Citizen helped stall the bill in committee in 1998 and 1999. In 2000, Schering-Plough's friends in Congress tried a more devious tactic: attaching a secret provision to a military construction appropriations bill then in a House-Senate conference committee. Again, Public Citizen's vigilance helped win an important battle for consumers. "Working with our allies, we blocked the Claritin extension, and that saved the public billions of dollars," said Clemente.

Between the 1996 election cycle and March 2001, Schering-Plough spent $28 million on lobbying and campaign contributions. That included more than $800,000 in soft money to political parties for the 2000 elections. Ultimately, the company failed to reach its goal, in part because of Public Citizen. Claritin's patent expired, and in November 2002, the FDA announced that Claritin and its generic versions, called loratadine, could be sold over the counter without a prescription. Consumers were now able to buy loratadine for about 50 cents per pill — saving about $2.50 from Schering-Plough's price.

The Fight for a Medicare Drug Benefit

In an effort to bring relief to consumers, Public Citizen in 1998 embarked on a wide-ranging campaign to highlight the drug industry's unfair pricing practices and to press for legislative reform. A bill sponsored by Maine Democratic Representative Tom Allen sought to lower drug prices for Medicare beneficiaries by requiring drug manufacturers to sell their products to pharmacies at the same price paid by federal agencies and other large purchasers. This could allow up to 39 million Medicare beneficiaries to save about 40 percent on their prescription costs. Public Citizen also advocated adding a prescription drug benefit to the Medicare program, a move that would bring immediate relief to seniors and give the government the power to negotiate lower prices.

To build public support, Public Citizen coordinated a series of drug price surveys across the country, designed to show that drug makers were gouging the nation's most vulnerable citizens: the elderly, ill and infirm.

The findings in Pennsylvania were typical of those in other states.[28] There, a local consumer group recruited volunteers from labor, senior and faith-based groups to gather price data from 98 pharmacies. "Over the course of two months, people went to pharmacies and asked the pharmacists to write down the prices of 10 common senior medications, and one taken by people with disabilities," said Alisa Simon of Citizens for Consumer Justice in Pennsylvania.

At an April 2000 press conference in Harrisburg, Public Citizen and Citizens for Consumer Justice released findings showing that Pennsylvania seniors without prescription drug coverage were being charged an average of 113 percent more than the drug companies' most favored customers, such as the Departments of Defense and Veterans Affairs. For the 11 drugs surveyed, Pennsylvania residents were paying between 48 percent more (for the ulcer drug Pepcid) and 231 percent more (for the cholesterol drug Zocor). Overall, the average retail price in Pennsylvania for the 11 drugs was more than double that for favored customers — $173 versus $81.[29]

"It's embarrassing when I walk into a pharmacy and I have to ask how much my medications will cost before I know if I can buy them," Carol Martin of the Harrisburg, Pennsylvania, area told the researchers. "Sometimes I can't pick up medication I've ordered because I realize I don't have the money to pay for it because the medications are so expensive."

Surveys in Arizona, Arkansas, California, Illinois, Massachusetts, New Hampshire, New Jersey, New Mexico, New York, Wisconsin and the District of Columbia told the same story. On average, consumers without prescription drug coverage were paying double the price charged to the drug companies' most favored customers.

To add insult to injury, consumers in many foreign countries, including Canada and Mexico, were able to buy the same drugs made by the same companies at a fraction of the cost. In January 2000, as presidential aspirants began campaigning in earnest, Public Citizen sponsored a bus trip from New Hampshire to Montreal so that participants could fill their prescriptions at Canadian pharmacies. New Hampshire resident Olive Karpinski joined Claybrook, former television host Phil Donahue and other seniors for the ride to Montreal. Buying a three-month supply of her most expensive medicines, she saved more than $500.

Karpinski pointed to the money that the drug companies spent on marketing as one of the reasons prices were so high. "All this advertising on TV and magazines, it's a tremendous price," Karpinski said. "Why advertise there? Let the doctors decide."

The other seniors saved a bundle as well and in the process gave newspaper and TV reporters grist for the front page and the evening news. Calling themselves "drug price refugees," the bus-riding seniors discovered, for instance, that a prescription for Vanceril (a steroid used to treat asthma and allergies) cost $10.49 in Canada and $48 in the United States. A three-month supply of the blood pressure medication Adalat cost $102.26 in Canada and $227 in the United States. Every drug they sought was far cheaper in Canada.[30]

The citizens of virtually every industrialized nation pay far less for their drugs than Americans do. So why did Congress turned a blind eye to the problem? A simple answer: campaign contributions.

The pharmaceutical companies in the 1990s had become masters of the political game. They showered legislators with campaign cash. They hired well-connected lobbyists and public relations firms. They spent millions on "issue ads" that helped re-elect their friends in Congress, and they warned Americans about the dangers of letting "big government into your medicine cabinet." They also distorted the facts about their profits and their spending on research and development of new drugs.[31]

Above all, the industry wanted to keep Congress from enacting a prescription drug benefit under the Medicare program, because the federal government then would have the incentive and the leverage to negotiate steep price discounts on behalf of all seniors. So as the debate heated up, the drug industry opened its money spigot.

Public Citizen's Congress Watch, which was helping to lead the fight for drug coverage under Medicare, produced a report in July 2001 documenting pharmaceutical industry spending totaling $262 million during the 1999–2000 election cycle. That included $20 million in campaign contributions, of which $11.8 million was soft money donations to the parties. Eighty percent of those contributions went to the GOP. After the election, the drug industry contributed $625,000 to Bush-Cheney inaugural events.[32]

What was truly remarkable, however, was the industry's spending on lobbying: $177 million during the two-year period. That included money to hire 625 lobbyists — more than one for every member of the House and Senate — from more than a hundred different lobbying firms. Most of the lobbyists had either served or worked in Congress or in other federal positions. The industry seemed to have Washington, D.C. wired.

The industry also operated a campaign of deception to call into question any government role in making medications more affordable. In 1999, it formed a front group called Citizens for Better Medicare to scare and confuse seniors about President Bill Clinton's proposal to add a prescription drug benefit to the Medicare program. In a $64 million TV advertising campaign, Citizens for Better Medicare featured an actress playing a worried fictional character named "Flo," reminiscent of the "Harry and Louise" characters the insurance industry had invented to help derail Clinton's 1994 health care plan.

A widely publicized Congress Watch report in July 2000 exposed Citizens for Better Medicare for what it was: a sham. Its director had been a marketing chief for the Pharmaceutical Research and Manufacturers of America, or PhRMA, the drug industry's lobbying organization, and had acknowledged that Citizens for Better Medicare was overwhelmingly funded by PhRMA.[33] Congress Watch researchers also found evidence that Citizens for Better Medicare was coordinating its issue ads with the Republican National Committee and its campaign for George W. Bush. Some 98 percent of Citizens for Better Medicare's spending from July through September 2000 went to a GOP media consultant that also produced campaign ads for the Republicans and Bush.

Despite the drug industry's cash outlay, Public Citizen made great strides in the battle for public opinion. The industry for years had claimed that astronomical research and development costs required it to make high profits. It also claimed that it cost an average of $500 million to develop each new drug, counting both successes and failures, a figure that the news media usually accepted uncritically.

But using government studies, company filings with the Securities and Exchange Commission and documents obtained via the Freedom of Information Act, Congress Watch researchers issued a report in July 2001 that exposed the $500 million figure as a false claim.[34] The real figure was no more than $110 million, and possibly as low as $57 million. Even this sum might have been inflated, because it included the cost of bringing dozens of "me-too" drugs to market — drugs that represented no significant upgrade over existing therapies.

The study, "Rx R&D Myths: The Case Against The Drug Industry's R&D 'Scare Card,'" also exposed the fact that taxpayer-funded scientists, not corporate labs, had conducted 55 percent of the research projects that led to the discovery and development of the five top-selling drugs in 1995. The report documented the many ways in which government subsidized the industry. Its effective tax rate was about 40 percent less than the average for all other industries, for example. And contrary to drug company claims about needing high profits to fund research and development, it turned out they allocated just 12 percent of their revenues to research and development — and 30 percent to marketing.

The report garnered widespread media coverage. This research and Public Citizen's grassroots organizing helped turn the tide of public opinion and galvanized support for a prescription drug benefit for Medicare recipients.

By the summer of 2001, the Democratic and Republican parties both considered the drug benefit a political priority, with one fundamental difference. Democrats wanted to administer the benefit through Medicare. Republicans wanted to give seniors money to buy private insurance, which would undermine Medicare.

By 2003, the Republican-controlled Congress yielded to grassroots pressure and passed legislation revising Medicare to cover prescriptions for seniors, and President George W. Bush signed it into law. But the industry had had a heavy hand in writing the measure — so heavy that Public Citizen opposed the bill. The law provided meager benefits to seniors but would cost taxpayers an estimated $400 billion in its first decade (revised upward a few months after passage to $534 billion).

The bill required seniors using Medicare to get their "Part D" prescription coverage through private insurers and provided billions in subsidies to insurers to lure them into covering the seniors' needs. It would have been much cheaper and more efficient to simply add the new coverage to the existing Medicare program. To make matters worse, the legislation forbade the government from using its procurement authority to negotiate with drug makers for lower prices for seniors.

The bill barely passed the House, and did so only after Republicans kept the vote open late into the night to arm-twist lawmakers into supporting the bill. DeLay, the majority leader, bullied Republicans opposed to passage to change their votes. He was later admonished by the House ethics committee for offering to endorse the House candidacy of Michigan Republican Representative Nick Smith's son in return for Smith's vote.

Leading the charge for passage was Republican Representative Billy Tauzin of Louisiana, who soon retired from Congress to head PhRMA, the powerful drug industry trade group. And in the Department of Health and Human Services, the bill was pushed by Tom Scully, administrator of the Centers for Medicare and Medicaid Services, who then took a job as a lawyer at Alston & Bird LLP, an Atlanta-based law firm that lobbies for health care industry companies.

Scully had made several trips to negotiate the Medicare drug legislation while also negotiating for possible future employment with three lobbying firms and two investment firms that had major stakes in the legislation.[35] His agency subsequently whitewashed that behavior by waiving its conflict-of-interest rules.

In response, Public Citizen called on the U.S. Office of Government Ethics to investigate the basis for Scully's waiver. In January 2004, the White House moved to prohibit agencies from granting that kind of waiver. And in July 2006, Scully settled with the U.S. Attorney's Office, paying $9,782. The agreement stated, correctly, that Scully's trips had improperly combined his public sector work with his private sector job search.[36]

Reforming Campaign Finance

It is one thing to win reform of congressional travel policies and ethics rules; it is another challenge entirely to reform the campaign finance system itself. This battle continues today as one of the organization's most grueling — and fighting it remains a top priority.

Many, if not most, politicians have come to depend on large campaign contributions from corporate executives, labor unions and the wealthy, and naturally resist changing a system that keeps them in office. While landmark reforms occurred in the Watergate era, entrenched incumbents and their funders have thwarted attempts to win broader, more meaningful reforms ever since.

The relationship between campaign money and policy has been a matter of public concern since the Civil War. But Congress did not attempt to rein in the power of money until 1907, when it outlawed direct campaign contributions from corporations. In 1925, Congress passed the Federal Corrupt Practices Act, but its reporting provisions and spending limits were feeble. In 1943, alarmed at the rising power of unions, Republicans joined with Southern Democrats to pass a temporary ban on direct union contributions to candidates, making the ban permanent four years later.[37]

With the rising popularity of television ads as a campaign medium in the 1950s and 1960s, concern about escalating campaign spending began to mount. When Dwight D. Eisenhower first ran for president in 1952, the total spent on campaigns for federal office was $140 million.[38] By 1968, it had more than doubled to $300 million.[39] Congress passed mild reforms in 1971, but they were shown to be ineffective in the 1972 races and by the subsequent Watergate scandal, which set the stage for major reforms in 1974.

The Federal Election Campaign Act Amendments of 1974 were the most comprehensive campaign reforms ever adopted. The act established the Federal Election Commission (FEC), strengthened reporting requirements and created an optional public funding system for presidential campaigns, funded by taxpayers who checked a box on their tax returns. It also set limits on campaign spending and contributions. The spending caps were later struck down as unconstitutional, and the candidates for office quickly learned to stretch and dodge the new rules.

Throughout the 1980s, during the Reagan and Bush years, it became apparent that candidates and parties were shredding the intent of the 1974 law. One unintended consequence, for example, was the rise of the political action committee, or PAC. This heretofore little-known entity had first surfaced in 1943 as a response to the outlawing of political contributions by unions. Under the 1974 law and previous reforms, neither corporations nor unions could contribute directly to campaigns, and individuals were limited to $1,000 per candidate for each of the primary and general elections.

But PACs provided a way for corporations and unions to circumvent the rule. They could collect voluntary contributions from corporate employees and stockholders, or union members and other individuals, and thereby could give a total of $5,000 per election to each candidate. Corporations and unions could pay for the PAC's operating costs and control the disbursement of its funds.

The number of PACs had been growing over the years, but slowly. Then in the wake of the Watergate reforms, 608 PACs registered with the new FEC, blooming like dandelions across Washington, D.C. By the end of 1984, just a decade after the most comprehensive reforms ever, more than 4,000 PACs were collecting and handing out political money.[40]

Funds from corporations, unions and trade associations still flowed to politicians, just through different channels, as PACs became their surrogates. They became the conduits for money that was otherwise prohibited. But PACs were required to report all money collected and disbursed to candidates and parties.

"PAC money is destroying the electoral process," complained Republican Senator Barry Goldwater of Arizona in the early 1980s. "It feeds the growth of special interest groups created solely to channel money into political campaigns. It creates the impression that every candidate is bought and owned by the biggest givers."[41] This has long been Public Citizen's view: Big money not only distorts the electoral process, it debases the legislative process as well, because big donors inevitably expect big returns.

Public Citizen's research in the late 1980s showed that the 1974 campaign finance reforms did little to reduce money's influence. Incumbents still enjoyed a massive financial advantage over their opponents. In 1988, despite public outrage at the S&L meltdown and the large role that members of Congress played in it, 98 percent of House incumbents were re-elected. In 1990, 74 incumbents ran with no major party opposition in primary or general elections—and still raised a total of $19.6 million, including more than $10 million from PACs.[42] The majority of winning House members received more than half their money from PACs.

Congress Watch documented another disturbing new trend: No longer were PACs simply choosing sides in an election. Instead, they were hedging their bets by giving money to both candidates in a race.

In a July 1991 study, "PACking the Deck: How PACs guarantee access by giving to both candidates," Congress Watch researchers found that in the 15 House races where challengers had defeated incumbents, 158 PACs had given to both sides. Some who had backed both sides then even gave bonuses to the winner to help pay off campaign debts. "In every case, PACs gave to both candidates and ignored character, stance and party," the report said.

Why? Because a PAC contribution is not an expression of ideological support as much as a way to gain access to lawmakers. Access leads to influence, and special interest influence leads to skewed legislation, corruption and scandal.

Even as PACs gave to both sides, incumbents still enjoyed an overwhelming advantage because PACs tended to give more to those already in positions of influence. This was and remains true of the leaders of powerful congressional committees, who can decide whether legislation lives or dies, and whether special provisions are slipped surreptitiously into bills. From 1980 to 1990, PAC giving to congressional candidates nearly tripled — from $55 million to $150 million. Then it doubled again by the 2008 election cycle, to $369 million.[43]

The "Soft Money" Loophole

In 1991, Public Citizen and allied groups began a major push for reforms against soft money. Congress in 1992 approved legislation to create a system of voluntary spending limits and partial public campaign funding, but in a blow to reformers, President George H.W. Bush vetoed the package.

Public Citizen's ultimate goal was public financing of elections, but it welcomed incremental changes. After the veto, Public Citizen's lobbyists and researchers went back to work. They churned out report after report detailing the stark relationship between campaign funds and legislative matters. They staged protests outside million-dollar fundraisers going on in swank Washington hotels. They introduced a costumed, cigar-chomping "fat cat" to the scene, making the issue more visual for TV news producers.

It was already apparent that soft money was a monstrous loophole in campaign laws, allowing corporations, unions and wealthy individuals to evade the prohibition on direct contributions. In the 1992 elections, the Democratic Party's committees raised more than $36 million in soft money and the Republican Party's committees raised even more — $50 million.[44] Under the law, the parties that got the checks could not use soft money to expressly advocate the election of specific candidates, only for such activities as "party building" and "get out the vote" efforts. For example, the Democratic National Committee could not legally purchase television ads that said "Vote for Bill Clinton for president." But ads attacking his opponent and promoting Clinton's views were fair game as long as they did not have to ask directly for a viewer's vote.

By 1996, the soft money loophole had made a farce of the ban on direct contributions, and everyone knew it. Yet the Federal Election Commission did not use its authority to regulate soft money. In the 1996 election, the two major parties raised an astonishing $262 million in soft money, much of it for an unprecedented blizzard of political party TV commercials promoting their presidential nominees — Bill Clinton and Bob Dole — in a wholesale but legal evasion of campaign laws. Some Democratic Party contributors were rewarded with White House coffees and sleepovers.

After the scandalous 1996 elections, Public Citizen joined allied groups such as Common Cause to renew the push for change. The next year, reformers had a legislative vehicle that was gaining popularity — a bipartisan bill proposed by Arizona Republican John McCain and Wisconsin Democrat Russell Feingold in the Senate and Connecticut Republican Christopher Shays and Massachusetts Democrat Marty Meehan in the House.

McCain and Feingold had worked in 1995 with Public Citizen and other groups to enact a successful tightening of lobbying registration requirements. Their campaign reform bill sought to ban soft money outright and regulate so-called "issue ads" that were really campaign ads in disguise. The bill enjoyed support by virtually the entire Democratic caucus in Congress but was bitterly opposed by GOP leaders.

To the dismay of his Republican colleagues, McCain campaigned vigorously for the legislation. Through the summer of 1997, Public Citizen pressured Senate leaders to bring the bill up for a vote, targeting key senators by communicating with voters in their home states. The bill finally hit the Senate floor in October. And even though eight Republicans joined all 45 Democrats in voting for it, they failed to get the 60 votes needed to overcome a filibuster — which was led by two of the Republican Senate's chief money raisers, Majority Leader Trent Lott and Kentucky Senator Mitch McConnell.

In the years that followed. Public Citizen and its allies led a grassroots campaign that eventually forced House Speaker Newt Gingrich to bring up the Shays-Meehan reform bill in 1998. In a heartening victory for reformers, the House in August passed the bill by a decisive, bipartisan margin. But once again, Lott and McConnell stymied the bill in the Senate by tying it up with a filibuster. In 1999, the House passed the bill again, but reformers still could not break through the Senate Republican blockade.

GOP leaders insisted that the McCain-Feingold legislation would curtail free speech. But their true objection became clear when McConnell was quoted in *The Washington Post*: "Take away soft money and we wouldn't be in the majority in the House and the majority in the Senate, and couldn't win back the White House," he said. "Hell's going to freeze over first before we get rid of soft money."[45]

By October 1999, however, 55 senators favored some version of the legislation, a significant improvement, and only five more were needed to break the GOP filibuster. Public Citizen and its partner groups kept up a campaign of lobbying, organizing constituents in the states of key senators and publishing timely reports on the influence of special interest money.

McCain, meanwhile, made campaign finance reform a key issue in his candidacy for the 2000 Republican presidential nomination. So did former New Jersey Senator Bill Bradley, who was challenging Vice President Al Gore for the Democratic nod. In a major speech in New Hampshire in July 1999, McCain decried the political climate and called the campaign system "nothing less than an elaborate influence-peddling scheme in which both parties conspire to stay in office by selling the country to the highest bidder."[46]

Although politicians rarely acknowledged the link between campaign cash and specific legislation, McCain did. Referring to the 1996 Telecommunications Act, McCain said that "every company affected by the legislation had purchased a seat at the table with soft money." But consumers had no seat there, and as a consequence, he said, "Lower prices that competition produces never materialized. Cable rates went up. Phone rates went up. And huge broadcasting giants receive for free billions of dollars in digital spectrum, property that belonged to the American people."[47]

Although McCain lost the 2000 nomination to Texas Governor George W. Bush, he propelled the issue of campaign finance reform to a new level of public awareness.

The "527" Groups Emerge

In 2000, with the election campaign in full swing, a deeply divided and bitter Congress hadn't even considered fundamental campaign finance reform. However, Congress did approve legislation to close a loophole that had allowed secretive tax-exempt organizations (named "Section 527 groups" after a provision of the Internal Revenue Code) to raise and spend millions of dollars to influence elections without disclosing their donors. It was the first important campaign finance reform enacted in more than two decades.

Liberals and conservatives alike had used 527 groups. Among the most prominent were the Sierra Club, the Republicans for Clean Air, and the drug industry front group Citizens for Better Medicare. Politicians also were major abusers. For example, during the 2000 election cycle, dozens of congressional and presidential candidates formed Section 527 "state leadership PACs" to attract unlimited soft money from corporations, unions and the wealthy. This represented a new level of corruption.

After the reform passed, lawyers for some candidates tried to protect their soft money by arguing that the new law didn't cover those "state leadership" PACs as long as their "hard money" federal branches reported to the FEC. Public Citizen promptly wrote to the IRS director showing that this argument was contradicted by law and by existing FEC disclosure requirements. On August 9, 2000, the IRS upheld the position of Public Citizen and other congressional reformers.

Although the McCain-Feingold bill was languishing, the 2000 elections altered the political landscape. Soft money contributions nearly doubled again, to $495 million from $262 million in 1996.[48] Democrats picked up seats in the House, but not enough to take control, and achieved a 50–50 split in the Senate. Because Vice President Dick Cheney could cast the deciding Senate vote, however, the GOP remained in power, giving Republicans control over the White House and both chambers of Congress for the first time since the Eisenhower administration. But Lott was weakened. Increasingly, GOP moderates were bucking the party leadership.

Sensing an opening in the Senate, Public Citizen worked closely with reformers to draft legislation, provide research and develop a strategy for the floor debate. The group's field organizers courted Republicans from Arkansas, Illinois, Ohio, Oregon and Rhode Island. Public Citizen worked to educate reporters and editorial writers about the need for the McCain-Feingold bill and the pitfalls of poison pill amendments.

The groups prepared a report showing that the leading alternative measure, sponsored by Republican Senator Chuck Hagel of Nebraska, would stop only about 40 percent of the soft money flowing to national parties. Lobbying and grassroots campaigning helped persuade senators in a dozen states to oppose an increase in hard money contributions that individuals and PACs could give. Public Citizen issued a report demonstrating that raising the individual hard money limit from $1,000 to $3,000 would increase the amount of money that a senator received from wealthy contributors from 47 percent of the total donated to 64 percent.

Campaign Finance Reform Passes

Finally, in April 2001, after two weeks of dramatic debate, the Senate passed the McCain-Feingold reform bill with its ban on soft money. Lawmakers amended the bill to double the amount that individuals could give directly to candidates in each election cycle from $1,000 to $2,000. Public Citizen vigorously opposed that provision but felt successful in keeping the contribution limit below $3,000, a level that had considerable Democratic support. The corrupting effect of the increase paled in comparison to the perils of the soft money system that the legislation was set to abolish.

The House had passed campaign finance reform relatively easily in earlier years, but this time its approval was not so simple. The Shays-Meehan bill became bogged down in partisan bickering as GOP leaders tried to erect procedural barriers to the legislation. Campaign reformers were thwarted for the moment, but after decades of working on the issue, Public Citizen was not about to give up.

In July 2001, House Speaker Dennis Hastert of Illinois declared that he would allow a vote on the bill only if compelled to do so by a "discharge" petition signed by a majority of the House (218 members). So Public Citizen aimed its grassroots organizing and media efforts toward getting those signatures. By the end of the year, 212 signatures had been secured.

The stars aligned in 2002. Enron Corporation, the nation's seventh-largest energy company, collapsed amid a huge and complex accounting scandal (see Chapter 9). Public Citizen reports detailed the ways the company had used investors' money and its political connections to win regulatory and legislative favors. Giveaways from Congress had aided its rise to power and helped it concoct the fraudulent schemes that ripped off consumers, defrauded investors and sapped the pensions of its employees.[49] For weeks, newspapers and televisions networks were filled with shocking revelations about Enron's massive accounting fraud (and later, its manipulation of energy prices).

The scandal turned out to be just the first ripple in an epic corporate crime wave that came to light over the next few years. It propelled the McCain-Feingold bill, called the Bipartisan Campaign Reform Act of 2002 (BCRA), to final passage. This new law prohibited national political parties from raising or spending soft money and restricted state parties from serving as conduits. It also reined in the use of bogus issue ads that flouted campaign finance rules, and raised the limit on individual contributions to $2,000 per election.

The battle wasn't over yet. A broad array of special interest groups challenged the law's constitutionality in court: Senator Mitch McConnell, the Republican National Committee, the U.S. Chamber of Commerce, the National Manufacturers Association, the National Rifle Association, the AFL-CIO and even the American Civil Liberties Union. In all, more than 80 plaintiffs filed 10 separate lawsuits that were eventually consolidated into one.

Public Citizen's Alan Morrison, a constitutional law expert, assisted a high-powered legal team charged with defending BCRA. After a special three-judge court issued a mixed verdict in May 2003, the U.S. Supreme Court, which generally hears cases for just one hour each, scheduled an extraordinary four-hour hearing on it.

In December 2003, in a strongly worded opinion, the Supreme Court voted 5 to 4 to uphold nearly all elements of the law. Opening the door to further reform, the *McConnell v. FEC* ruling admonished the Federal Election Commission for the proliferation of money in politics, rejecting the argument that such funding played little role in legislative outcomes. "Particularly telling is the fact that, in 1996 and 2000, more than half of the top 50 soft money donors gave substantial sums to both major national parties," the court wrote, "leaving room for no other conclusion but that these donors were seeking influence, or avoiding retaliation, rather than promoting any particular ideology."

Opponents of campaign finance reform didn't give up. The new Supreme Court tilted 5-4 to the right thanks to President George W. Bush's appointment of conservatives Samuel Alito and Chief Justice John Roberts. In 2007, it issued a landmark ruling in *Federal Election Commission v. Wisconsin Right to Life, Inc.* The case centered around ads during the 2004 campaign season in which the Wisconsin group asked people to urge their senators to hold votes on judicial nominees. At the time, Wisconsin's Senator Feingold was up for re-election, and the Federal Election Commission barred the ads as violating campaign finance law.

An appellate court said the ads should have run. The Supreme Court concurred, ruling that ads that contain no express advocacy — such as "vote against Feingold" in this case — or electioneering messages (for example, mentioning an election, candidacy, political party, or a candidate's character or fitness for office) may qualify as "issue ads" that are not subject to limits in the campaign finance law.

The 5–4 ruling on this class of advertisements was viewed by good-government groups like Public Citizen as a setback that would undermine — but not entirely eliminate — limits on electioneering funded by corporate and union "soft money."[50] And in the 2008 election cycle, total PAC spending for all races again set a new record, reaching a staggering $1.5 billion as Barack Obama was elected president.[51]

The *Wisconsin* decision set into motion additional court challenges and regulatory actions seeking to roll back the 2002 limits, but they held firm for the rest of Claybrook's tenure at Public Citizen. A year after her departure, in 2010, came the Supreme Court's *Citizens United v. Federal Election Commission* decision that erased all bounds to political spending by corporations, unions and wealthy individuals — and on that very day, Public Citizen's new president, Robert Weissman, launched a campaign for a constitutional amendment to specify that corporations do not have free speech rights. The organization would remain, as ever, in the thick of the fight to restrain corporate power.

Draining the Swamp

Although the 2006 attempt to reform lobbying and ethics in Congress fizzled under Republican rule, Public Citizen and other reform-minded groups began pushing from new angles. One battle involved a Republican drive to repeal the estate tax, the tax on large inheritances. Congress had voted in 2001 to gradually raise the lower limit for escaping the tax from $675,000 that year to $3.5 million by 2009. Critics called any estate tax a "death tax" that would hurt small businesses, widows and minority children and discourage hard-working investors. In 2005, they moved to repeal the tax completely.

Congress Watch produced a study in 2006, "Spending Millions to Save Billions; The Campaign of the Super Wealthy to Kill the Estate Tax,"[52] revealing that members of 18 super-wealthy families — not small businesses — were financing and coordinating the massive publicity campaign against the tax. Their members included 23 billionaires such as the owners of Wal-Mart, Campbell's Soup, Nordstrom, Mars, Black Entertainment Television, Gallo and Koch Industries, among others. The report showed the 18 families had spent nearly half a billion dollars to lobby Congress between 1998 and 2006. Their net worth was more than $185.5 billion — and they would deprive the U.S. Treasury of a whopping $71.6 billion if their repeal bid succeeded. Only one-quarter of one percent of all estates would owe anything in 2006.

"It was a huge media success," recalled Taylor Lincoln, research director at Congress Watch. "It was the biggest blog issue on the Web at one point. [Then-Senator] Hillary Clinton pulled Joan [Claybrook] aside and complimented her. The '18 families' became the symbol of the lobbying effort for repeal." In the end, the tax was repealed for one year only, 2010, and legislation that year set the applicable level "permanently" at $5 million, to be indexed for inflation thereafter.

Democrats, who had launched their campaigns while the Abramoff scandal was at its peak, regained control of Congress in the 2006 midterm elections on a pledge to "drain the swamp." At the victory party, future House Speaker Nancy Pelosi, a California Democrat, announced that "the Democrats intend to lead the most honest, most open and most ethical Congress in history."

In 2007, Public Citizen held lawmakers to their word and pressed them to make dramatic changes. Government affairs lobbyist Craig Holman consulted with Pelosi and helped shape new legislative language. On the first day of the new congressional session, Pelosi proposed new House ethics rules aimed at fundamental change to business as usual.

No longer would lobbyists — nor organizations that employ lobbyists — be able to give lawmakers meals and gifts. House members would have to pay the face value of tickets to sporting events and concerts. Organizations that employed lobbyists could no longer arrange or pay for most congressional travel, except for one-day trips such as to give a speech. Corporate jet use would be banned, but members could be reimbursed for traveling commercial business class. Registered lobbyists could not tag along.

Information about earmarks — those taxpayer-funded highway projects, museum grants, post offices named after lawmakers and other goodies doled out to enrich specific constituents — was now to be made public, including sponsors' names. This represented a significant reform because this "pork" had soared from $12.5 billion in 1996 to $29 billion in 2006, according to Citizens Against Government Waste. The new rules passed the House two days later.

The momentum reached the Senate as well. Similar lobbying and ethics reforms were introduced as the Senate's first bill, and passed days later on a vote of 96 to 2. Only one problem remained: The House measures were mere rules that could be repealed by any new leaders. They were not the law of the land.

Moves to turn the House rules into a statute faced resistance from many of the "old bulls" in the Democratic Party's middle ranks. They steadily chipped off bits of the package as it moved through committee, even the "revolving door" restriction to require former House members to wait two years before lobbying former colleagues. The disclosure of bundled contributions, a highly controversial reform, became a separate measure. In a final attempt to kill both bills, Republicans moved to reattach the two pieces, restored the "revolving door" provision and added other aspects they believed would be nails in the coffin.

But prodded by Public Citizen lobbyists and under intense public and news media scrutiny, the House approved the entire package on May 24, 2007, on a 396 to 22 vote. Neither Democrats nor most Republicans dared to cast a public vote against reform once the bill came to the floor.

Now a House-Senate conference committee had to reconcile the differences between the two measures, giving opponents one last shot. Senator Jim DeMint, a South Carolina Republican, tried to kill it by placing a "hold" on the appointment of conferees so that they could not meet. In a masterful political maneuver, Pelosi sat down with Senate Majority Leader Harry Reid and redrafted the entire reform package as one single bill for both chambers.

The resubmitted legislation passed days later in both the House and the Senate. And because there were no House-Senate differences, no conference committee was needed, evading DeMint's blockade. President Bush reluctantly signed the "Honest Leadership and Open Government Act of 2007" into law on September 14, 2007.

It included key reforms that Public Citizen had long championed. One was an open book on lobbyists and campaign money, requiring online posting of the dollar amount of direct and bundled campaign contributions, the names of lobbyists who host fundraising events and the amounts they raised. The measure ended anonymous "bridges to nowhere" by requiring online disclosure of the names of the sponsors and recipients of earmarks 48 hours before final approval of appropriations and tax bills. Travel junkets were limited to one-day trips — not on corporate jets — and lobbyists were not allowed to accompany lawmakers. But the rules contained exceptions for educational and charitable groups, including their lobbyists, and were later eased further to allow seven-day foreign trips and four-day domestic trips.

The Challenges Ahead

Public Citizen's goal of public financing of congressional elections remained unmet, but the group kept pushing. During the 2008 presidential race, Public Citizen and its allies persuaded both the Obama and McCain campaigns to reveal more information about their donors and bundlers. Additionally, a report detailing the ways corporations used free entertainment and parties to gain influence at the national party conventions succeeded in keeping some members of Congress away from some of those events. But the parties' candidates alone still collected a record $416.9 million from PACs.

In the years after the Supreme Court's *Citizens United* decision, Public Citizen's petition drive for a constitutional amendment to reverse the ruling has "made more progress than anyone thought feasible at the outset," President Robert Weissman said in 2015. Sixteen states and the District of Columbia had passed supportive resolutions along with more than 650 cities and towns and more than 150 civic organizations. More than 50 organizations gathered more than five million petition signatures supporting the amendment, and in September 2014 a U.S. Senate majority voted to overturn *Citizens United* and other court decisions. The drive to empower the people to impose reasonable restraints on campaign spending continues.

Congress saw many changes in the four decades after Public Citizen first sent emissaries to Capitol Hill to be the advocates and voices for ordinary citizens. Gone are some of the most abusive practices. No longer can members of Congress pocket money from favor-seeking corporations just for making speeches or showing up at corporate retreats. Innumerable corporate welfare proposals have been exposed—and often eliminated—thanks to the watchdogs in Public Citizen's Congress Watch program and its allies.

On many issues, Public Citizen manages to build public support and win despite massive industry spending. Because of Public Citizen's founding generation, Americans are better informed about the political issues that affect them. They better understand the role of corporate interests in crafting public policy and are better equipped to hold their senators and representatives accountable. To this day, Public Citizen still seeks to rise to the challenge that Nader posed in *Who Runs Congress?*—to take back Congress for the American people.

Endnotes

1   Michael Isikoff, Holly Baily and Evan Thomas, "A Washington Tidal Wave," *Newsweek*, Jan. 16, 2006.
2   R. Jeffrey Smith, "DeLay Airfare Was Charged to Lobbyist's Credit Card," *The Washington Post*, April 25, 2005.
3   Karen Tumulty, "The Man Who Bought Washington," *Time*, Jan. 16, 2006.
4   Lobbying Database, Center for Responsive Politics, based on data from the Senate Office of Public Records, at www.opensecrets.org/lobby/index.php. Accessed Sept. 25, 2013.
5   Mark J. Green, James M. Fallows and David R. Zwick, *Who Runs Congress?*, Bantam Books, 1972, p. 5.
6   *Congressional Travel: Justified Journeys or Junkets?*, Public Citizen's Congress Watch, August 1983, p. 9.
7   *Flights of Fancy, Foreign Travel by the U.S. Congress*, Public Citizen's Congress Watch, 1986.
8   *Free Flying Congress*, Public Citizen's Congress Watch, 1989.
9   *They Love to Fly ... And It Shows!*, Public Citizen's Congress Watch, 1991.
10 *Aid For Dependent Corporations: A Study of the Fiscal 1984 Corporate Welfare Budget*, Public Citizen's Congress Watch, April 1983.
11 Michael Waldman and the staff of Public Citizen, *Who Robbed America? A Citizen's Guide to the Savings and Loan Scandal*, Random House, 1990, pp. 14–19.
12 Ralph Nader, in introduction to *Who Robbed America? A Citizen's Guide to the Savings and Loan Scandal*, Michael Waldman, Random House, 1990, pp. xiii–xiv.
13 *The Resolution Trust Corporation: Secrecy in the Savings and Loan Bailout*, Public Citizen's Congress Watch, July 1989 p 2.
14 Timothy Curry and Lynn Shibut, "The Cost of the Savings and Loan Crisis: Truth and Consequences," FDIC Banking Review, Federal Deposit Insurance Corporation, Dec. 2000. www.fdic.gov/bank/analytical/banking/2000dec/brv13n2_2.pdf.
15 Michael Waldman et al., *Who Robbed America? A Citizen's Guide to the Savings and Loan Scandal*, pp. 92–99.
16 Ralph Nader, in introduction to *Who Robbed America? A Citizen's Guide to the Savings and Loan Scandal*, Michael Waldman, Random House, 1990, pp. xiii–xiv.
17 Patrick Woodall and Peter Eliot, *Take the Money and Run: How the Bush Administration is Letting S&L Crooks off the Hook*, Public Citizen's Congress Watch, September 1992, p. 9–11.
18 Kitty Calavita, Henry N. Pontell and Robert H. Tillman, *Big Money Crime: Fraud and Politics in the Savings and Loan Crisis*, University of California Press, Berkeley and Los Angeles California, 1997, pp. 156–9. www.ncjrs.gov/pdffiles1/Digitization/176104NCJRS.pdf.
19 Calavita, Pontell and Tillman, *Big Money Crime: Fraud and Politics in the Savings and Loan Crisis*, University of California Press, Berkeley and Los Angeles California, 1997, p. 159.
20 *Betting on Trent Lott: The Casino Gambling Industry's Campaign Contributions Pay Off in Congress*, Public Citizen's Congress Watch, June 1999.
21 Hedrick Smith, *The Power Game: How Washington Works*, Collins, 1988, p. 257.
22 See www.citizen.org/congress/reform/state_rx_price/articles.cfm?ID=821.
23 *The Rx R&D Myths: The Case Against the Drug Industry's R&D "Scare Card,"* Public Citizen's Congress Watch, July 23, 2001, pp. 13–14.

24 Schering-Plough Corporation Annual Report, 2000.

25 *Aggressive Lobbying Behind Claritin Patent Extension Bill That Could Cost Consumers $1.6–$3.2 Billion*, Public Citizen's Congress Watch, June 30, 1999.

26 Edward R. Silverman, "'America's Family Doctor' Takes on Drug Maker's Case," *Star-Ledger*, June 20, 1999.

27 "Senate Judiciary Committee to Vote on Nov. 17 on Special Interest Patent Extension for Claritin," Public Citizen press release, Nov. 16, 1999; and report, *Aggressive Lobbying Behind Claritin Patent Extension Bill That Could Cost Consumers $1.6–$3.2 Billion*, June 30, 1999. Hatch used the Schering-Plough corporate jet at least five times in July and August 1999. He reimbursed the company the price of a first-class air ticket for each passenger, as the rules require. However, the total of $18,691 was just a fraction of actual costs of operating the plane, which would have cost $5,000 an hour to charter.

28 *Public Citizen Investigations into Prescription Drug Price Gouging in Selected States*, Public Citizen's Congress Watch, Oct. 23, 2000.

29 "Study Shows Pharmaceutical Companies Are Price-Gouging Pennsylvania Consumers," Public Citizen press release, April 18, 2000.

30 *U.S. vs. Canadian Price for Selected Drugs Used by Seniors on New Hampshire-Montreal Bus Trip*, Public Citizen's Congress Watch, Jan. 18, 2000.

31 *Rx R&D Myths: The Case Against the Drug Industry's R&D "Scare Card,"* Public Citizen's Congress Watch, July 2001 www.citizen.org/documents/ACFDC.pdf. Accessed May 14, 2015.

32 *The Other Drug War: Big Pharma's 625 Washington Lobbyists*, Public Citizen's Congress Watch, July 23, 2001.

33 *Citizens for Better Medicare: The Truth Behind the Drug Industry's Deception of America's Seniors*, Public Citizen's Congress Watch, June 2000, p. 1.

34 *Rx R&D Myths: The Case Against the Drug Industry's R&D "Scare Card,"* Public Citizen's Congress Watch, July 23, 2001.

35 "In Wake of Scully Fiasco, Public Citizen Calls on the Office of Governmental Ethics to Improve Procedures for Granting Ethics Waivers," Public Citizen press release, Jan. 14, 2004.

36 Amy Goldstein, "Former Bush Adviser Agrees to Pay for Trips," *The Washington Post*, July 11, 2006.

37 Anthony Corrado, "Money and Politics: A History of Federal Campaign Finance Law," *Campaign Finance Reform: A Sourcebook*, Brookings Institution Press, Washington, D.C., 1997.

38 Mark J. Green, James M. Fallows and David R. Zwick, *Who Runs Congress?*, Bantam Books, 1972, p. 9.

39 Anthony Corrado, "Money and Politics," p. 31.

40 Frank J. Sorauf, "Political Action Committees," p. 129.

41 Hedrick Smith, *The Power Game: How Washington Works*, Harper-Collins, New York, 1988, p. 253.

42 Karen Hobert, *Running with the Money: An Examination of Campaign Fundraising by Unopposed House Incumbents in the 1989-90 Elections*, Public Citizen's Congress Watch, 1990.

43 The Campaign Finance Institute, "PAC Contributions to Congressional Candidates, 1978–2010," www.cfinst.org/data/pdf/VitalStats_t10.pdf. Washington, D.C.

44 Anthony Corrado, "Party Soft Money," *Campaign Finance Reform: A Sourcebook*, Brookings Institution Press, Washington, D.C., 1997, p. 175.

45 Terry M. Neal, "Fired Up and Financially Flush, Forbes Plans to Run Ads in Key States," *The Washington Post*, April 11, 1999.

46 Alison Mitchell, "McCain Exhorts His Party to Reject Campaign System," *The New York Times*, July 1, 1999.

47 David Broder, "McCain: Campaign Finance Will Be a Campaign Issue," *The Washington Post*, July 1, 1999.

48 Center for Responsive Politics, www.opensecrets.org.

49 *Blind Faith: How Deregulation and Enron's Influence Over Government Looted Billions From Americans*, Public Citizen's Critical Mass Energy and Environment Program, December 2001.

50 "Supreme Court Weakens, But Does Not Overturn, Federal Campaign Finance Law," Public Citizen press release, June 25, 2007.

51 Center for Responsive Politics, *Top PACS by Total Expenditures 2007–2008*, www.opensecrets.org/pacs/toppacs.php?cycle=2008&party=A. Accessed Sept., 26, 2013.

52 Public Citizen's Congress Watch and United for a Fair Economy, *Spending Millions to Save Billions: The Campaign of the Super-Wealthy to Kill the Estate Tax*, April 2006.

Photographs

Photographs

Ralph Nader testifies in 1968 at a Senate hearing.

Public Citizen
attorneys at the
U.S. Supreme Court
in 1988. From
left to right, Con
Hitchcock, Paul
Alan Levy and Eric
Glitzenstein. All
three argued cases
before the Supreme
Court that year.

Dr. Sidney Wolfe, founder and longtime
director of Public Citizen's Health Research
Group, in a mid-1970s photo.

Alan Morrison, co-founder and longtime
director of the Public Citizen Litigation
Group, in the mid-1970s.

Joan Claybrook was president of Public
Citizen from 1982 to 2009. She is pictured
here in the late 1970s when she was
administrator of the National Highway
Traffic Safety Administration.

Ralph Nader and his "Nader's Raiders" in front of the U.S. Capitol in 1969.

In 1993, TV talk show host Phil Donahue holds up the
second edition of the best-seller *Worst Pills, Best Pills*,
a Public Citizen book that provided vital drug safety
information to millions.

David Vladeck joined the Public Citizen
Litigation Group in 1977 and succeeded
Alan Morrison as director in 1993.

Ralph Nader speaks at
the U.S. Capitol in 1990.

Dr. Sidney Wolfe, founder and longtime director of Public Citizen's Health Research Group, at a staff meeting around 1980.

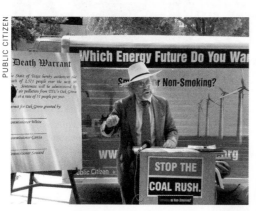

Tom "Smitty" Smith, director of Public Citizen's Texas office, led a successful effort to block new coal-fired power plants in that state.

Joan Claybrook speaks at a 1994 press conference to highlight the dangers of a General Motors pickup truck designed with "side-saddle" gas tanks outside the main frame, which made them prone to explode in crashes.

SIDNEY WOLFE, M.D.
"WORST PILLS, BEST PILLS"

Dr. Sidney Wolfe, founder and longtime director of Public Citizen's Health Research Group, appears on the "Phil Donahue Show" in 1988 to talk about Public Citizen's best-seller, *Worst Pills, Best Pills*.

Public Citizen often used a costumed, cigar-chomping Fat Cat while holding demonstrations calling for campaign finance reforms.

Joan Claybrook with congressional allies in 2002 at an event to deliver thousands of Public Citizen petitions for campaign finance reform. Congress passed the McCain-Feingold campaign finance legislation in 2002. From left to right, Rep. Christopher Shays of Connecticut, Senator Russell Feingold of Wisconsin, Senator John McCain of Arizona and Rep. Marty Meehan of Massachusetts.

Lori Wallach, director of Public
Citizen's Global Trade Watch,
at a 2001 demonstration.

Senator Edward Kennedy of Massachusetts
speaks at a press conference with Joan
Claybrook, first on the left. The event was
held in the Senate during the 1980s.

Alan Morrison, co-founder and longtime director of the Public Citizen Litigation Group.

Joan Claybrook and others at a 1992 press conference to promote the Anti-Car Theft Act.

Joan Claybrook testifies Sept. 12, 2000, at a Senate hearing investigating Firestone tire safety.

7

CITIZEN SAFEGUARDS UNDER SIEGE: REGULATORY BACKLASH

———

WHEN TERRORISTS CRASHED AIRLINERS into the World Trade Center and the Pentagon on September 11, 2001, Americans reacted with an outpouring of grief and rage and patriotism—and not a small bit of anxiety about their security. The inevitable questions arose: How vulnerable are we to future attacks, perhaps even more deadly ones? Where are the chinks in our armor and how do we shore up our defenses?

For President George W. Bush, the security of Americans became the rhetorical and policy centerpiece of his presidency. During his State of the Union address in January 2002, he promised to protect Americans from terrorists: "Our government is doing everything it can to stop another attack." His political fortunes soared from the spirit of unity that swept the country.

New laws to improve U.S. national security followed rapidly. Airline vigilance was transformed by creation of the Transportation Security Administration, putting the federal government in charge of screening passengers and cargo. Congress ordered a massive government reorganization, creating the Department of Homeland Security to oversee and coordinate 22 security-related agencies and organizations. Many executive orders and laws authorizing government tracking of telephone calls and Internet communications were approved in secret, not to be revealed until at least a decade later.

But there was one thing Bush and Congress generally refused to do. They declined to impose any significant new security requirements on the private sector, which controls 85 percent of the nation's critical infrastructure.

Any quick survey could spot many rich targets, most notably nuclear reactors and chemical plants, that terrorists could conceivably attack to kill thousands, maybe even millions of people. The Environmental Protection Agency (EPA) identified more than 100 lightly guarded chemical plants where a leak caused by an accident or attack could threaten the lives of a million people. But the Bush administration failed to require industry to increase security.

For example, 90-ton rail cars containing enough chlorine to kill 100,000 people routinely passed through Washington, D.C., within four blocks of the Capitol. But the administration — and the railroad companies — actively opposed efforts by the Council of the District of Columbia to require that those dangerous loads be rerouted. Even though the nation's 104 commercial nuclear reactors were vulnerable in the eyes of many security experts to a ground attack by a small armed force, Bush resisted placing new security requirements on the utilities that own the plants. Representative Edward J. Markey, a Massachusetts Democrat, tried to pass such legislation year after year but was rebuffed by Republican leaders each time.

Public Citizen believed the administration was dangerously derelict in its duties to secure vulnerable nuclear, chemical, water, port and hazardous materials transportation facilities. In October 2004, its report "Homeland Unsecured: The Bush Administration's Hostility to Regulation and Ties to Industry Leave America Vulnerable," outlined the risks of inaction.[1] The report also noted that those industries had contributed $20 million to Bush and the Republican National Committee since the 2000 election cycle. Thirty of Bush's top fundraisers hailed from those industries, which had spent more than $201 million on lobbying since 2002.

"This administration, which has filled the top levels of government with corporate CEOs, lobbyists and lawyers, simply does not want to regulate business — even when the safety and security of Americans is at stake," said Joan Claybrook at the time.

Throughout Bush's first term and well into his second, the White House and Republican congressional leaders ignored calls to beef up security for critical infrastructure. It was not until 2006, when Bush's popularity had plummeted after years of the Iraq War, his failed attempt to privatize Social Security and his administration's anemic response to Hurricane Katrina, that he was forced to address legitimate security concerns.

The administration had approved a business deal that would have allowed Dubai Ports World, a company operated by the United Arab Emirates, to operate six major ports in the United States. Conservatives were aghast that an Arab country, even one that Bush said was an ally in his "war on terror," would be in control of the nation's ports, where very few cargo containers were ever inspected.

Many of Bush's staunchest defenders in Congress demanded the deal be cancelled. Eventually, Dubai Ports World sold the port rights to an American-owned corporation. From Public Citizen's viewpoint, the issue had less to do with the company's Arab ownership than with the fact that the tough-talking Bush reliably put global commerce before U.S. security. The White House later washed its hands of the entire debacle, insisting that the initial decision to give the deal the go-ahead had not even reached Bush's desk.

Within weeks, Homeland Security Secretary Michael Chertoff announced he wanted to tighten security at chemical plants. But he said businesses should have the leeway to decide how to secure their facilities. *The Boston Globe* quoted Chertoff as saying that under no circumstances would chemical plants be required to switch to safer processes, and that any legislation would have to avoid government "micromanaging." Public Citizen and other critics dismissed the initiative as a plan the chemical industry had drafted to avoid the expense of meaningful security measures that might actually prevent terrorists from creating a toxic cloud.[2]

In 2005, Congress ordered the Nuclear Regulatory Commission (NRC) to revise its rule describing the kinds of terrorist threats that nuclear power plants must protect themselves against. But instead of deciding what threats the reactors were likely to face and requiring the operators to have security to meet those threats, the NRC proposal was based on what it thought it reasonable to require of a private security force. In 2008, as the rulemaking was finally in process, Public Citizen declared that approach an outrageous endangerment of public safety. It filed suit challenging the threat description on behalf of the San Luis Obispo Mothers for Peace, but an appeals court rejected the suit the following year.

Defending Regulation

The business backlash against regulations sparked by the consumer movement had begun in 1971, with Lewis F. Powell's memo calling on the business community to unite and pay for opposition efforts. It grew in the late 1970s, during Jimmy Carter's presidency, but it really gained momentum with President Ronald Reagan's election in 1980. Reagan famously promised during a period of economic stagnation to "get government off our backs." The federal government, in his view, was an impediment to personal freedom and economic vitality.

"It is no coincidence," he said in his first inaugural address, on January 20, 1981, "that our present troubles parallel and are proportionate to the intervention and intrusion in our lives that result from unnecessary and excessive growth of government." In a ringing phrase, he added, "Government is not the solution to our problem; government *is* the problem."

Reagan's message, refined and amplified by conservatives ever since, was that government is inherently wasteful and ineffective at solving society's problems. Far better to unleash private enterprise to "create wealth" and to "starve the beast" of regulation by cutting its funding. Translated into policy terms, this meant slashing social programs aimed at fighting poverty and reducing inequality, while shredding the regulatory system designed to ensure that products are safe and effective and that corporations do not defraud consumers, damage the environment or abuse worker and civil rights.

Veteran political reporter William Greider wrote on Reagan's death in 2004 of a "chilling meanness" at the heart of Reagan's agenda, saying, "he used this meanness like a razor blade to advance his main purpose — de-legitimizing the federal government."[3]

On Jan. 22, 1981, just two days after his inauguration, Reagan announced that Vice President George H.W. Bush would head a new Task Force on Regulatory Relief, with the mandate to "cut away the thicket of irrational and senseless regulations."

Less than a month later, the president issued an executive order that established the procedures by which the task force would eliminate "unnecessary" regulations. All executive branch agencies, including the Departments of Labor, Transportation, and Health and Human Services as well as the EPA and others, would henceforth be required to obtain permission from the White House's Office of Management and Budget (OMB) before issuing major regulations.

The OMB was staffed by conservative political operatives, not by experts in the fields subject to regulation. That was the point. To gain the OMB's approval, an agency had to demonstrate that the "potential benefits to society" of a regulation outweighed the "potential costs to society" and that the agency had selected the least costly alternative — not necessarily the most protective one.[4]

This new regime of "cost-benefit analysis" purported to be fair and open-minded. But in fact it was an elaborate ruse to justify dismantling the regulatory safety net. Cost estimates often relied on dubious and inflated data, much of it supplied by industries being regulated. Meanwhile, the benefits often were far more difficult or even impossible to quantify — and therefore weren't counted at all. What is the cash value of a healthier population, of air that doesn't cause lung disease, of water and food that don't make you ill, of workplaces that don't maim, cripple or harass their employees, of lakes and rivers again alive with fish and safe for swimming?

One of the first regulations the task force targeted, oddly enough, was a 1978 Department of Agriculture (USDA) rule requiring the meat industry to disclose on labels of hot dogs and other processed meats that the product contained powdered bone. The bone was a byproduct of a mechanized process to separate bits of meat from the skeletal remains of cows, pigs and lambs. The meat industry's argument: Consumers would not eat products that they knew contained crushed bone, even if they couldn't taste it, so the industry would be effectively prohibited from using hundreds of millions of pounds of perfectly good meat (plus bone) each year. That would mean a rise in the price of beef and pork cuts by three to four cents per pound, the industry said.

Those few cents were enough justification for the Reagan White House to go after the rule. Never mind that consumers — by the industry's own admission — did not want to eat crushed bone. Or that mandatory labeling simply gave people a choice. By July 1981, six months into Reagan's first term, the USDA announced that it intended to change the labeling standard. The meat industry no longer would have to disclose the amount of crushed bone in processed meat products. Instead, man-ufacturers could now state on the labels that the product contained "calcium." The revision was made final a year later and was cited in an August 1982 administration "progress report" as the source of a major cost saving.[5]

Such political meddling in consumer and other public interest regulations became common. The OMB, for example, refused to approve an EPA proposal to ban certain asbestos products, arguing that industry's costs far outweighed the benefits. In calculating the benefits, however, the OMB refused to include savings such as reduced medical care and increased productivity that would stem from controlling the serious lung diseases caused by asbestos.

In addition, because diseases caused by asbestos do not become apparent for 10 to 20 years, the OMB used a technique called "discounting" — normally used to estimate the future value of money — to devalue the lives of asbestos victims. The OMB figured that the "discounted" value of a human life saved through the rule would be $208,000.[6] Calculating that the rule's cost to corporations would be far greater than that, the OMB rejected the rule.

Vice President Bush took to his regulation-cutting task with zeal. In March 1981, he sent letters to corporations to solicit lists of rules they found burdensome and suggestions for rewrites. Barely a month later, the White House issued a report that credited the Bush task force with persuading the EPA and the National Highway Traffic Safety Administration (NHTSA) to "rescind, revise and repropose" 34 regulations that had been aimed at reducing air pollution and decreasing highway deaths and injuries.[7] But those were the statutory missions of these programs; helping auto companies' bottom line was not.

Bush and OMB officials met often in secret with industry representatives, adopting their recommendations but leaving little or no paper trail. That meant little evidence survived that could be used in court to support charges that the administration was ignoring the Administrative Procedure Act. That 1946 law requires agencies to solicit comments from the public about a proposed regulation, consider those comments and justify the final regulation based on the public record. This record then provides the basis for all parties — regulated industries as well as those benefiting from the regulation — to mount a legal challenge to the rule and for a court to decide whether to uphold the agency's decision.

Reagan attacked consumer protections in other ways. He slashed regulatory agency budgets, sometimes by a third or a half, eviscerating their rulemaking and enforcement abilities. "They just decided not to enforce the law," marveled the young Democratic Representative Al Gore of Tennessee. "This sets up a conflict between those who would obey the law and those who would violate it, and gives the advantage to the violators."[8]

The Reagan and Bush attacks were so brazen that they quickly ran afoul of federal law. Many of the rules they targeted were the product of laws that gave the executive branch little discretion over whether or how they should be implemented. The rulemaking process also included requirements for public participation that the administration routinely disregarded. Public Citizen quickly launched a spirited defense in the courts, Congress and the news media.

One of its first lawsuits compelled the Food and Drug Administration (FDA) to issue a new regulation requiring that aspirin labels include warnings about a deadly children's disease called Reye's Syndrome (described in Chapter 3). Public Citizen sued the administration again when the OMB employed its cost-benefit analysis to water down proposed FDA standards for the nutritional value of infant formula. That suit failed, but Congress did enact legislation requiring the administration to issue stronger standards. Later, Public Citizen sued to force issuance of a requirement for uniform absorbency labeling for tampons, to help prevent toxic shock syndrome, a rare but potentially deadly bacterial infection associated with women's use of high-absorbency tampons.

Again and again, Public Citizen filed administrative petitions and lawsuits demanding that the Reagan administration comply with federal statutes dealing with such issues as dangerous food additives, workplace hazards, air bags, tire safety and environmental pollutants. Most of these suits were successful, as the administration had routinely ignored the law. One such suit, for example, stopped NHTSA from entering a "cooperative research" program with automakers to serve as the basis for new regulations.

Joan Claybrook returned to head Public Citizen in 1982 after serving in the Carter administration for four years as NHTSA administrator. There, she had gained valuable regulatory experience that would help the organization defend health and safety rules. Two years later, Claybrook concluded that "Reagan's deregulation has been a rampage that has brushed aside rational, scientific arguments and scorned due process and democratic participation."[9]

Because of the vigilance of Public Citizen and other like-minded groups, the Reagan anti-regulatory agenda was only partially successful. A series of investigations revealed scandal within Reagan's EPA in late 1982. Daily reports of cover-ups and conflicts of interest within the agency led to heightened public and media awareness of White House machinations. Reagan was forced to fire EPA Administrator Anne Burford, and five months later, the Task Force on Regulatory Relief quietly shut its doors.

The Reaganites then turned to Congress to implement their anti-regulatory agenda. Reagan called on Congress to abolish the Consumer Product Safety Commission (CPSC), created in 1972 to issue product safety standards and force dangerous products off the market. He called for enactment of a Regulatory Reform Act (which would codify his early executive order on procedure into law) to create a web of regulatory hurdles and exclude the public from the regulatory process. The bill died in the House of Representatives after Public Citizen helped convince committee chairs that it would undermine their authority to oversee the regulatory process.

Reagan also lobbied for a much weaker Clean Air Act when the law was up for reauthorization in 1982. He opposed reauthorization of the Superfund hazardous waste cleanup law and proposed a radical restructuring of food safety laws to give the FDA virtually unlimited discretion to approve food additives.

By the end of the 1980s, Public Citizen had contributed mightily to the defense of the regulatory system. In addition to lobbying Congress and challenging administration actions in the courts, the group had churned out report after report to document the Reagan abuses and had published two books on the subject — *Retreat from Safety: Reagan's Attack on America's Health,* by Claybrook and the staff of Public Citizen, and *Freedom from Harm: The Civilizing Influence of Health, Safety and Environmental Regulation,* by Claybrook and David Bollier.

Donating for Deregulation

A few months after President George H.W. Bush entered the White House in 1989, he announced that Vice President Dan Quayle would head a new task force called the Council on Competitiveness. It was the direct descendant of Bush's earlier Task Force on Regulatory Relief and took up where that group had left off. Its chief goal was to provide a backdoor, extra-legal means for business lobbyists and big campaign donors to eliminate unwanted regulations.

Like the task force, Quayle's council kept a stranglehold on regulatory agencies that dealt with consumer, environmental and workplace standards. It worked with the OMB to review final regulations before they were published. And like the Task Force, it met secretly with representatives of the regulated industries and flouted federal law that required openness in regulatory decision-making. The net effect was to allow a politicized office of corporate-minded economists to subvert years of agency regulatory decisions crafted by scientists and public health experts.[10]

When Quayle's council blocked or changed a proposed regulation, it left no record of who influenced its decision or what information was considered. Like the earlier task force, the council inserted itself without accountability into countless highly technical and scientific matters that were clearly the purview of experts at the agencies — such as how long the ground must be saturated and what types of vegetation must be present for an area to be defined as a wetland subject to federal protection.

The council forced the EPA to roll back protections for wetlands, exposing as much as 30 million additional acres to development. It torpedoed EPA rules that would have kept reusable items and toxic lead batteries out of incinerators. It blocked protections for workers exposed to formaldehyde. It delayed important new standards for medical laboratories. The list was long.

Quayle's council, however, refused to disclose all but the most rudimentary information about its operations, even to members of Congress. Public Citizen filed a Freedom of Information Act (FOIA) request in 1991, asking for information about the council's formation, structure and budget; a list of its staff members, their education and work experience; and all records of council meetings with outside groups on regulatory matters.

The council denied the request, claiming "executive privilege." It also refused an information request from committees in the House and Senate about its role in regulatory matters. Public Citizen knew a lawsuit would be futile; it had lost an earlier suit, *Meyer v. Bush,* against the Reagan administration's task force when an appellate court ruled that a task force was not a federal agency and therefore was not subject to such open records requests.

In January 1992, the Quayle council's executive director, Allan Hubbard, was forced out amid revelations in *The Washington Post* that he had violated federal ethics laws on conflicts of interest. *Post* reporters Bob Woodward and David Broder revealed that during Bush's re-election campaign against Bill Clinton, Quayle and Hubbard regularly asked campaign contributors for suggestions about regulations to weaken or block. In a January 9, 1992, article, they wrote:

> Word quickly spread throughout the business community that the Competitiveness Council was ready and able to help on regulatory matters, and its agenda filled up. In almost every city he visits as a campaigner, Quayle holds closed-door round tables with business people who have made sizable contributions to the local or national GOP. Hubbard, who also has the title of deputy vice presidential chief of staff, often travels with Quayle and sits in on these sessions.

A few months later, Public Citizen documented a clear relationship between campaign contributions and four regulatory actions the council took—on the FDA drug approval process, wetlands regulation, air pollution standards and airplane noise reduction. "In each of these four cases, affected corporations kicked in massive campaign contributions—and later saw the Quayle Council intervene on their behalf to weaken particular regulations," the report said.[11]

With the 1992 presidential elections looming, Bush pleased corporate contributors by announcing in his State of the Union address that year that he was ordering a three-month freeze on the issuance of regulations. He later extended the moratorium for a full year, stalling or killing dozens of proposed health, environmental and worker safety protections. Quayle's later claim that the freeze had saved $10 billion to $20 billion was exposed as dubious when Public Citizen filed a FOIA request with federal agencies to obtain the data for the "savings" figures.

"None of the agencies provided information about 'cost savings' that was even remotely understandable," said the report, "Voodoo Accounting: The Toll of President Bush's Regulatory Moratorium, January–August 1992." One agency sent hand-scribbled notes that were largely illegible.[12]

By the end of the Bush administration, deregulation had taken a heavy toll, as recounted in an October 1992 report by Public Citizen and allied groups, called "Who's Protecting Consumers? Federal Neglect of Consumer Protections." Timed to highlight the hypocrisy of Bush's proclamation of a National Consumers Week, the report noted that the CPSC was a mere shadow of its former self; that hundreds of new federal advisory committees gave industry representatives an inside path to decision-makers; that key government publications for consumers had been abolished or now cost so much that most could not afford them; and that public participation in government actions on consumer issues had been seriously undermined.[13]

After 12 years of such efforts by Reagan and Bush, consumer advocates were relieved to see Bush lose in 1992 to Bill Clinton. However, the Clinton-Gore team had come from a business-friendly wing of the Democratic Party called the Democratic Leadership Council. The Clinton administration repeatedly "triangulated" controversial issues by seeking a "third way" of compromise between the public interest and corporate interests.

In this case, that meant that Clinton did not ditch the Reagan-Bush approach to regulatory review, as Public Citizen and other public interest groups had urged. Instead, he left in place the anti-regulatory apparatus of OMB review and cost-benefit analysis. He issued Executive Order 12866, which moderated some of the harsh language of Reagan's earlier order and narrowed somewhat the draft regulations subject to OMB review, but it wasn't enough. Clinton entreated the public interest community to endorse his order, but Public Citizen and its colleagues refused.

Meanwhile, anti-regulatory forces continued their march in Congress. In 1994, Georgia Representative Newt Gingrich led a Republican resurgence that captured control of both the House and Senate. As part of his business-oriented "Contract With America," Gingrich sought legislation setting up more procedural barriers to hamstring the Clinton administration's ability to issue new regulations. He pledged to enact key elements of the "Contract" within the first 100 days of the 104th Congress.

In February 1995, the strongly partisan House passed H.R. 9, a comprehensive attack on health and safety standards. Rather than try to amend the dozens of statutes that protected consumers, workers and the environment, the legislation set up a flawed and inappropriate cost-benefit analysis process as a hurdle for new standards. It required a blizzard of paperwork and costly, irrelevant new analyses and procedures. It gave corporate America new avenues to challenge regulations in court, even though business interests already dominated the rulemaking process, and gave political operatives at the OMB power to block new standards.

In the Senate, Majority Leader Bob Dole, a Kansas Republican who was contemplating a campaign for president in 1996, proposed similar legislation, adding a "reach-back" provision to allow regulated industries to seek repeal of long-established standards on the basis of financial considerations. It was a great fundraising device for Dole and could affect every industry in America. The battle was on once again.

"The Dole bill said in essence three things," explained David Vladeck, then-director of the Public Citizen Litigation Group. "First, it said that the existing system of regulation doesn't place appropriate emphasis on cost-benefit considerations and we're going to make certain that all regulatory efforts take rigorous account of costs and benefits — even in instances where it's very hard to make a quantification. Second, it said, we are going to amend all substantive law — civil rights laws, environmental laws, worker safety laws — to say that an agency may not impose a regulation unless it can demonstrate the regulation is in fact cost-beneficial.

"That gets dicey when you're dealing with things like curb cuts [for the disabled]," Vladeck continued. "How do you place a dollar value on the ease with which someone in a wheelchair can get around? How do you value the habitat of an endangered species? The federal government ... has not been able to do it. Third, the Dole bill included what we called a super-mandate. That was a provision that trumped all existing laws, requiring cost-benefit considerations to prevail. In many ways, it made explicit a bias against regulation. And so we fought it mightily."

Congress was on the brink of rolling back a century of progress in protecting Americans' health and safety. To counter this threat, Public Citizen played a leading role in organizing a formidable united front of 230 labor, environmental, consumer, civil rights, religious and disability rights groups. The coalition, named Citizens for Sensible Safeguards, produced reams of materials and studies to demonstrate the widespread benefits of regulation and the flaws in business groups' arguments. Corporate America countered with a propaganda barrage promoting regulatory "reform" with specious images of federal bureaucracies run amok, government "red tape" and attacks on freedom.

But strong public support for health and safety protections survived this assault. Americans could plainly see that the air and water had gotten cleaner since the 1960s and that air bags and other innovations had made cars much safer. Auto safety standards, for example, had saved an estimated 250,000 lives over the previous three decades. Workplace rules had saved 140,000 lives since the Occupational Safety and Health Administration (OSHA) was created in 1970. The CPSC estimated that standards in four product categories alone had saved $2.5 billion in emergency room visits. Levels of toxic lead in the air had fallen by 98 percent since leaded gasoline was phased out, reducing brain damage, kidney disease and anemia in children.[14]

Public Citizen and its allies pointed out that these benefits would not have occurred had the government relied on "market forces" or if all new protections had to meet spurious cost-benefit standards concocted by industry allies.

The 1995 Senate battle was fierce, and Public Citizen took a lead role in organizing opposition to the Dole bill and providing intellectual underpinning for the effort. Vladeck and other Public Citizen lawyers testified before Congress. Claybrook was in the center of the effort, visiting senator after senator. She urged involving Democratic Senator John Kerry of Massachusetts as one of the leaders, even though he was not on the pertinent committee, because of his advocacy and legal skills. He became a key leader of the opposition and a new source of energy to stop the bill.

Claybrook also worked with the coalition to design a legislative strategy. Congress Watch orchestrated meetings and workshops with members of Congress and their staffs, and activated its field network. Public Citizen leaders wrote opinion articles for the news media and held regular press briefings. Meanwhile, corporate America, sensing the chance for a landmark victory, poured massive resources into the battle.

"This was war for us," Vladeck said. "This was our Battle of Britain. We fought them on the beaches, we fought them in the trenches, we fought them on the land, we fought them on the seas. Everywhere we went, we were always outmanned, out-numbered and outgunned. And yet we won."

But only by a whisker. Democratic Senators Kerry and John Glenn of Ohio, and Republican Lincoln Chaffee of Rhode Island led the battle for consumers. They gath-ered the 41 Senate votes needed for a filibuster that kept the legislation from coming to a final vote. Several minor components of the regulatory bill were enacted—but by and large, the main thrust of corporate America's anti-regulation offensive was turned back.

"I think once again the business community overplayed its hand," said Vladeck. "They thought this was their year. They thought they were going to win and come away with the big enchilada. Instead, they came away with a few chips."

Regulatory rollback remained on the Republican agenda throughout the 1990s and into the next millennium, though in some years it faded to the back burner. In 1998, legislation with many of the same elements as the 1995 legislation turned up as the Regulatory Improvement Act, this time with a Democratic co-sponsor, Senator Carl Levin of Michigan. It failed to pass but resurfaced again in 1999. Each time, Public Citizen and allied organizations stood in the doorway to block the corporate takeover of regulatory agencies.

Like Father, Like Son

By the beginning of the 21st century, corporate America's two-decade cam-paign to portray businesses as overregulated had managed to damage the regulatory system by layering it with multiple new procedural requirements — "paralysis by analysis." Regulated industries dominated the rulemaking process. Reagan's execu-tive orders remained largely in effect, agency budgets had been slashed and several new laws succeeded in slowing down the process of writing and enacting new rules. Government agencies were experiencing a "brain drain" as conscientious scientists and regulators left government service. Years of attacks on "pointy-headed bureau-crats" undermined the prestige and integrity of the federal agencies.

The process of writing new rules to protect consumers had become so encrusted with laborious procedures that OSHA, for example, now took an average of eight years to issue new regulations. Some rules, like one on workplace ergonomics, were subject to being overturned by Congress. OSHA became so understaffed that it had fewer than 100 people working on standards for the thousands of toxic substances used in workplaces every day. For most dangerous chemicals, essentially no stan-dards existed. NHTSA, charged with regulating the politically and economically powerful automobile industry, had just 625 employees by 2000, only 15 of whom were investigators. The agency's budget also was 30 percent lower, in inflation-ad-justed dollars, than before Reagan took office.[15]

Yet Public Citizen and its allies had largely succeeded in beating back the worst assaults on the regulatory system. They had filed dozens of successful lawsuits, particularly against the administrations of Reagan and both Bushes. Most basic protective statutes — with the notable exception of laws covering drinking water and prescription drug safety — remained virtually intact. Some, including automobile safety and pesticide laws, were even substantially improved.

In 2001, following the disputed presidential election results in Florida, former Texas Governor George W. Bush was sworn in as the nation's 43rd president. On Inauguration Day, January 20, he signaled a disdain for government and its safeguards that echoed that of his father George H.W. Bush and Ronald Reagan: his chief of staff, former automotive industry lobbyist Andrew Card, sent a memorandum to the heads of all federal agencies postponing by 60 days the effective date of new regulations that had already been published in the Federal Register but had not taken effect. This "Regulatory Review Plan" put scores of new safety standards approved late in the Clinton administration in abeyance, giving Bush's business allies another opportunity to lobby against their implementation.

Fearing a return to the anti-regulatory attacks of Reagan and Bush I, Public Citizen immediately compiled a report listing the standards that could be affected. Among them were rules to reduce arsenic in drinking water; set standards for organically grown crops; curtail logging in national forests; increase the energy efficiency of home appliances; reduce pollution from diesel engines; strengthen the protection of wetlands; prevent lead poisoning in children; phase out damaging snowmobile use in several national parks; provide HMO protections for Medicaid patients; and protect iron workers and miners from job hazards.[16] All had been approved after years of research, public hearings and formal rulemaking procedures.

"No law gives Mr. Card the authority to stay rules that have been signed, sealed, delivered and published," Claybrook said in a statement to the media. "It's urgent that these protections, which represent years of work by agency experts, move forward. If industry groups object to any final standards, they can petition for reconsideration, not use their financial connections to the Bush administration to try to rescind, delay, defang or derail these standards."

The Card memo sought to do even more than delay published rules. It required agencies to withdraw new proposed and final standards that had been sent to the Federal Register but had not yet been published. These included EPA rules to improve air quality and require monitoring of the environmental and health effects of genetically modified crops, and a USDA proposal to require packagers of hot dogs and ready-to-eat meats to test for the potentially deadly listeria pathogen. The memo set no time limit for the administration review and placed no restrictions on incoming Bush officials' ability to make wholesale changes or cancel the standards outright.

"The Card memo is just the opening skirmish in what we expect to be a protracted war between special interests and the public's interest under the Bush administration," said Congress Watch Director Frank Clemente. "We anticipate a return to the ways of the former Reagan and Bush I administrations, when important safeguards proposed by the agencies were sent into an OMB 'black hole,' where they were delayed for years, eviscerated or buried under the guise of administration 'review.' "

Card's memo was indeed the opening salvo in a new war on regulation. Bush soon announced he would reverse his campaign pledge to control emissions of carbon dioxide, the "greenhouse gas" that is a major contributor to climate change. He supported a successful congressional move to rescind an ergonomics rule to protect workers from repetitive stress syndrome, which had been under development for nine years. He said he would rescind a requirement that federal contractors comply with civil rights, workplace safety, environmental, tax and other laws.

The administration also announced plans, pushed by the meat industry, to eliminate salmonella testing of ground beef used in federal school lunch programs. That news made headlines. A day later, the administration backed away from the plan and blamed a low-level employee of the USDA for the announcement.[17]

While Bush was attacking individual health and safety standards, he also was moving to undermine government regulation in a more systematic way. In March, he appointed a Harvard academic named John D. Graham to head an obscure but powerful part of the OMB known as the Office of Information and Regulatory Affairs (OIRA). Graham, in effect, would be the nation's regulatory gatekeeper, with power to block or alter any new standards federal agencies had promulgated, even though such standards usually emerged only after years of scientific, engineering and economic analysis and with input from the public and regulated industries.

Public Citizen campaigned against his Senate confirmation. Researchers found that Graham — as director of the Harvard Center for Risk Analysis (HCRA) — had deep financial ties to regulated industries and that his research was based on methods that were biased toward corporate interests and against new protections. HCRA, founded 12 years earlier, had received money from more than 100 corporations and trade associations — a Who's Who of America's largest chemical, oil, energy, agribusiness, pharmaceutical, automotive and manufacturing companies. Companies like Exxon, Monsanto, Philip Morris (through a subsidiary) and others provided 60 percent of HCRA's funding.

Graham also had a long personal history of research and public relations work intended to discredit federal regulators and shoot down safety standards through the use of "cost-benefit" and "comparative risk" analyses that masqueraded as objective science. Graham had often downplayed risks from sources such as secondhand smoke and dioxin when talking to the news media and before Congress — without mentioning that he was being funded by the businesses involved.

Public Citizen's 100-page investigative report, "Safeguards at Risk: John Graham and Corporate America's Back Door to the Bush White House," written in Claybrook's office by legislative counsel Laura MacCleery, contained numerous examples of Graham's anti-regulatory bias.[18] It helped coalesce opposition to his Senate confirmation among many public interest groups and academics who became appalled by the nomination.

The Senate Governmental Affairs Committee, at the time controlled by the GOP, refused to allow Graham's opponents to testify in person. But Claybrook submitted written testimony summarizing the concerns of Public Citizen and its allies. "In ways the public and Congress may never know, the appointment of John Graham to this powerful office within the OMB could dramatically diminish the quality of the air we breathe, the wholesomeness of the food we eat and the safety of the cars we drive," Claybrook wrote to the committee.

Despite these alarms and a robust debate led by Senator Richard Durbin, an Illinois Democrat, the Senate confirmed Graham's nomination by a 61 to 37 vote on July 19, 2001. However, a clear message had been sent: that Public Citizen and other groups would monitor Graham's performance very closely.

Graham immediately went to work extending the Reagan-Bush anti-regulatory policies. He developed a set of controversial one-size-fits-all guidelines to make cost-benefit analyses even more demanding and time-consuming. He created so-called "peer review" guidelines, which barred agencies from using scientific data or releasing information to the public unless it had first gone through a cumbersome and industry-favored review process. He sought to burden the scientific evaluations that help agencies make health and safety decisions, and proposed to extend OIRA's purview to cover all agency "guidance" documents (non-binding advisory statements and information).

Public Citizen responded with its own critiques, congressional testimony and vigorous advocacy that cast light on this otherwise obscure OMB office. In the end, the peer review guidelines were watered down in ways that would not have happened without citizens' involvement and the risk-assessment bulletin was withdrawn.

Graham was just one of dozens of Bush appointees with strong ties to industry. Many had served as lawyers, lobbyists or executives for businesses that had contributed a total of $200 million or more to Bush's 2000 campaign and the Republican National Committee. Now those donors were getting their reward: Their operatives were moving into position to undermine public safeguards and change government policy.

Some examples: Mark Rey, a lobbyist for the timber industry, was named to head the Forest Service. Jeffrey Holmstead, a lawyer who had represented energy companies trying to block pollution regulations, became administrator for air and water at the EPA. Gail Norton, a protégé of former Reagan Interior Secretary James Watt and a longtime proponent of opening federal lands to industry exploitation, became Interior Secretary. Steven Griles, a lobbyist for the coal and oil industries, became deputy secretary at the Interior Department. Chuck Lambert, who had spent 15 years at the National Cattlemen's Beef Association, was put in charge of meat inspections at the USDA. Jacqueline Glassman, former senior counsel for DaimlerChrysler, was named chief counsel at NHTSA. Tom Scully, former CEO of the Federation of American Hospitals, was appointed to head the Centers for Medicare and Medicaid.

These were just a few of the industry foxes now guarding the public interest henhouse.[19]

The New Source Review Battle

Bush's appointees wasted little time before attacking all manner of health, safety and environmental safeguards. To illustrate the way the administration was working with industry to undermine public protections, Congress Watch produced a groundbreaking report in October 2003 — "EPA's Smoke Screen: How Deception of Congress, Campaign Contributions and Political Connections Gutted a Key Clean Air Rule" — about the administration's evisceration of an important rule called "new source review." It was a classic case study of the way the Bush administration and its allied industry insiders hijacked public policy for private gain.

Under the Clean Air Act of 1970, dozens of old coal-fired power plants had been "grandfathered," meaning they did not have to meet the act's new pollution control standards. To ensure that these old plants were eventually cleaned up, the EPA in 1977 established "new source review" rules requiring utilities to outfit the older plants with modern equipment to control pollution whenever an expansion or upgrade significantly increased emissions. But for more than two decades, the EPA had failed to enforce this law.

Finally, in 1999 and 2000, President Clinton's Justice Department and several states filed suit against nine utilities, claiming that 51 plants had been upgraded without the required pollution controls and were illegally emitting massive amounts of pollutants such as sulfur dioxide, a major cause of acid rain, and nitrogen oxides, a component of smog. The EPA estimated that bringing these plants into compliance with the law would reduce air pollution by nearly seven million tons per year, about half of all power plant air emissions.[20]

The utilities had a major financial stake in fighting these suits: Potential penalties could reach $50 million per plant,[21] and the required upgrades would cost billions. They found hope in the form of the pro-business governor from Texas who was starting his run for the presidency.

In May 1999, Thomas Kuhn, president of Edison Electric Institute, the industry's main trade association, solicited industry donations to Bush's 2000 campaign fund. A Public Citizen report showed that employees, executives and political action committees of the electric utility industry ponied up $4.8 million for the Bush campaign, the National Republican Committee and Bush's inauguration. That total included more than $2.3 million from utilities facing lawsuits.

The utilities got what they wanted. In October 2003, the EPA implemented a severely weakened new source rule that would allow utilities to spend as much as $160 million on upgrading old plants without worrying about whether they would be required to scrub pollutants more effectively.[22] "This appears to be the biggest rollback of the Clean Air Act in history," said Senator James Jeffords, the Vermont Republican who became an Independent in 2001.

Fourteen states, several cities and some environmental groups sued to stop the new rule, winning a December 2003 court order delaying its implementation. But the rule undermined the Justice Department's suits even while tied up in court. In

September 2004, EPA's inspector general reported that despite the court stay, the rule revision "has seriously hampered OECA [Office of Enforcement and Compliance Assurance] settlement activities, existing enforcement cases, and the development of future cases."[23]

Finally, in March 2006, a three-judge panel of the U.S. Court of Appeals for the District of Columbia Circuit ruled unanimously that the administration had acted in violation of the Clean Air Act in gutting the new source rule. New York Attorney General Eliot Spitzer, who led the state challenge, hailed the ruling as "a major victory for clean air and public health."[24]

The new source review rule was just one case in which the Bush White House used executive powers to try to undermine the federal safety net and environmental protection. A 2004 report by the Center for American Progress and OMB Watch, to which Public Citizen contributed, documented many other instances. Bush's EPA abandoned 62 rules that were under development during the Clinton years, while OSHA dropped 21 rules and the FDA dropped 57. The administration slashed EPA enforcement personnel by 12 percent. Average penalties for OSHA violations fell by 25 percent. FDA enforcement actions against misleading drug advertisements fell by almost 80 percent. And on numerous occasions, the White House suppressed or distorted scientific information.[25]

Bush also collaborated with Congress to attack regulations. In one of the biggest regulatory changes in decades, he sought and obtained congressional action to abolish the Public Utility Holding Company Act, a Depression-era law that regulated the financial transactions of electric and natural gas utilities. The law was widely credited with stabilizing an industry that had seen 53 holding companies go bankrupt in the Depression. It prevented utility executives from using ratepayer profits to finance risky investments unrelated to their core business. Public Citizen warned that repeal would lead to a wave of utility mergers that would bring higher prices and poorer service to consumers — and that is precisely what happened (see Chapter 9).

John Graham left OIRA in 2006, but that did not slow the attacks on regulation. Bush named Susan Dudley of the George Mason University-based Mercatus Center to replace him. Public Citizen geared up again and co-authored a report with OMB Watch, "The Cost Is Too High: How Susan Dudley Threatens Public Protections." It detailed some of Dudley's extreme views, winning key media coverage. This time the persistent advocacy by Public Citizen, OMB Watch, the Natural Resources Defense Council and others proved effective; the Republican-controlled Senate could not move the nomination out of committee, and Bush was forced to resort to a recess appointment.

Worse was yet to come. Bush decided to amend the Clinton executive order governing regulatory review. The White House opened 2007 with Executive Order 13422, which extended regulatory review to what it called "significant guidance documents," defined so broadly as to cover almost anything an agency might publish.

With this order in hand, Dudley drafted a memorandum on risk assessment that, as Public Citizen showed, would impose the very same industry-backed restrictions on calculating risks to the public that Graham had wanted. Dudley's memorandum went into effect and held until President Barack Obama revoked it soon after taking office in 2009.

Patrolling the Ramparts

Public outrage at President George W. Bush's attempts to eliminate regulations for business gave Joan Claybrook and Public Citizen's founding generation some real cause for hope that Americans still believe in a strong protective role for government. "The amazing thing is that considering these attacks on regulation, if you look at public opinion polls, whether it's 1983 or 1993 or today, there is strong public support for clean air and water rules, auto safety rules and workplace rules," Claybrook said.

As the end of Bush's second term neared, Claybrook's relentless optimism proved correct once again. The under-resourced Consumer Product Safety Commission had "suffered death by a thousand cuts" under Bush and Reagan, Public Citizen and its allies argued, failing to protect American consumers. Thousands of children had been hurt or sickened or even died from unsafe products.

These included 16-month-old Danny Keysar of Chicago, who was killed when a portable crib collapsed around him in 1998. Many millions of products had been recalled since then, shaking the confidence of parents in the safety of the toys and juvenile products on the market. So many recalls occurred in 2007 that media outlets dubbed it "the year of the recall."

Public Citizen and a coalition of other activist groups reasoned that members of Congress would hesitate to vote against a CPSC cleanup labeled "Danny's Law" after Danny Keysar. It worked. In mid-2008, Congress approved the Consumer Product Safety Improvement Act, making reforms at the CPSC that Public Citizen had been advocating almost since the agency came into existence. Not only did the measure ban lead and phthalates in toys (see Chapter 3), but it also created an open consumer complaint database, increased resources for the commission, raised its penalty powers and established protections for whistleblowers that remain today.

David Arkush, director of Public Citizen's Congress Watch division, summed up the organization's view after winning the decades-old fight: "This is a huge victory for consumers over big business," he said.

Endnotes

1   *Homeland Unsecured: The Bush Administration's Hostility to Regulation and Ties to Industry Leave America Vulnerable*, a Public Citizen report, October 2004.
2   Charlie Savage, "Chertoff Touts Chemical Plant Plan: But Industry Critics Contend Security Proposal Caters to Industry," *The Boston Globe*, March 22, 2006.
3   William Greider, "The Gipper's Economy," *The Nation*, June 28, 2004.
4   Executive Order 12291, issued by President Ronald Reagan, Feb. 17, 1981.

5 Standards and Labeling Requirements for Mechanically Separated (Species) and Products in Which It Is Used, 9 CFR Parts 317, 318 and 319, published in Federal Register on June 29, 1982.

6 Guy Darst, "EPA Officials Criticize White House Approach to Asbestos Proposal," Associated Press, April 16, 1985.

7 "Auto Makers Push for Reduced Regulation, Dow Jones News Service, Aug. 14, 1981. See also *Risking America's Health and Safety: George Bush and the Task Force on Regulatory Relief,* Public Citizen, October 1988, p. 4.

8 Joan Claybrook and the staff of Public Citizen, *Retreat from Safety: Reagan's Attack on America's Health,* Public Citizen, 1984, pp. xvi–xvii.

9 *Retreat from Safety: Reagan's Attack on America's Health,* p. xiv.

10 Nancy Watzman and Christine Triano, *All the Vice-President's Men: How the Quayle Council on Competitiveness Secretly Undermines Health, Safety and Environmental Programs,* Public Citizen and OMB Watch, September 1991, p. 1.

11 *The Quayle Council on Competitiveness: The Campaign Finance Connection,* Public Citizen's Congress Watch, March 1992, pp. 2–3.

12 Nancy Watzman and Christine Triano, *Voodoo Accounting: The Toll of President Bush's Regulatory Moratorium, January–August 1992,* Public Citizen's Congress Watch and OMB Watch, Aug. 27, 1992, p. 23.

13 *Who's Protecting Consumers? Federal Neglect of Consumer Protection,* prepared by Center for Media Education, Center for Science in the Public Interest, Citizen Action, Institute for Injury Reduction, National Consumers League, Public Citizen, and Public Voice for Food and Health Policy, October 1992.

14 *Saving Money, Saving Lives: The Documented Benefits of Federal Health and Safety Protections,* Public Citizen's Congress Watch, June 1995.

15 David Vladeck, "Under-Regulated?: Big Business Fights Health, Safety Standards that Save Lives, Money," *Public Citizen News: Special Anniversary Issue,* Vol. 21, No. 1, March 2001.

16 *Public Safeguards at Risk! A Compendium of Important Consumer, Workplace, and Environmental Safeguards Likely to be Affected by the Bush Administration's Recent Regulatory Freeze,* Public Citizen, Jan. 30, 2001 (updated Feb. 21, 2001).

17 Marc Kaufman and Amy Goldstein, "USDA Shifts Stance on Testing of School Beef; Agency to Continue Salmonella Screen," *The Washington Post,* April 6, 2001.

18 *Safeguards at Risk: John Graham and Corporate America's Back Door to the Bush White House,* Public Citizen, March 2001.

19 *Special Interest Takeover: The Bush Administration and the Dismantling of Public Safeguards,* The Center for American Progress and OMB Watch for The Citizens for Sensible Safeguards, May 25, 2004.

20 Internal EPA memo from Office of Enforcement and Compliance Assurance circulated to the Office of Air and Radiation prior to June 2002. Document obtained by the Natural Resources Defense Council and provided to Public Citizen.

21 U.S. Justice Department, Office of Legal Policy, "New Source Review: An Analysis of the Consistency of Enforcement Actions with the Clean Air Act and Implementing Regulations," January 2002.

22 "New Source Review Rule Change Harms EPA's Ability to Enforce Against Coal-fired Electric Utilities," Report No. 2004-P-00034, Office of Inspector General, U.S. Environmental Protection Agency, Sept. 30, 2004.

23 "New Source Review Rule Change Harms EPA's Ability to Enforce Against Coal-fired Electric Utilities," Report No. 2004-P-00034, Office of Inspector General, U.S. Environmental Protection Agency, Sept. 30, 2004.

24 Juliet Eilperin, "States Win Suit to Stop New EPA Regulations: Proposal Violated U.S. Clean Air Act," *The Washington Post,* March 18, 2006.

25 *Special Interest Takeover: The Bush Administration and the Dismantling of Public Safeguards,* The Center for American Progress and OMB Watch for The Citizens for Sensible Safeguards, May 25, 2004.

8
THE PHONY
"LAWSUIT CRISIS"

——

KIM TUTT WAS A LOYAL REPUBLICAN FROM TYLER, Texas, who proudly helped elect George W. Bush as her governor and then as president of the United States. In May 2001, four months after Bush moved into the White House, Tutt's life took a bad turn. What began as a toothache turned into a personal nightmare: She learned she didn't have long to live. Doctors removed a suspicious mass from her jaw, and laboratory reports said she had small-cell neuro-endocrine carcinoma, a fatal form of cancer. It was an extremely rare cancer for a young, otherwise healthy woman.

She said goodbye to her friends and family and told her two young sons they would have to grow up without her. At 34, the homemaker drafted her will and made other arrangements to spare her family as much pain as possible. "I had my funeral plan," she recalled. "I met with my preacher. I met with the people who were going to sing at my funeral."[1]

Then she learned of one way to steal some precious time, perhaps three months extra to spend with her family. It would be painful, but she figured she had nothing to lose after being given her diagnosis. So surgeons cut away the right side of her lower jaw, from the front of her mouth to behind her ear, in an attempt to excise the cancer. They took the fibula from her right leg and fashioned it into a new jaw to rebuild her face.

In July, as she awaited a second surgery, this time on her lungs, she received the second most profound shock of her life. Her death sentence had been over-turned. "The doctor called and said, 'I think we've got a problem.' What can be worse than 'you're going to die'?" she wondered. The surgeon then told her there had been a terrible mistake. Somewhere along the line, procedures had broken down in the pathology lab where her biopsy tissues were sent. In fact, she had never had cancer at all.

Tutt's excruciating pain, her disfigurement, her emotional scars had all been for naught. "I was in shock, and then I went from being in shock to being furious." Later, she discovered her sample had been contaminated by cancerous tissue from another patient, who later died from the disease Tutt had thought she had.

Almost two years later, Tutt learned that her president was complaining about lawsuits filed by people like her who faced debilitating and sometimes fatal injuries at the hands of medical professionals. On January 16, 2003, Bush appeared at the University of Scranton in Pennsylvania, surrounded by doctors in white coats, to campaign for a new law limiting payments to patients injured unnecessarily by doctors or hospitals. Belittling those who exercised their rights to sue doctors, he suggested that the court system was like a "giant lottery" and claimed the courts were clogged with "frivolous" and "junk" malpractice suits. He contended that these suits were driving up the cost of doctors' insurance premiums, forcing many out of business and making health care unaffordable.[2]

In an obviously coordinated public relations campaign, doctors began to hold large rallies and stage dramatic "walkouts" in states including Pennsylvania, New Jersey, West Virginia and Florida, where they claimed there was a "crisis" of unwarranted lawsuits against them. For the most part, journalists covered the events with barely an acknowledgment that there might be another side to the story. And Bush continued to call for limiting patients' right to sue.

The president, the insurance industry and the American Medical Association wanted Congress to pass a law dictating that juries could award malpractice victims only their economic losses — meaning lost wages, medical expenses and such — plus up to only $250,000 to compensate for their anguish, pain and disfigurement. The bill similarly protected nursing homes, hospitals and pharmaceutical companies from most liability.

Tutt felt betrayed by the president she had trusted. "I was absolutely livid," she said, "because I was living it. I had the inside scoop." She scoffed at the notion that she had won a lottery. It was true that her own economic losses amounted to very little. The medical bills were covered by her health insurance, although she had to reimburse those sums from the settlement she eventually received in a lawsuit against the pathology lab. But under Bush's proposal, her injury wasn't worth more than that — not nearly as much as if she had been a CEO making millions of dollars a year, whose restored wages would be enormous. "I thought, 'How can Republicans be this wrong? How can they think I'm not worth anything because I'm a housewife and a mother?'"

Tutt had suffered immensely. She endured 22 subsequent operations, including many to remove raging infections surrounding the metal implants that connected her teeth to her reconstructed jaw. She tore ligaments and tendons in her right knee because of her weakened, fibula-less leg.

Because of her experience, Tutt took issue with Bush's assertion that many lawsuits against doctors were unjustified or frivolous. Despite the obvious, horrible mistakes in her treatment, "it was so hard to even get my lawsuit filed because of all the red tape. You can't just make an accusation and get millions of dollars."

Blaming the Victims

Bush and the doctors had one thing right: Malpractice premiums were, in some states for some specialties, going through the roof. But Bush was blaming lawyers and injured patients for something that wasn't their fault. No evidence supported his claim that spiking insurance rates were caused by a surge in patient lawsuits. On the contrary, plenty of evidence showed that rising premiums were the direct result of a poor investment climate and bad business decisions by major insurers. Bush's explanation simply was not true.

Led by Joan Claybrook and Frank Clemente, who headed Congress Watch until 2006, Public Citizen mounted a furious campaign to refute the charges by Bush and the doctors' lobby. Combining meticulous research with aggressive outreach to the news media and lobbying on Capitol Hill, Public Citizen eventually released more than a dozen fact-based reports, some targeting states where lawmakers were considering similar restrictions. The organization also held press conferences featuring victims of negligent doctors who told their heart-rending stories to the news media.

The truth was that stock prices had nosedived after the technology market bubble burst in 2000 and again after the terrorist attacks of September 11, 2001. Interest rates on bonds remained extremely low. Insurers made their profits from investing the premiums paid by doctors, so when their investment income dropped, they raised rates sharply to cover their losses.

A former Texas insurance commissioner, J. Robert Hunter, documented this phenomenon in a 2002 study. Hunter, an actuary who had been head of the Federal Insurance Administration, examined all malpractice payouts over the previous three decades, as well as premiums doctors paid and the economic cycles of the insurance industry. He found that malpractice payments to injured patients, when adjusted for the rate of health care inflation, had remained virtually flat since the mid-1980s. He further showed that malpractice premiums rose and fell with the overall economy.[3]

Public Citizen then added a new element to the debate by analyzing information from the National Practitioner Data Bank—a database run by the Department of Health and Human Services with information about physicians who were disciplined by state medical boards, paid malpractice claims or had hospital privileges restricted or revoked. (Some statistical information from the data bank is public, but the names of doctors are available only to health maintenance organizations, hospitals, and state and federal regulators.) Public Citizen researchers discovered that just 5 percent of doctors in the country were responsible for 54 percent of all malpractice payouts.

The problem was that state medical boards, typically made up mostly of doctors, were loath to discipline their own. Just 17 percent of doctors who had made five or more malpractice payouts had been disciplined by their state board.[4] This statistic reinforced Public Citizen's argument that, beyond fundamental reform of the insurance industry, one way to rein in malpractice premiums was to crack down on the relatively few bad doctors who were responsible for most of the malpractice. The fact was picked up and used in hundreds of newspaper accounts of the malpractice debate, and it helped to turn the tide of public and media opinion.

While Bush was intent on limiting patients' rights, the truth was — and is — that medical mistakes are alarmingly common, and the vast majority of victims never manage to sue. In 1999, the Institute of Medicine reported that between 44,000 and 98,000 Americans die each year in hospitals due to preventable medical errors, costing society between $17 billion and $29 billion annually.[5] Yet little was being done about that. No federal program existed to reduce this preventable violence.

Instead, the medical lobby and insurers blamed the legal system and attacked personal injury lawyers as a proxy for patients and the court system. "Doctors are falsely demonizing America's legal system rather than saving tens of thousands of lives and litigation costs by preventing careless or unnecessary medical errors, such as operating on the wrong part of the body," Claybrook said in 2003.

Public Citizen argued its case on the grounds of fundamental fairness and morality. A $250,000 cap on noneconomic damages would discriminate against seniors, children and people like Kim Tutt who worked at home or otherwise earned little or nothing in wages. A well-paid CEO who suffered a crippling injury at the hands of a negligent doctor could be awarded millions in lost wages, but the jury award for a retiree with no salary would be limited to medical bills and $250,000 for a lifetime of pain and suffering. It would be the maximum compensation even for confinement to a wheelchair, loss of childbearing ability or permanent disfigurement.

Public Citizen pointed out that the boss of one major malpractice insurer earned $250,000 in just 10 days.

Another likely pernicious outcome of Bush's proposal was virtually ignored by the news media: The proposed cap would, in many cases, prevent legitimate victims of malpractice from ever getting their cases heard by a court — so there would be no accountability for negligent doctors. That's because plaintiff lawyers are paid only if they win. In many cases, these lawyers must invest large sums — often $200,000 or more — to fight deep-pocketed insurance companies. Bush's proposal limiting pain-and-suffering compensation would make it difficult for lawyers to recover their costs and fees in cases with little prospect of a sizable economic damage award. It meant that people with low-wage jobs, retirees, disabled people and homemakers would be much less likely than high-wage earners to receive any justice.

Overall, however, Public Citizen's arguments found a receptive audience among journalists and editorial writers; dozens of prominent newspapers nationwide opposed the caps. But the most dramatic event of the debate came in February 2003, when Public Citizen and the New York-based Center for Justice & Democracy hosted a forum for members of Congress and the news media to give malpractice survivors an opportunity to speak out in public.

One of those survivors was Linda McDougal, a U.S. Navy veteran who lived with her husband, also a Navy veteran, and her sons in the small town of Woodville, Wisconsin. Her story is eerily similar to Kim Tutt's. Like 182,000 other women each year, she had been diagnosed with breast cancer after a routine mammography and follow-up tests. She decided that a double mastectomy would give her the best chance for long-term survival. So she went under the knife. Only 48 hours later, her surgeon told her that she had never had cancer.

"My breasts were needlessly removed," she told a joint committee of Congress. "The pathologist switched my biopsy slides and paperwork with someone else's. Unbelievably, I was given another woman's results." Like Tutt, she continued to have complications, which in her case prevented reconstructive surgery. And like Tutt, her injuries were mostly noneconomic: serious pain and suffering.

"It is unfair to suggest that all victims should be limited to the same one-size-fits-all, arbitrary cap that benefits the insurance industry at the expense of patients," McDougal said. "Victims deserve to have their cases decided by a jury that listens to the facts of a specific case and makes a determination of what is fair compensation based on the facts of that case."[6]

Kathy Olsen of Chula Vista, California, also spoke at the press conference. Eleven years earlier, Olsen's 2-year-old son Stephen fell on a twig so that it penetrated his sinuses. Doctors operated and released him the same day. But when he became feverish and lethargic, his parents returned him to the hospital. The hospital refused to perform a CT scan, which would have cost $800 but also would have detected the abscess that was causing his problems. Untreated, Stephen was left blind and brain damaged.

At trial, a jury decided to award the family $7 million for Stephen's pain and suffering. Jurors were not told that the award would be reduced to $250,000 because California lawmakers had enacted that limit to damage awards in 1975. "Last month the president said the system looks like a giant lottery, and to that I say my son never purchased a ticket for this lottery," Kathy Olsen said. "If you think malpractice victims are somehow winners in some kind of lottery, I say look at Stephen Olsen."[7]

California Governor Jerry Brown later said he regretted signing the $250,000 cap, which was not indexed to inflation, but the number became a model for many other states and it remains California law today, with no effort by Brown to overturn it.

In July 2003, six months after doctors began walking out and on the eve of a Senate vote on the malpractice legislation, Public Citizen released startling data to journalists, demonstrating conclusively that the "lawsuit crisis" was a myth. No correlation existed between patient lawsuits and rising premiums. The number of malpractice payouts had actually declined by about 8 percent from 2001 to 2002—from 16,669 to 15,304. The money paid to injured patients also had fallen—from $4.5 billion in 2001 to $4.2 billion in 2002,[8] less than what Americans spent in 2000 on cat food.[9]

Payouts clearly weren't the cause of doctors' spiking insurance rates. Bush and the doctors were perpetuating a fraud on the public.

In the end, a Democratic-led effort to block a vote on the bill managed to kill the pernicious legislation. A handful of states (Texas, Florida, Ohio, Colorado, Oklahoma and West Virginia) did enact various limits on noneconomic damages in malpractice cases, and in 2004 and 2005, Alaska, Georgia, Illinois, Mississippi, Missouri and South Carolina passed similar restrictions.[10] Challenges by Robert Peck of the Center for Constitutional Litigation overturned some of these harsh laws. And legislation failed in other states the medical lobby had targeted. In most states, the limits, while still unfair to injured patients, are still not as draconian as the uniform national caps that Bush had sought.

In several states, voters rejected ballot initiatives to institute caps. Public Citizen played a major role in defeating initiatives in Oregon and Washington by issuing detailed reports and analyses refuting industry claims about a shortage of doctors and the cost of liability claims.[11] But Bush continued pressing for limits on malpractice lawsuits and even made it a major part of his second-term domestic agenda. With a new Democratic Congress in 2007, and Barack Obama's election in 2008, the prospects for enactment faded further. So business interests tried to open up a new front in the war — in the courts.

Under the corporate lobbying group with the Orwellian name "Common Good," led by Covington & Burling attorney Philip K. Howard, the doctors' and insurance associations proposed something they called "health courts." Far from promoting either health or justice, this clever variation on workers' compensation practices sought to remove judges and juries entirely from the court system. Instead, victims charging medical malpractice would present their cases to a tribunal of insurance company assessors who matched injuries to a pre-set schedule of compensation. In other words, representatives from the industry would determine how much compensation, if any, the industry should pay.

The industry mounted an aggressive campaign to sell this concept at the state and federal levels during the rest of Claybrook's time at Public Citizen. The organization fought back with persuasive information about the perils of a bureaucratic substitute for the time-tested jury system, and proof that false claims of excessive jury payout awards were unsubstantiated. The debate continued without resolution well into the next decade, but Congress passed no new limits.

The Treasure of the Tort System

Protecting consumers' legal rights is one of Public Citizen's primary missions, because the judiciary is the one branch of government that ordinary Americans can use to hold powerful institutions directly accountable for their actions. In the courts, the rule of law can trump politics. The U.S. tort system, which addresses complaints of civil harms, is a triumph of American democracy, in Public Citizen's view. A robust system of civil justice with trial by jury is key to ensuring a fair, safe marketplace for consumers and was written into the U.S. Constitution as the Seventh Amendment to combat autocratic rule as a product of the American revolt against King George III.

The government's regulatory system is charged with *preventing* harm, not compensating for it. The tort system advances both objectives. Regulation seeks to protect consumers from deceptive business practices, expose fraud and recall dangerous products, such as automobiles with design defects or prescription drugs that cause adverse reactions.

But regulation has its limits, in part because the agencies are controlled by the president and may be subject to political pressures. Regulations can be compromised by budget cuts, delays in rulemaking, congressional interference or politically appointed administrators more loyal to regulated industries than to the public. And regulatory standards can become obsolete over time as products and technologies change.

In contrast, the civil justice system of tort law helps ensure that manufacturers, and anyone in society, acts consistently with a forward-looking duty of care toward others. A vehicle, for example, may meet federal minimum standards and still be unreasonably dangerous. A jury would be justified in such a case to find that the vehicle manufacturer was negligent — and many juries have made just that finding.

Over time, information and pressure produced by litigation over harms can spur improvements in both product manufacturing and regulatory safeguards. The tort system therefore complements the regulatory system but plays a distinct role in identifying dangers that the regulatory system may overlook.

Another fundamental purpose of the civil justice system is to compensate people after they are injured as a result of wrongdoing and to deter misconduct that causes injury. Through punitive damages, it punishes corporations that recklessly and knowingly harm the public. Lawsuits decided by citizen juries reflect the community's conscience and ethical standards. When the regulatory system fails, as it too often does, the courts are there to ensure that people who are injured — often horribly — can seek redress and punish malfeasance.

"The regulatory and court systems mutually reinforce each other and they separately place disciplines on the market that have been there for five or six centuries, since the advent of English common law," said David Vladeck, former director of the Public Citizen Litigation Group.

When consumers or the environment are harmed, the ensuing costs must be borne by someone. If the entity causing the harm is shielded from this cost, it falls on the individual, or on society as a whole, to care for that person or clean up that place. Shielding those responsible means there is no deterrent to irresponsible behavior or hazardous products, so it is more likely that the cumulative costs will grow.

The Launch of "Tort Reform"

Over the past half century, citizen lawsuits have served a powerful societal purpose by cleaning up and deterring pollution, forcing lethal products off the market and publicly disclosing information about dangerous products, deceptive practices and malfeasance. This is precisely what enrages many corporate investors and executives: Lawsuits impose a measure of accountability and costs that they would prefer to avoid.

Limiting the ability of citizens to pursue justice in the courts has long been a Big Business goal. In the 1980s, corporate political strategists introduced the term "tort reform" to the nation's political lexicon. They pushed so-called "reform" legislation in state legislatures and Congress to limit consumers' access to the courts and to shield various industries from accountability for injuries and illnesses they caused.

Several large consortia of major companies mounted a long-running smear campaign against plaintiff lawyers, attacking the fundamental rights of Americans to seek redress in court from companies that produce or sell harmful products. In the ensuing two decades, the companies spent billions of dollars on this crusade.

Presidents Ronald Reagan and George H.W. Bush ignored the flimsy evidence of citizen abuses in the civil justice system and lent their personal support to the "reform" drive. This gave the effort significant momentum. Tobacco companies and other industries poured rivers of money into the public relations war chest, and Vice President Dan Quayle's Council on Competitiveness took up the issue with zeal. Solicitor General Kenneth Starr, a lawyer who had worked for Big Tobacco as well as General Motors (and who later gained fame as President Bill Clinton's Whitewater inquisitor), was assigned to develop a plan to overhaul the nation's civil justice system.

In a speech before the American Bar Association in August 1991, Quayle unveiled the "Starr Report" and its 50 recommendations for "tort reform," that he claimed were necessary to remedy a "self-inflicted competitive disadvantage." Most of the recommendations, such as severe limits on punitive damages, had been on corporations' wish lists for years and were part of their litmus test for campaign donations. President George H.W. Bush embraced the report and promised to make "reform" a top priority; he knew corporations hated to be sued.

In his speech, Quayle recited a long list of complaints about the existing justice system — most of them wildly distorted or inaccurate, it turned out. In remarks the following April before the National Practice Institute, Claybrook examined some of Quayle's claims.

Were there really, as Quayle asserted, 18 million civil cases filed in the United States in 1989 — one for every 10 adults, "making us the most litigious society" on the planet? Well, only if you counted all the many millions of small-claims complaints, traffic court disputes, divorces, child custody battles, wills and probate filings.

Had punitive damages, as the vice president declared, become routine, and were they being applied in an "arbitrary," even "freakish" manner? Not by any stretch.

Studies confirmed that punitive damages were only rarely awarded and were not increasing in severity. Quayle, like his business allies, could make his case only with distortions — what Ralph Nader called "Tort Deform." But because of Quayle's lofty position, the media often initially treated his untruthful statements as fact.

The Truth About the Horror Stories

An essential part of industry's campaign was dissemination of phony anecdotes. Almost always, these lawsuit "horror stories" depicted innocent businesses being forced to pay millions to undeserving plaintiffs or defend against "frivolous" claims. But in fact, the industry stories typically were inaccurate, incomplete and misleading.

President Reagan, for example, mocked an Oregon mechanic who sued Ford Motor Co. when a horse leaped in front of his Ford Pinto and crushed the car's roof, killing the man's wife. Why not sue the horse? But the trial revealed that the Pinto's roof did not comply with the federal roof strength standard.

Another tale, one that gained national notoriety, was about a woman who sued McDonald's restaurant after spilling hot coffee on herself. Business lobbyists used the story to suggest that the court system was seriously out of whack even to listen to such a charge. But the truth about Stella Liebeck was very different from what McDonald's and the business lobby led the public to believe.

Here's what really happened: Liebeck, 79, was sitting in her grandson's car as he pulled into a drive-through McDonald's in Albuquerque in 1992. She bought a cup of coffee, and he stopped the car while she lifted the lid on the Styrofoam cup to add cream and sugar. It was then that she spilled the entire contents on her lap. The coffee soaked through her sweatpants, causing third-degree burns to her thighs, buttocks and groin area.

A third-degree burn means full penetration of the burn through the skin. Nerves and sweat glands are destroyed, and skin grafts are required. Liebeck was hospitalized for eight days for skin grafting and was disabled for two years. She had permanent scarring. When she asked McDonald's to pay her $10,000 medical bill, the company offered her only $800. So she exercised her right to have a jury of her peers hear all the facts and arguments in her claim against the company.[12]

During the court case, it emerged that McDonald's had ordered its restaurants to serve coffee at between 180 and 190 degrees, hot enough to inflict third-degree burns in a few seconds and about 40 degrees higher than most other food establishments used at the time. Prior to the lawsuit, McDonald's had been warned that its coffee was served dangerously hot. In the 10 years before Liebeck's injuries, the company had received at least 700 complaints about serious scaldings and had settled claims for amounts as high as $500,000. At the trial, McDonald's officials testified that although they knew of the risks, they consciously decided not to lower the temperature of the coffee (they said it tasted better hot) or give any warnings — and they had no intention of changing their policies.

Shocked by the company's cavalier attitude toward customer safety, the jury awarded Liebeck $160,000 in compensatory damages and $2.7 million in punitive damages. The $2.7 million figure wasn't pulled out of a hat; it equaled two days of the company's profit on coffee sales. The judge reduced the award to $480,000. Either side could have appealed, but Liebeck reached a settlement with McDonald's. The amount of the final settlement was not disclosed but was lower than $480,000.

Despite the facts of the case and the obvious harm to Liebeck, advocates of restricting consumer rights seized upon her case as evidence of a crisis in the civil justice system. The idea, of course, was to spread the image of greedy lawyers, unwarranted lawsuits and massive punitive damages charged to blameless companies. Liebeck could not respond because she had agreed as a condition of her settlement with McDonald's not to discuss the case.

But McDonald's was not similarly limited and began publicizing its version of the case. Public Citizen then contacted Liebeck's daughter, who told the real story, and *Newsweek* magazine gave it several pages of coverage. But it was too late. The version told by McDonald's became the new reality, and decades later, her case is still the subject of ridicule by late-night talk show hosts. Later, Public Citizen assisted director Susan Saladoff in making "Hot Coffee," a film that told the real story. It was shown at the Sundance Film Festival in 2011 and on HBO.

Big Tobacco Weighs In

The early 1990s saw the rise of an "astroturf" — or fake grassroots — campaign to back legislation curbing consumers' legal rights. The American Tort Reform Association had been formed in 1986 as a coalition to coordinate more than 300 major corporations and trade associations in this effort. In the early 1990s, as documented in a Public Citizen report published in 2000,[13] the group contracted with a Washington, D.C. public relations firm connected to the tobacco industry to build a network of local organizations that would be mouthpieces for tort law change, creating the illusion of a citizen movement.

By the end of the decade, dozens of such organizations operated in at least 18 states. They were known generally as Citizens Against Lawsuit Abuse groups (although they had no citizens as members) and received much of their financial and organizational support from the American Tort Reform Association and Big Tobacco, which had started pouring millions into the product liability campaign in the mid-1980s. Other corporate front groups, such as Citizens for a Sound Economy, joined the fray.

Big Tobacco's role in the tort movement was largely invisible to the public, and that's the way tobacco companies wanted it. But the Public Citizen report, "The CALA Files: The Secret Campaign by Big Tobacco and Other Major Industries to Take Away Your Rights," was based in part on internal industry documents released during lawsuits against tobacco companies. It showed that the industry played a major role in helping to create the political climate to "reform" away citizens' legal rights.

In 1985, the industry faced a consumer lawsuit that it feared could open the door for future liability claims by injured smokers. So the Tobacco Institute, the industry's chief lobbying outfit, formed the "Ad Hoc Committee on Tort Reform" to "pursue the industry's interests in tort reform and product liability legislation being considered in the states." Two years later, in 1987, the industry celebrated two huge victories: New Jersey and California both passed laws that helped protect tobacco companies from future claims by smokers. After the New Jersey vote, it was revealed that the industry had poured an astonishing $940,000 into the effort to get the bill passed.

Big Tobacco quickly took its campaign to statehouses across America. In 1989, the industry spent nearly $7 million on state efforts. It also formed a "Tort Reform Project" that grew into a sophisticated, $15-million-a-year operation by 1995. In addition to funding Citizens Against Lawsuit Abuse groups, often covertly, Big Tobacco sought to undermine the credibility of scientific studies about the dangers of secondhand smoke and, in the report's words, to associate "fear studies with plaintiff-lawyer greed."

Scores of new restrictive tort laws passed in every state except Delaware. Most of them made it more difficult for consumers to collect adequate damages for their injuries — 34 states enacted new restrictions on punitive awards.[14] Public Citizen actively opposed the limitations in a number of states as well as in Congress. The courts later viewed many of these anti-consumer tort law restrictions with suspicion, however, and dozens of them have since been struck down on constitutional grounds.

While industry had little success with legislation at the federal level and while some state tort law changes were thrown out, the system was damaged. "They've done enough damage that in some states, certain kinds of lawsuits are no longer brought because recoveries are inadequate," said Vladeck.

He described an auto injury case of the 1990s that was dropped in Michigan, which has a statutory cap on pain and suffering damages. "The defect in the car was rare enough and hard to prove, and it would have cost the plaintiffs more money in experts than they could have possibly gotten in damages — even though their experts were absolutely convinced that there was a design defect in the car."

One of the states where big business enjoyed the most success was Texas, where George W. Bush was elected governor in 1994. Bush had earlier served on an advisory board to the right-wing Texas Public Policy Foundation, where he wrote to other businessmen about a "runaway tort system" that gave plaintiffs huge punitive damages.

As soon as he entered the governor's mansion in 1995, he declared a "state of emergency" in the civil justice system. He pressed state lawmakers to enact sweeping changes in product liability laws to protect corporations from Texans who had been injured and were seeking justice. Much of his agenda, including a punitive damages cap of $750,000, was signed into law.[15] His chief adviser, Karl Rove, understood that lawyers who represented Texas consumers were significant contributors to Democratic candidates and that limiting their lawsuit recoveries would pinch them financially. The political capital Bush earned with business interests in Texas helped propel him to the GOP nomination for president five years later.

Defending the right of the American people to seek compensation in court for deaths and injuries caused by faulty products is one of Public Citizen's most enduring principles. Standing up for this principle, Public Citizen fended off both narrow and broad federal tort law changes that would have had the effect of denying citizens the right to be compensated for injuries caused by defective products and to punish corporate wrongdoers for deliberate acts that kill or maim.

Public Citizen also helped defeat many bills designed to immunize some corporations, such as asbestos manufacturers and tobacco companies, from liability. The tobacco industry especially deserved its days in court for the decades in which it lied to the American public, manipulated nicotine levels and marketed deadly products to teens.

The Gingrich Attack

In the 1994 elections, Republicans took control of the House of Representatives, and Speaker Newt Gingrich pledged to enact his 10-point "Contract with America" within the first hundred days. One of the planks was called "The Common Sense Legal Reform Act." Purporting to "stem the endless tide of litigation," the legislation was little more than the same set of proposals that corporate America had been pushing for more than a decade.

A pitched political battle erupted as Public Citizen and hundreds of other groups coalesced to fight the GOP's attempt to impose uniform federal restrictions on the courts.

As had been the case in earlier corporate campaigns, no "crisis" that warranted congressional action in fact existed. First, there was no explosion in product liability claims. Data showed that product liability suits made up fewer than four of every 1,000 civil filings in state courts.[16] Excluding asbestos cases, these suits had declined in federal courts by almost 40 percent since 1985.[17] According to the Rand Institute for Civil Justice, a group funded in part by the insurance industry itself, only one in 10 people injured by dangerous or defective products ever filed suit for compensation.[18]

One of the primary myths the American Tort Reform Association tried to sell was that product liability suits were driving up the cost of insurance for businesses to levels that harmed the economy. The facts, however, were that such insurance at the time cost just 26 cents per $100 of retail product sales—a small price to pay to preserve the consumer's right to sue and the deterrent effect of that right on manufacturer decisions. Since 1987, total product liability insurance premiums had in fact dropped by 47 percent, from $4 billion to $2.6 billion in 1993.[19] By comparison, Americans were spending about the same—$2.86 billion a year—on bottled water.[20]

The centerpiece of the Gingrich tort legislation was again the cap on punitive damages at $250,000 or twice the compensatory damage award, whichever was greater. This alone would have shredded the system that had served Americans well for so long.

As the name implies, punitive damages are meant to punish defendants for wrongful acts and deter reckless or malicious misbehavior. Many dangerous and defective products — including the hazardous Ford Pinto gas tanks, the Dalkon Shield intrauterine device and silicone breast implants — had been removed from the market in part because of punitive damages. In addition, an untold number of products had been made safer in response to such awards — such as children's sleepwear that is now flame-retardant, toxic household chemicals that now contain warning labels, tractors that are now equipped with roll bars and chainsaws that have safety hand guards.

Clearly, removing the threat of large punitive damage awards would permit corporations to produce and sell products they knew were dangerous without fear of being held accountable. Besides, no evidence existed for any epidemic of frivolous awards.[21] Between 1965 and 1990, in fact, only 355 punitive damages were awarded in all the state and federal product liability lawsuits nationwide — an average of just 14 per year, according to a study by law professor Michael Rustad of the Suffolk University School of Law.[22] Of these, only 35 were larger than $10 million, and all but one of those were reduced. Eleven of the 35 were reduced to zero.[23]

The proposed cap on punitive damages, like medical malpractice award limits, would have had a particularly harsh impact on injured people with low incomes. Unless a state allows full "pain and suffering" compensation, only awards punishing the offending company assure that low-income people will be treated fairly.

Public Citizen realized that with anti-consumer corporate interests firmly in control of the House, the product liability bill probably could not be stopped there. But the Senate looked more promising. As Senate debate was about to begin, Public Citizen invited victims of defective products to come to Washington, D.C., to tell their stories. In a dramatic press conference in April 1995, these citizens appealed to the Senate to defeat the measure that would deprive them of justice.

Ray Romine of Miami told of losing his wife and suffering debilitating burns when his General Motors pickup truck burst into flames after a car hit it on the passenger side. The company had designed the truck with "side-saddle" gas tanks outside the main frame, and despite knowing for years that fuel-fed fires in these vehicles were causing hundreds of deaths and injuries, the company had failed to fix the defect or warn owners.

Internal documents revealed that GM executives consciously chose not to make the repair after a cost-benefit analysis said fixes to prevent fire deaths would benefit GM's bottom line only if they cost less than $2.20 per vehicle. By removing the threat of punitive damages, the proposed Senate bill "will encourage corporations to engage in this type of cost-benefit analysis," Romine said at the press conference. "Do not allow corporations to make this callous type of calculation. The corporate accountants cannot calculate their company's potential liability if the size and frequency of punitive damages are unpredictable."

Public Citizen poured great energy into the public relations and lobbying campaign to defeat the legislation. Claybrook and others worked for months to bring out the truth. Industry, meanwhile, put its more massive resources into the battle. Business lobbying coalitions represented by the American Tort Reform Association and The Product Liability Alliance had contributed nearly $62 million to House and Senate members in the previous six years, not counting unlimited "soft money" donations to the political parties.[24] The two business-funded groups also reportedly spent $6 million on radio ads that perpetuated falsehoods about the civil justice system.[25]

After a fierce debate lasting almost two weeks, the Senate overcame a defensive filibuster and approved the regressive legislation by a 61 to 37 vote. It was the first time the Senate had ever passed a measure curbing product liability, despite considering similar bills since the early 1980s. In a last-ditch effort, Public Citizen and its allies, including many victims, submitted a series of appeals and extensive documentation of the reality to President Bill Clinton, and — fortunately for consumers — he vetoed the bill.

Three years later, in 1998, corporate America revived its attack. This time, Senators Jay Rockefeller of West Virginia, a Democrat, and Republican Slade Gorton of Washington negotiated what supporters called a "reasonable compromise" with Vice President Al Gore. But the bipartisan bill still would have imposed what Public Citizen regarded as intrusive federal mandates. "This bill," said Claybrook, "would relieve corporations of full responsibility for their misconduct — even if their acts are intentional and no matter how grievously their products injure."

With Public Citizen and its allies again denouncing the legislation, proponents failed to muster the 60 votes needed to force a vote, and the bill died. Rockefeller, after conversations with Clinton about the broad impact of product liability limits, became an opponent of those limits and never authored such a measure again.

Accountability on Asbestos

Although the combined might of global corporations failed to rewrite America's product liability laws, individual industries and companies frequently have demanded that Congress grant separate, special legal protections. In one such episode, manufacturers of asbestos products tried to escape legal liability for the countless deaths and incidence of disease associated with their products.

Asbestos was used for decades as a fire retardant and in insulation in consumer products, buildings and machinery. Its fine grains and fibers caused tens of thousands of deaths from lung cancers and related illnesses, and many victims filed and won hundreds of lawsuits. In 1993, a coalition of 20 companies that manufactured or used asbestos products persuaded a federal judge to approve the settlement of a class-action lawsuit that would cover as many as 20 million people.

The settlement established a workers' compensation-style system that included future asbestos victims — people who had already been exposed in the workplace but were not yet diagnosed with cancer or another asbestos-related disease, which often emerges years later. Public Citizen, representing a number of asbestos advocacy groups, labor unions and class members, challenged the settlement on the grounds that it provided only miserly compensation to many, particularly to future claimants, and would effectively prevent millions of people from seeking a remedy in court.

In 1996, Public Citizen and other lawyers representing the class members persuaded an appellate court to overturn the settlement. That victory later was upheld by the U.S. Supreme Court.

Undeterred, one of the companies, GAF Corporation, embarked on an extraordinary lobbying campaign in 1998 and 1999 to persuade Congress to approve a similar scheme that would tie the hands of future asbestos plaintiffs. GAF had in previous years manufactured building products containing asbestos, so GAF and its multi-millionaire owner, Samuel Heyman, wanted Congress to require many workers and their families to forgo compensation for any injuries asbestos had caused.

Under the proposal, asbestos victims would face new, restrictive criteria for the types of lung cancer for which they could recover damages. Awards to most workers with pleural plaques (thickening of the wall of the lungs) caused by asbestos would be barred. The bills would have protected corporations even when they had full knowledge that the asbestos exposures might cause severe injury or death.

Heyman, reckoned to be worth $800 million, owned 97 percent of the stock in GAF, which ranked 187th on the Forbes Top 500 Private Companies list. By March 2000, the company had paid out $1.2 billion in asbestos claims and had more than 100,000 claims still pending.[26] Heyman was fighting all of those, and when talking to legislators, they knew his pockets were deep. Researchers at Public Citizen's Congress Watch found that GAF, its political action committee, and Heyman and his family had given $360,220 to parties and candidates between 1995 and 1999. The researchers also found that the money given to politicians had risen sharply after the company's defeat in court.

"Based on the timing of these campaign contributions and pro-GAF legislative action by both Republicans and Democrats," the researchers wrote, "there is a strong circumstantial case of a relationship between a candidate's and a party's receipt of GAF/Heyman financial support and congressional support of the company's asbestos legislation." For example, in 1998, GAF gave $70,000 to fundraising committees controlled by Democratic New York Senator Charles Schumer, and in 1999, Schumer became a co-sponsor of the GAF-inspired bill.

Similarly, the 12 House co-sponsors of the bill each received $1,000 from GAF's political action committee within four months. And apart from such direct donations, GAF spent vast sums on lobbying: $1.5 million in 1998 and a staggering $4.9 million the following year.

Public Citizen saw that its Supreme Court victory was in danger of being overtaken by new legislation. Its lobbying intensified, along with work with allies to expose the connection between asbestos industry money and members of Congress. Key to the battle was a Sunday article in *The New York Times* that laid out the industry

lobbying campaign and its connections to individual members of Congress supporting the measure. The proposal was defeated in both 1998 and 1999.

The losses weakened asbestos industry influence, but it wasn't long before
another generation of companies entangled in asbestos litigation saw new opportunities to press their interests.

At the beginning of George W. Bush's administration, the industry injected
significant cash into campaigns and unleashed an army of high-priced lobbyists on
Congress. By 2005, Senator Arlen Specter, the moderate Pennsylvania Republican (later
Democrat) who chaired the Judiciary Committee, and Vermont Senator Patrick Leahy,
the committee's ranking Democrat, sponsored a bill to ban all state-law asbestos lawsuits, instead giving a select group of victims access to a meager compensation scheme.
Most important, the new bill drastically slashed the future liability of companies that
used asbestos (such as auto companies) for injuries caused during their years of deceit.

Bipartisan sponsorship made this bill the most formidable threat to date. Public
Citizen jumped in with its signature multi-pronged defense. Researchers produced
an investigative report that laid bare the secretive lobbying campaign of the asbestos
industry and companies that use asbestos, and the staggering financial savings it
hoped to win in return. At the same time, Public Citizen's Health Research Group
rallied leading lung specialists around a blistering critique of the bill's unscientific
medical standards.

Public Citizen lobbyists, able as usual to cross the partisan divide, teamed up
once again with fiscal conservatives to warn that inadequate financing would leave
taxpayers holding the tab. As the coup de grâce, Public Citizen debunked the industry's fraudulent claims that justified the bill in the first place — that courts were
buckling under a crushing load of asbestos cases and that corporate bankruptcies
driven by asbestos lawsuits were hurting the economy. The bill seemed headed for
passage in the Senate, but at the eleventh hour, in a victory for asbestos victims, it
was defeated by a single vote.

Federal vs. State Regulations

Government agencies and the standards they set are a first line of protection
for citizens against dangerous products or unsafe workplaces. But sometimes agencies' standards don't afford adequate protection for consumers. Standards also may
become outdated by new technology or the passage of time, or an agency may set no
standards at all for particular hazards, even if it has authority to do so.

In an attempt to insulate themselves from state laws, companies often argue
that the mere existence of a federal regulation, however weak or flawed, overrides
state authority and provides immunity from accountability for state-law claims. This
theory is known as "federal pre-emption."

Fast-food companies, for example, used the pre-emption argument in an
attempt to invalidate a 2008 New York City law that required restaurants to include

the calorie content of dishes on their menus. The companies pointed to the federal law giving restaurants choices about menu labeling and argued that this requirement pre-empted any effort by New York City to impose menu labeling requirements, such as calorie content. Representing a group that included a member of Congress and the American Medical Association, Public Citizen helped persuade the federal judge that the city ordinance should prevail — a victory for consumers' waistlines.

Regulated industries routinely lobby the executive branch to weaken or remove federal safeguards. Then, when their products cause harm, they sometimes try to hide behind those same safeguards, arguing that because the federal government regulates the products, consumers cannot bring state-law claims — claims based on defective design or failure to warn of hazards associated with their products — seeking redress for that harm. Because federal law offers consumers no means to sue for harm caused by consumer products, the argument that federal regulation pre-empts state-law claims, when accepted, leaves consumers with no avenue for seeking redress for injury caused by a company's harmful product.

For example, medical device manufacturers have argued since the early 1990s — and the federal courts have often held — that Food and Drug Administration (FDA) regulations should override state laws that provide a remedy for defective medical devices. (Medical devices include pacemakers, knee implants and a wide variety of medical products.) Although FDA regulations were designed to protect consumers from defective medical devices, companies were invoking the rules to escape liability under state law when their devices injured patients — even when the FDA had conducted little or no review of the particular devices' safety before allowing them on the market.

One notable lawsuit involved Lora Lohr, a young Florida woman whose defective pacemaker nearly killed her. The pacemaker was manufactured by Medtronic, Inc., the world's largest medical device manufacturer. When Lohr sued under Florida law for compensation for her injuries, Medtronic argued that because the FDA had permitted the company to market its pacemakers, it was immune from accountability when the devices injured patients.

Public Citizen attorneys represented Lohr on appeal and in the U.S. Supreme Court, arguing that federal regulation did not block her right to sue. In 1996, the Supreme Court agreed, allowing Lohr's claims to go forward. "The Supreme Court precedent is important, because it makes clear that general federal regulatory requirements ordinarily do not destroy an injured party's right to compensation under state law," said Brian Wolfman, the Public Citizen lawyer who argued the case. "But this area of law is fraught with peril for consumers, which is why we watch it closely and help lawyers less familiar with this area."

Despite the Supreme Court victory, businesses kept pressing the issue, with support from President Bush's FDA. In a 2007 case, the FDA reversed the position it had taken under the Clinton administration. Now it argued that federal marketing approval of medical devices did bar injured patients from filing state-law tort suits.

Again, Public Citizen represented an injured patient at the Supreme Court. This time, however, the court sided with the company.

Around the same time, Public Citizen also argued at the Supreme Court for 18 patients who had suffered serious liver damage after taking the diabetes drug Rezulin. Here again, the manufacturer argued that it should be immune from liability — even though the drug had been withdrawn from the market in 2000 after causing 63 deaths from liver damage. The FDA sided with the company. In this case, however, the patients prevailed in a 4-4 Supreme Court decision in 2008.

In 2005, Public Citizen discovered that the Bush administration had begun a new strategy to grant immunity to manufacturers of dangerous products. It was inserting expansive language into regulations governing things like automobiles and prescription drugs, asserting that federal regulations pre-empted state common law.

In November 2005, for example, the National Highway Traffic Safety Administration (NHTSA) proposed a new standard governing the amount of force that a motor vehicle's roof must withstand in a rollover crash. Such crashes were killing 10,000 people every year, mainly because roofs routinely crushed in when vehicles flipped. But the new standard was so feeble that even NHTSA acknowledged it would save fewer than 50 lives per year. And embedded within its long introductory section was an assertion that, because NHTSA regulated the safety of motor vehicle roofs, consumers injured by crushed roofs could not sue automakers that complied with the rules — even if they were severely hurt or killed because of the unsafe design.

This pre-emption language would not carry the force of law, but Public Citizen feared it could strengthen the hand of business lawyers arguing to dismiss liability cases. This would further chip away at consumer protections. The strategy was a new one on the part of the Bush administration, and Joan Claybrook spelled it out for the public:

"This is an attempt to effectively shut the courthouse doors on consumers, and it would remove incentives for manufacturers to make safe vehicles when minimal government standards are insufficient or outdated, or are not well enforced," she said in a 2005 statement. "It also would burden the taxpayers with the costs of these crashes."

In 2008, actor Dennis Quaid and his wife made pre-emption a national news story. The previous year, their infant twins had nearly died because they were mistakenly given adult doses of the blood thinner Heparin instead of an anticoagulant for infants, Hep-Lock. The two drugs' blue labels were confusing and their bottle sizes were similar, but Baxter Healthcare Corp. had refused to recall the bottles then on the market. Quaid sued, and Baxter used the pre-emption argument in asking the courts to drop the suit.

"My family blessedly survived a huge drug error," Quaid testified at a congressional hearing, where he was represented by Public Citizen attorneys. If Congress allows broad pre-emption of state-law remedies, he warned, "society will lose one of the most effective incentives for safer drugs."

Pre-emption remained a battlefield through the rest of Claybrook's tenure, and Public Citizen and its allies continued to prevail. No federal pre-emption statute had been enacted by 2015.

Improving Class-Action Lawsuits

Public Citizen has always supported the proper use of class actions as a crucial way to ensure that consumers who cannot afford to sue individually can group together to hold corporations and the government accountable for wrongdoing. Increasingly, though, corporations began to include pre-dispute binding arbitration provisions in consumer and employment contracts. In these clauses, the consumer or worker "agrees" to resolve any dispute in arbitration, not in court, and agrees not to raise any disputes as class actions.

Companies began to try to enforce these provisions in courts around the country, knowing that, in many cases, individual consumers did not lose enough money to justify a lawyer's costs in bringing separate suits. Therefore, the ban on class actions would effectively make the companies immune from liability.

Initially, the lower courts held such provisions to be unenforceable under state contract law. In 2010, however, the Supreme Court agreed to hear a case called *AT&T Mobility v. Concepcion*, which presented the question of whether the Federal Arbitration Act overrides state laws invalidating these provisions. Public Citizen stepped in to argue before the high court. Unfortunately, in a 5 to 4 decision, the court held that the Federal Arbitration Act pre-empts state law disallowing class actions bans, when the bans are included in arbitration agreements. Many disputes subject to forced arbitration agreements involve wrongdoing that affects large numbers of people but for only small amounts of money, making individual cases infeasible. The *Concepcion* decision, therefore, has effectively barred redress for numerous consumers injured by corporate abuses.

While recognizing the value of class-action lawsuits, Public Citizen also recognized that some class actions mostly end up benefiting the lawyers for both parties more than they benefit class members. This not only is bad for consumers, but it also helps business interests intent on curbing consumer rights. Public Citizen therefore has represented class members who object to unfair settlements.

One type of abuse that Public Citizen fought was the bogus coupon settlement, in which class members received nearly worthless and often nontransferable discounts for future purchases of the defendant's product in exchange for giving up their claims. Corporate defendants like coupon settlements because they cost the company very little (most recipients never use them) and provide free product promotion. To secure these inexpensive endings, they are happy to pay large fees to plaintiff attorneys who agree to such settlements, corrupting the class-action process.

A prime example was a case involving more than five million GM pickup trucks equipped with side-saddle gas tanks. When other vehicles hit these trucks from the side, they tended to explode into flames. More than 1,800 people died in these fiery crashes between 1973 and 2000 — 20 times the carnage from the infamous Ford Pinto, which could explode when hit from the rear.

Although NHTSA investigated the defect in the GM pickups, political appointees in the Justice Department pressed the agency to reach a financial deal with GM rather than requiring a vehicle recall. GM also faced a flurry of class-action lawsuits. Under a proposed settlement, truck owners would receive coupons worth $1,000 toward the purchase of a new GM truck or van. If the recipient or a close family member did not want to buy a new vehicle, the coupon was worthless. This settlement also did nothing to repair the four million dangerous GM trucks still on the road.

Public Citizen challenged the settlement, representing its allied organization the Center for Auto Safety and a group of truck owners, and got the settlement overturned by the 3rd U.S. Circuit Court of Appeals. After several more years of litigation, a final settlement was reached. Under this one, truck owners would still receive the $1,000 coupons, but a secondary market would be created where class members could sell the coupons for cash if they didn't want another GM product. GM later challenged the way the sales mechanism was structured as going beyond the agreement, and its appeal derailed the secondary market. But Public Citizen had made its point about coupons.

GM also paid $3 million into an independent fire-safety research fund under the settlement, while fees received by plaintiff attorneys established another independent $1 million fund to research a way to retrofit the trucks to make them safer. Such a retrofit, costing about $300 per truck, was developed and announced jointly in April 2001 by the Center for Auto Safety and Public Citizen.

The GM case also was an important precursor to a landmark 1997 Supreme Court decision in which Public Citizen attorneys, working with members of the private bar, established critical rights for consumers in class actions. In *Amchem Products v. Windsor*, a group of class-action plaintiffs' lawyers and 20 major asbestos companies had agreed to replace the court system with a compensation system for future asbestos victims. Public Citizen argued that lawyers should not be able to bargain away the rights of future plaintiffs. The Supreme Court agreed and disallowed the settlement.

"Sometimes a Supreme Court victory is more important not for where it takes the law, but because of what would have been had we lost the case," said Brian Wolfman, the Public Citizen lawyer who handled *Amchem*. "If the Supreme Court had allowed the class-action device to replace the court system for future asbestos cases, it would have been only a matter of time before the auto industry, the pharmaceutical industry and the financial services industry would be constructing class actions to escape future liability. Victims would not be compensated, and the civil justice system would no longer serve as a deterrent to wrongful corporate conduct."

Public Citizen also has intervened to improve the administration of class-action settlements and ensure that recoveries are fairly distributed to the victims. One case involved a fund that a settlement had created for victims of a defective bone screw that tended to break once implanted in a patient's spine. The court set a deadline for filing claims that was strictly enforced, even though late filers posed no harm to the class—and in fact, most late filers learned of the settlement only after the deadline had passed.

Amazingly, lawyers for the class supported the strict deadline despite its devastating effect on their clients. Public Citizen challenged these decisions and won a victory in the 3rd U.S. Circuit Court of Appeals (*Sambolin v. Acromed*). As a result, 208 claimants obtained some $4.5 million in damages.

In some class actions, some plaintiffs filed valid objections to a proposed settlement. Other times, an objection was little more than extortion, in which the objectors agreed to drop the complaint in exchange for a cash payment. These payments typically were made under the table, outside the judicial process.

Public Citizen lawyers argued that these side agreements were improper and should be illegal. "We've objected to this practice, but it has accelerated and it is a real bane to class-action practice, because what it is doing is setting up a market where people who object are being bought off," Vladeck said. "We think that is a very serious and bad turn of events. By all appearances, these are bribes."

Due largely to a Public Citizen case and testimony before a federal judicial panel, the federal class-action rule was changed to require that settlements with objectors be publicly disclosed and approved by the court.

Public Citizen's efforts had helped strengthen the class-action system, but many members of Congress were still intent on disabling it if they could. In 2000, Congress took up legislation to move most multi-state class actions and many single-state ones from state court to federal court. Public Citizen lobbied hard for five years against the bill, because class-action suits usually are based on state laws, and federal judges may be reluctant to let them to go forward.

A filibuster initially stopped the bill in the Republican-controlled Senate, but it was finally broken by a few Democrats, including Mary Landrieu of Louisiana and Chris Dodd of Connecticut, subsequently joined by Charles Schumer of New York and the newly elected Senator Barack Obama of Illinois. All knew their votes would lock many meritorious claims out of court, and Public Citizen lobbying helped moderate some of the most restrictive provisions. But the business drive to federalize many class actions succeeded in 2005.

The end of 2005 also witnessed one of the Bush administration's most aggressive assaults against the civil justice system. As the first session of Congress was ending, Senate Majority Leader Bill Frist, a Tennessee Republican, defied legislative procedure and democratic process by sneaking an early holiday present for the drug industry into a defense spending bill. The measure, unrelated to military spending, gave drug companies virtual immunity from lawsuits involving products used in an epidemic. It trumped state law, prohibiting states from offering their citizens additional protections. And it included only the façade of a compensation plan—all words, no funding—so that victims of defective or dangerous drugs would have to fend for themselves.

A Public Citizen report showed that Frist's midnight maneuver came after members of the House-Senate conference committee negotiating the bill had already signed off on the final version that both chambers would be asked to pass. Only then did Frist and House Speaker Dennis Hastert insert the 40-page liability shield—which had never been seen, debated or voted on by any member of Congress—above the signatures of the committee members.

This subterfuge, the product of White House negotiations with the drug industry, provoked an outcry from both sides of the aisle when the language was discovered. But members of Congress feared that holding up military spending in a time of war would make them vulnerable to being branded unpatriotic. Congress passed the bill overwhelmingly, with the drug company immunity provision intact, and it remains in place today.

━━━━━

If the fight to assure consumer safety and justice has proven anything, it is that winning new laws is not enough. Corporations have a history of using underhanded tactics to bypass or neutralize laws they oppose and exploiting back channels—from Congress to regulatory agencies, to the Office of Management and Budget, to enforcement funding and so on. But they tend to fear the power of the courts precisely because the courts operate in a public process that is less susceptible to the corrupting influences of politics and money. The courts' basic function is to preserve the rule of law.

Public Citizen's work in preserving access to the courts is therefore crucial. It is not a splashy enterprise that generates big headlines, nor is it particularly well understood by non-lawyers. Yet to deter reckless manufacturers, vigilance and legal action have long been essential to protecting citizens' ability to bring class actions and personal injury lawsuits, to imposing punitive damages and to affirming state-based standards of accountability. This life-defending and life-saving work was a signature mission of Public Citizen during its first several decades and has continued ever since.

Endnotes

1 Interview with Kim Tutt, and her statement at a Public Citizen press conference on Feb. 11, 2003.
2 Speech by George W. Bush, delivered Jan. 16, 2003, at University of Scranton, Scranton, Pennsylvania.
3 J. Robert Hunter, *Medical Malpractice Insurance: Stable Losses/Unstable Rates*, Oct. 10, 2002.
4 *Medical Misdiagnosis: Challenging the Malpractice Claims of the Doctors' Lobby*, Public Citizen's Congress Watch, March 2003.
5 Institute of Medicine, *To Err is Human: Building a Safer Health System*, November 1999.
6 Testimony of Linda McDougal before the Joint Judiciary and Health, Education, Labor and Pensions Senate Committees, Feb. 11, 2003.
7 Statement of Kathy Olsen, delivered at Public Citizen press conference, Feb. 11, 2003.

8   "New 2002 Government Data Dispute Malpractice Lawsuit 'Crisis,'" Public Citizen, July 7, 2003.

9   "Pet Food Sales," Pet Food Institute, 2012.

10   Tort Reform Record, American Tort Reform Association, July 22, 2005.

11   *Oregon's Increased Number of Doctors: Government Data Refutes Medical Lobby Claims,* Public Citizen, Aug. 4, 2004; and *Fewer Lawsuits and More Doctors: The Myths of Washington State's Medical Malpractice Crisis,* Public Citizen, September 2005.

12   This account of Stella Liebeck's lawsuit against McDonald's is from "Legal Myths: The McDonald's Hot Coffee Case," a Public Citizen fact sheet based on newspaper reports.

13   Carl Deal and Joanne Doroshow, *The CALA Files: The Secret Campaign by Big Tobacco and Other Major Industries to Take Away Your Rights,* Center for Justice & Democracy and Public Citizen, July 2000.

14   Tort Reform Record, American Tort Reform Association, July 22, 2005.

15   Public Citizen, "George W. Bush: A Tort 'Deformer' With Results," fact sheet.

16   National Center for State Courts, The Conference of State Justices Statement on S. 687, The Product Liability Fairness Act of 1993, submitted to the U.S. Senate Committee on the Judiciary, Courts and Administrative Practice Subcommittee, March 15, 1994, p. 7.

17   Marc Galanter, "Pick a Number, Any Number," *Legal Times,* Feb. 17, 1992.

18   Deborah R. Hensler et. al., *Compensation for Accidental Injuries in the United States,* Rand Institute for Civil Justice, 1991, p. 19.

19   J. Robert Hunter, *Product Liability Insurance Experience, Consumer Federation of America,* 1984–1993.

20   Kathleen J. Ransome, "Bottled Water: A Perspective on the New Titans," *Water Conditioning and Purification,* October 2002, p. 45.

21   A Justice Department study, *Civil Jury Cases and Verdicts in Large Counties,* Bureau of Justice Statistics, U.S. Department of Justice, NCJ-154346, July 1995, confirmed the rarity of punitive damages, finding they were awarded in just over 2 percent of product liability cases tried by juries and won by plaintiffs in the nation's 75 most populous counties during a year-long period ending in June 1992.

22   Michael Runstad, *Demystifying Punitive Damages in Product Liability Cases: A Survey of a Quarter Century of Trial Verdicts,* The Roscoe Pound Foundation, 1991, pp. 23, 27.

23   ABC News segment on product liability, March 9, 1995.

24   Citizen Action, analysis of FEC campaign filing data, April 19, 1995.

25   "The Facts About Products Liability Litigation: Facts Belie Need for Proposed Changes," Public Citizen fact sheet, 1995.

26   For most figures in the following account, see Public Citizen report, *How Special Interests Make Law: GAF Corporation Tries to Buy Liability Protection From Asbestos Claims,* March 2000.

9
SAVING YOUR ENERGY

—

EVERY DAY THAT KAREN SILKWOOD walked into work at the Kerr-McGee Nuclear Corp.'s plant in Crescent, Oklahoma, she passed under a giant "SAFETY FIRST" sign above the entrance. She worked as a laboratory technician at the plant, which manufactured fuel rods used to power a government-owned nuclear reactor.

Silkwood, 28, also was a union activist who was battling the company's plan to decertify the union. Working with her union's national legislative director, Anthony Mazzocchi (who later joined Public Citizen's board), she was assigned to investigate health and safety concerns at the plant. What she uncovered alarmed her. In addition to safety hazards, she discovered evidence of faulty welds that seemed to compromise the integrity of the fuel rods. She found indications that the company was falsifying X-rays and other data to cover up the problems. Nuclear activists feared such defects not only could jeopardize the safety of workers but also might even lead to an explosion.

In September 1974, when the plant had been operating for about six years, Silkwood filed her concerns and those of several other workers with the federal Atomic Energy Commission. She charged that the company had failed to educate or train workers properly about the dangers of radiation; had failed to keep exposures as low as practicable or take proper hygienic precautions; and had failed to adequately monitor workers' exposure to radiation.

Six weeks later, during a shift in which she was grinding and polishing plutonium pellets that would be used in the fuel rods, she decided to check herself for radiation. Inexplicably, her hands and clothes were contaminated. Over the following days, plutonium was detected in her apartment kitchen, bedroom and bathroom, and even in the chicken, bologna and cheese in her refrigerator. The company said it could not determine how she had been contaminated. She was sent, with her roommate and boyfriend, to Los Alamos, New Mexico, for further testing. Physicians there found a significant amount of plutonium in Silkwood's lungs and traces of the deadly substance in her roommate.

Silkwood returned to work on November 13. That night, she attended a union meeting in Crescent and afterward departed alone in her car. She was planning to meet David Burnham, an investigative reporter for The New York Times, and union representative Steve Wodka, an assistant to Mazzocchi, to deliver documents she claimed would prove that the safety of the fuel rods had been compromised.

About an hour later, the Oklahoma state police received a call about a single-car crash seven miles south of town. Karen Silkwood's car had run into a ditch, and she was dead.

The documents she was purportedly carrying were never found. Union investigators later said there was evidence that Kerr-McGee had kept Silkwood under surveillance, that her phone had been tapped and that her car might have been forced off the road. Police, however, never established any plot to kill Silkwood.

The news of Silkwood's mysterious death reached Washington, D.C., just as more than a thousand activists worried about nuclear power plants were gathering at a conference organized by Ralph Nader, then president of Public Citizen, and Joan Claybrook, who was then Congress Watch director. Stunned, the activists asked Public Citizen to organize a new group to monitor the nuclear industry.

The Critical Mass Energy Project was born. "The announcement of [Silkwood's] death gave people at the conference real momentum to believe that this is a real life-and-death battle," recalled Wenonah Hauter, an early anti-nuclear activist. More than two decades later, in 1997, she became director of what is now a broader Public Citizen division, the Energy Program.

In the years that followed that first conference, Public Citizen's Critical Mass played the role of nuclear watchdog, ferreting out information from industry insiders and government agencies, and producing hundreds of reports documenting safety problems with nuclear reactors and the dangers of nuclear waste. These reports — released to the news media and grassroots anti-nuclear groups and allies across the country — provided vital ammunition in the struggle for nuclear safety. In later years, the Energy Program branched out to work on other related concerns, including energy efficiency, electric utility deregulation, oil prices and the irradiation of food.

The Origins of Nuclear Activism

The nuclear industry was in its heyday at the time of that first Public Citizen conference. Its roots reached back almost three decades to the World War II era, when Enrico Fermi created the first successful nuclear chain reaction on December 2, 1942, under the west stands of Stagg Field at the University of Chicago. Fermi's reactor was 20 feet high and 25 feet wide, and cost about $1 million to build.[1]

In the postwar period, the U.S. government's Manhattan Project quest for the atomic bomb yielded to the idea of using the heat from splitting atoms to produce electricity. The first official government report on the development of nuclear power, the 1946 Acheson-Lillienthal report, recognized that "the development of atomic energy for peaceful purposes and the development of atomic energy for bombs are in much of their course interchangeable and interdependent."[2]

In 1946, Congress established the Atomic Energy Commission (AEC), which took over operation of the Manhattan Project the following year. It was overseen by Congress' only combined House and Senate legislative committee, the Joint Committee on Atomic Energy. The committee met in secret rooms accessible only by a private elevator and sent its recommended bills simultaneously to the House and Senate floors. That made it very difficult for oversight groups to monitor its work or promote amendments.

As the United States and the Soviet Union sank deeper into the Cold War, the AEC's primary task was to expand the U.S. nuclear arsenal. It undertook a study by Dow Chemical and Detroit Edison to develop "a large-scale reactor to produce power and fissionable materials as joint products."[3]

A guiding assumption was that the government would need the bomb-making materials the reactors would produce. However, in the summer of 1952, "the Commission made it plain that there would be no guaranteed government market for fissionable material, and therefore the study groups, if still interested, should direct their efforts toward an unsubsidized power reactor or, as it was called, a 'power only' reactor."[4]

On December 8, 1953, President Dwight Eisenhower began the "Atoms for Peace" program with a speech to the United Nations. The following Labor Day, in 1954, Eisenhower broke ground in Shippingport, Pennsylvania, for the first commercial nuclear power plant. Atomic Energy Commission Chairman Lewis L. Strauss, in a speech 10 days later to the National Association of Science Writers, elaborated on Eisenhower's Atoms for Peace program: "It is not too much to expect that our children will enjoy electrical energy too cheap to meter."[5]

This famous claim failed to impress Ralph Nader. His skepticism first arose at a scientific conference in 1964. It flared in 1970 when two scientists funded by the AEC, forerunner of the Nuclear Regulatory Commission (NRC), publicly questioned the safety of radiation exposure levels then allowed under federal standards. When John W. Gofman and Arthur R. Tamplin estimated that more than 16,000 additional cancer or leukemia cases would afflict Americans every year if the public were exposed to the permissible doses of radiation from nuclear power plants, Nader persuaded the Senate to hold hearings on nuclear power plant safety.

By the early 1970s, as the civil rights movement, the women's rights movement and anti-Vietnam war protests were roiling the country, citizen activists sprang up in dozens of communities to challenge the nuclear industry. Nader arranged the November 1974 conference to provide a national focal point for them.

Critical Mass '74 was the first national anti-nuclear gathering, taking its name from the industry's jargon: "Critical mass" refers to the amount of fissile material (uranium 235, uranium 233 or plutonium 239) needed to sustain a nuclear chain reaction. To Nader, "a critical mass of people can make the critical difference."[6]

The theme of the first Critical Mass conference was, "A nuclear catastrophe is too big a price to pay for our electric bill." Workshops gave the activists some of the technical and political knowledge and skills they would need to hold the industry and government regulatory bodies accountable. The premise was that citizens should have a voice in power generation decisions. Each participant took home a manual, written by Nancy Ignatius and derived from the experience of Nader's Raiders on Capitol Hill and with the media, on the basics of nuclear power and on how to lobby and agitate.

"Our mass convocations in Washington ... were largely mass training seminars for the thousands who attended, who took home with them not only information but also the early civic strategies that the speakers found workable," Nader said later. "The coalition is intended not only to serve as a citizen advocate against nuclear power before the Congress, but also to vividly demonstrate the growing strength and vitality of the anti-nuclear movement."

One major challenge at the time was simply obtaining information about the industry. "Today's energy activists, overwhelmed with supporting data and achievements for their cause, would find it hard to believe there was such secrecy, suppression and intimidation over information that should have been public, and over the few whistleblowers who spoke up for the right to know and for independently reviewed scientific analysis," wrote researchers Jerry Brown and Rinaldo Brutoco in their 1997 book on the movement.[7]

Alarmed at the prospect that activists would focus attention on the industry's safety practices, the industry sent spies to the conference. "They didn't know what to wear," said Claybrook, who the year before had founded Public Citizen's lobbying arm, Congress Watch. "So they all wore jeans, all starched and new-looking, and you could spot them immediately."[8]

Wenonah Hauter was a teenager drawn to citizen activism in the 1960s. "I was in the tail end of the peace movement, and many of us who were involved saw those issues involving corporate power and nuclear energy, and it seemed like the new battleground to fight those very same interests," Hauter said in an interview. "In those days, there were thousands of nuclear plants planned in this country, and the connection between nuclear power and nuclear weapons was very clear."

President Richard Nixon predicted that a thousand U.S. nuclear reactors would be operating by the end of the century. But Nader had a different vision. He foresaw that nuclear power would become the country's "technological Vietnam."

Activists surfaced from all over the country to join the new people's movement. "The anti-nuclear movement was a fluid movement that bubbled up out of the grassroots without money to organize, without a national strategy," Hauter said. "It was one of those movements like civil rights when everything was ripe, and it was the most powerful environmental movement of our lifetime."

Vera Moore Squires of Biloxi, Mississippi, had been campaigning against nuclear plants since before the first one was built in the 1950s. Her son had worked to help develop nuclear weapons in the Manhattan Project during World War II and had helped plan the Oak Ridge National Laboratory in Tennessee. Despite his pioneering role in nuclear energy — or perhaps because of it — he appreciated better than most the perils of atomic energy and began writing about them.

Among those the young scientist persuaded was his mother. "You can learn a lot after you're 90," she told the *Critical Mass* newsletter in 1977, at the age of 93.[9] Vera Moore Squires wrote dozens of letters to Mississippi newspapers about safety threats from reactors and nuclear waste. She joined religious and environmental groups that opposed nuclear power and helped organize a national petition drive.

Faced with mushrooming local resistance and another Critical Mass conference looming in 1975, the nuclear industry fought back — with money. It spent more than $1 million that year to set up a lavish public relations organization called the Atomic Industrial Forum. A leaked memo from the new industry group identified the greatest threats to the industry as being the decline of congressional support for nuclear programs and "the proliferation of anti-nuclear citizen groups, particularly Ralph Nader's forces and the Boston-based Union of Concerned Scientists." Rather like Lewis Powell's Chamber of Commerce memo of a few years before (see Chapter 1), the AIF plan outlined a sophisticated strategy to combat local activism by influencing the media.

"There is an urgent need to initiate frequent and substantive news events, to counter the pseudo press conferences held regularly by the national critics, and to provide a news peg for media attention," the memo advised. It went on to urge that positive articles about nuclear power be ghostwritten on behalf of distinguished experts to be published in prominent publications and disseminated through news media syndicate services.[10]

The nuclear industry realized that bad publicity could threaten the cozy relationship it had with government regulators and Washington politicians, which had proved extremely beneficial. The Price-Anderson Act, which took effect in 1957, for example, created corporate welfare of monumental proportions for the nuclear industry. It insulated the industry from full financial accountability in the event of a catastrophe and shifted potentially hundreds of billions of dollars in liability costs to the government.

The act's idea was to encourage commercial exploitation of nuclear power by placing a ceiling on the total amount each utility would have to pay to settle private claims in the event of an accident. This approach masks the true cost of nuclear energy. Without such protection, it is doubtful that utilities would take the risk of building nuclear plants, because even a single accident could bring financial ruin.

Under the Price-Anderson Act, which Congress extended for 20 years in 2005, owners of licensed reactors must purchase just $300 million in private insurance. If damage claims from an accident at any one reactor exceed that utility's policy, then all other commercial reactors are assessed a share of the excess, up to $95.8 million each. That limits the total liability for the nuclear industry and all its contractors for any single accident to about $10 billion.[11] Since that amount could fall woefully short, the law calls for the rest of the cost to come from the U.S Treasury.

Undeterred by the industry's legislative and public relations drive, the anti-nuclear movement and Public Citizen's Critical Mass surged through the 1970s, accumulating popular support and political experience every year.

In 1974, Public Citizen gave critical support to Philip Burton, a powerhouse from California, in his successful move to disband the Joint Committee on Atomic Energy and give oversight of nuclear power to the committees handling energy issues. This one move in the Energy Reorganization Act of 1974 made the entire industry more accountable to the public. The law also established the Nuclear Regulatory Commission with responsibility for overseeing nuclear safety, power production and nuclear medicine, and gave oversight of military nuclear weaponry to a new agency, the Energy Research and Development Administration. In 1977, ERDA was expanded into the Department of Energy.

In 1976, Critical Mass helped train local activists who got nuclear initiatives on the ballot in eight states. The victorious Missouri initiative prohibited utilities from charging consumers for the construction costs of nuclear plants before they produced electricity.

By 1977, Critical Mass had doubled its newsletter circulation and become a full-fledged department of Public Citizen. (Previously it had operated under Congress Watch.) It coordinated more than 175 local citizen groups on a wide range of energy issues, eventually involving nuclear power, energy conservation and the development of renewable technologies such as solar and geothermal energy. That year, Nader and John Abbotts published their book *The Menace of Atomic Energy*.

In 1977, Critical Mass mobilized thousands of activists to press the new President, Jimmy Carter, to cancel the Clinch River Breeder Reactor Project near Oak Ridge, Tennessee. The project, begun in 1972, was designed to test a new generation of nuclear reactors that proponents believed would power the United States in the 21st century. Called "liquid-metal fast breeder reactors," they were cooled by liquid sodium rather than water and in the critics' view were inherently more volatile. The lure of fast breeders was that they produced more nuclear fuel than they consumed, guaranteeing an endless supply of plutonium to fuel more reactors or to make bombs.

The U.S. experience with fast breeder reactors was not encouraging. In November 1955, the EBR-1 (experimental breeder reactor) in Arco, Idaho, had melted down during testing. Rather than shutting it off as the test ended, an operator had mistakenly hit the wrong button. In the few seconds he took to realize the mistake and press the correct one, about half the reactor core had melted. Regulators and the public were not told of this meltdown until Lewis Strauss, head of the Atomic Energy Commission (the man who claimed nuclear power would be "too cheap to meter") was confronted by *The Wall Street Journal* and had to admit his ignorance of the accident.[12]

Carter halted construction of the Tennessee breeder reactor in 1977, marking a milestone in the battle against the nuclear industry. Six years later, after a full-bore organizing and lobbying effort by Congress Watch, Critical Mass and conservative groups upset over the spiraling cost to taxpayers, Congress overrode Senate Majority Leader Howard Baker of Tennessee to officially kill the project in his home state. Fully $1.1 billion had been spent. In 1978, Critical Mass attracted 700 activists to its Washington, D.C., conference on safe energy issues and pushed the number of newsletter subscribers past 10,000. It looked like the tide was beginning to turn against nuclear power.

Three Mile Island

On March 16, 1979, "The China Syndrome," a Hollywood blockbuster starring Jack Lemmon and Jane Fonda, premiered in New York City. The film told the fictional story of a nuclear plant accident that came perilously close to a catastrophic meltdown of the reactor core. In the story, a frightening but plausible chain of events revealed faulty materials and unchecked safety systems. What followed in the film was an equally plausible cover-up by the government and the utility company.

The film was an instant box-office smash. The industry dismissed the plot as pure fantasy, claiming that what had been portrayed could never happen.

Exactly 12 days later, things went terribly wrong at the brand-new Unit 2 reactor at the Three Mile Island nuclear plant, situated on the Susquehanna River less than 10 miles from the Pennsylvania capital of Harrisburg.

Events unfolded as if Hollywood scriptwriters had plotted them. At about 4 a.m. on March 28, a series of mechanical failures occurred. Emergency procedures went wrong. Coolant water began to rush out of the reactor at a rate of 220 gallons per minute. Emergency pumps malfunctioned. Reactor operators in the control room refused to believe what their meter readings were telling them and overrode the plant's safety backup equipment. The reactor's 36,000 fuel rods began to overheat as the water rushed out of the reactor, leaving the reactor's core uncovered.

"It seemed to go on and on, surprise after surprise," said radiation protection supervisor Thomas Mulleavy afterward. Four hours and 20 minutes after the initial failure, officials declared the first-ever general emergency at an American nuclear power plant.[13]

In the following days, a hydrogen bubble formed in the reactor and officials feared a catastrophic explosion. Such a blast might destroy the entire plant and spread radiation across many miles. Alternatively, if the reactor core continued to overheat, it might melt through the containment building and into the ground below, spewing a vast amount of radiation into the air and water. These stark scenarios spurred the federal government into a desperate effort to get supplies of potassium iodide manufactured and flown into the area to prevent a mass outbreak of thyroid cancer that likely would follow any large radiation release.

Pennsylvania Governor Richard Thornburgh ordered all schools closed and advised pregnant women and children within 10 miles of the plant to flee. More than 140,000 people did not wait for the government's evacuation plan to go into effect — they clogged highways leading out of the area in every direction.

After several days of worldwide tension, the hydrogen bubble shrank, operators were able to begin cooling the reactor core and greater disaster was averted by the narrowest of margins.

The NRC would later determine that almost one-third of the Three Mile Island reactor core had melted. The resulting radiation had not been completely contained, however. Some radioactive gas was released into the atmosphere, and some 400,000 gallons of radioactive water were released into the Susquehanna River.

In the subsequent investigation, Public Citizen's Critical Mass program disclosed to the American public for the first time that failures of major safety systems at the reactor had forced operators to shut it down a year earlier, from mid-April to September 1978 (before the plant's commercial operation had started). The organization also revealed that, despite continuing safety problems, Metropolitan Edison had rushed the reactor into commercial operation on December 30, 1978 — just 25 hours before the end of the calendar year — to reap $40 million from a special federal tax break. Two weeks later, the reactor was shut down again when safety relief valves ruptured during a routine test.[14]

Later, Critical Mass discovered a serious conflict of interest involving the NRC's reliance on Radiation Management Corp. for analyzing radiation monitors at Three Mile Island: The company had been founded by General Public Utilities, the parent company of plant operator Metropolitan Edison.[15]

Critical Mass and the Public Citizen Litigation Group petitioned the NRC to declare the meltdown at Three Mile Island an "extraordinary nuclear occurrence." Such a designation would have precluded the reactor owner from using certain legal defenses against claims brought by citizens, many of whom were exposed to radiation. The petition was dated July 24, 1979, and the NRC did not respond immediately, to put it mildly. The answer finally came in a letter the NRC sent to Public Citizen in 2000 — fully 21 years later! The petition was denied.

The Three Mile Island crisis made 1979 the most active year for Critical Mass since its launch. Its annual budget rose from $95,000 in 1978 to $234,000, and its public profile soared as staffers testified before House and Senate committees on radiological emergency planning and the breakdown of evacuation plans in Pennsylvania. Critical Mass also helped organize more than 100,000 people for a rally in Washington, D.C., in May and 200,000 in New York City four months later.

For seven years, the accident at Three Mile Island stood as the most pivotal moment in the anti-nuclear movement. Then, in April 1986, the worst nightmare of nuclear activists and the industry alike came true when the Soviet Union's Chernobyl nuclear power plant exploded in the Ukraine.

Multiple blasts killed at least 31 people immediately, injured more than 1,000 and forced hundreds of thousands of people to be relocated. The disaster discharged up to 400 times the amount of long-lived radionuclides released in the bombing of

Hiroshima.[16] A radioactive cloud drifted over Northern Europe and even into North America, raising the fear of cancer among millions of people. The blasted area became an abandoned no man's land open only to scientists for decades afterward.

The Nuclear Option

After Three Mile Island and Chernobyl, the safety of nuclear plants came under scrutiny as never before. The industry insisted its plants were safe and that a Chernobyl-type disaster could never happen in the United States. But Critical Mass continued to unearth increasingly disturbing data. In 1986, Public Citizen published the "1979–1985 Nuclear Power Safety Report," documenting the safety performance of every reactor in the country.[17]

Critical Mass investigators had worked to pry information from a reluctant industry, and soon they began hearing from insiders who were alarmed at lax safety standards. Critical Mass also worked with local activists such as Ann Harris, who discovered longstanding safety problems at Watts Bar, a nuclear plant being built by the Tennessee Valley Authority (TVA) near her home in Ten Mile, Tennessee.

"When Ann first asked me to help her fight the licensing of Watts Bar, I told her that it was probably too late to stop construction because they had already spent $7 billion on Watts Bar, and TVA was nearly $30 billion in debt from the nuclear construction program," said Jim Riccio, who tracked nuclear safety problems for Critical Mass. "They were going to turn on the switch. But we could try, and at least we could force the TVA and the NRC to address safety issues and make the reactor less dangerous. Ann cried for three days, called me back and we rolled up our sleeves and got to work."

Ann lived in a log house on land granted to her family by the King of England prior to the American Revolution. Her mother had worked at Oak Ridge on the Manhattan Project during World War II and had grown ill as a result. Three generations of her family had ties to that land, and it was now within the emergency planning zone of the nuclear reactor.

Some in Ann's family were not pleased that she was being heard raising safety issues. Southern women were expected to be seen and not heard, like children, Ann said. "A woman's name is only supposed to appear in the paper three times: when she's born, when she's married and when she dies."

The industry didn't know what to make of the Harris-Riccio team, Harris said. "There was this crazy old woman and this activist lawyer." But workers in the plant secretly supplied the duo with evidence about untrained staff and skipped safety inspections. "Sometimes documents would be slipped through the window of my parked car," Harris said. "Packets were anonymously left behind my screen door."

Public Citizen staffers knew how to use that material in dealing with regulatory bodies and how to get verified information into the newspapers. "The media had a field day," said Harris.

The reactor's opening was delayed until 1996. Public Citizen's pressure forced the TVA to correct longstanding safety problems with the plant's electrical wiring, which controls the reactor. Public Citizen also documented the fact of the TVA's $30 billion debt, enabling the group to argue successfully that funds had to be set aside for decommissioning, rather than relying on a letter of credit.

"Without Public Citizen's help, the plant would have opened as an even more dangerous plant in 1994," Harris said.

Insider information often proved crucial. In Texas, whistleblowers came to Public Citizen about faulty welds and wiring and poor concrete quality at the South Texas nuclear plant construction site. The resulting publicity, including a major exposé on CBS' "60 Minutes," led to a 13-month delay in licensing and a billion dollars worth of repairs to the plant.

A week after Critical Mass released its 1993 report "Nuclear Lemons," a large box arrived at the group's office. It contained internal industry reports on about half the country's reactors, sent by someone within the industry-funded Institute for Nuclear Power Operations (INPO). This was an alleged self-monitoring group the industry had formed in the wake of Three Mile Island as a way to avoid increased government scrutiny.

The INPO routinely inspected reactors, reviewed significant events and maintained databases on plant operations. But the organization's findings, while provided to the NRC, were not open to the public. Public Citizen had tried and failed in 1984 to obtain INPO documents through the Freedom of Information Act, and had then filed a lawsuit, but eight years later, a federal appellate court ruled the documents were not subject to public disclosure.[18] The court ruled that the INPO had voluntarily given the documents to the NRC on the condition they not be disclosed, even though the NRC had the power to subpoena them. The ruling, in Public Citizen's view, allowed the industry and government to conspire to get around the Freedom of Information Act.

Now, however, Public Citizen's Critical Mass staffers had the documents they had been seeking. Riccio and others immediately began the tedious task of comparing the secret industry documents with reports the NRC had made public. The resulting report, "Hear No Evil, See No Evil, Speak No Evil," "found gross disparities between what the two [INPO and the NRC] were saying," Riccio said.

In other words, the NRC reports were painting a much rosier picture of the industry than even the industry's own internal inspectors were seeing. The Public Citizen report documented that the NRC had, in fact, failed to address about two-thirds of the safety concerns the industry itself had identified in the INPO inspections.

Reports such as these, aided by the political and psychological fallout from the meltdown at Three Mile Island, further tarnished the image of the nuclear power industry and cast doubt upon the NRC's ability and willingness to ensure safety. But the risk of reactor accidents was only part of the problem. Despite Strauss' prediction of bountiful electricity "too cheap to meter," the reality was that reactor construction costs were spiraling out of control. Meanwhile, no resolution was in sight for the problem of radioactive waste disposal, with its potentially huge costs. Nuclear power had become an economic albatross around the neck of the American consumer.

In 1986, the Department of Energy compared nuclear construction price estimates to the actual final costs for 75 reactors. The original estimate was $45 billion; the actual cost was $145 billion. According to *Forbes* magazine, this "failure of the U.S. nuclear power program ranks as the largest managerial disaster in business history, a disaster of monumental scale." The magazine added, "only the blind, or the biased, can now think the money has been well spent."[19]

A subsequent Public Citizen report, released in June 2001, found that electricity rates in the 31 states that used nuclear power were, on average, 25 percent higher than in the states that did not use it.[20] Their rates were generally still higher a decade later, according to independent reports.[21]

Coupled with public understanding of safety risks, the economic disaster of nuclear power led to its decline. U.S. utilities cancelled almost as many reactors as they built, and none were ordered and subsequently built after 1973. This was largely because of construction costs. Between 2002 and 2008, for example, cost estimates for new nuclear plant construction rose from between $2 billion and $4 billion per unit to $9 billion per unit, according to the Union of Concerned Scientists. No new license was issued until 2012. The last to be completed was the TVA's Watts Bar reactor. It cost nearly $8 billion and took 23 years, opening in 1996.

Nixon had predicted a thousand U.S. reactors by the year 2000, but the U.S. reality in 2015 was just 99 commercial nuclear reactors in 61 plants operating in 30 states. They now produce about 20 percent of the nation's electricity.

The Dirty Little Secret

As public awareness of nuclear plants' dangers and drawbacks grew more acute, so too did concern about nuclear waste, the industry's dirty little secret. Scientists have yet to agree upon a safe method for dealing with the "spent" fuel that is removed from reactor cores. It is highly radioactive and remains so for thousands of years. An unprotected person standing one yard away from a spent fuel rod for 30 seconds would suffer a significantly higher risk of cancer or genetic damage. A three-minute dose of that radiation would be lethal.

In the absence of an agreed-upon method to treat the waste and a secure place to dispose of it, the industry has stored each reactor's waste "temporarily" in pools of water at the plant. It remains one of the industry's most intractable problems.

In the 1980s, seeking to expand nuclear power, the industry sought to shed its waste disposal responsibility. Congress, awash in campaign money from the nuclear industry, was happy to comply. Lawmakers passed the Nuclear Waste Policy Act of 1982, essentially telling the government to take over the waste problem. The measure said the costs of centralized waste treatment and repositories would be borne primarily by ratepayers in the form of a special assessment added to their monthly electricity bills.

The law instructed the Department of Energy (DOE) to find an eastern and a western site for permanent "geologic" waste repositories, and then build them. This decision followed decades of fruitless research and debate about disposal options. Some of those actually discussed included such harebrained schemes as burying the waste in polar ice caps, or in salt formations, or under the ocean floor; or launching it into outer space to be either stored on the moon or sent into the sun.

The DOE initially studied nine sites in six states, and President Ronald Reagan narrowed them down to three: Hanford, Washington, which already was thoroughly contaminated from DOE nuclear weapons facilities and waste tanks; Deaf Smith County, Texas; and Yucca Mountain, Nevada. In 1987, Congress directed the DOE to further evaluate only Yucca Mountain, a six-mile long, 1,200-foot high volcanic ridge just 80 miles northwest of Las Vegas.

Public Citizen, the state of Nevada and many other environmentalists and activists looked into the matter and decided it was a risky boondoggle designed more to relieve the nuclear industry of its burden than to safely dispose of the toxic byproducts of nuclear power.

"The proposal to build a repository at Yucca Mountain does not resolve the nuclear waste problem," said Lisa Gue, who worked on nuclear waste issues for Critical Mass at the turn of the century. "In fact, it implicitly encourages the continued generation of nuclear waste while transferring the risk to the state of Nevada and to communities unlucky enough to be located along transportation routes."

Like nuclear projects decades earlier, the project's early cost projections proved far too low. The government poured billions into the plan, mostly to conduct environmental studies to find out whether the waste could be safely isolated for the tens of thousands of years it will remain lethal. That massive investment, coupled with the political momentum to find a "solution," led Public Citizen and others to question whether the DOE would ever abandon Yucca Mountain — even if the environmental studies demonstrated it would not be suitable for the task.

In fact, Public Citizen cited the DOE's own studies to make its case that Yucca Mountain was not an appropriate site for a nuclear dump. Some studies showed that radiation could seep into an important source of drinking water for nearby residents and farms, an aquifer that likely would be used by the growing population of Las Vegas in the coming years. There also were concerns that volcanic and earthquake activity in the area could open fissures in the earth that could lead to massive contamination of the surrounding environment. Public Citizen urged that nuclear utilities continue to store the waste at individual nuclear plants until a safer long-term solution could be found.

In the 1990s, the industry pushed legislation that would establish a "temporary" storage facility for waste at Yucca Mountain — even before the site received final approval for a permanent repository. The effect of that proposal was clear. If waste were taken to Yucca Mountain for "temporary" storage, the debate over the site's suitability would in effect become moot, because no one would want to suffer through another rancorous debate process or risk moving the waste again.

Working with senators and representatives from Nevada and other groups, Public Citizen played a leading role in stopping the legislation year after year. But the more money the industry poured into congressional campaigns, the harder it became. The measure passed Congress in 1997 and again in 2000, but President Bill Clinton vetoed it both times.

One problem facing Public Citizen's Critical Mass division was that the anti-nuclear movement had waned by the 1990s, in part because the industry itself had lost steam and stopped planning new reactors. Foundations and individual funders had long since moved on to other crises. And it was difficult to convey to ordinary citizens outside Nevada why they should be concerned about Yucca Mountain.

But Public Citizen noticed a previously understudied aspect of the project: the complex transportation effort that would be necessary to move 42,000 metric tons of high-level radioactive spent fuel to Yucca Mountain from the 104 reactors where it was stored. The safe-handling issues were delicate, the amount of waste that needed moving was already daunting, and the waste was expected to double by 2035.

Projections showed that trucks and trains would carry the waste through 43 states, potentially exposing 50 million Americans to serious risk in the event of an accident or terrorist attack. These routes went straight through many of the country's largest cities, where hospitals, police and rescue personnel probably lacked sufficient training and equipment to respond effectively to a radiation emergency.

In the summer of 2000, Public Citizen and the Nuclear Information and Resource Service (NIRS) launched the Radioactive Roads and Rails campaign. Working with local and state organizations, the campaign featured public workshops, press conferences and meetings with elected representatives along proposed transportation routes.

Even with this concerted effort, Public Citizen and NIRS found it difficult to attract the attention of the national news media. Rank-and-file journalists rarely, if ever, get instructions from media executive suites outside the newsroom, but activists couldn't help but suspect that the owners of large media corporations influenced editors' decisions about the way journalists framed this issue for the public.

A decision by the NBC network in 1999, for example, while not directly involving the news operation, raised activists' eyebrows. In May of that year, as Congress was debating an industry-backed amendment to the Nuclear Waste Policy Act, NBC planned to show a made-for-TV movie called "Atomic Train," starring Rob Lowe. The plot: A runaway train hauling nuclear waste and a nuclear weapon bears down on Denver, ultimately causing a nuclear catastrophe.

NBC vigorously promoted the thriller for weeks, emphasizing the threat of trains carrying nuclear waste. "Because the issue of secretly transporting radioactive materials and waste is so threatening, many viewers might want to dismiss it as 'make-believe.' That is simply not true," declared an NBC press release.[22]

Seeking to capitalize on the hype for the movie, Public Citizen issued press releases to NBC affiliate stations throughout the country, with maps depicting proposed nuclear waste transportation routes through their states. The resulting coverage apparently touched a nerve. Just days before the action film was to be screened, NBC executives hurriedly ordered the movie re-edited. References to "nuclear waste" were changed to "hazardous materials." NBC officials claimed the story had to be changed because the casks carrying the waste on the fictional train were not portrayed accurately.

Many suspected that wasn't the whole story. "The more likely scenario is that the nuclear industry — including the NBC network's corporate parent, General Electric (GE) — leaned hard on NBC," said Claybrook at the time. GE built about a third of the nuclear plants operating in the United States, including some identified as the most dangerous, and GE owned NBC. The company's nuclear division, GE Nuclear Energy, still supplied parts and service for reactors.

In 2002, President George W. Bush and Congress formally approved construction of the Yucca Mountain project. But controversy continued, and public confidence in the project was again damaged in 2005 when news media revealed that U.S. Geologic Survey scientists, in emails, had falsified scientific data used to justify the Yucca Mountain site. Candidate Barack Obama promised in 2008 to scuttle the project, and Senate Majority Leader Harry Reid of Nevada used his powerful position to block funding for it into the second Obama administration. In 2015, the project remained mired in political and scientific uncertainty.

The Deregulation Fiasco

Nuclear power has never come close to living up to the rosy early predictions of cheap electricity, even with federal laws relieving the industry of full accountability for an accident and setting up a waste repository. That fact came into stark relief in the late 1990s, when states began to deregulate electric utilities.

For decades, utilities had operated as state-regulated monopolies whose rates were based on their costs. That meant they could spend virtually any amount to build power plants and still be guaranteed steady profits. For consumers, it meant reliable service and predictable rates, even though utilities were notoriously wasteful.

In the early 1990s, large industrial users of electricity began clamoring for deregulation of power utilities so they could search for cheaper suppliers outside their own utility's coverage area. They argued that this would promote competition and greater efficiency. And because some utilities had made wiser investments — not relying heavily on nuclear power, for example — they were in fact able to offer better rates than others. Companies that wanted to serve as energy middlemen also joined the deregulation campaign, and many utilities decided it was easier to join the deregulation movement than to fight it.

By 2001, 24 states and the District of Columbia had passed laws to end state-controlled energy monopolies and ostensibly bring competition into the market. But using their political muscle, nuclear utilities laid down a condition for deregulation that Public Citizen found unacceptable: In most states, lawmakers agreed to bail the utilities out for "stranded costs" — mostly investments in nuclear plants — that they would be unable to recover in a competitive market. This bailout, borne by ratepayers, was estimated to cost $300 billion nationwide.

In theory, competition among electricity providers made sense for consumers, in that it would help turn investors away from expensive, long-term boondoggles like nuclear power. But Public Citizen predicted that not only would it bring higher prices and less reliable service, but the environment also would suffer. A 1996 publication called "Power for the People," which Public Citizen wrote and released with several grassroots organizations, warned that individuals and small businesses likely would see rate increases while large industrial users got discounts; that an increase in fossil fuel use could pollute more air and water; and that energy efficiency programs could be eliminated or cut back.

In Texas, Public Citizen's office couldn't stop deregulation in 1999, but did lobby successfully for power plant cleanup and for state programs requiring more energy efficiency and use of renewable energy sources.

Many of Public Citizen's fears about deregulation were eventually realized in California. The state deregulated its utilities in 1996 and a classic disaster followed.

The deregulation measure included a $28 billion ratepayer bailout for the nuclear utilities, in exchange for which the utilities agreed to a temporary cap on retail rates that would be phased out over four years. In an October 1998 report called "California Dreaming: The Bailout of California's Nuclear Industry," Critical Mass demonstrated that one of every five dollars that Californians paid each month for electricity went toward subsidizing nuclear power plants that otherwise might not be able to continue operating.[23]

Ratepayers should not be forced to pay off the utilities because of their expensive mistakes, the group argued. "This 'free capital' gouged from consumers with the help of the California Assembly will be used to stifle competition and innovation, and prolong the use of dirty power plants," warned Wenonah Hauter, director of Critical Mass. "This is one of the biggest consumer rip-offs in recent memory."[24]

Public Citizen organized a coalition of more than 100 groups to reverse the industry bailout and reform elements of California's deregulation law. Called Ratepayers for Affordable Green Electricity, or RAGE, the coalition included Nader and David Brower, the visionary who had transformed the Sierra Club from a hiking club into a political powerhouse. Like Nader, Brower was extremely critical of deregulation, especially the California legislation.

In California, the Foundation for Taxpayer and Consumer Rights, the Utility Reform Network and other consumer organizations gathered enough signatures to put forth a ballot initiative that would reduce the bailout by $14 billion, mandate a 20 percent rate cut and reform the state's deregulation law. Public Citizen helped support the initiative, known as Proposition 9.

Brower, who died in 2000 at the age of 88, co-wrote a letter with Nader in support of Proposition 9. "Make no mistake: Collaboration with the utility companies can only result in the failed approach that is now the law in California," the letter said. "After all these years, have we not learned that it is only from a position of strength, backed by public support, that a truly enlightened energy policy will proceed?"[25]

The warnings went unheeded. Several environmental groups, including the Natural Resources Defense Council, joined California's three largest utilities, which poured $39 million into a lavish campaign to defeat Proposition 9 in 1998.[26] The utilities claimed the measure would wreck the state's robust economy, harm the environment and frighten away investors. The utilities' money and scare tactics prevailed, and 73 percent of the voters opposed Proposition 9.

Utilities had gotten what they wanted, but they would soon come to regret it. And so would consumers.

The deregulation law required the state's major utilities to sell some of their power generating plants. They ended up divesting all their fossil fuel plants to out-of-state energy corporations, retaining only their nuclear and hydroelectric plants. These out-of-state firms included one that few people had heard of at the time — the Enron Corporation. The name would soon be only too familiar to suffering taxpayers.

In a complex scheme, both the California utilities and the new out-of-state owners sold their electricity into a wholesale power pool, where prices were no longer regulated by the state of California. It was from this power auction that the utilities purchased electricity to be delivered to consumers. That meant that the out-of-staters, freed from regulatory constraints, suddenly could — and did, as it turned out — withhold power from the auction pool at times of high demand to drive up prices. In August 2000, for example, almost five times as much power generating capacity was turned off as in the entire previous year.[27]

This ability to manipulate prices and supply came directly from deregulation. In May 2000, consumers served by San Diego Gas and Electric became the first to experience the full impact; their electric bills nearly tripled. Proponents of deregulation had predicted that competition in the marketplace would lower prices by 20 percent, but instead, the wholesale price of electricity soared 240 percent within two months for the entire state. Electricity that had previously sold for $20 to $40 per megawatt hour now was trading for hundreds of dollars on the open market. But only the San Diego utility was allowed to pass its new higher costs on to consumers.

The other two major utilities — Pacific Gas & Electric and Southern California Edison — were required to supply power at controlled rates whatever its cost, and so sank deeper and deeper into debt. By the end of the year, California's wholesale electricity costs had reached $27 billion, compared to $7 billion the year before.[28] The two utilities often could not afford to buy enough power to meet demand.

On January 17, 2001, California's electricity supply ran short. The state ordered rolling blackouts for the first time since World War II, affecting some half a million customers. With little or no warning, elevators stopped working, trapping people inside. Traffic lights blinked off. Automatic bank machines shut down. Businesses shuttered and schools closed early.[29] The next day, more extensive blackouts affected about 1.5 million people in Northern and Central California.[30] Governor Gray Davis declared a state of emergency, allowing the state to begin spending up to $50 million per day of taxpayer money to purchase electricity for the embattled utilities.

Three days later, then-Texas Governor George W. Bush was inaugurated as the nation's 43rd president. Joining a chorus of other energy interests, the former oilman immediately seized on the California crisis — not as the deregulation disaster it was, but as an opportunity to dig the hole deeper. "California just didn't deregulate enough," Bush administration supporters argued. They falsely claimed that strict environmental standards had prevented new power plants from coming on line. The White House solution: suspend environmental and safety standards for building new power plants and laying transmission lines — that is, enrich energy companies further at the expense of consumers and the environment.

The facts, however, were that California's utilities had been meeting the power needs of residents until deregulation disrupted the marketplace. On January 30, 2001, Public Citizen released a report called "It's Greed, Stupid! Debunking the Ten Myths of Utility Deregulation." The report rebutted the list of excuses for the failure of electricity deregulation in the nation's most populous state.

By April 2001, Pacific Gas & Electric was so deeply indebted to its electricity suppliers that it filed for bankruptcy protection. As California officials grappled with the crisis, Davis and other Western governors, some of them Republicans, beseeched the new Bush administration to impose caps on wholesale prices, arguing that energy suppliers were gouging consumers and that the market was not functioning as deregulation proponents had envisioned.

The Federal Energy Regulatory Commission (FERC), agreed, having ruled earlier that the marketplace was not functioning properly and that power generators were no longer charging "just and reasonable prices."[31] FERC alone had the power to curtail the profiteering. In fact, the California governor argued that the 1935 Federal Power Act obligated FERC to impose "just and reasonable" prices.

Technically, the agency did not answer to Bush, but in practice, the president could influence the agency's actions. So FERC did impose modest price controls, but only in emergency situations, and power generators reacted by resorting to "megawatt laundering" — getting around the weak controls by selling power out of state and then reimporting it.

Bush steadfastly refused to intervene — even as wholesale prices rose by 1,000 percent at times. He contended that "free market forces" would resolve the problem by giving companies the incentive to increase production and ultimately bring down prices. Meanwhile, the California Assembly passed legislation to ease the financial pressure on the two foundering utilities by raising retail energy prices 40 percent.[32]

Energy wholesalers and traders raked in enormous profits. California officials estimated that wholesale electricity costs for the year 2001 would top $50 billion — up from $7 billion just two years earlier.[33] Still, Bush and other industry supporters in Congress insisted on a laissez faire approach to the matter — that it was California's problem and there was no need to interfere in this "free market."

Bush's hands-off approach perhaps could be explained by ideology. But many suspected something more insidious. Some of the companies benefiting the most from California's failed deregulation experiment had close ties to him.

Public Citizen's Texas office filed a Freedom of Information Act request that yielded six boxes of documents from Governor George W. Bush's files that documented the close ties between Bush and Kenneth Lay, chairman of Enron Corp. In February 2001, Critical Mass produced a report, "Got Juice? Bush's Refusal to End California Electricity Price Gouging Enriches Texas Friends and Big Contributors." It detailed these associations, including naming the financial giant Enron as a culprit in manipulating the market. The top 10 suppliers of electricity to California had contributed $4.1 million to Republican candidates and committees for the 2000 election, compared to $1.8 million to Democrats. Three of those companies were based in Texas and had given $1.5 million to the Bush-Cheney campaign, his inauguration committee and the Republican National Committee.[34]

Investigations by California and FERC later uncovered illegal energy market manipulation on a massive scale. The Independent System Operator, the agency that served as the traffic cop for California's electricity distribution system, by May 2001 had identified $6 billion in overcharges by generators.[35]

In June, Vermont Senator James Jeffords defected from the Republican Party to become a Democrat, returning control of the Senate to the Democratic Party. Only days later, Senate Democrats promised to hold investigative hearings into the California situation. In the same month, the Justice Department announced it had launched an antitrust investigation into whether two companies, Williams Energy Services and AES Southland, had agreed to limit their power plant expansion so as to restrict supplies, and whether AES had improperly kept generating units out of operation.[36]

The Enron Connection

At the center of the California controversy was the Houston-based Enron Corp., an energy-trading powerhouse whose political and financial ties to the Bush administration ran very deep. Enron and its chairman Lay had been the president's single biggest financial backer since Bush's first foray into electoral politics. A personal friend of Bush, who called him "Kenny boy," Lay also had hired two former Cabinet members of Bush's father, President George H.W. Bush — James A. Baker III and Robert Mosbacher — when they left office in 1993.

Lay and Enron contributed $127,525 directly to the younger Bush's 2000 campaign and another $713,200 to the Republican National Committee. The company also gave $250,000 of its shareholders' money to the GOP convention that nominated Bush for president, and Enron and Lay each later chipped in $100,000 to help make Bush's 2001 inauguration a glitzy affair. Lay was a member of the Bush campaign's "Pioneers," who each pledged to raise at least $100,000 for the 2000 campaign, and he served on Bush's transition team as an adviser on energy policy. All told, Lay, Enron and other company executives gave $2 million to benefit Bush after 1993.[37]

When Bush arrived in the White House, he stocked his administration with men who had ties to Enron. Army Secretary Thomas White was a former Enron vice president. Senior political adviser Karl Rove owned at least $100,000 worth of Enron stock. Economic adviser Lawrence Lindsey had earned $50,000 as a consultant to Enron. U.S. Trade Representative Robert Zoellick had served on an Enron advisory board for $50,000 a year. Marc Racicot, new head of the Republican National Committee, was a former Enron lobbyist.[38] Attorney General John Ashcroft received $57,499 from Lay and Enron in his failed 2000 Senate re-election bid. White House legal counsel Alberto Gonzales, who later became attorney general, was Enron's lawyer at Vinson & Elkins. Enron paid Bush's campaign manager, Ed Gillespie, $75,000 a month after the election to lobby the White House and Congress.

Enron and its chairman were among the earliest and most aggressive proponents of deregulating electricity markets. As governor of Texas, Bush had worked with Lay to deregulate that state's electric utility industry, and Lay hoped for deregulation nationwide. But Enron, which once had been primarily a natural gas pipeline company, didn't want to own power plants. It wanted to make money by buying and selling electricity as a middleman in a deregulated market, such as California's. It also wanted to operate its power auction without government scrutiny.

A series of government actions helped Lay achieve his goal. A key moment came in late 1993 when Wendy Gramm, a Reagan appointee who chaired the Commodity Futures Trading Commission, was about to leave office. Apparently in response to a request from Enron, she muscled through a rule that exempted energy-trading operations from government oversight. She resigned a few days after the rule was adopted and five weeks later joined Enron's board of directors. There she was paid between $915,000 and $1.85 million between 1993 and 2001 in salary, fees, stock option sales and dividends.[39]

At the time, Enron also was a major financial contributor to Gramm's husband, Senator Phil Gramm, a Texas Republican who chaired the influential Senate Banking Committee. He was the second-leading recipient of Enron campaign cash in Congress: $97,350 from 1989 to 1993.[40]

In 2000, Senator Gramm co-sponsored what would turn out to be major legislation, the Commodity Futures Modernization Act. It wrote Wendy Gramm's regulatory exemption for energy traders into law and broadened their deregulation.

A Clinton administration advisory board opposed the measure, warning that it would allow manipulation of energy markets, and initially the bill went nowhere.

But mysteriously, as Congress was winding up its business in December, the legislation was attached to an 11,000-page, must-pass appropriations bill — without the benefit of a committee hearing or other congressional debate. After that passed, Enron could buy and sell billions of dollars worth of electricity without disclosing the price, volume or terms of its contracts — a major difference from the transparency required at major stock and commodity exchanges.[41]

California's energy crisis had been simmering prior to passage of that federal deregulation law. Afterward, as *The Village Voice* reported, "all hell broke loose."[42] A 2001 report by Public Citizen showed that in the six months before deregulation, California experienced only one "stage 3 emergency" requiring rolling blackouts. In the next six months, there were 38 such emergencies.[43]

Public Citizen found that because of Enron's ability to control a large portion of California's electricity flow, its "Wholesale Services" revenues had quadrupled — from $12 billion in the first quarter of 2000 to $48.4 billion in the first quarter of 2001. This astonishing increase came on top of the record revenue gain the company posted from 1999 to 2000, when full-year "wholesale services" revenues increased from $35.5 billion to $93.3 billion — a 163 percent increase.[44]

The 2001 Public Citizen report, "Blind Faith: How Deregulation and Enron's Influence Over Government Looted Billions from Americans," also exposed Enron's web of more than 2,800 subsidiaries — more than a third of them in the Cayman Islands and other tax and banking havens where illicit profits could be stashed. President Clinton had promoted a plan to crack down on these havens, but the Bush administration shelved that idea.

The Public Citizen report and testimony in Congress were widely quoted by the news media and helped focus attention on the link between Enron's campaign contributions and the public policies it helped to shape. It was this public pressure that finally forced FERC to impose its limited price controls in June 2001. Although weak, that act, said the *Village Voice*, "basically killed Enron's auction system."[45]

By this time, Enron had become the nation's seventh-largest company. But it was about to tumble from that lofty perch.[46] Bereft of its rigged auctions, Enron disclosed a major loss in October 2001, and it then came out that company executives had used questionable accounting techniques and created outside "partnerships" to keep massive debts off their balance sheets. These shell partnership entities had no other visible function.

Shocked investors hurried to dump their holdings, and Enron stock prices plummeted from a high of $90 in mid-2000 to less than $1 in November 2001. Tens of billions of dollars in shareholder equity evaporated, and thousands of employees lost not only their jobs but the majority of their retirement accounts, which were heavily invested in company stock.

Enron collapsed. In December 2001, the company filed the largest bankruptcy in history. The implosion sparked criminal investigations by the Securities and Exchange Commission and the Justice Department as well as inquiries by a dozen congressional committees. It was later revealed that Lay and other top executives had dumped more than $1 billion they owned in company stock as the firm was sinking, while preventing employees from selling shares they held in retirement accounts.

In an attempt to distance itself from Enron, the Bush administration pointed out that Bush had taken no action to help the company during its death throes. It was clear, however, that Enron had earlier held disproportionate influence over the administration's energy policy. Democratic Representative Henry Waxman of California said in January 2002 that he had documented 17 provisions in Vice President Dick Cheney's new energy plan that benefited Enron.

Under pressure, the administration acknowledged that Cheney had met personally with Lay while overseeing the plan's development. In fact, Enron officials met six times with the administration. But the administration refused to release records of all administration contacts with representatives of the energy industry.

After Enron fell apart, state and federal investigators unraveled the whole sordid story. The accounting scandals at the heart of the operation led to multiple indictments, plea bargains and convictions of former Enron executives at the highest level, as well as of officials at other companies that abetted the fraud. The government brought Lay and former Enron CEO Jeffrey Skilling to trial in January 2006. Four months later, on May 25, a federal jury convicted Lay on all six fraud and conspiracy charges against him and found Skilling guilty on 19 of 28 charges. Lay died in July 2006, before he could be sentenced; Skilling was sentenced to 24 years and four months in prison.

The proceedings revealed not only accounting fraud but ironclad proof that Enron had helped rig the deregulated California electricity market to cheat residents and businesses there out of billions of dollars — just as Public Citizen had warned years earlier might happen. Confidential Enron memos described the schemes company traders had used to drive up prices as Californians suffered through rolling blackouts. Some of these tricks had colorful nicknames, like "death star," "ricochet" and "fat boy." They included sham sales among company affiliates, power plant shutdowns to create artificial shortages and phony reports of congestion on transmission lines, which triggered payments from the utilities — and then from taxpayers to the utilities — to relieve the nonexistent problem.

One revelation followed another. In 2004, the Snohomish Public Utility District, a Seattle utility that Enron had victimized, obtained and released thousands of hours of audio tapes of Enron traders gloating, often in crude language, about exploiting California's crisis and scheming to cause new shortages. One trader mentions "the money you guys stole from those poor grandmothers in California." Another responds: "Yeah, Grandma Millie, man." Excerpts from the tapes were widely aired nationwide on radio and television. CBS News reported that the tapes appeared to show that Lay and former CEO Skilling were aware of the trading fraud.

The energy crisis was the result of energy firms' lobbying for deregulation and then intentional manipulation by Enron and others of the system they helped design, and it cost California more than $70 billion.[47] For its part, the Bush-Cheney administration never admitted it had wrongly blamed the California crisis on environmental regulations. But the move toward deregulation largely stalled after that, and utilities in about half the country remained under state supervision.

Corporate Policy Goes Nuclear

The new Bush administration's Energy Task Force (officially called the National Energy Policy Development Group) was a study in corporate influence. The secretive panel worked for three months in early 2001, meeting with more than 400 people from 150 groups. Energy companies such as Enron and industry trade associations apparently had broad access. "The task force put out the word they were open to input," Tom Kuhn, head of the Edison Electric Institute, an industry lobbying group, told The New York Times.[48]

Cheney had turned down a meeting with the leaders of about two dozen environmental groups, sending mid-level staff members to meet with them for about 40 minutes. But his office had more time for the energy industry. In mid-March, a group of nuclear industry executives had an hour-long session with Bush's and Cheney's political adviser Karl Rove, economic adviser Lawrence Lindsey and task force head Andrew Lundquist. Their goal: to raise the dead.

"We said, 'Look, we are an important player on this energy team and here are our vital statistics, and we think that you should start talking about nuclear when you talk about increasing the nation's supply,'" said Christian H. Poindexter, chairman of the Constellation Energy Group. They got swift results. "It was shortly after that — as a matter of fact I think the next night — when the vice president was being interviewed on television, he began to talk about nuclear power for the first time."[49]

When the Bush energy plan was revealed, it held few surprises. It virtually ignored proven energy-efficiency strategies such as renewable source technologies and tighter motor-vehicle fuel-economy standards. Instead, it recommended billions in taxpayer subsidies to expand production of fossil fuels and nuclear power. The plan offered no relief for California or for consumers facing rising gasoline prices.

Bush also withdrew U.S. support for the Kyoto Protocol, which was aimed at halting the steady worldwide rise in carbon dioxide emissions that are the major contributor to global climate change. Even after the National Academy of Sciences issued a report — at his request — that found solid scientific consensus about the reality of global warming, Bush continued to express his own unfounded doubts.

Energy industries and their friends in Congress hailed the Bush-Cheney plan, but much of the public reacted with skepticism. Democrats on Capitol Hill said many plan elements stood little chance of being enacted. But opponents feared that the short-term instability in energy markets and skyrocketing prices from deregulation might give proponents an edge in pushing for new nuclear reactors or relicensing old ones.

Public Citizen launched a spirited campaign, against long odds, to defeat the regressive legislation. One little-noticed aspect sought to repeal the Public Utility Holding Company Act, known as PUHCA. This 1935 law, passed after dozens of utility holding companies went bankrupt in the 1929 stock market crash, had firmly protected electricity ratepayers and utility shareholders ever since. It regulated the finances of multistate utility holding companies, strictly limited mergers and prevented non-utilities from owning utilities. The New Deal statute had fostered a stable, financially strong electricity sector, and Public Citizen became the primary voice for retaining it.

Public Citizen organized to defeat the repeal, spoke out in the media and testified on Capitol Hill. The measure remained bottled up in Congress throughout Bush's first term, partly because of a dispute over a provision to shield manufacturers of a gasoline additive called MTBE from liability. The chemical had contaminated groundwater in a number of states and would cost billions to clean up. Not until Bush's second term did Congress finally approve the Energy Policy Act of 2005. The final bill did not include the MTBE provision, but it did repeal PUHCA, and it contained more than $25 billion in subsidies to energy companies.

Before the bill passed, several large utilities anticipated PUHCA's demise and announced mergers it would likely have barred. Public Citizen predicted that the industry would be transformed as deregulation led to further consolidation and opened the way for banks, oil companies and other conglomerates to own utilities. The combination of state deregulation and PUHCA repeal portended higher prices for consumers, many of whom already were seeing dramatic increases in their electricity bills.

Democrats took control of Congress in the 2006 elections, but still needed Republican support to pass measures that could withstand a veto by President Bush. Public Citizen and its allies tried again for comprehensive energy legislation to repeal $12.5 billion in subsidies for the oil industry, arguing that it had earned $315 billion in profits since 2005 and didn't need the money. Another target was a $50 billion loan guarantee program for the nuclear industry. The goal was to defeat both provisions and shift the funds into support for clean energy and efficiency measures. Public Citizen also wanted to increase fuel economy standards for cars and light trucks.

Public Citizen's Energy Program Director Tyson Slocum testified before a congressional subcommittee in May 2007, saying Big Oil should be required to invest its record profits into projects to help consumers. He added that nuclear power plants often can't repay their loans and that the $50 billion guarantee program likely would end up on taxpayers' shoulders instead.

Congress listened — in part. The nuclear loan guarantees were taken out of the energy bill. But a separate measure restored $20 billion worth of guarantees, without funding them, and in 2008, limited them to $18.5 billion. The oil subsidies survived, although the final 2007 legislation did expand Federal Trade Commission authority to regulate oil markets. It also mandated the first fuel economy increases for passenger cars and light trucks in 30 years, since Claybrook issued them as National Highway Traffic and Safety Administrator under Carter in 1977. The 2007 law required the combined fleet to reach 35 miles per gallon by 2020, a standard that held until President Obama significantly increased it.

As the national economic meltdown hit in 2008, Public Citizen and its allies again called on Congress to end oil subsidies and won a partial scale-back, by $7.1 billion. Congress softened the blow to the industry, however, with a new $900 million tax giveaway for oil and a $1.2 billion break for coal-fired plants.

The Texas office of Public Citizen, established in 1984, organized opposition to proposals for new coal-fired power plants in that state, hosting a 2009 movie tour of the documentary "Fighting Goliath: Texas Coal Wars." Narrated by actor Robert Redford, it showed Texas activists, including those from Public Citizen's Texas office, as they succeeded in blocking all but three of 11 new coal-fire power plants proposed by TXU (later called Energy Future Holdings). "There's no such thing as 'clean' coal,'" they argued.

In the Wall Street bailout of October 2008, Congress extended a $5.8 billion tax credit for renewable energy production that had been about to expire, and expanded tax credits for families who install solar panels or buy new plug-in hybrid vehicles. Claybrook, in one of her final trips to the Capitol as Public Citizen president, insisted to Congress that the auto industry bailout bill had to include binding measures for safety improvements and greater fuel economy. And although Congress decided not to bail out the automakers, the Obama White House did it anyway, without including Public Citizen's recommendations.

The Fuel Efficiency Battle

What Bush's 2007 energy bill did not do was address the related problems of global climate change and soaring gasoline prices. Gas prices had hit $3 a gallon by 2005 and were still rising, and Americans clamored for relief. Public Citizen's answer to both problems was to make automobiles more efficient. This would reduce gasoline demand to lower prices while cutting carbon emissions at the same time.

When Claybrook served as head of the National Highway Traffic Safety Administration (NHTSA) under Carter, she issued and oversaw implementation of the nation's first rules requiring automakers to produce more fuel-efficient cars and trucks. Called Corporate Average Fuel Economy (CAFE) standards the law had passed in 1975 in response to high gasoline prices and the national dependence on foreign oil, especially after the Arab oil embargo.

The CAFE standards, issued in 1977, set out an ambitious schedule that doubled passenger car miles per gallon by 1985. The law also gave NHTSA the authority to establish similar standards for light trucks, including SUVs, minivans and pickups. They were a rousing success. According to the government's Energy Information Administration, the nation's oil consumption dropped 20 percent in five years — from 18.9 million barrels per day in 1978 to 15.2 million in 1983.

But in the mid-1980s, Congress and Reagan administration regulators began allowing vehicle fuel economy to stagnate. Large, gas-guzzling cars reappeared, and the 1990s brought a boom in SUVs. These included many hulking vehicles too heavy to be covered by the CAFE rules. Oil consumption rose steadily from its 1983 low. In fact, the Environmental Protection Agency found that the average vehicle in 2005 was getting 21 miles per gallon — a 5 percent decline from the 22.1 miles per gallon average in 1988.[50]

Public Citizen fought these trends. In 1990, the organization supported a bill offered by Senator Richard Bryan, a Nevada Democrat, to raise standards to 40 miles per gallon over 10 years. The measure fell short in Congress by only a few votes, failing to overcome a filibuster. Throughout the 1990s, in 2001 and again in 2003, Public Citizen joined environmental groups to support fuel economy bills that would have sewn up the many loopholes in the law and set the nation on a clear path to reduced oil consumption. They all failed by ever-larger margins; the auto industry was going all out to defeat forward-looking bills and punish their supporters.

Congress also placed crippling restrictions on NHTSA's budget from 1995 to 2001, prohibiting the agency from spending money to develop new fuel economy standards and hamstringing the fuel economy program. A large coalition including Public Citizen managed to get these restrictions lifted in 2001. Then it launched a lobbying campaign to persuade NHTSA to use its regulatory authority to improve fuel economy, as the CAFE law required.

Then came the terrorist attacks of September 11, 2001. The consequences for national security of the country's addiction to oil were immediately apparent, and public awareness skyrocketed. Other prods to action included the cost to consumers and the clear scientific consensus that the burning of fossil fuels was contributing greatly to global warming. Public Citizen worked with state governments, including California, that were moving to address greenhouse gas emissions in the absence of federal leadership.

Five years later, in 2006, the Department of Transportation reluctantly issued new CAFE standards for SUVs, minivans and pickup trucks. For the first time, the rules included vehicles weighing more than 8,500 pounds. However, the rules were set under a restructured method influenced by high-level Bush administration officials, including Cheney, and were so weak that a *Wall Street Journal* article called them "mostly a victory for automakers."[51] As Public Citizen showed with documents obtained under a series of Freedom of Information Act requests, the basis for these changes had come out of Cheney's Energy Task Force.

The feeble standards emerged even though the previous year had seen sharp spikes in gasoline prices. Public Citizen believed they were largely the result of increasing concentration in the oil industry. In September 2006, Tyson Slocum, then research director for Public Citizen's Energy Program, released "Hot Profits and Global Warming: How Oil Companies Hurt Consumers and the Environment." The report showed that recent mergers meant the top five oil refiners now controlled more capacity that the largest 10 refiners had controlled a decade earlier.

Such consolidation boosted the industry's pricing power. In 1999, oil refiners earned 18.9 cents for every gallon refined. By 2005, they were making 48.8 cents. Profits soared. Between the time Bush took office in 2001 through June 2006, the five biggest U.S. oil companies recorded profits of $375 billion.

"We have seen what happens when companies like Enron are able to buy off our politicians and write our nation's energy policies," said Hauter, Critical Mass' director. "We can't let the profiteers run roughshod over the public. After all, the decisions that we make on energy today — from nuclear power to coal and other fossil fuels — will affect the children of many, many generations to come."

The Intergovernmental Panel on Climate Change, set up in 1988 under United Nations auspices, issued its "Fourth Assessment Report in 2007," saying flatly that global warming was a reality and was "very likely" due to greenhouse gas emissions. Public awareness rose further from the alarming headlines that resulted, along with anger at rising gas prices. So Congress moved at last to pass new energy legislation. Public Citizen saw it as a chance to achieve the first meaningful fuel economy standards since the 1970s, knowing the debate would include many familiar opposition arguments about threats to safety and the auto industry's limited capacity to increase fuel economy.

Many powerful members of Congress wanted to weaken the rules by adding "economic analysis" to NHTSA's criteria for standards. As approved, the 2007 energy law did secure a change the Bush administration wanted: Standards would be set using a size-based scheme cooked up by Cheney and the Energy Task Force. However, Public Citizen succeeded in keeping cost-benefit analysis out of the law.

Meanwhile, California and the Environmental Protection Agency (EPA) pursued other routes to curbing greenhouse gas emissions for motor vehicles. The Supreme Court held in *Massachusetts v. EPA* in 2007 that greenhouse gases could be regulated under the Clean Air Act. That permitted California to renew its request for the EPA's permission to enforce its own emission standards. The decision also instructed the EPA to determine whether greenhouse gases posed a threat to public health and welfare.

The Bush administration's EPA denied California's request in March 2008, blocking it and 13 other states from pursuing their own standards, which would have required cars and light trucks to reach 36 miles per gallon by 2016. The EPA argued that the fuel economy standards mandated by Congress in 2007 was the way to control greenhouse gas emissions from motor vehicles.

Responding to the pressure, however, NHTSA proposed in April 2008 requiring cars and light trucks to reach 31.6 miles per gallon by 2015. Public Citizen argued that this was not the highest technologically achievable level and ridiculed NHTSA's economic assumption that the price of gas would be just $2.31 per gallon in 2015. It reached more than $4 per gallon three months later, in July 2008.

NHTSA did not issue final fuel economy standards before the end of the Bush administration, and on January 26, 2009, President Obama issued directives requiring NHTSA and the EPA to re-evaluate motor vehicle efficiency for fuel economy and greenhouse gases. His administration had inherited a disastrous effort to restructure the domestic auto industry, which had by January 2009 received some $20 billion in government bailout funds.

In May 2009, President Obama announced plans to raise fuel economy standards for passenger cars and light trucks to 35.5 miles per gallon by 2016. His plan included a joint rulemaking by NHTSA and the EPA to set parallel fuel economy and greenhouse gas standards for motor vehicles. The target was consistent with technologically achievable gains that would reduce oil consumption and greenhouse gas emissions. By the time Claybrook left Public Citizen, the long, difficult battle to achieve significant increases in fuel economy was well on its way to realization.

The Texas Office

In 1984, when Southwestern Bell was attempting to raise Texas phone rates after federal telephone deregulation, Public Citizen opened a temporary office in the state. Based in Austin, the office successfully organized Texans to oppose the proposal, and it was eventually withdrawn. But Public Citizen decided to stay.

With energy companies being big business in Texas, and several Texas members of Congress holding powerful committee chairs, the organization had a full agenda from the start. It moved immediately to expose the high cost of new nuclear plants in the state, and its work on that issue — as Public Citizen organizers so often have found — opened doors to many other consumer concerns.

Under the guidance of director Tom "Smitty" Smith, the Texas office lobbied to clean up the state's notoriously weak air pollution laws and won important pesticide regulations. It helped pass and improve the state's lemon law for car buyers and successfully pushed for rules to prevent the sealing of court records in public health and safety cases.

For many years, Smith and his team focused on campaign finance reform and lobbying disclosure, fighting successfully for campaign finance limits on Texas judicial campaigns. The office provided some of the evidence that the Travis County district attorney used to convict former House Majority Leader Tom DeLay of felony money-laundering. Another major win was the establishment of the Texas Ethics Commission.

In due course, Smith became one of the state's most prominent citizen advocates, finding himself in the thick of virtually every major state issue affecting consumers and the environment.

Energy issues, however, have remained the Texas office's chief concern. It was instrumental in the creation of the Texas Emissions Reduction Plan, which cut emissions from the dirtiest diesel engines by 30 percent and raised new home energy efficiency by 15 percent. It fought off efforts by utility companies in 1989, 1993 and 1995 to push up rates that would have cost Texans more than $1 billion a year, and by its 30th anniversary in 2014 had managed to block 17 of 22 proposed coal-fired power plants in the state, as well as six of eight proposed nuclear plants.

The office pushed successfully for a law requiring 3 percent of Texas' energy to come from renewable sources by 2009 and to source at least 10,880 megawatts from renewables statewide by 2025 — a target that was met 15 years early, in 2010. It won a power plant cleanup program to reduce smog-forming nitrogen oxide emissions by up to 88 percent, and won safety improvements at the South Texas and Comanche Peak nuclear power plants.

These wins added up to "an amazing record of achievement in the tough Texas political climate," Claybrook said at the Texas office's 20th anniversary celebration in 2004.

"We have seen success when we've built coalitions with unlikely allies," said Smith. "We've won some and we've lost some, but we are getting stronger every day."

Leverage for Consumers

When it became clear in the early 1980s that the government under President Reagan was not going to do much for consumers, Ralph Nader had an inspired idea: Why not try to harness collective consumer buying power to lower the costs of goods and services while creating a constituency to hold sellers and producers accountable? The idea was to enable consumers to drive progressive change through the market, from the bottom up. Public Citizen would act as an intermediary, not as a direct provider.

In 1983, Nader asked a young staffer, Jason Adkins, to research where Public Citizen might usefully organize consumers around homeowner services. (Fast forward: Adkins began serving as chair of Public Citizen, Inc.'s board of directors in 2009.) Adkins found that No. 2 home heating oil — a simple, necessary commodity used by low- and moderate-income communities — offered an ideal vehicle for leveraging consumers' buying power. Similar group purchasing projects had shown some success with that oil in Massachusetts, Connecticut and New York.

The result was Public Citizens' Buyers Up program. "If we don't build that private sector out there in the consumer area, then there's never going to be the constituency to demand enforcement of consumer laws, tough safety and health standards," said Nader of the early effort.

Buyers Up officially launched as a program of Public Citizen in December 1983. In essence, it served as an agent for consumers, negotiating for them with suppliers who agreed to offer group discount rates for goods and services. To participate, households paid a yearly membership fee of $15. Buyers Up took care of administrative matters, negotiated prices and drew up the contracts that assured price discounts and product quality.

A household that used 1,100 gallons of heating oil annually, for example, could save 25 percent on its bills, or $200.[52] The oil distribution companies in turn were assured of high-volume business, a reliable consumer base and steady profits. The program was targeted to serve low- and moderate-income families and nonprofit organizations such as homeless shelters, community centers and religious institutions, as well as small businesses.

At a time of great concern about energy prices and availability — the Iranian Revolution of 1979 was still fresh in everyone's minds — the emergence of Buyers Up was a good-news story that won extensive TV, radio and print media coverage. Buyers Up members were portrayed as empowered consumers taking on big business. Buyers Up was the subject of hundreds of positive news stories, both local and nationwide. These included many feel-good stories on the group and spotlighted ways that consumers could benefit.

Heating oil distributors were wary at first, saying they feared the program would be unreliable. Over time, Buyers Up dispelled such fears and even began to influence energy markets. In its first year, it had only 348 paid subscribers. But then advertising, word-of-mouth and grueling door-to-door promotion, along with several press conferences spotlighting oil market abuses, led to a nearly sevenfold leap in membership.[53] Members collectively saved more than $500,000 in 1984, paying prices 15 to 20 percent below the average market rate.[54]

This early success allowed expansion. By late 1986, five offices served more than 11,000 household and institutional members: in Washington, D.C.; Baltimore, Maryland; Wilmington, Delaware; Philadelphia, Pennsylvania; and Richmond, Virginia. The reach of each office extended to its greater metropolitan area, and in the case of Maryland and Delaware, to the whole state. Buyers Up members purchased oil through 12 participating companies, saving more than $1 million in 1986.[55] Savings rose to $1.3 million in 1988, when 18 oil companies took part.

An unlikely ally in the campaign appeared in the summer of 1985: Abe Pollin, owner of Washington, D.C.'s professional basketball team, the Washington Bullets (now the Wizards). He set up a lottery where Buyers Up members could win up to $1,200 in free heating oil for one year for two members. Drawings were held at basketball games, further increasing Buyers Up's presence in the community. Pollin donated the oil as a community service and lent his support every year until 1992.

To further demonstrate the capacity of group purchasing power and help consumers, Buyers Up soon became involved with a broader array of energy-related programs. In 1986, it began offering cost-effective, high-quality energy conservation products and services, such as conducting free energy audits, upgrading furnaces, insulating homes, closing off cold air leaks and improving hot water systems. Buyers Up-approved energy specialists did the work at negotiated discount rates and according to the exacting specifications that the staff developed from best practices.

To expand the program's reach, Buyers Up successfully negotiated with the D.C. electric utility, Pepco, for subsidies to reduce the cost of weatherization work by non-profit institutions. This enabled Buyers Up to improve dozens of leaky buildings and helped preserve those groups' resources for serving clients.

Buyers Up also raised questions about indoor air quality. Adkins was concerned that pollutants in homes became more concentrated once the homes were insulated. Further research validated what Adkins called "one of the great public health dangers," which led to the group's campaign to educate members on the importance of keeping cleaning products and paint in closed containers or outside to avoid putting toxic chemicals into the indoor air.

Adkins also was concerned about radon, an inert, naturally occurring radioactive gas that can cause lung cancer when inhaled. It is usually attached to house dust or cigarette smoke. The fear was that radon concentrations would grow to unsafe levels in weatherized homes and buildings. However, relatively inexpensive mitigation work could be done to reduce radon levels once they were detected. So Buyers Up began testing home radon kits in 1987 to help consumers pick the best.

The office had consumers buy test kits from providers around the country and then expose the kits to known amounts of radiation. The consumers then returned the kits and forwarded the results to Buyers Up, which evaluated the accuracy of the test kit company's readings by comparing the exposure levels reflected by the kits to the true exposure levels. Surprisingly, three of the seven largest kit companies failed the Buyers Up analyses — although all three had passed a pre-test notification program run by the EPA.

In response, the EPA changed its protocols to perform double-blind tests to ensure more accurate results. In early 1989, Public Citizen published "A Citizen's Guide to Radon Home Test Kits," which rated 35 companies on the quality, pricing and convenience of their do-it-yourself tests.

In addition to extensive coverage of Buyers Up oil-buying, conservation and radon programs, the media covered the many policy reports that Adkins and his staff produced. These included an investigation of oil industry data that disclosed multiple incidents of market manipulation by refineries and pipeline distributers attempting to artificially inflate oil prices. National coverage also followed the Buyers Up discovery that the U.S. still was importing oil from Iran despite a U.S. embargo.

Perhaps most important, Buyers Up assembled and released county-by-county data for Virginia, Washington, D.C., and Maryland showing that an astoundingly high number of low-income families would be left in the cold, without federal heating oil assistance, under cuts proposed by the Reagan administration. By localizing the dramatic cuts and focusing on stark human suffering, Buyers Up drove home the message to Congress and most of the cuts were averted.

Buyers Up also published its own quarterly newsletter containing consumer tips and stories on energy and safety matters and helpful resources on a wide array of subjects — from energy conservation to the benefits NASA had discovered of certain household plants for improving indoor air quality, to the details and locations of businesses and credit unions that cooperated for cost savings.

Buyers Up membership remained fairly constant at 11,000 with an 85 percent renewal rate throughout the late 1980s, when Adkins left Buyers Up to attend law school. The program operated into the early 1990s, but as oil prices stabilized in the late 1990s, reducing consumer savings, more and more households switched to natural gas. Membership declined and, having served its purpose of saving consumers money and stimulating reforms, Buyers Up ended its run in 2005.

Public Citizen has a long history of pushing for safe, clean and efficient energy and fighting industries that favor more self-serving profit goals. The organization confronted the nuclear industry at its zenith and helped stop the construction of new nuclear power plants, while opening up the entire regulatory process to greater transparency and citizen participation.

Fighting nuclear waste, abusive rate controls, the price gouging that came with utility deregulation, weak fuel efficiency standards for motor vehicles — Public Citizen's founding generation was in the thick of all of these battles, as well as launching pro-consumer innovations like Buyers Up to leverage consumer purchasing power. The struggle for fair and eco-friendly energy policies will continue as a major part of Public Citizen's agenda in the years ahead.

Endnotes

1 Rhodes, Richard, *The Making of the Atomic Bomb*, Simon & Schuster, 1986, pp. 431–442.
2 Hilgartner, Bell and O'Conner, *Nukespeak*, Sierra Club Books, 1982, p. 40.
3 U.S. Atomic Energy Commission, *Information Report to the Project Companies of the Dow Chemical — Detroit Edison and Associates, Nuclear Power Development Project*, Dec. 1, 1953, De-classified Aug. 12, 1957, pp. 16–17.
4 U.S. Atomic Energy Commission, *Information Report*, p. 16.
5 U.S. Atomic Energy Commission press release, remarks prepared for the Founders Day Dinner, National Association of Science Writers, Sept. 16, 1954, p. 9.
6 *Public Citizen News*, 1997 Anniversary edition, p. 20.
7 Brown, Jerry and Brutoco, Rinaldo, *Profiles in Power: The Antinuclear Movement and the Dawn of the Solar Age*, Twayne Publishers, 1997, p. xii.
8 See David Bollier, *Citizen Action and Other Big Ideas: A History of Ralph Nader and the Consumer Movement*, Center for Study of Responsive Law, 1991, p. 56.
9 *Critical Mass* newsletter, Vol. 2, No. 12, March 1977, p.1 and 3.
10 *Critical Mass* newsletter, Vol. 1, No. 1., April 1975, p. 9.
11 U.S. Nuclear Regulatory Commission fact sheet, "Nuclear Insurance: Price-Anderson Act."
12 May, John, *The Greenpeace Book of the Nuclear Age*, Pantheon, 1989, p. 126.
13 Judith Cook, *Red Alert: The Worldwide Dangers of Nuclear Power*, New English Library, 1986, p. 82.
14 Richard Pollock, "The Harrisburg Syndrome," *The Public Citizen*, Spring 1979.
15 *Public Citizen Annual Report 1979*, pp. 6–7.
16 Brown, Jerry and Brutoco, Rinaldo, *Profiles in Power: The Antinuclear Movement and the Dawn of the Solar Age*, Twayne Publishers, 1997, p. 26.
17 *1979–1985 Nuclear Power Safety Report*.

18 Jim Riccio and Matthew Freedman, *Hear No Evil, See No Evil, Speak No Evil, Public Citizen's Critical Mass Energy Project,* Dec. 15, 1993.

19 James Cook, "Nuclear Follies: Nuclear Power is a Failing Due to Internal, Not External Problems," *Forbes,* Feb. 11, 1985.

20 *States Pay the Price for Relying on Nuclear Power,* Public Citizen report, June 12, 2001.

21 Brian Zajac, "Ten States that Run on Nuclear Power," 24/7 *Wall St. website,* Feb. 21, 2012. http://247wallst.com/energy-business/2012/02/21/the-ten-statesthat-run-on-nuclear-power/.

22 NBC promotional material, quoted in Public Citizen press release, May 12, 1999.

23 *California Dreaming: The Bailout of California's Nuclear Industry,* Public Citizen, Oct. 30, 1998.

24 "Electric Utilities Seeking Nuclear Bailout are 'California Dreaming," Public Citizen press release, Oct. 30, 1998.

25 "An Urgent Letter from David Brower and Ralph Nader," undated.

26 Thomas D. Elias, "3 California Utilities Bankroll Coalition Backing Bailout," *The Washington Times,* Nov. 3, 1998.

27 Chip Commins and Rebecca Smith, "For Power Suppliers, the California Market Loses its Golden Glow," *The Wall Street Journal,* Jan. 25, 2001.

28 Gray Davis, "Bush's Mistake in California," *The New York Times,* May 31, 2001.

29 Rene Sanchez and William Booth, "California Forced to Turn the Lights Off," *The Washington Post,* Jan. 18, 2001.

30 William Booth and Rene Sanchez, "Blackouts Hobble Calif. for 2nd Day," *The Washington Post,* Jan. 19, 2001.

31 Joseph Kahn, "U.S. Energy Regulators Plan Effort to Limit Prices in West," *The New York Times,* June 14, 2001.

32 John Howard, "Lawmakers Wrap Up San Diego Plan," Associated Press, Sept. 1, 2000.

33 Gray Davis, "Bush's Mistake in California," *The New York Times,* May 31, 2001.

34 *Got Juice: Bush's Refusal to End California's Electricity Price Gouging Enriches Texas Friends and Big Contributors,* Public Citizen, Feb. 2001.

35 *Got Juice: Bush's Refusal to End California's Electricity Price Gouging Enriches Texas Friends and Big Contributors,* Public Citizen, Feb. 2001.

36 Peter Behr, "Justice Probes AES's Electricity Deal," *The Washington Post,* June 6, 2001.

37 *Blind Faith: How Deregulation and Enron's Influence Over Government Looted Billions from Americans,* Public Citizen's Critical Mass Energy and Environment Program, December 2001; *Got Juice: Bush's Refusal to End California's Electricity Price Gouging Enriches Texas Friends and Big Contributors,* Public Citizen, February 2001; Dan Morgan and Juliet Eilperin, "Campaign Gifts, Lobbying Built Enron's Power in Washington," *The Washington Post,* Dec. 25, 2001; and Bob Davis, "Chairman's Deep Political Connections Run Silent," *The Wall Street Journal,* Nov. 29, 2001.

38 Dana Milbank and Glenn Kessler, "Enron's Influence Reached Deep into Administration: Ties Touched Personnel and Policies," *The Washington Post, Jan. 18, 2002.*

39 *Blind Faith,* December 2001.

40 *Blind Faith ,* December 2001; and James Ridgeway, "Watchdog: Senator Pushed End to Oversight for Campaign Contributor: Phil Gramm's Enron Favor," *The Village Voice,* Jan. 16, 2002.

41 Ronald Brownstein, "After Enron, Bush Has Little Wiggle Room," *Los Angeles Times,* Jan. 17, 2002.

42 James Ridgeway, "Watchdog: Senator Pushed End to Oversight for Campaign Contributor: Phil Gramm's Enron Favor," *The Village Voice,* Jan. 16, 2002.

43 *Blind Faith,* December 2001.

44 *Blind Faith,* December 2001.

45 James Ridgeway, "Watchdog: Senator Pushed End to Oversight for Campaign Contributor: Phil Gramm's Enron Favor," *The Village Voice,* Jan. 16, 2002.

46 This account of Enron's collapse is based on news articles over several months in late 2001 and early 2002, primarily from *The Wall Street Journal, The New York Times* and *The Washington Post.*

47 Jason Leopold, "Enron's Trading Schemes: New Documents Reveal What Was Known," Znet, June 7, 2004.

48 Katharine Q. Seelye, "Bush Task Force on Energy Worked in Mysterious Ways," *The New York Times,* May 16, 2001.

49 Katharine Q. Seelye, "After Lobbying, Nuclear Industry Finds Itself Back on Political Map," *The New York Times,* May 23, 2001.

50 Testimony of Tyson Slocum, research director of Public Citizen's Critical Mass Energy Program, before the U.S. Senate Committee on Commerce, Science and Transportation, Sept. 21, 2005.

51 Laura Meckler, "Fuel Standards Set for Auto Makers: Despite Higher Gas Prices Rules Offer Little Change From Last Year's Proposal," *The Wall Street Journal*, March 30, 2006.

52 Belden, Tom. "Consumer Group Will Pay 25% Less for Fuel Oil," *Philadelphia Inquirer*, October 22, 1986.

53 *Public Citizen News,* Spring 1985.

54 *Public Citizen News,* December 1984.

55 Buyers Up pamphlet, 1986.

10
GOING GLOBAL

———

WEDNESDAY, DECEMBER 1, 1999 — The streets of Seattle resembled a war zone. Phalanxes of police officers in riot gear blocked key avenues and intersections around the downtown convention hall. Throngs of protesters roamed the streets of the vibrant West Coast city under a dreary sky, bundled against the chill and the intermittent drizzle. Inside the convention hall, 3,000 delegates to the World Trade Organization (WTO) were hammering out an agreement to govern a new "Millennium Round" of international trade talks.

The gathering was trying to expand the WTO's power and scope, empowering multinational corporations and rolling back decades of hard-won consumer, worker and environmental safeguards. Public Citizen staff had played a key role in organizing the demonstrators against WTO expansion and were scattered across the city, linked by walkie-talkies and cell phones. They sensed they were on the brink of a historic moment.

Suddenly a voice pierced the crackling static of the organizers' handsets. It was Lori Wallach, the head of Public Citizen's Global Trade Watch division. "Trade team! Trade team!" she shouted. "We did it! The WTO expansion is stopped! We have won! There will be no new WTO round!"

Mike Dolan's face lit up where he stood on the corner of Pine Street amid a sea of 30,000 people. He grabbed a megaphone and shouted out the news. "We've won!" The crowd roared. Inside the convention center, Wallach held up her own walkie-talkie so the jubilant activists there could hear the celebration in the street.

Cheering, the activists hoisted Wallach and campaigners from India, Canada, Malaysia and France onto chairs for an impromptu news conference. Public Citizen's Margrete Strand-Rangnes linked arms with her counterparts from Africa, Europe and Asia in a spontaneous jig, and a bemused press corps began to gather.

The week of protest in Seattle proved to be the turning point in a growing debate about globalization. Before 1999, few Americans knew much, if anything, about the powerful global commerce agency called the World Trade Organization. But some 50,000 people had come a long way to point out that the talks were set to undermine hard-won U.S. regulations protecting Americans from health, environmental and labor abuses. World media — and President Bill Clinton — took notice.

The protesters and speakers included progressive luminaries such as Ralph Nader, author and radio host Jim Hightower (a Public Citizen board member), French farm leader Jose Bove, Canadian activist Maude Barlow, Indian author Vandana Shiva, filmmaker Michael Moore and the heads of many U.S. and foreign environmental, consumer, religious, human rights and labor organizations. Massive network television and nationwide newspaper coverage of their speeches and the street demonstrations seared the term "WTO" into the national consciousness.

"The WTO, which was a little-known entity dominated by corporate interests, is now a household word because of one of the largest demonstrations since the Vietnam War and civil rights protests of the 1960s," said Joan Claybrook at the time. From California to Maine, people began to wonder what the buzz was about.

It was a seismic shift in U.S. public awareness about the WTO and its role, and about citizens' own ability to affect what was happening worldwide. The message was electrifying: Even in the country where government and corporations were pushing the corporate globalization agenda, people were fighting back — and winning. A new generation of Americans awoke to the power and excitement of uniting to win an important battle.

Not Just Tariffs and Quotas

December 1999 may have been the first time many Americans realized corporate globalization had broad implications for their lives, but it was a discovery Public Citizen had made almost a decade earlier.

Ralph Nader, ever sensitive to new corporate strategies aimed at dominating markets and consumers, had begun raising questions about the way new universal and mandatory rules were being proposed for international trade deals, starting with the 1988 Canada-U.S. Free Trade Agreement. In 1991, as Congress began debating President George H.W. Bush's request for "Fast Track," a uniquely undemocratic process to railroad such agreements into place, Nader urged Claybrook to get Public Citizen involved.

Meanwhile, Lori Wallach, a young Harvard-trained lawyer, was working as a lobbyist for Public Citizen's Congress Watch division on issues such as pesticide regulation and food safety and labeling. Then she noticed something odd. "I would be testifying at a hearing and industry representatives would say things like, 'Well, you can strengthen that pesticide law, Congressman, but that's not going to be allowed under the GATT [the General Agreement on Tariffs and Trade].' I was thinking, 'What are these people talking about? GATT is just about a bunch of tariffs and quotas.' I began to get a bad feeling that we were missing something."

Indeed they were, and so was virtually everyone else in the U.S. public interest community. Under prodding from Nader, Wallach and Litigation Group attorney Patti Goldman delved deeper into agreements then under negotiation. They saw that the agreements represented a serious threat to the public good. "I felt like I was the security guard at a bank," Wallach told her Public Citizen colleagues. "And what's in the vault is the public interest, and I am 24/7 protecting the front entrances. But the problem is, someone's raiding the entire vault via sneak attack through a door I can't see, and it's somehow related to trade. I know it sounds paranoid, but I sensed that something like that was going on."

In 1991, Claybrook authorized Wallach to engage in the debate about the renewal of an arcane trade procedure called "Fast Track," which President Richard Nixon had concocted in 1973. The procedure turned over to the president numerous powers the Constitution had given to Congress — authority to set the terms of foreign trade, select negotiating partners, decide agreement terms and sign pacts — *before* Congress voted on the matters. Fast Track in effect let the executive branch usurp Congress' legislative process — to propose new laws as needed to conform with trade pacts. A vote on the pacts was guaranteed in both houses of Congress within 90 days after the White House submitted them, with limited debate and no amendments allowed.

Congress had renewed Fast Track several times with little controversy, but had used it previously for only three trade pacts, all focused mainly on traditional tariffs and quotas. However, Nader's antennae twitched when he heard how enthusiastically corporate America was embracing Fast Track this time around. It seemed especially suspect in the context of the anti-regulatory aspects of two proposed future agreements also under negotiation at the time — the North American Free Trade Agreement (NAFTA) and a transformation of the GATT into a new and expansive body called the World Trade Organization.

Several years earlier, in 1988, Nader had worked with citizen groups in Canada to raise concerns about anti-consumer, anti-environment provisions in the U.S.-Canada "free trade" pact. Now he, Claybrook and Wallach discovered that a monumental change had occurred, and the more they learned about the GATT negotiations, the more outraged they were.

The good name of world trade was being hijacked to provide cover for some expansive and binding provisions in pending pacts that had little to do with tariffs and quotas. Rather, the agreements had become backdoor delivery mechanisms for policies designed to limit any government's role in regulating its consumer, labor and environmental markets and corporate conduct.

The United States was an original signatory to the 1948 General Agreement on Tariffs and Trade. That consensus-oriented agreement set basic principles for postwar global trade in goods, providing common tariff and quota schedules for all its country signatories. GATT was so non-controversial that few Americans even knew it existed.

But starting in the mid-1980s, the Reagan administration and Margaret Thatcher's UK government began working quietly to transform the GATT into a new global commerce agency. Its new regulations started imposing *nontrade* policies that would bring to life the Reagan-Thatcher economic worldview, undermining government regulation of markets and privatizing public services.

This Reagan-Thatcher laissez faire agenda had not fared well in the sunshine of public scrutiny. But the obscure "Uruguay Round" of GATT negotiations, launched in 1986, had begun creating a comprehensive set of policies that would be imposed worldwide, a one-size-fits-all model. The pact required every signatory country "to ensure ... the conformity of its laws ... with the provisions of this Agreement." In other words, countries that failed to rewrite their domestic laws and regulations to "harmonize" with the terms of the pact could be subject to economic retaliation from other signatory nations—for having "illegal trade barriers."

It wouldn't matter that those "illegal trade barriers" might be rules about environmental protection or workplace conditions or banking operations that a country had drawn up over decades of domestic debate to protect consumers or public health and safety. Under the new proposal, the trade agreement terms would take precedence.

In 1991, few people were aware of this alarming situation. Mark Ritchie, a Minneapolis-based family farm advocate, was one of them. He had awakened to the GATT talks through his work for Minnesota's agriculture secretary and had taken a leave of absence to explore GATT issues in Europe. He returned with a copy of the secret new treaty draft, and he shared it with Wallach.

"My legal training was very useful, because the text was written in technical jargon and inaccessible to a lay reader," Wallach said. "But [Public Citizen attorney] Patti Goldman and I translated it out of GATTese." Wallach said she then understood that all the retrograde rules would be strongly enforced in international tribunals that could impose trade sanctions. "As I connected with the handful of consumer and environmental advocates in other countries that had become savvy to the deal, I began to recognize its dire implications—on consumer access to affordable medicine, on natural resource and environmental policies, on regulation of services like health care and banks, and more."

The documents showed that powerful multinational corporations and their allies in certain rich-country governments had moved their war against public interest accountability to the international stage. Unable to use the democratic process at home to undercut popular environmental, health and safety laws and consumer-friendly regulation of corporate practices, they were moving quietly to eliminate such rules under the GATT. And a new global commerce agency would be the judge of whether a country's rules conformed to the pact. That agency was first dubbed the "Multilateral Trade Organization" but ultimately was named the World Trade Organization.

A Quiet Corporate Takeover

The draft WTO rules that Public Citizen now examined were written in secrecy under the influence of the world's largest multinationals: 500 U.S. corporations were officially designated as formal U.S. government advisers during the talks. Public interest representatives were not similarly included. The new agreement would subject U.S. health, safety and environmental standards — even those that treated foreign and domestic goods exactly the same — to review by WTO bureaucrats in international tribunals where basic U.S. rules of open due process did not apply. It would impose global uniformity even on value-related decisions — such as a society's chosen level of environmental protection, or how it balances consumer priorities (such as access to affordable medicines) with companies' interests (such as patent protection for drug products).

The draft pact also added new protections for corporations seeking to relocate production to low-wage areas, and new rights allowing foreign firms in the service sector — such as banking, medicine, water, transportation and energy — to acquire or establish businesses and operate them according to WTO rules. In every case, local laws could be undermined.

Mary Bottari was working for the Judiciary Committee in the Wisconsin Legislature in 1991 when, through Wallach, she first heard about the GATT-WTO proposal. "Wisconsin has great environmental laws, great recycling laws, great food safety laws — all sorts of strong consumer laws — but when I took a look at the GATT, it overwhelmed me with its ability to undercut Wisconsin law," said Bottari.

"The agreement would become federal law, which trumps state law. GATT and NAFTA meant 'trade' agreements would be setting the parameters on all sorts of regulatory matters unrelated to trade." Bottari joined Public Citizen and soon became a talented advocate, writer and researcher for many trade reports over the next decade.

Claybrook recognized that the new trade deals cut to the very core of Public Citizen's primary mission of promoting public health, consumer safety, environmental protection and economic justice. She saw that the pact's terms shifted decision-making on matters that would affect people's everyday lives to a distant impersonal venue (such as the closed tribunals in Geneva, Switzerland) where those living with the result would have no role. That seemed to undermine the very principle and practice of democracy itself — a stark and disturbing change from GATT's earlier limited realm of tariffs and quotas. Public Citizen set out to raise funds to tackle this whole new set of concerns.

Public Citizen's initial goal was to block the U.S. government from making deals at the secretive talks that it could later use as an excuse not to address public demands. As an anonymous WTO official later told the *Financial Times*, "The WTO is 'the place where governments collude in private against their domestic pressure groups.'"[1]

"One by one, we reached out to U.S. labor, environmental, family farm, faith and consumer groups whose work was silently being undone in the context of these [trade] negotiations," Wallach said. "It was a tremendous amount of work to get things going. Even other public interest organizations were cool, if not hostile, to the notion that criticism of these seemingly arcane trade issues was not protectionist or that they needed to pay attention."

But Public Citizen soon realized that opposing the WTO's creation in the United States was not sufficient. Stopping this corporate power grab would require coordinated campaigning in many countries at once. Activists were helped by the sheer scope of WTO ambition. It was so audacious that even many governments protested WTO invasion into nontrade matters, often pushed by citizen movements more aware of the threat than U.S. activists. Working with Nader, Wallach began to sound the alarm.

One shocking development under the old GATT rules helped Wallach make her point. In 1990, the Mexican government had complained to GATT that the U.S. Marine Mammal Protection Act of 1972 violated trade rules by barring U.S. sales of tuna caught using purse seine nets. These deadly nets, used in Mexico, had drowned millions of dolphins, appalling consumers. "Dolphin-safe tuna" caught without such nets was now required for any U.S. sale. But the GATT tribunal agreed with Mexico: The U.S. law was an "illegal trade barrier."

This startling 1991 ruling, that the United States should allow imports of dolphin-deadly tuna, could not be enforced under existing GATT rules, which retained some safeguards for national sovereignty. But the new WTO terms would eliminate those safeguards. The new pact would impose trade sanctions on the United States if dolphin-deadly tuna imports were barred.

In short order Public Citizen turned this possibility into Exhibit No. 1, papering much of Washington, D.C., with colorful "GATTzilla vs. Flipper" posters depicting a GATTzilla monster strangling a dolphin, above the caption, "WTO is coming! What you don't know will hurt you!" The "smoking dolphin," the group argued, proved "that trade commitments *do* lead to the erosion of domestic public interest policies." It became an enduring and powerful argument in the battles to come.

The Fast Track Connection

With these developments in mind, Public Citizen geared up to try to halt the pending Fast Track extension that would accelerate the passage of the WTO and NAFTA. Both were being negotiated behind closed doors. Then-Representative Byron Dorgan, a North Dakota Democrat, offered a resolution that would stop an extension of Fast Track, the first time the procedure had been seriously opposed.

It was defeated, but it got 192 votes, only 26 short of passage. The corporations pushing NAFTA and the WTO were shocked, as previous trade votes had often sailed through the House with only single-digit opposition. The change would not have happened without the hard work and growing influence of labor unions on trade issues.

The fight gave global trade critics a major political and psychological boost. Some members had seen what was at stake: Large corporations were quietly trying to shape policy on nontrade matters normally under the jurisdiction of Congress and state legislatures. It also provided a focus for organizing, uniting a small but passionate network of allies — even some conservative businessmen such as Roger Milliken and other textile magnates. And Public Citizen had shown that it could tackle the nuts and bolts of trade deal minutiae and translate technical language to make it comprehensible to the general public.

"We learned a lesson from the Fast Track fight that shaped all the work going forward. That was the power of what we call the 'you can't run, you can't hide' coalition," Wallach said. "Time and again, environmentalists would meet with a representative who would say, 'I would love to be with you on this, but I have to support my union friends.' Meanwhile, the union folks would be asking for the same position as the environmentalists, but get the same story about not being able to get support because the representative had to help his environmental friends. The farm and consumer groups were also being played off each other.

"After a lot of relationship-building work to overcome past differences, we were able to build a cross-sectoral coalition that put everyone in the room together," Wallach said. "That meant that the members of Congress either had to be with their base or had to tell us all straight that they were against the public interest and for the corporations."

Out of this initial effort grew a coalition of labor and environmental advocates and conservative business owners who feared the impact of new trade rules on their companies. It was a left/right coalition that expanded into new grassroots power as more conservative groups got involved.

The NAFTA Battle

In 1991, the George H.W. Bush administration wanted more Fast Track authority because it was negotiating not just the new WTO but also NAFTA. Corporate America was excited because the pact would provide new foreign investor protections that would make it safer and cheaper for firms to relocate to Mexico, where wages were $6 to $10 per day. Labor leaders warned that U.S.-based corporations would use NAFTA to make that move, as not only wages but also workplace and environmental rules were much weaker in Mexico.

NAFTA represented an extreme experiment in merging into a single economy two countries with very different levels of development and public interest regulation. Public Citizen was not alone in foreseeing a race to the bottom as NAFTA threatened to weaken an array of public safeguards, including many that Congress had previously decided not to roll back.

For example, NAFTA privatized enforcement of its rules by empowering corporations and foreign investors to sue governments in secret tribunals outside domestic courts for cash payments when the firms thought domestic regulations or court verdicts would undermine their future profits. Congress had rejected this notion of government compensation for "regulatory takings" because it would eviscerate congressional authority to enact policies in the public interest. But NAFTA would open a back door that would let it sneak into law.

Public Citizen and its allies realized that they faced an enormous gap in U.S. public and congressional understanding of these high stakes. They went on the offensive.

Health and environmental champion Representative Henry Waxman, a California Democrat, and House Democratic Majority Leader Richard Gephardt of Missouri sponsored a resolution that proved an excellent educational and organizing hook for future fights. Its key provision stated: "The Congress will not approve legislation to implement any trade agreement (including the Uruguay Round of the GATT and the United States-Mexico Free Trade Agreement) if such agreement jeopardizes United States health, safety, labor, or environmental laws (including the Federal Food, Drug, and Cosmetic Act and the Clean Air Act)."

The resolution would not have the force of law, but the very idea roused the corporate lobby to fury. Democratic House Speaker Tom Foley of Washington and powerful Ways and Means Chair Dan Rostenkowski, an Illinois Democrat, urged their party members not to be co-sponsors. But a massive grassroots and lobbying effort, led by Public Citizen, resulted in 219 co-sponsors — more than half the House. That set the measure up for a vote.

As the tally began in August 1992, Nader, Claybrook, Wallach and their allies stood on one side of the hallway leading onto the House floor signaling "thumbs up" for yes votes. Corporate lobbyists on the other side of the gauntlet were signaling "thumbs down" — but then they suddenly switched. Thumbs up from everyone!

The resolution passed in a lopsided vote. What had happened? Trade was becoming an election issue, and pro-NAFTA and WTO forces did not want a clear on-the-record tally that would reveal to the public where their representatives stood.

The NAFTA issue played a role in the 1992 presidential election anyway when Reform Party candidate Ross Perot warned that NAFTA would create a "giant sucking sound" as jobs drained south to Mexico. His campaign attracted a sizable number of GOP voters, and their defection helped deliver the election to Democratic nominee Clinton.

Bush signed the NAFTA agreement in the last days of his administration, but it still needed congressional approval. Candidate Clinton had pledged to renegotiate the pact, but President Clinton made passing NAFTA a top priority of his first year in office. This about-face was a shock that put Public Citizen and the rest of the NAFTA opposition into high gear.

House Democratic Whip David Bonior of Michigan, who later joined Public Citizen's board, led the House resistance. U.S. activists worked with their counterparts in Mexico and Canada, including the Council of Canadians President Maude Barlow. They brought useful lessons from their work against the 1988 U.S.-Canada Free Trade Agreement that Nader had questioned.

In 1992, Public Citizen helped launch a national coalition called the Citizens Trade Campaign (CTC), with Public Citizen on its board. Headquartered in the National Farmers Union office, with former Democratic Member of Congress Jim Jontz of Indiana as its first director, CTC united representatives of national labor unions with family farm, consumer, environmental and faith groups. Public Citizen brought to the table research, analysis and media savvy that helped mobilize the large organized memberships and grassroots capacity of the other groups.

The energy of this sudden campaign against NAFTA startled the trade pact's corporate backers and the new Clinton administration. Corporate America responded by throwing $30 million into a public relations and lobbying bombardment to promote the pact. The Mexican government also spent millions on lobbyists and PR firms. Clinton added billions in presidential pork to lure support from members of Congress.

Goldman, the Public Citizen lawyer and an expert in environmental law, then raised a critical question: the National Environmental Policy Act (NEPA) required an Environmental Impact Statement to accompany significant policy decisions. How could NAFTA go forward without such an assessment?

Goldman's NEPA lawsuit against NAFTA convinced a federal district court judge, who ordered such an assessment — an outcome that crashed the Mexican bond market for several days. The Clinton administration then won an appeals court ruling that the assessment wasn't required because NAFTA didn't yet exist. Goldman, relentless, launched a similar NEPA suit against the WTO on the day the WTO pact was signed — and an appeals court this time ruled that the assessment was moot because the organization existed already. "They got us coming and going," Goldman said. The Supreme Court declined to review both decisions.

As the fall of 1993 arrived, however, NAFTA opponents had organized a majority of House members to oppose the deal. The Clinton administration then moved to split the environmental movement. Its tactic was to create a side agreement promising environmental protections, which won support from the National Wildlife Federation, the World Wildlife Fund, the Environmental Defense Fund and the Natural Resources Defense Council.

The agreement was unenforceable, as was an equally unenforceable side agreement on labor issues. But these maneuvers provided cover for some Democratic members of Congress who wanted to vote with Clinton — and the corporations that were lavishing campaign contributions on them.

The result was that Congress approved NAFTA in late 1993. It passed the 435-member House by just 18 votes after Clinton clinched a series of desperate pork-barrel deals in the final days — promising military planes, bridges, highways and even fund-raising help to members of Congress in exchange for their votes. NAFTA went into effect on January 1, 1994.

"We won the debate, but not the vote," Wallach said. "But the national debate over NAFTA changed the face of the issue forever."

The GATT Gambit

While Public Citizen was fighting NAFTA in Congress, it also was doing somewhat lonelier work on the pending GATT-WTO agreement. Some unions and consumer groups were inclined to support the GATT, thinking that expanding "free trade" would deliver benefits to workers and consumers. Public Citizen pointed out that the alluring term was being used to mislabel a policy package that was not about trade alone, and that this was not just another GATT round. It was rather a transformation of GATT into a new powerful global commerce agency (the WTO) that would be able to use new binding rules to roll back basic consumer and labor rights and environmental protections in scores of countries worldwide.

Again, the Clinton administration managed to divide and conquer some domestic forces. President Clinton signed the new GATT with its WTO incarnation two weeks after the NAFTA vote. But it still had to be ratified by its then-123 signatory nations, including the United States.

Many in the public interest sector and in Congress remained unaware of what was at stake because there had been virtually no public debate or input about how the WTO should operate — or even if it should operate at all. Public Citizen worked to block its ratification.

"In the course of two months in 1993, I met face-to-face with more senators than I have lobbied in all my years since," said Wallach. "Ralph [Nader] could just walk into an office without an appointment and see many a senator. But the challenge was enormous. Because there had never been anything like the WTO, and its negotiation has been so secretive, and no one had read the WTO text, even old friends of Public Citizen had a hard time believing that what we said about the WTO's threats to food safety and access to medicine and environmental laws could possibly be true."

Trade was already an election-year issue because of U.S. political fallout from the NAFTA battle. So the Public Citizen team got creative. In one memorable episode that captured national media attention and generated buzz on Capitol Hill, the team delivered to every member of Congress a full-sized pillow in a pillowcase bearing a custom-printed warning — "WTO: Dangerous to Your Political Health" — and urging legislators not to rush the United States into the organization but to "sleep on" the momentous decision.

Republican Senator Bob Dole, a NAFTA supporter, brought the pillow to the Senate floor and held it up to the cameras as he gave a speech warning of the WTO's implications for U.S. sovereignty. Congress listened. It recessed for the 1994 elections to "sleep on" the proposal without taking action.

Nader then challenged any senator to sign an affidavit stating that he or she had read the entire GATT text. Not one would sign. Finally, one senator took the challenge: Colorado Republican Hank Brown. He read the text and then surprised everyone by announcing he would oppose the pact. A free trader, he had supported NAFTA but said he was horrified by the WTO's anti-democratic provisions.

The 1994 elections fired or retired many members of the 103rd Congress, so when it returned for its lame-duck session, the Clinton administration rammed through the new GATT with the support of departing members who had reconsidered their opposition to likely future corporate employers. This locked the United States into a WTO future.

The December 1, 1994, vote represented the last act of a Democratic Congress that had been swept from power — and that was in part because election turnout by labor households had plummeted. Post-election opinion polls documented that working people had stayed home in anger and disgust over NAFTA's passage by a Democratic president and Congress.[2]

Global Trade Watch Arrives

Public Citizen managed to raise some public and congressional awareness that these new agreements meant a radical power shift toward corporations. One success story in the WTO fight was that the Clinton administration was forced to drop a multiyear Fast Track expansion from the WTO implementation bill because it became too controversial to push right then. But Public Citizen could see that the future held more "trade agreement" assaults on its core agenda of protecting health, safety and democracy. To face this challenge, in 1995, Claybrook launched Public Citizen's fifth division, Global Trade Watch, with Lori Wallach as director and Chris McGinn as her deputy.

Wallach had bonded during the GATT/WTO struggle with scholars and activists from several countries who became an international network. Through the insight of San Francisco author Jerry Mander and support from the Foundation for Deep Ecology, this group became the International Forum on Globalization (IFG). Public Citizen was a founding board member.

"Working together as IFG, we set out on a series of teach-ins, newspaper advertisements and books, and gave the name 'corporate globalization' to the pervasive corporate rollback of our most basic rights and safeguards via 'trade' agreements," Wallach said.

While Public Citizen was expanding its trade-related operations, the Clinton administration was expanding its trade-related goals. In 1994, it initiated talks among leaders of all Western Hemisphere nations except Cuba toward what it dubbed the Free Trade Area of the Americas (FTAA) — to extend NAFTA from the Arctic to the Antarctic by 2005. And at the WTO, the administration was pushing to include expanded rights for foreign investors, limits on procurement policy and other provisions that WTO signatories had rejected during the Uruguay Round.

In a moment of unusual candor, Renato Ruggerio, then-director general of the WTO, declared at the WTO's 1996 Singapore Ministerial summit: "We are writing the constitution of a single global economy."[3]

At that Singapore gathering, however, many developing countries rejected this push for WTO expansion. Many battles later, the drive was renamed "the Millennium

Round" of trade talks — the one that Public Citizen and its worldwide allies later derailed at the 1999 Seattle WTO summit.

Meanwhile, totally under the radar, the Clinton administration in 1997 signed a new WTO Financial Services Agreement. Promoted quietly by then-Treasury Undersecretary Timothy Geithner and his boss Treasury Secretary Larry Summers as a simple continuation of discussions predating WTO creation, this pact locked in domestically — and exported internationally — the model of extreme deregulation of financial services that most analysts now consider a prime cause of the 2008 global financial crisis.

Congress never voted on this WTO expansion, which is one reason that many members do not realize to this day that the Financial Services Agreement exists and that it in fact conflicts with the re-regulation of financial practices.

Let the Sunshine In

Like a globalized Hydra, the Multilateral Investment Agreement (MIA) that was beheaded at the 1996 Singapore meeting sprouted a new face later that year: the MIA became the MAI, the Multilateral Agreement on Investments. After developing countries rejected the addition of new investor privileges to the WTO, the 29 wealthy nations of the Organization for Economic Cooperation and Development (OECD) began negotiating at OECD's headquarters in Paris to put them in the MAI — with no input from public interest groups, citizens or elected legislatures. Clinton administration officials at first even denied the MAI's existence.

Public Citizen knew better, thanks to Martin Khor, director of Third World Network. In February 1997, Canadian activists obtained a copy of a draft MAI text, which Public Citizen released to the media. It was shocking. It showed that the MAI would limit the rights of governments — and, by extension, their citizens — to regulate the flow of capital across borders, to determine the degree and shape of foreign investments, to impose standards of behavior on foreign investors, and to shape investment policy so as to promote social, economic and environmental goals.

Foreign firms could demand compensation for having to comply with U.S. laws such as the Community Reinvestment Act, which requires banks to lend money in local communities as a condition for opening branches. Governments would be barred from halting currency speculation, even during a financial crisis. Rules requiring foreign mining and timber firms to meet environmental standards would be subject to attack in foreign tribunals. And as in NAFTA, corporations would have the right to sue governments in special foreign tribunals for compensation if they thought their rights under the agreement had been violated.

To Public Citizen's Global Trade Watch, the MAI seemed an outlandish example of corporate overreaching — an obvious and astonishing attempt to grab as much power for the wealthy elite as possible. And perhaps because the agreement had never been intended for public review, its language was relatively straightforward — and extreme. "We knew that if this horrifying proposal could be exposed to the sunshine of public scrutiny worldwide, we could kill it," Wallach recalled.

Public Citizen and allies launched what they dubbed the "MAI dracula strategy," a coordinated "sunshine" campaign in several countries. It became the model for linking country-based efforts against globalization hazards. Activists listed OECD countries as either prospective allies, relatively neutral players or unrelenting enemies. Finalizing the deal would require consensus among all the countries, so the idea was that countering the most ardent proponents' zeal might allow political space to develop in the more skeptical countries for governments to break consensus and stop the pact.

The Clinton administration was one of the most relentless advocates, and with Congress in Republican hands, Public Citizen saw that efforts there might be futile. On the theory that state legislators might be more worried about sovereignty, Public Citizen and its allies launched a national "campaign of inquiry" involving letters to members of Congress and state legislators posing basic questions about the MAI. Because the pact was so extreme, simply quoting its language and asking about the implications started a considerable buzz. Policymakers scrambled to find out more in order to answer the worrying questions coming in from their constituents.

Public Citizen then set up a debate tour on the pact, inviting Clinton administration officials to discuss it in town meetings. At the first debates, state legislators, members of Congress and activists became so incensed about the proposal that Clinton administration officials stopped taking part. The national MAI debate tour continued, using an empty chair labeled with an official's name.

By late 1998, arch-conservative Senator Jesse Helms of North Carolina was grilling Secretary of State Madeline Albright about the deal in a Senate Foreign Relations Committee hearing. Many congressional letters of inquiry and considerable congressional ire ensued. Several states and localities passed "MAI-Free Zone" resolutions. The Clinton administration showed no intention of stopping the negotiations, but criticism was mounting.

Meanwhile, allies in Canada and France designed campaigns tailored to their political systems. Public Citizen staff spent significant time on the ground with allies in these and other countries. Canadian activists pitted provinces against the central government and ultimately forced the government to demand certain exceptions to the deal, making it vulnerable to similar attacks elsewhere.

After almost two years of pitched campaigning by citizen activists in scores of countries, the French government slammed the lid on the MAI's coffin by announcing in October 1998 that it would not join the required consensus.

NAFTA *Hits Home*

The MAI had been defeated, but the Clinton administration was still pushing to complete the 34-nation Free Trade Area of the Americas, a NAFTA expansion. To

pave the way, the administration in 1997 launched a new drive for Fast Track authority. Public Citizen decided to make the debate a referendum on NAFTA and the very
serious damage it was causing. Then Lindsey Doneth got sick.

On Valentine's Day in 1997, 10-year-old Lindsey and her classmates in Marshall,
Michigan, were served strawberry shortcake as part of their school lunch. Four weeks
later, Lindsey developed flu symptoms and stayed in bed for the day. She got worse
and started vomiting. "After three days at home we knew something was wrong,"
said Sue, her mother. "We took her to the emergency room, and she was diagnosed
with hepatitis A." About 270 other people in five states, including 130 children in
the Marshall community, also became ill.

"I have never seen a child so sick," said Sue Doneth. "I cannot describe to you
what it is like to witness a child so ill, especially when that child is your own. I
remember my child whispering to me through dehydrated, cracked lips, 'Mommy,
it hurts everywhere.' She was hospitalized for six days and lost 10 percent of her
body weight."

Lindsey's illness was traced to the frozen strawberries that had been imported
from Mexico and provided to public schools through the government's school lunch
program. Sue Doneth became incensed about what had happened to her daughter.
"I'm warned when I travel to countries like Mexico not to eat fresh fruit, not to eat
fresh vegetables," she said. "I did some research on growing conditions in countries
like Mexico and was sickened when I learned what sort of conditions exist where
these crops are grown."

Doneth investigated the chain of events. A private company, Andrews and
Williams, had the federal contract to supply food for school lunches. When Doneth
asked how the company managed to get contaminated food through the U.S. system
of safety checks, she found "there were no safety checks. We're essentially taking the
word of these companies to be honest with us and tell us what they're doing, which
is just ridiculous when you're talking about a billion-dollar food industry.

"It wasn't a matter of the system failing. There were no systems in place," she
continued. "The government is only inspecting two percent of what's coming in."
Actually, despite (or perhaps because of) surging produce imports under NAFTA,
inspections that once covered 8 percent of these imports now cover less than 2 percent.

In addition to contaminants that might cause illness like hepatitis A, Mexican
produce often had pesticide residues greater than were allowed in fruits and vegetables grown in the United States. Before NAFTA, spot checks found 18.4 percent
of imported Mexican strawberries had illegal levels of pesticide; after five years of
NAFTA it was 31 percent. In other words, by 1997, almost one-third of the *inspected*
strawberries coming from Mexico had illegal pesticide residues — and since so little
was inspected, most imports sailed easily across the border with their pesticide cargo.[4]

Doneth had never given much thought to trade legislation before 1997, but what
happened to Lindsey made her wonder how trade deals affected ordinary families
like hers. "I used to say I'd spent most of my life becoming an expert in becoming

actively involved in nothing. I was not a joiner. You know, 'Don't sign me up, don't ask me.' I'm as shocked as anyone else that I'm labeled a political activist."

Doneth travelled across the country to tell community groups about the dangers of NAFTA. "I told them this isn't something that just happens to somebody else. I wanted people to know it can happen again, it can happen tomorrow, it can happen the next day — and until regular people like myself become outraged and start putting the pressure on, things aren't going to change."

She was another American galvanized by Public Citizen's founding principle: One determined individual can get results. "I had been one of those people walking around saying, 'Well, what difference does one person make?' It became really clear to me after I became involved in Public Citizen that one person *can* make a difference, and you get a couple of people together and you can make a huge difference."

Tricks for Truckers

A similar speaking tour spotlighted a border truck inspector who had been grievously injured by toxic cargo that had not been labeled. Under NAFTA, goods once made in the United States and now produced in Mexico were flowing north in a new and heavy parade of trucks. Inspection was lax. The trucks initially had to offload their cargo onto U.S. carriers at the border, but NAFTA required Mexico-based trucks to be allowed to travel throughout the United States starting in 2000.

That "market access" rule had a firm start date, but a NAFTA provision calling for "harmonization" of the two countries' safety and environmental standards for trucks had no firm deadline. The debate over what that meant proved to be a politically powerful example of how NAFTA extended far beyond trade to undermine the most basic public safety rules on which all Americans rely.

Claybrook, Public Citizen highway safety allies and the Teamsters worked to force the Clinton administration to review environmental, safety and insurance standards for the Mexico-based trucks and their drivers. What the review found was alarming: Mexican commercial driver's licenses could go to 18-year-old drivers, even if they were colorblind, and required no medical exam or drug testing. The government had no system for tracking driver violations, insurance or hours of service. The truck fleet was older and emitted many more air pollutants than U.S. trucks. Public Citizen pointed out that Americans' safety was at stake.

For the rest of Claybrook's time at Public Citizen, the organization held off an influx of unsafe NAFTA trucks by raising these concerns repeatedly in lobbying efforts and lawsuits. In 2001, Mexico won a NAFTA tribunal ruling that ordered the United States to allow access for Mexico-based trucks or face permanent trade sanctions, and one of President George W. Bush's first actions in office was to try to implement the order. But Public Citizen and a coalition of consumer, labor and environmental groups successfully sued in federal court to block it on grounds the administration had failed to conduct an environmental impact assessment.

That decision was overturned in a 2004 Supreme Court ruling, *Department of Transportation v. Public Citizen,* that had chilling implications: The high court said the domestic requirement for an environmental statement was trumped by the president's foreign affairs authority to enforce an international agreement. But Congress, awakened to the danger, limited the administration to a series of 18-month "pilot" programs that allowed Mexican trucks only restricted access to American roads.

Congress defunded that program in 2007, and prompted by congressional demands for better safety standards, President Barack Obama formally ended it in 2009. But Mexico immediately launched trade sanctions under NAFTA in retaliation, and the controversy continued well into Obama's second term.

Fast Track III

In 1996, Public Citizen started working to ensure that the Clinton administration did not obtain renewed Fast Track authority. The organization knew that if the debate was about giving the administration some general authority for some general thing called "trade expansion," Americans' collective eyes would glaze over. Public Citizen therefore set out early to frame the next Fast Track fight as a referendum on the unpopular NAFTA, labeling Fast Track as "NAFTA Expansion Authority." That frame was adopted by activists across the nation.

Global Trade Watch Research Director Patrick Woodall began compiling the outcomes of NAFTA into a series of well-documented national reports. These showed that every promise of NAFTA boosters—from border environmental cleanup to job creation and more (which the team had meticulously collected and archived)—had failed to materialize, and that damage was accruing instead. Despite roaring economic growth through most of the 1990s, at least 215,000 U.S. workers lost their jobs to NAFTA just in its first years as companies moved factories producing apparel, electronics, autos and other products to Mexico.

Woodall also created state-level NAFTA mini-report cards and released them at scores of local press events. Bass Shoes, which had operated in Maine for 122 years, idled 350 workers on its way south. A Thomson Consumer Electronics plant in Bloomington, Indiana—the self-styled "color television capital of the world"—moved to Mexico, leaving 1,200 workers jobless. Just 8 percent of them found jobs with equal or better pay, according to the Indiana Department of Workforce Development.[5]

In the border town of El Paso, Texas, more than 10,000 workers were laid off due to NAFTA. Cheap imports of tomatoes, hogs, wheat and other commodities had enriched agricultural resale companies but depressed prices for domestic farmers. Real income losses hit 45 percent of U.S. small and medium-sized farms. Mexican tomato imports to the United States grew by 63 percent while more than 100 Florida tomato growers were forced out of business between 1993 and 1998, costing the state $1 billion. And did U.S. consumers benefit? No, consumer prices rose by 16 percent.

In Mexico, NAFTA was also dealing a devastating blow to many, though the trade pact had been touted as opening the route to a higher standard of living. An estimated 28,000 small businesses were destroyed by competition with subsidized U.S. and foreign multinationals. Many peasant farmers were forced off their land because their crops were no longer "competitive." Eight million Mexicans were pushed out of the middle class and into poverty. Meanwhile, pollution rose and health and environmental conditions deteriorated along the U.S.-Mexico border. By the late 1990s, the Mexican government found that 1.5 million small farmers had lost their livelihoods to NAFTA corn imports and emigration to the United States had doubled.

Then a Public Citizen Freedom of Information Act lawsuit won access to the raw figures of a Department of Labor database on NAFTA job losses. The team quickly designed a NAFTA casualty list searchable by zip code, industry and more, and this soon became the most visited page on the Global Trade Watch section of Public Citizen's website. In monthly reports, it compared the official count of jobs lost to the administration's rosy pre-passage claims, showing that NAFTA opponents' worst predictions were coming true. The Department of Commerce soon shut down its NAFTA job creation website, which had shown a gain of only a few hundred jobs.

Many Americans whose economic fortunes were not directly affected had felt NAFTA's impact in other ways. Working with the Teamsters, Public Citizen helped organize national speaking events that allowed Doneth and others injured by NAFTA to tell their stories. Public Citizen's NAFTA Accountability Campaign tracked NAFTA damage in the congressional districts of the key representatives whose votes had won NAFTA passage, and these made news as well.

All this contributed to a satisfying victory in 1997. As the congressional vote on a five-year extension of Fast Track moved into the wee hours, the Global Trade Watch field team worked the phones while Wallach stalked the Capitol halls with powerful labor and environmental allies. Representative David Bonior led a team whipping up "no" votes on the floor. It worked.

To avoid a formal defeat, President Clinton asked Speaker Newt Gingrich to withdraw Fast Track from the House floor. It was the first time a Fast Track request had failed in Congress since Nixon cooked up the idea in 1973. And when Clinton tried again in 1998, the House voted Fast Track down officially, depriving Clinton of this extreme power for all of his administration except the first two years.

The win seemed to signal a shift in the balance of power over the trade issue. By the end of 1998, NAFTA had been in effect for five years, so Global Trade Watch issued a damning report, "NAFTA at Five," which compiled and documented its failings. Consumer groups like Public Citizen and its civil society allies could now stall some of these abuses despite the vast corporate resources deployed against them. The seemingly inexorable corporate globalization juggernaut had at least been slowed.

Stalling WTO Expansion

Energized by the MAI and Fast Track victories of 1998, Global Trade Watch again set its sights on the prime delivery mechanism for corporate globalization — the World Trade Organization. Now three years old and at that time still largely unknown to the U.S. public, the WTO was gearing up to launch the "Millennium Round" of negotiations at a summit planned for 1999. U.S., European, Japanese and other developed-country governments — and a bloc of powerful multinational corporations — wanted to revive the expansion agenda that had died at the 1996 Singapore gathering.

The Clinton administration and other supporters hoped to expand the WTO's jurisdiction to cover global investments, biotechnology and more service-sector fields such as health and education. Some countries wanted to include the discredited elements of the MAI.

Global Trade Watch and its other allies had other plans. They geared up too — for a yearlong "WTO: No New Round — Turnaround!" campaign that would focus on getting rid of many WTO rules, rather than expanding the mess. The campaigners identified the Achilles heel of the expansion drive — deep conflicts among the powerful interests and countries of the WTO. Each national opposition campaign therefore focused on the aspects that were most politically untenable in that country.

Many nations had experienced major public controversy over the WTO's initial launch, with massive protests in India, the Philippines and elsewhere. But in the United States, NAFTA and its increasingly visible job losses were still trade topic No. 1. Public Citizen sought a way to communicate to the American people just exactly what the secretive WTO was doing and how it related to NAFTA.

Media interest and coverage had been scant. WTO headquarters was in Geneva, Switzerland, and few, if any, of the largest U.S. media organizations covered it full time. Global Trade Watch had managed to draw attention to some of the more outlandish WTO rulings. One was the declaration that U.S. Clean Air Act rules limiting gasoline pollution were an illegal trade barrier. Another said that so were Endangered Species Act rules protecting sea turtles from being killed by shrimp fishing.

Global Trade Watch also scored on the news that the Clinton administration had pushed through a major rollback of dolphin protections to avoid WTO sanctions in that old case about dolphin-deadly tuna imports. However, a poll found that most Americans still thought "WTO" referred to the call letters of a radio station.

Wallach and her colleagues at Global Trade Watch set out on two tracks: a research project to gather a comprehensive record of WTO outcomes to date, and a public education campaign using simple fact sheets on each possible subject of interest, from food safety to the environment to jobs.

Through 1998 and the first half of 1999, the team labored to document, in meticulous detail, the record of WTO challenges and rulings with public interest implications. The team also examined WTO processes and economic trends related to what it had caused in the United States and in developing countries. What they found was so shocking it made the serious concerns they had raised during the WTO ratification fight in 1994 seem mild.

Few had noticed, for example, that the U.S. Department of Agriculture had obeyed the WTO's order that it could no longer require imports of fresh and processed meat to conform to U.S. standards. Now Americans had to accept meat imports that met whatever the Agriculture Department declared were "equivalent" standards. Global Trade Watch found that the standards in 43 countries had been declared "equivalent" even though many of the countries had inadequate safety systems, and imports of their processed and fresh meats were on grocery store shelves nationwide.

For instance, U.S. law forbade company-paid meat inspectors, but the USDA had declared Australian chicken "equivalent" to USDA-inspected chicken, even though it had been inspected only by meatpacking companies — and salmonella poisoning in Australia had risen by 20 percent in the first year of such company inspections.

In other abuses, U.S. consumer prices for medicine had increased, thanks to the WTO's requirement that the United States extend its 17-year drug patent terms to 20 years before cheaper generics could compete. In developing countries, millions of people were being displaced from farming by WTO-approved imports, so that hunger and migrations were rising. The damage list went on, and Public Citizen kept track.[6]

The group discovered — and pointed out to allies — that even state laws were under WTO attack. Massachusetts had passed a boycott law aimed at the military dictatorship in Myanmar, formerly Burma, that was identical to a law that had helped fight apartheid in South Africa. The intent was to keep American taxpayer dollars from shoring up repressive governments. But Japan and the European Union challenged the Massachusetts law on the grounds that WTO rules forbade considering noncommercial factors, such as human rights abuses, in government purchasing decisions.

That case was suspended after a U.S. corporate front group called USA Engage challenged the law separately in U.S. courts. But the Clinton administration used the WTO attack on the Massachusetts law as Exhibit No. 1 to kill a similar proposal in Maryland that was aimed at the military regime in Nigeria. The State Department argued that the proposed law would run afoul of WTO rules, and the legislation, which had been expected to pass easily, failed by one vote.

In other countries, conflicts also were common. Nations challenged each other's health and safety standards for imported products, typically on behalf of large corporations whose only motive was profit. Public Citizen's Global Trade Watch staff was often called upon for advice in resisting those challenges. On behalf of Chiquita, which was headquartered in Ohio but produced bananas on plantations with terrible labor records in Ecuador and other Latin American countries, the Clinton administration challenged a European Union effort to open its markets to poor Caribbean island banana producers. "We pointed out what was involved there," Wallach recalled.

On behalf of Big Pharma, the Clinton administration went after Brazil's policy on access to anti-AIDS medicines, but dropped the case after a huge public outcry. Another U.S. challenge on behalf of Big Pharma, against India's ban on the patenting of seeds, medicines and life forms, resulted in an adverse WTO ruling that required India to change policies that had helped to safeguard the lives and food security of its large population of poor people.

On behalf of the U.S. Cattlemen's Beef Association, the Clinton administration challenged a European ban on meat grown using artificial growth hormones. Even though Europe banned its own farmers from using these chemicals, some of which were known human carcinogens, the WTO ordered the European Union to admit the U.S. meat, over Public Citizen objections. Canada challenged France's ban on asbestos imports, but the case had such an explosive possibility for bad publicity that a WTO tribunal found a creative way to reject it quietly.

The United States then threatened to take WTO action against Japan, Australia and the EU over their requirements for labeling genetically modified food. In another case, South Korea, to avoid a threatened U.S. challenge, extended its allowable shelf life for processed meat from 30 to 90 days. Guatemala was forced to weaken its UNICEF-Nestle Code baby formula labeling requirements — meant to ensure that illiterate mothers are not tricked into abandoning breast feeding — because baby food maker Gerber got the U.S. government to threaten WTO action.[7]

"In each of those cases we helped make it clear what was going on and got a number of other groups involved — wildlife and natural resource groups, anti-apartheid movement activists and so on," Wallach said. "Issue by issue, Public Citizen helped other groups recognize the situation."

Each case found corporations seeking to replace existing national product standards with global ones, which they had written themselves under NAFTA and WTO requirements for the "harmonization" of standards across the world. In theory, harmonization could require countries with lower standards to accept higher ones, but unfortunately — if predictably — that's not how it worked. Instead, the WTO and NAFTA set a ceiling on safety — so that laws above their standards were subject to challenge — but failed to set a floor of standards that all goods must meet. This lack of baseline standards became a major Public Citizen talking point in its opposition to expanding the WTO.

The more Public Citizen researchers discovered, the clearer it became that the WTO was a vehicle for big business to ride over and crush any country's regulations that could hinder their push for short-term profits and higher stock prices. It seemed to Public Citizen that democratic governance itself hung in the balance.

"WTO rules go way beyond basic trade principles, such as treating domestic and foreign goods the same. They actually impose value judgments on how much environmental or food safety protection a country will be allowed to provide its people," Wallach said. "The WTO's five-year track record looked like a quiet, slow-motion coup d'état against democratic and accountable policymaking and governance worldwide."[8]

Girding for the Battle of Seattle

Global Trade Watch saw the plans for a 1999 WTO meeting of trade ministers as a real opportunity to ratchet up the visibility of these issues for the public. The day Seattle was announced as the site for a December gathering, Public Citizen began reserving youth hostels and hundreds of hotel rooms, plus large venues for rallies, teach-ins and other events. Wallach named Global Trade Watch's field director, Mike Dolan, as the protest organizer.

"Within two weeks, I was there," Dolan recalled. "I knew if we didn't take the lead in organizing things, they wouldn't happen." He rented a cheap Seattle storefront slated for demolition the following year, and volunteer carpenters built a makeshift office. Phones and computers were donated and furniture came from yard sales. In March, a website went up to be a central source of information. Dolan and other Public Citizen activists traveled the country organizing turnout for the coming protests.

"We opened a press center and built a makeshift radio studio from which we persuaded three national, hour-long shows to broadcast live each day," Wallach said. "Organizing for Seattle was a herculean task, and involved training and coordinating nearly 3,000 volunteers."

Dolan called it "pure, unadulterated grassroots organizing." He met regularly with city police to ensure that Public Citizen's demonstrations would be peaceful.

In mid-October, Public Citizen released a groundbreaking 229-page paperback book called *Whose Trade Organization? Corporate Globalization and the Erosion of Democracy,* authored by Wallach and Global Trade Watch Research Director Patrick Woodall. News media gearing up for Seattle could use the book for the information they needed to flesh out the debate. It also gave organizers a morale boost as they distributed copies to appreciative activists around the world. Less than a year after publication, 10,000 copies were in circulation and 5,000 more were ordered.

As protesters gathered in Seattle in late November 1999, a *Wall Street Journal* writer sniffed at the carnival atmosphere of costumes, concerts, parades, giant puppets and street theatre, dubbing it the "Woodstock of anti-globalization."[9] But participants knew it was serious. A dockworkers' union had its 9,600 members stop work on December 1, the conference opening day, to shut down West Coast cargo movement in solidarity with the protesters. Longshoremen lined up beside people dressed as monarch butterflies. Activists from around the world had united to stop WTO expansion and force a rethink of the corporate globalization agenda it imposed.[10]

Mike Dunlap, a burly steelworker from West Virginia, was standing on a corner by the Methodist Church when he saw some environmentalists parading by in turtle costumes. "Passers-by were giving these young students, mostly female, a hard time about being environmentalists and being dressed as turtles," said Dunlap. "I thought, 'I'm not going to stand by and let this happen.' So I went and I put a turtle suit on. If they want to talk bad to the turtles, let them talk bad to me."

Pictures of the 6-foot-4 machine worker marching along in a turtle suit flashed around the world, the perfect illustration of the new broad political front against the WTO. *Newsweek* and other publications prominently featured it. Dunlap's gesture encapsulated years of coalition-building by Public Citizen and others, bringing disparate and often competing groups together to fight the common threat of job losses and attacks on human and consumer rights.

"By me putting that turtle suit on, we made a bridge between those folks and organized labor," Dunlap said in an interview. "Since then, I've spoken to many student groups about world trade. I'm very proud I did that. I didn't know the impact it would have at the time."

Dunlap said he went to Seattle because he was concerned about American jobs disappearing overseas as corporations rushed to exploit weak labor and environmental policies in developing countries. "We're not against trade," he said. "But we have to have a level playing field. We can't compete against child labor. But it's not just about money. Trade involves the losing of jobs but also conditions in other countries where people bathe and wash dishes in the same water. It involves human rights."[11]

As the WTO opening day dawned, thousands of protesters — a "guerrilla army," said *The Washington Post* — surrounded the Washington State Convention and Trade Center. Many chained themselves together across the entrances.[12] Before dawn, activists had organized to block every major intersection in downtown Seattle. Some WTO delegates were turned away while others remained trapped in their hotels, unable to get to the convention hall. A morning opening ceremony was canceled. At noon, tens of thousands of protesters from the Steelworkers, Machinists, Teamsters, the Washington state AFL-CIO and other labor unions converged for a massive rally and a peaceful march through the city.

The tranquility wouldn't hold. Under Clinton administration pressure to remove the demonstrators, Seattle police began to use pepper spray and tear gas, beating protesters who resisted. Then a small band of people dressed in black and wearing full-face ski masks began overturning trash containers and smashing store windows. The organizers and many protesters implored the police and the window-smashers to stop, to no avail. Indeed, police stood by as property was damaged and instead attacked the non-violent protesters. They used a barrage of tear gas, pepper spray and rubber bullets to disperse them, hauling hundreds off to jail.

As the tear gas swirled, Dolan peered through the smoke and saw California state Senator Tom Hayden, the former Vietnam War protester and one of the famed Chicago Seven who disrupted the 1968 Democratic Convention. "The difference between Chicago '68 and Seattle '99," Hayden told him, "is that you're winning."

And win they did. The WTO meeting was unable to open until 3 p.m., and by then the world was watching — and wondering. Nader, Jim Hightower and other national figures gave so many speeches and interviews that President Clinton was forced to comment on the protests. He noted that many Americans were worried about globalization and said the WTO needed to include improved labor rights.

This comment only fanned the flames of activists inside the convention center, where scores of trade ministers from developing countries had been watching the street action on television. Quickly, the U.S. and a few other countries' representatives met behind closed doors to work out a take-it-or-leave-it deal.

Marches, teach-ins and rallies continued through the week. On the last scheduled day of the meeting, a bloc of African countries and then Latin American and Caribbean countries announced their rejection of the WTO expansion agenda the U.S. and its small group had offered. They declared it would result in more hungry people, more people without access to life-saving medicines and more power for the world's largest corporations over developing countries' natural resources.

The WTO expansion had stalled. The outcome gave civil society new political relevance. Media coverage had forced the debate on corporate globalization onto front pages everywhere for a week, a huge coup in itself. And trade rules now became a front-burner issue, with major news organizations covering the issues in far greater depth than they ever had before.

For many activists, the fair trade campaign became their civil rights movement, and Seattle was their March on Washington. "In every era, different phenomena end up affecting every aspect of our lives," Wallach said. "The phenomenon of globalization is that issue for our generation."

The New Millennium

In 1998, the Clinton administration had begun to push what TransAfrica's founding president Randall Robinson called "NAFTA for Africa." The African Growth and Opportunity Act (AGOA) was billed as a way to expand African countries' access to U.S. and other markets, especially for textiles and clothing. However, it was drawn up with little, if any, input from African countries themselves.

Public Citizen successfully opposed it for three years. The organization pointed out that AGOA would require each African nation to submit to an annual review by the U.S. president to determine if its protections for investors and intellectual property, among other policies corporations favored, qualified it to continue in special status. Decisions, predictably, would rely heavily on U.S. industry views, not on any required benefit to the African countries or to American consumers.

Public Citizen worked with TransAfrica and the Congressional Black Caucus to promote an alternative measure called the Human Rights, Opportunity, Partnership and Empowerment (HOPE) for Africa Act. But Congress was not open to these arguments and AGOA was approved in 2000.

That year also brought a battle in Congress over whether to grant China Permanent Normal Trade Relations (previously Most Favored Nation) status. In prior years, Congress had reviewed China's human rights and economic conduct and determined annually whether to allow it certain trade benefits. The Clinton administration wanted to dispense with the annual reviews and make the preferential status permanent as part of China's bid to join the WTO. Many in Congress opposed this plan, and Public Citizen worked intensely for a year with California Representative Nancy Pelosi and Tiananmen Square student refugees to stop it.

Corporate America, salivating over the prospect of tapping into China's huge cheap labor pool, poured contributions into the campaigns of relevant members of Congress. Public Citizen issued a study showing that corporations also had spent $13 million to $15 million on advertising for the proposal, dwarfing the $4 million mustered against Clinton's health care plan earlier in the decade.[13] Lobbyists swarmed over the Capitol, and Congress approved the China legislation. But the need for such massive spending and the bad publicity demonstrated that a dramatic political shift had taken place: Americans were now deeply suspicious of trade deals.

"It had taken 10 years to move the issue, which is about what Ralph Nader told me in his office in 1991 when I first showed up with the GATT text," said Wallach. "He said it could be done with 100 percent focus and 200 percent effort. We went from being laughed at in 1990, when we tried to talk to the press, most of Congress or the [first Bush] administration, to [being] an unavoidable factor in the most crucial policy debate of our time, globalization."

The "Seattle coalition" of civil society groups from 77 countries capitalized on that position with the December 1999 launch of Our World Is Not for Sale, a global network dedicated to rolling back corporate globalization and replacing it with rules to benefit people and the environment. The network's WTO Turnaround Agenda called for elimination of the WTO's nontrade rules and for new global trade controls based on a "floor of decency" — the international standards for labor, environmental preservation, health care and human rights to which most WTO signatory countries had agreed in various UN and other treaties.

"The WTO must be cut back so that these already-agreed public interest standards can serve as a floor of conduct that no corporation can violate if it wants the benefits of global trade rules and market access," the founding statement said.[14] "What we want is for countries to be free to prioritize these other values and goals. And as long as a country treats domestic and foreign goods and investors the same, it's up to the country to decide the values it seeks for its domestic policies."

The United States had banned child labor, for example, so it should have the right to bar imports made with child labor. If India prioritized the World Health Organization treaty on access to essential medicines more than the WTO's intellectual property rules, so be it — as long as it treated foreign and domestic firms the same way.

"This was a campaign about what we are for," Public Citizen declared. "We are for internationalism — where different cultures, countries and people trade and exchange goods and ideas and work together towards common goals — not for corporate economic globalization, which imposes a one-size-fits-all model of economic and social policy worldwide."

With the contested election of President George W. Bush in 2000, corporate influence seemed entrenched in Washington, D.C. Still, the broad movement against corporate globalization was gearing up for major protests at the annual fall World Bank and International Monetary Fund meetings. Then came the attacks on the World Trade Center of September 11, 2001.

National security became the Bush administration's standard defense thereafter for a broad array of controversial measures both public and secret, whose reach is still being uncovered today. The proposed measures immediately included another run at the trade policies that citizen campaigning had derailed.

The Doha Round

Preparing for a WTO ministerial meeting in Doha, Qatar, in November 2001, only weeks after the 9/11 attacks, the U.S. and the European Union resurrected the same WTO expansion agenda that had failed twice. They renamed it the "Doha Development Round" and pitched it as a new deal for developing countries. A large bloc of 100 such countries were not fooled, however, and united behind an alternative agenda to fix WTO rules, one that overlapped with the citizens' "Turnaround" agenda.

At Doha, U.S. officials warned the trade ministers that anyone who did not support "increased international cooperation" in the form of WTO expansion was implicitly supporting terrorism. Developing countries rejected that argument and continued to block the expansion until the scheduled meeting ended. But the talks were then extended. Many diplomats had to depart, and with fewer opponents present, the meeting agreed to launch the Doha Round of WTO expansion talks.

Back in Washington, D.C., the Republican-controlled Congress moved to resurrect Fast Track for President Bush, renaming it Trade Promotion Authority. Public Citizen and its allies blocked it for 18 months, winning repeated skirmishes, but then the president made it a top priority. In a post-midnight vote at the end of the session, with the clock held open for an hour while members' arms were twisted, Fast Track was reauthorized by a two-vote margin. The 2002 decision gave the president authority for the next five years to bypass Congress in negotiating and implementing so-called "free-trade" agreements.

A flood of such proposals began to surge worldwide in a corporate drive to extend existing NAFTA rules wherever possible. Global Trade Watch found itself working with activists in South Africa, Thailand, Malaysia and elsewhere against NAFTA-style pacts, helping to inform local allies in detail just what was at stake for them. Public Citizen and its international allies also worked to build opposition to the Doha Round WTO expansion and its dangerous agenda.

The first victory came at a September 2003 WTO ministerial meeting in Cancun, Mexico. Many countries' trade ministers reiterated their opposition to aspects of the Doha Round agenda, and the talks collapsed after four days. In 2004, the U.S and other Doha Round boosters realized their plan was in dire trouble and agreed to jettison half of the expansion proposal to add new foreign investor rights and limits to competition and procurement policies. That year, Lori Wallach and Michelle Sforza updated and the New Press republished Public Citizen's 1999 book *Whose Trade Organization? A Comprehensive Guide to the WTO*. It detailed the whole sorry history.

For the next five years, Public Citizen and its civil society allies around the world continued their efforts and further Doha round meetings foundered again and again on the same issues. Public Citizen's Global Trade Watch activists and allies were so relentless at WTO ministerial meetings in Geneva and Hong Kong that the WTO stopped holding ministerial meetings for a time.

Many meetings, deadlines and declarations followed in the next several years, but WTO expansion terms remained undecided, and as the civil society campaign grew and the dire results of the original WTO rules became more apparent, the prospect of the Doha Round's demise began to haunt Obama's second term.

The Battle Goes South

With the Doha Round deadlocked, the Bush administration renewed a push for the stalled Free Trade Area of the Americas (FTAA) pact in negotiations among 34 countries of the Americas. The FTAA was intended to be the most far-reaching such agreement in history and was based on the NAFTA model. But it went far beyond NAFTA in its scope and power. The FTAA sought to introduce into the Western Hemisphere all the provisions of the proposed WTO agreement on services plus those of the failed agreement on investments, as well as new limits on access to affordable medicines that would boost Big Pharma profits. It would create a new corporate globalization powerhouse with sweeping new authority.

Public Citizen was among opponents who had campaigned since 1994 to stop this dangerous pact. Staff worked with allies throughout the Americas in national-level campaigns and at FTAA ministerial meetings in Lima, Quebec City and other locales. Brazil, Argentina and several Caribbean nations began to declare opposition to the extreme new corporate privileges the FTAA would establish.

By 2002, national polling showed that American sentiment had begun to turn against "free trade" agreements in general. So the call went out for demonstrators to come to the November 2003 FTAA ministerial meeting in Miami. Public Citizen joined a team of renowned musicians and actors on a monthlong, multicity Tell Us the Truth concert tour, ending in Miami.

Miami officials declared unconditional support for the trade talks. Police harassed activists at campaign headquarters in a Miami storefront and swore that protesters would not be allowed to block streets or meeting access as they had in Seattle. The city became a militarized zone.

Downtown businesses were asked to close as an army of extra police clad in riot gear converged on the protesters. In the ensuing melee, scores of people were beaten and arrested, including journalists and Miami residents. Some were beaten again in jail, and lawsuits against the police reverberated for years thereafter, keeping the issues in the news.

At the meeting, meanwhile, key countries' delegates refused to accept the full NAFTA-style "single undertaking" list of rules binding every country, as the United States wanted. They insisted on an "FTAA-lite" approach that included a few "core" obligations for all, with additional terms optional. The United States would not relent, as corporate interests declared it was better to have no deal if they could not get what they wanted. The meeting closed with an official announcement that negotiations would continue. But in fact, the NAFTA-on-steroids agenda had been derailed and later talks sputtered to an end. In a major setback for corporate globalization, the FTAA was officially declared dead in 2007.

The Bush administration's fallback strategy was to make deals with a "coalition of the willing" — countries that had supported its FTAA agenda. Thus in 2004, it signed a Central America Free Trade Agreement (CAFTA) with the Dominican Republic and five Central American nations — Guatemala, El Salvador, Honduras, Costa Rica and Nicaragua.

Public Citizen, its NAFTA allies and new allies from the Latino civil rights movements campaigned for a year in Congress against U.S. approval. On July 27, 2005, the pact passed the House, but in the middle of the night and by only one vote — that of veteran Republican Representative Robin Hayes of North Carolina. Public Citizen immediately launched the CAFTA Damage Report, which regularly documented the consequences of this agreement. In 2008, Hayes lost his seat in Congress to a political novice whose campaign hammered on his vote and the pact's damage to the U.S. economy.

Promoting Fair Trade

In 2005, to rally such grassroots support for "fair trade" rather than "free trade" and to increase public awareness of globalization's threats, Public Citizen launched the New Accountability Project. The goal was to educate state and local officials on why they should become involved in trade policymaking and how to do it. In part as a result, several states passed legislation in 2007 asserting their right to vote on whether they must be bound by new pacts, and more than a score of states passed resolutions asking Congress to replace Fast Track with a more accountable system for trade negotiations.

The 2006 midterm elections featured trade issues for the first time. "We found at least 100 ads that used the trade issue and attacked incumbents for their votes in 2005," Wallach said. When voters returned the House to Democratic control, front-page news stories declared that voters had punished NAFTA supporters, adding 31 members who supported "fair trade." Polls then found that majorities of Democrats, Republicans and Independents alike were opposed to a continuation of the Bush administration's trade agreement agenda. "The public has internalized the notion that these agreements are bad for us," Wallach said.

In January 2007, Wallach submitted testimony to a congressional hearing about the economic carnage of CAFTA and other deals negotiated under Fast Track. The average American worker was making only a nickel more per hour in inflation-adjusted terms than in 1973, the year before Fast Track went into effect, she said. Were it not for trade agreements that pit U.S. workers against poverty-wage laborers worldwide in a race to the bottom, wages in all countries would better track productivity increases. Meanwhile, in 2006, the United States had only 14 million manufacturing jobs left—nearly 3 million down from the pre-NAFTA-WTO level.[15]

"Fast Track, like eight-track tapes, belongs in a Smithsonian display of outdated technology," Wallach said. Congress listened to her and other opponents and voted down Fast Track, a major victory for consumers. With the authority's massive political liability established, President Obama declared during his 2008 campaign that he would replace it with a new process. Public Citizen activists bird-dogged the 2008 Democratic primaries, extracting written commitments from all candidates to renegotiate NAFTA and more.

In 2008, Public Citizen also helped promote a major motion picture, "Battle in Seattle," directed by Stuart Townsend and featuring Charlize Theron, Woody Harrelson and other stars in a drama about a dozen fictional characters during the five days of the protests in 1999. Opposition to the old trade regime became a theme of the 2008 elections; Public Citizen issued a report documenting the more than 200 television ads that were run against NAFTA, CAFTA and trade-pact job offshoring.

The fall elections brought in 51 new House members, and Public Citizen set out to educate them all, as it did in every new Congress, about the dangers of being uncritical supporters of sweet-sounding "free trade" agreements. With congressional and civil society allies, Public Citizen sought to build consensus about what sorts of trade agreements and negotiating processes to support.

More than 160 representatives and senators co-sponsored legislation that detailed this vision. The Trade Reform, Accountability, Development and Employment (TRADE) Act, sponsored by Maine Representative Michael Michaud and Ohio Senator Sherrod Brown, outlined terms that agreements must and must not include and detailed a replacement for the Fast Track process. The TRADE Act proposals have resonated ever since.

A Public Citizen book, *The Rise and Fall of Fast Track Trade Authority*, became another tool. The book, authored by Wallach and Global Trade Watch Research Director Todd Tucker in 2008, provided the first primary-source history of trade authority since the nation's founding. It documented Fast Track as a historical anomaly, used only 16 times in American history. Many noncontroversial pacts had passed without it. Public Citizen was hopeful that the new members and the Obama administration might become allies in preventing further trade pact damage. "We look forward to a future new mechanism that can reduce political tension about trade policy and secure prosperity for the greatest number of Americans," the authors said, "while preserving the vital tenets of American democracy in the era of globalization."

The issues have only intensified since Claybrook left Public Citizen. "We've been outspent and outgunned in communicating to the public, but we've managed to connect these agreements to the disasters they have caused in people's lives," Wallach said. "Perhaps the most lasting and pervasive contribution of Public Citizen was in creating debate where there was none. We've helped the public understand the threat from these trade agreements to people's day-to-day lives and the basic principles of democratic governance — that those living with the results must make the decisions. We stopped the new WTO round, the FTAA and the MAI, and although we're still fighting for the necessary turnaround, globalization is now a viable, dangerous issue in American politics."

Endnotes

1   Lori Wallach and Michelle Sforza, *Whose Trade Organization? Corporate Globalization and the Erosion of Democracy,* Public Citizen, 1999, pp. 4 , 71.
2   Karen Hosler, "World Trade Agreement Wins Senate's Approval," *Baltimore Sun,* Dec. 2, 1994.
3   Public Citizen fact sheets, found at www.citizen.org/trade.
4   *NAFTA at Five,* Public Citizen's Global Trade Watch, December 1998, p. 9.
5   *NAFTA at Five,* Public Citizen's Global Trade Watch, December 1998.
6   Lori Wallach and Michelle Sforza, *Whose Trade Organization?,* Public Citizen, 1999.
7   Lori Wallach and Michelle Sforza, *Whose Trade Organization?,* Public Citizen, 1999.
8   "Five-Year Record of WTO Reveals Disturbing Trends: Food Safety, Environment Undermined, Accountable Governance Eroded," Public Citizen press release, Oct. 13, 1999.
9   Helene Cooper, "Some Hazy, Some Erudite and All Angry," *The Wall Street Journal,* Nov. 30, 1999.
10 *Public Citizen News,* Jan/Feb 2000, p. 7.
11 Mike Dunlap, interview, April 20, 2000.
12 John Burgess and Steven Pearlstein, "Protests Delay WTO Opening," *The Washington Post,* Dec. 1, 1999.
13 *Purchasing Power: The Corporate-White House Alliance to Pass the China Trade Bill over the Will of the American People,* Public Citizen, October 2000.
14 *International 'Seattle Coalition' of Civil Society Groups Launch WTO Turnaround Campaign,* Public Citizen statement, Aug. 8, 2000.
15 L. Josh Bivens, "Trade Deficits and Manufacturing Job Loss: Correlation and Causality," Economic Policy Institute Briefing Paper 171, March 14, 2006.

11

THE FIFTH BRANCH
OF GOVERNMENT

I N 1967, SIX MONTHS AFTER RALPH NADER had exposed dangerously unhealthy standards at meatpacking plants and prodded Congress into action, President Lyndon Johnson signed the Wholesome Meat Act. Nader was invited to the ceremonial signing at the White House, as was Upton Sinclair, whose legendary novel "The Jungle" had first alerted the public to unsanitary conditions in the meat industry back in 1906.

Sinclair was 89 when he and Nader were introduced at the signing, and he struggled to rise from his wheelchair to shake hands with the young activist. "I sort of felt that two historic consumer ages were meeting—Upton Sinclair and I were together at the White House," Nader marveled years later.

But Nader wondered whether another generation of activists would pick up the torch Sinclair passed to him that day. "It's hard to get people to make a lifetime career out of this," he said. "It was the aura of the times [in the late 1960s] that got people committed—the whole civil rights and anti-war, environmental and student rebellions. They never considered alternative careers. It's hard to find the same kind of people. When Sid [Wolfe] was first hired [in 1971], the press asked him how long he would do this, and he said it would be his last job. It's hard to replicate that every five or 10 years."

He needn't have worried.

True, the Raiders of the 1960s and 1970s were probably a one-time phenomenon in their excitement at being pioneers and in the staggering list of their accomplishments (See Appendix). It is ironic that as a direct result of those achievements, the business and government worlds mobilized by the beginning of the new millennium for massive resistance to the sort of citizen demands that once led to so many reforms.

But in 2009, when Joan Claybrook left the position she had held for 27 years, a new generation of activists was in place and already carrying that torch on a very different battlefield. Internet-wise and social media-savvy, the new leaders still draw upon the idealism that recognizes democracy as forever a work in progress and forever an uphill struggle. They know that the persistence and vigilance of citizens — traits that have defined Public Citizen's work since 1971 — are as essential to democracy today as the checks and balances set up by the Constitution.

Public Citizen, in short, managed within four decades to institutionalize a progressive populist presence in American political life, doing work that is valued as essential to the functioning of America as a free society, and very much aware that its work will never be finished.

In the late 1960s and 1970s, the organization was able to face down pro-business forces in Congress and the White House. Congress responded to threats posed by the industrial society and exposed by consumer crusaders. But the Reagan-Bush and Bush II years witnessed incessant administration attacks on those new health, safety and environmental regulations that had become the bedrock of citizen protections. Globalization pressures and a right-wing Congress in most of the Clinton years did the same.

"I'm stunned at how brash and confident we were to think we could make a difference in determining the policies of this nation," Claybrook reflected at Public Citizen's 40th anniversary dinner in 2011. "It's an amazing story. What we've done since then has been crucial in terms of retaining many of the legislative and regulatory achievements between 1966 and 1980."

The sharp federal veer to the right thereafter required Public Citizen to adopt a more defensive posture than Nader had originally envisioned. But the organization proved flexible enough to adapt. Nader created the organization without a rigid political ideology, and this helped it cope with the surge in corporate power and administrations that often were hostile to consumer concerns.

"In this country, if you start out with an ideology, you can be stereotyped, which has happened throughout history," said Nader. "Also, ideology tends to freeze innovation and creativity. To avoid these pitfalls, we started a very empirical organization. People were getting hurt by unsafe cars, drugs and other dangerous products; by pollution; and by government secrecy and misconduct. So we worked on those problems."

Solving them for citizens' benefit was the goal of Public Citizen's founding generation, and its triumphs in legislation, regulation and court rulings were significant and enormously satisfying. But losses were frequent as well. Fortunately, losing never seemed to bother Claybrook or anyone else at Public Citizen. Defeated in court or in Congress, they immediately got busy figuring out another road to victory.

"We're an action organization," Claybrook said, pointing to the river of meticulous studies and reports that flow from Public Citizen into the public debate arena every year. "We don't do research just to find out things but to support our actions. We litigate, we petition, we lobby, and the reports all are designed to help us with that."

full-time employees, its general administration spending was $1.35 million — still frugal in relation to the organization's reach.

"Because we don't take any government or business money, Public Citizen has a profile of an organization that is hard-hitting and honest," Claybrook said. "We tell it like it is. We name names. And we can move on a dime. That ability gives us a huge amount of power and is one of the reasons corporations cannot influence our decisions." Another reason, she added, is that "none of the staff is for sale — our work is our passion — it is so essential, so energizing, so exciting." As she put it at a retirement dinner, "That makes us fearless, and thus we are feared."

Much of Public Citizen's political leverage in Washington, D.C., was based on that reputation as a fearless independent operation. "It speaks to justice and human values beyond short-term profit or the protection of narrow pecuniary interests," said Fellmeth and Adkins. It is this determination not to be compromised that has given Public Citizen credibility with the public.

"The work never ends," Claybrook added. "With each new administration and new Congress, we need to be there, in the middle of the debates, researching the facts, educating the decision-makers, lobbying and — if necessary — suing, to be sure the public has a voice. Too many other groups have lost their souls."

In the late 1990s, Joan Yarbrough worked in the member services department, where she often spoke with Public Citizen contributors. "People call in all the time and say, 'We know Sid Wolfe isn't in it for the money, that he's here to help people,'" she said. "Three or four times a day people call to thank us for the work we do. They call all the time to say that the *Worst Pills, Best Pills* book or the newsletter has saved their lives. That's when I know it's working."

Because of the organization's frugality and the deep trust of its membership, Public Citizen has become a permanent fixture in the advocacy world. In 1995, the organization moved out of its cramped, old rented headquarters and took up residence two blocks away in a four-story, red-brick Victorian townhouse in the heart of Dupont Circle in Washington, D.C. Public Citizen snatched up the building at a bargain price from the Resolution Trust Corp., which was created by the federal government in 1989 to liquidate the assets of failed financial institutions following the savings and loan crisis.

Five years after the purchase, Claybrook paid off the mortgage on the building with the profits from selling two million copies of Sidney Wolfe's *Worst Pills, Best Pills*, ensuring that the organization would have a home for many years and that future contributions would go straight into the fight for consumer rights. Claybrook knew a permanent home would strengthen the group's authority and staying power.

Nader once confided a deep concern that he and the consumer movement would wind up "a footnote in history ... a nice little vignette" that "the power structure" would offer as a testament to its own tolerance. It hasn't happened. Central figures who joined Public Citizen in the early 1970s, including Morrison, Wolfe and Claybrook, stayed on into their third decade of activism, and the organization emerged from the wars of the Reagan-Bush years more resilient than ever.[1]

"Ralph, Public Citizen, Common Cause, the Sierra Club and some others estab-lished the legitimacy of the citizen advocate in America," Claybrook said. "If media is the fourth branch of government, we're the fifth branch. Agencies worry about us, and members of Congress know they're at risk when they battle with us."

Fellmeth, one of the original Raiders, regards the group's contribution to democ-racy at the structural level as its most significant achievement. "Public Citizen is not a service provider except in a few cases, and that's its strength," Fellmeth said. "It under-stands that we're a mass society and a lot of outcomes depend on the rules of the game, like statutes and rules of law. Those rules of law are very important, and the represen-tation before bodies that make decisions is badly skewed against the impoverished and consumer interests. Public Citizen is at its best when it changes the rules of the game."

At the end of Claybrook's tenure, changing the rules to benefit consumers was in many ways much more difficult than in the early days. Although Public Citizen in 2009 was a much larger, more experienced organization than it was in 1971, its corporate adversaries also were far more powerful, and the political climate was much more forbidding. Former Litigation Group Director David Vladeck predicted that in the future, "playing defense will become harder and harder as the [political] bargaining chips we have become fewer. Paradoxically, that makes it all the more important that we're at the barricades."

The story of Public Citizen's first 38 years is ultimately one of triumph and per-sistence in the face of adversity. The organization's many achievements on behalf of consumers came in spite of opposition from conservative administrations and an exponential expansion in the political power of corporations.

"The more of a grip the corporations have, the weaker labor is, the weaker the democratic tradition is, the more they can go abroad, the more they can bring politicians to their knees," Nader said. "We're up against an indifferent or hostile or trivialized media; a corporate state where corporations merge with government power to use it for the perpetuation of corporate power; a severely weakened trade union movement; and a culture where millions of youngsters grow up devoid of any history of the struggle for justice."

Nader's analysis of the challenges facing Public Citizen might sound over-whelming, but his conclusion was characteristically optimistic: "Despair is an admis-sion that you can't find another way to prevail. It's also a self-indulgence. If you're 19 or 20, maybe you're able to despair and get away with it without being criticized. But for veterans like us — it's like a doctor after 30 years of practice going to a hospital and wringing his hands and saying, 'Every year I go to this hospital and there are sick people here.' [But] you're always thinking you can develop the strategies that will have an electric impact off of colossal overreaching blunders by corporations — and they are providing us with those!"

In many ways, the transformation of communications technology has enabled Public Citizen and its allies to level the playing field somewhat with corporate lobbies. Public Citizen's website offers a wealth of tools for citizen activists and detailed back-ground and information on every public policy battlefield that has engaged the organization since its founding. The Internet allows cheap and fast grassroots communication, as well as document distribution that used to require expensive and laborious hand-delivery to the media, government agencies, opposing counsel and Congress.

Global Trade Watch routinely exploits the power of the Internet and social media to organize protesters and publicize the texts of pending agreements aimed at giving international investors new rights at the expense of public interest protections. In 2009, for example, it videotaped a 20-year-old intern as she called one of the many firms in Panama that set up shell companies where people — and corporations — can park funds to dodge U.S. taxes.

How easy was it? Very easy: Jessica could have been the head of her own tax-evading corporation while still in college. This two-minute video proves it: www.youtube.com/watch?v=5jtsgDBL7Mc.

In his 40th anniversary speech, Nader called upon the new generation of Public Citizen leaders to continue creating new groups, to work across coalitions and not to give up on old battles lost. "Leave slack time" to allow new offensives as developments occur, he said; permit a "residential thinker" to ponder new directions, and "think incredibly big" in terms of funding and policy goals.

"I hope the younger generation will aspire to be more effective than their precursors," he said, "refusing to be discouraged, being resilient and sharing credit." The goal, he said, should be "to build more and more oak trees in the deforested area of our deteriorating democracy."

Unfinished Business

Musing on goals she would like to have completed, Claybrook said she hoped Public Citizen would be able in the future to defend against abuses by multinational corporations, to work more at the state level with state attorneys general, to take on Chambers of Commerce and their tax-exempt status, and to look into ways the Securities and Exchange Commission regulates or fails to regulate American businesses.

"There's so much to do: tax law reform, the resurgence of secret budget earmarks, the arbitrariness of budget allocations, waste — you wouldn't believe how much the Defense Department spends on military bands!" As always, she was energized and optimistic on Public Citizen's behalf, focused on the victories ahead.

Perhaps Public Citizen's most valuable contribution to the consumer movement is just this kind of determination, with an inclusive view that knits together apparently diverse issues — showing the public, for example, how a corrupt campaign finance system translates into higher prices for prescription drugs. Or how efforts by big business to "reform" the regulatory system can lead to more dangerous automobiles. Or how so-called free trade can mean more pesticide residues and dangerous pathogens in school lunch strawberries.

Helping citizens reclaim the democracy Fellmeth discovered in his ninth-grade civics class is what Public Citizen does. It has empowered citizens in communities all over the country to work for democratic values and government policies that protect health, safety and the environment. This challenge, seeking a fair and just democracy, "calls for a lot of leaders at all levels — leadership that develops more leaders, rather than more followers," Nader said.

"And it calls for a broader discussion of the larger issue: how power is concentrated and abused to limit human possibilities and to inflict injustice on innocent people. Then the people can begin to take back their government, take back control, build their democratic independence and restore the true balance of power that the founders of this country began to envision more than two hundred years ago."

Making democracy work for citizens has been Public Citizen's guiding principle throughout its history. This mission has required independence, vigilance and persistence. Because of those traits — and the mostly anonymous work of its determined, courageous and expert staff — Public Citizen in its first four decades has been unafraid to raise difficult and controversial issues that have had a broad impact on life in America. That impact will continue under the new generation of leaders.

As Claybrook departed, Public Citizen announced its Citizen's Agenda for 2009 and beyond. It highlighted new approaches to goals the group has had since its founding: breaking ties between lawmakers and corporations, pushing sustainable energy investments, ensuring the safety of workplaces and medicines and other products, protecting access to government information, preserving free speech on the Internet and maintaining consumers' access to justice through the courts.

"We are the people's lobby, the people's lawyers, the people's doctors. We research and write petitions, feed the press, rabble-rouse and agitate," Claybrook told her farewell dinner gala. "We are passionate about this work and can name names and follow our conscience because of you, our supporters."

The supporters applauded the continuing goals: public funding of elections, an enhanced regulatory system to protect ordinary Americans, a single-payer system for health care, consumer protection in financial transactions, an end to corporate welfare and attacks on global warming on several fronts: halting coal-fired power plant construction, promoting fuel efficiency and renewable energy, and reallocating government subsidies away from fossil fuels.

It is a daunting agenda that covers most of American life. Taking it on as Claybrook's successor as Public Citizen president was Robert Weissman, a 20-year veteran of Nader's corporate accountability projects at Essential Action and the Center for Study of Responsive Law, and editor of *Multinational Monitor* magazine. Public Citizen, he said on taking office in late 2009, "is really something of a public trust."

Weissman reaffirmed the Citizen's Agenda and said he plans to build upon the legacy of achievements by the founders that has been recounted in this book: "Air bags. Safer drugs. Landmark U.S. Supreme Court cases. The Consumer Product Safety Commission. A thriving wind energy industry in Texas. Brakes on corporate globalization. A strengthened Freedom of Information Act. Lobbyist and campaign finance reform. Access to justice for victims of corporate wrongdoing. A healthier workplace. Wall Street reform. And much more."

The organization, Weissman promised, will continue to do everything it has done so well for nearly four decades. "It does no good to be discouraged," he said. "We still win many battles, on important things. We still identify new issues and emerging trends and policy solutions, based on what's right, not what's reasonable. We do a good job on moving the debate to incorporate the citizen perspective. And even when we don't win, more often than not, the outcome shifts in a discernible way because of our intervention."

High on Weissman's agenda: more work against climate change; better and more frequent communication via the Internet and social media with members and supporters; and relentless work on addressing corporate power. "There's no silver bullet, no one solution, and there's no end to it," he said. "Corporations never stop, and we won't either."

Public Citizen's fingerprints can be found whenever a homebuyer looks for the best-priced lawyer, whenever a bumped airline passenger is compensated, whenever a parent reads the warning label on an aspirin bottle, whenever a worker is free from breathing toxic chemicals in the workplace, whenever a life is saved by an air bag, whenever a journalist or an activist seeks information from the government. But Public Citizen's impact goes even deeper, to the core of democracy. It is a legacy of engaged citizenship, of people working in public forums to seek justice and equity for others.

"Public Citizen members have made this happen," Claybrook said. "These achievements belong to those people who have backed the organization in its fight for health, safety and democracy. When we started, we had no money, no power base, minimal experience and few allies. But we were part of something new in America. From our earliest days, millions of ordinary people have shaped the consumer move-ment — not by going to Washington, D.C., to investigate corruption, but by support-ing those who did.

"Citizen action is now ingrained in America's policy decisions, with thousands of advocacy organizations at the neighborhood, local, state and national levels, pushing all sorts of causes. New generations of advocates are bringing their talents and determination to the work of holding the powerful accountable.

"For nearly 40 years, Public Citizen has battled for citizens against corporate and government abuse, and its victories are those of its members. They are the real heroes of the consumer movement, the credit belongs to them, and any future Public Citizen success will be due to their support."

Endnotes

1 Nader quoted in Steve France, "Public Interest: Retooling for the '90s," *The Washington Lawyer*, May/June 1991, p. 40.

APPENDIX

TIMELINE OF MAJOR PUBLIC CITIZEN ACCOMPLISHMENTS AND HIGHLIGHTS OF ITS WORK 1971–2009

1971

— Public Citizen is founded by Ralph Nader to provide a full-time advocacy organization for citizens and consumers.

— Ralph Nader and Dr. Sidney Wolfe establish Public Citizen's Health Research Group.

— Public Citizen petitions the U.S. Food and Drug Administration (FDA) to ban the use of Red Dye No. 2 as food coloring, citing links to cancer.

1972

— Ralph Nader and Alan Morrison establish the Public Citizen Litigation Group.

— Ralph Nader is bumped from an airline flight, and Public Citizen files suit, leading to the U.S. Supreme Court decision that consumers who are bumped can sue for damages.

— Public Citizen plays a key role in creation of the U.S. Consumer Product Safety Commission.

— Public Citizen and the Oil, Chemical and Atomic Workers Union petition the U.S. Department of Labor to set an emergency temporary standard for 10 cancer-causing chemicals. The department issued the emergency standard the following year.

1973

— Public Citizen publishes a paper, "An Outline for Consumer Action on Prescription and Drug Prices."

— Ralph Nader and Joan Claybrook establish Congress Watch as Public Citizen's lobbying and legislative arm.

— Shortly after Public Citizen urges action, the FDA bans the Pertussin medicated vaporizer in the wake of the deaths of 18 children.

— President Richard Nixon's firing of Special Prosecutor Archibald Cox is ruled illegal in response to a Public Citizen lawsuit.

1974

— Public Citizen persuades Congress to pass major improvements to the Freedom of Information Act and override President Gerald Ford's veto.

— Public Citizen publishes a directory of doctors in Prince George's County, Maryland—the first of its kind in the nation—and challenges laws restricting consumer access to information about doctors.

— Ralph Nader creates Public Citizen's Critical Mass Energy Project to mobilize opposition to nuclear power and promote energy conservation and renewable sources.

— Public Citizen's "report cards" play a key role in the defeat of several House committee chairmen in the first caucus election since the seniority system was abolished in 1972.

— Public Citizen is instrumental in passing legislation giving the National Highway Traffic Safety Administration (NHTSA) subpoena power and authority to order a recall of unsafe cars and to set safety standards for school buses.

1975

— Public Citizen wins *Goldfarb v. Virginia State Bar*, a U.S. Supreme Court decision subjecting lawyers to federal antitrust laws and making standard fee-setting agreements illegal.

— Public Citizen wins *Train v. Campaign Clean Water, Inc.*, a U.S. Supreme Court decision barring President Richard Nixon from "impounding" funds appropriated by Congress.

— Public Citizen successfully lobbies Congress for energy conservation legislation, including the first fuel economy requirements for cars.

— Public Citizen publishes *Through The Mental Health Maze*, a consumer guide to finding a psychotherapist, and *Taking the Pain Out of Finding a Good Dentist*.

— A Public Citizen survey of America's 50 largest hospitals reveals most are violating government regulations to protect Medicaid recipients during surgical sterilization.

— Public Citizen petitions the FDA to require safety testing of the Dalkon Shield and other intrauterine contraceptive devices.

— After five filibuster votes defeated the Consumer Protection Act, Public Citizen helps persuade the Senate leadership to change the filibuster rules, cutting the number of votes needed to end debate from 67 to 60.

1976

— The FDA bans the carcinogenic food dye called Red Dye No. 2 after Public Citizen's four-year campaign.

— A Public Citizen petition leads the FDA to ban the use of cancer-causing chloroform in cough medicines and toothpaste.

— Public Citizen wins *Va. State Board. of Pharmacy v. Va. Citizens Consumer Council*, a major victory for consumers. The landmark U.S. Supreme Court decision allowed drugstores to advertise prices of prescription drugs.

— Public Citizen is a key advocate in passing three significant pieces of legislation: the Toxic Substances Control Act; medical device safety legislation; and antitrust reform legislation that empowered state attorneys general to enforce federal antitrust laws on behalf of citizens, thereby vastly expanding enforcement opportunities.

— Public Citizen uncovers a secret deal between the FDA and the Upjohn Company to conceal the contamination of the anti-diabetes drug tolanise with cancer-causing nitrosamine.

— Public Citizen forces the Senate Finance Committee to delete 20 special-interest tax giveaways from the 1976 Tax Reform Act.

— Public Citizen successfully lobbies for the Civil Rights Attorney's Fees Award Act of 1976, permitting successful civil rights litigants to recover costs and attorneys' fees from defendants judged to have violated civil rights laws; and for the Government in the Sunshine Act, requiring senior government officials to keep records and public logs; and for expanded provisions in the Freedom of Information Act.

1977

— President Jimmy Carter appoints Joan Claybrook, director of Public Citizen's Congress Watch division, to serve as NHTSA administrator in the Department of Transportation.

— Public Citizen mobilizes citizens in a movement that persuades President Jimmy Carter to halt construction of the Clinch River Breeder Reactor in Tennessee.

— Public Citizen launches an informational campaign against efforts to limit manufacturers' liability for consumer injuries caused by their products.

— The FDA bans the diabetes drug Phenformin, linked to hundreds of deaths each year, after a Public Citizen petition and lawsuit.

— Public Citizen files a class-action suit on behalf of 1,100 women who were given a synthetic form of estrogen called DES, which increases the risk of breast cancer, without their knowledge in the 1950s as part of a University of Chicago medical experiment. The case was not certified as a class, but the 1982 settlement was extremely favorable, including not only a payment, but also free exams and medical treatment.

1978

— Public Citizen calls for, and Congress passes, the Consumer Cooperative Bank Act, which encouraged the establishment of cooperatives by creating a bank modeled after the successful farm credit system to loan money and provide technical assistance to emerging cooperatives.

— Public Citizen issues a report on health and safety violations at the Central Intelligence Agency, suggesting that employees' health may be in jeopardy.

— Public Citizen publishes the first edition of *Getting Yours: A Consumer's Guide to Obtaining Your Medical Record* to help consumers gain access to their health records.

1979

— Public Citizen purchases a large building on Capitol Hill for its lobbying activities, with rental space to supplement its income.

— A Public Citizen petition leads the U.S. Environmental Protection Agency (EPA) to ban the use of DBCP, a pesticide that causes sterility in men and cancer in laboratory animals.

— Public Citizen exposes the history of safety problems at the Three Mile Island nuclear power plant in Pennsylvania after the nation's worst nuclear accident there.

— Public Citizen publishes a first-of-its-kind directory called *Cutting Prices: A Guide to Washington Area Surgeons' Fees,* listing fees by named surgeons in the area for 12 common surgical procedures.

— Public Citizen wins a landmark case in New York, *Gordon v. Committee on Character and Fitness,* which opens up competition among lawyers by striking down residency requirements that are barriers to working there.

1980

— Public Citizen publishes *Pills That Don't Work,* a consumer guide to ineffective drugs, which becomes a national best-seller after "The Phil Donahue Show" features the book.

— Public Citizen plays a critical role in passage of the Superfund law that requires cleanup of toxic waste sites without limits on liability.

— Public Citizen releases a progress report on the Three Mile Island reactor cleanup, "TMI: One Year in Retrospect." It documents safety mishaps at other nuclear power plants and lists accidents involving transportation of nuclear materials.

— Public Citizen leads a successful push for legislation that eased pricing rules governing the trucking industry, enabling more competition and saving each American family $70 to $105 a year.

— Public Citizen pressure leads to an FDA recall of Rely tampons, which are linked to toxic shock syndrome.

— *Public Citizen* magazine is introduced to give members regular updates on Public Citizen issues and activities.

— Ralph Nader steps down as president of Public Citizen and leaves the Board of Directors as well.

1981

— Public Citizen helps thwart President Ronald Reagan's attempts to dismantle the Clean Air Act and to diminish the authority of the Consumer Product Safety Commission.

— Public Citizen helps block Reagan administration efforts to eliminate the Legal Services program for low-income consumers and to cut funding for the Federal Trade Commission.

— Public Citizen urges the FDA to ban misleading advertising for the popular tranquilizer drug Valium, and the company withdraws the ads.

— Public Citizen publishes *Cataracts: A Consumers' Guide to Choosing the Best Treatment*.

— Public Citizen publishes *A Workers' Guide to Winning at The Occupational Safety and Health Review Commission*, informing workers of their rights.

— Public Citizen plays a major role in reducing dairy price supports, saving consumers an estimated 8 cents per gallon of milk.

1982

— Joan Claybrook returns to Public Citizen as its president.

— Public Citizen leads a successful effort to block passage of a far-reaching regulatory rollback bill.

— The arthritis drug Oraflex is withdrawn from the market after a Public Citizen campaign exposes the many deaths and injuries it caused.

— Public Citizen persuades Congress not to exempt doctors, lawyers and other professionals from Federal Trade Commission (FTC) oversight.

— Urea formaldehyde is banned for home insulation after an extensive Public Citizen campaign against this carcinogenic substance.

— Public Citizen leads the defense against congressional attacks on the Freedom of Information Act.

— Public Citizen's lobbying halts plans to extend drug manufacturers' patent monopolies on their products for up to seven more years.

— A Public Citizen study of Occupational Safety and Health Administration (OSHA) enforcement reveals a 50 percent drop in enforcement under the Reagan administration.

— *Over the Counter Pills That Don't Work* is published and becomes a national best-seller.

1983

— Public Citizen wins the landmark U.S. Supreme Court *Immigration and Naturalization Service v. Chadha* decision that overturns nearly 200 laws containing "legislative vetoes" Congress had used to block executive branch actions.

— Public Citizen assists State Farm counsel in the landmark U.S. Supreme Court decision, *Motor Vehicle Manufacturers Association v. State Farm Mutual Automobile Insurance*, overturning President Ronald Reagan's revocation of the auto safety standard requiring automatic restraints such as air bags.

— Based on a report by Ralph Nader on consumer cooperatives, Public Citizen founds Buyers Up to help consumers save money on heating oil.

— Public Citizen persuades Congress to halt funding for the Clinch River Breeder Reactor after Reagan revives the Tennessee program, defeating Senate Majority Leader Howard Baker of Tennessee.

— After intense Public Citizen lobbying, Congress upholds an FTC rule requiring funeral homes to itemize price lists and preventing the required inclusion of casket and embalming costs in cremations.

— Public Citizen wins a legal victory compelling the U.S. Department of Labor to commence rulemaking to control the hazardous workplace gas ethylene oxide.

— Public Citizen issues a report, "Aid for Dependent Corporations: A Study of the Fiscal 1984 Corporate Welfare Budget," part of an ongoing push to expose and reduce corporate welfare from the federal budget.

1984

— Public Citizen publishes *Retreat from Safety: Reagan's Attack on America's Health*, exposing the Reagan administration's efforts to roll back health and safety regulations.

— Public Citizen successfully opposes legislation easing restrictions on the use of cancer-causing food additives.

— Following AT&T divestiture, Public Citizen mounts a nationwide "Campaign for Affordable Phones" to oppose rate hikes for residential customers.

— Public Citizen opens a field office in Austin, Texas, after successfully defeating an effort by Southwestern Bell to drastically raise phone prices. (See Texas office accomplishments at the end of this appendix.)

— Public Citizen successfully pushes for a law encouraging states to set a minimum age of 21 for serving alcohol.

— After Public Citizen cites serious adverse reactions to the anti-inflammatory drugs Butazolidin and Tandearil, the FDA strengthens their warning labels.

— Public Citizen leads a successful fight against approval of the hazardous injectable contraceptive Depo-Provera.

— Public Citizen pressure defeats special antitrust provisions for beer distributors and preserves a law prohibiting U.S. companies from bribing foreign officials to win contracts.

1985

— Public Citizen successfully petitions the FDA to require a Reye's Syndrome warning on aspirin labels following a campaign that lasted several years.

— Public Citizen exposes the EPA's failure to accurately assess the dangers of toxic waste dump sites as part of a successful campaign to strengthen Superfund cleanup laws.

— Public Citizen releases names and locations of more than 250 work sites across the nation where workers have been exposed to hazardous chemicals.

— Public Citizen begins publication of *Health Letter* to provide consumers with critical information about health issues.

— Public Citizen wins a key amendment to banking legislation preventing out-of-state banks from siphoning off money from local communities.

— Public Citizen pressure on the FDA leads to a recall of large-model Bjork-Shiley heart valves, after risk of valve fractures is linked to 100 deaths worldwide.

— Public Citizen helps defeat industry-sponsored legislation to restrict the use of courts by victims of dangerous products to hold manufacturers accountable, and successfully opposes similar legislation in Congress over the next decade.

1986

— The U.S. Supreme Court rules in *Bowsher v. Synar* in favor of a Public Citizen lawsuit challenging the constitutionality of the Gramm-Rudman-Hollings deficit reduction law.

— Congress requires health warning labels on chewing tobacco and snuff, capping Public Citizen's two-year campaign.

— Public Citizen writes and publishes the book *Freedom From Harm: The Civilizing Influence of Health, Safety and Environmental Regulation,* explaining the importance of regulations in protecting consumers.

— Public Citizen publishes *Care of the Seriously Mentally Ill: A Rating of State Programs,* ranking states from highest to lowest in their provisions for mentally ill patients.

— Public Citizen plays an instrumental role in the 1986 Tax Reform Bill, especially in lowering taxes for low-income Americans.

1987

— Public Citizen issues a report evaluating the decisions of Judge Robert Bork on the U.S. Court of Appeals for the District of Columbia, helping to block his nomination to the U.S. Supreme Court.

— Public Citizen forces chemical producers of Agent Orange to make important information about its dangers available to the public.

— Public Citizen helps persuade Congress to pass a strong bill restricting the time banks can hold checks.

— Public Citizen publishes the first edition of *Unnecessary Cesarean Sections,* an in-depth investigation into the skyrocketing rate of cesarean section births.

— Public Citizen publishes its first "Nuclear Lemons" report, a nationwide listing of reactors with the worst safety records and other problems.

— After eight years of litigation, Public Citizen wins a victory for health care workers when OSHA imposes standards for exposure to cancer-causing ethylene oxide, used to clean medical instruments.

1988

— *Worst Pills, Best Pills,* a consumer guide to dangerous and ineffective drugs and their preferable alternatives, is published by Public Citizen and becomes a best-seller after being featured on "The Phil Donahue Show."

— Public Citizen actively supports Proposition 103, an auto-insurance rate reduction and regulation initiative that is then approved by California voters.

— Public Citizen leads a successful effort in Congress to strengthen a pesticide law.

— Public Citizen publishes the *Citizen's Guide to Radon Home Test Kits*.

— Public Citizen calls on the FDA to halt the use of silicone gel in breast implants.

— Public Citizen releases a report exposing the Nuclear Regulatory Commission's refusal to comply with a law governing nuclear worker training and revealing that more than two-thirds of 3,000 mishaps at U.S. reactors in 1987 involved personnel error.

— Public Citizen wins three U.S. Supreme Court cases: *Supreme Court of Virginia v. Friedman* (regarding Virginia's bar admission criteria for non-residents), *Lingle v. Norge* (protecting workers who are fired for filing workers' compensation claims from losing their right to file suit under union-management arbitration provisions) and *Department of Justice v. Julian* (establishing that pre-sentencing reports are available to the subjects of the reports).

1989

— Federal regulation requiring driver-side air bags or passive seat belts takes effect after a 20-year Public Citizen battle with automakers.

— Public Citizen releases a report detailing cesarean section rates in 30 states.

— Public Citizen wins a ruling in the U.S. Court of Appeals for the District of Columbia requiring FTC regulation of smokeless tobacco products.

— Public Citizen helps persuade California voters to shut down the Rancho Seco nuclear power plant.

— Public Citizen successfully campaigns to have R.J. Reynolds withdraw offensive cigarette ads.

— Public Citizen helps found a new consumer advocacy organization, Advocates for Highway and Auto Safety, with other consumer groups and insurance companies working jointly and exclusively on highway and auto safety issues. Joan Claybrook serves on the Board.

— In seeking electronic records from Oliver North's office concerning the Iran-Contra affair, Public Citizen wins the first court ruling requiring federal agencies to treat electronic records like paper records under the Freedom of Information Act.

— Public Citizen and Ralph Nader successfully lead the opposition to a $45,500 congressional pay raise recommended by President Ronald Reagan. Nine months later, Congress agrees to ban honoraria in exchange for a smaller pay raise.

1990

— Public Citizen publishes *6,892 Questionable Doctors*, the first edition of a nationwide listing of doctors disciplined for incompetence, substance abuse and other violations.

— A Public Citizen court victory forces the U.S. Nuclear Regulatory Commission to issue mandatory training requirements for nuclear power plant workers.

— Public Citizen initiates a "Doctor Bribing Hotline" for doctors to report unethical or illegal attempts by industry to persuade them to prescribe one drug over another.

Doctors could report to the Hotline, for example, offers of free dinners, airline tickets and cash.

— Public Citizen publishes the book *Who Robbed America?*, an investigation into the multibillion-dollar savings and loan scandal.

— Public Citizen begins developing a strategy for a comprehensive national health program for all Americans.

1991

— Public Citizen publishes *Women's Health Alert*, a handbook of vital health information for women.

— Public Citizen wins an important separation of powers decision in *Citizens Against Aircraft Noise v. Met. Washington Airports*, a U.S. Supreme Court case involving congressional control of two Washington, D.C., area airports.

— Public Citizen plays a key role in the passage of legislation requiring new car and truck safety rules, freezing the use of longer combination trucks (doubles and triples) to the fewer than 20 states where they were already authorized, and imposing mandates for air bags (no passive belts) on all cars, vans and light trucks.

— Public Citizen exposes lobbyist-funded travel by members of Congress with a widely publicized report, "They Love To Fly ... And It Shows."

— The Teamsters union elects new leadership, capping nearly two decades of Public Citizen legal support for the union's pro-reform movement.

1992

— Public Citizen's four-year campaign leads the FDA to severely restrict the use of silicone gel implants except for post-mastectomy patients.

— In New York's State Court of Appeals, Public Citizen wins the first case upholding the right of a lawyer to sue for damages when fired from a law firm after demanding that ethics violations be reported.

— Public Citizen exposes the threat to government health and safety standards posed by Vice President Dan Quayle's Council on Competitiveness.

— Public Citizen urges the FDA to ban Halcion, the most widely used sleeping pill, after it discovers links between the drug and adverse psychiatric affects.

— Public Citizen wins a court ruling allowing a dissident Teamsters group, Teamsters for a Democratic Union, to keep its list of contributors confidential.

— Public Citizen starts court proceedings to have 4,000 hours of tapes from the Nixon White House released to the public.

— Public Citizen plays an instrumental role in passing the federal Anti-Car Theft Act, which would reduce the incidence of motor vehicle thefts, facilitate the tracing and recovery of stolen motor vehicles, and require the federal government to create a database for used car buyers containing the mileage, title and history of theft or damage of vehicles.

— OSHA imposes a standard to protect workers from cadmium, linked to lung cancer and kidney damage, after Public Citizen wins a court order.

1993

— Public Citizen releases a report exposing the influence of tobacco money on Congress and uses rallies to support meaningful campaign finance reform.

— *Worst Pills, Best Pills II* is published with new information for consumers; two million copies will be sold by 1995.

— Public Citizen wins a landmark court victory preserving the electronic records of the Presidents Ronald Reagan and George H.W. Bush.

— Public Citizen plays a major role in galvanizing opposition to the North American Free Trade Agreement (NAFTA), the international trade agreement between the U.S., Mexico and Canada that was blamed for the loss of hundreds of thousands of U.S. jobs.

— Public Citizen releases findings on 680 privately funded trips by senators, including all-expense trips to Puerto Rico and Florida, paid for by corporations and trade associations.

1994

— Public Citizen helps enlist nearly 100 House co-sponsors for a single-payer health care reform bill.

— Public Citizen wins consumer protections against home equity loan scams.

— Public Citizen lobbying succeeds in blocking taxpayer funding for the proposed advanced liquid metal (breeder) reactor.

— In response to a Public Citizen lawsuit, the FDA announces it will withdraw approval of Parlodel for use as a lactation suppressant. Parlodel was linked with fatal strokes and seizures in breastfeeding mothers.

— Public Citizen publishes the *Green Buyer's Car Book* and a related consumer guide, providing detailed information on vehicles' emissions, fuel mileage and recycled components.

— Intense Public Citizen lobbying delays passage of damaging General Agreement on Tariffs and Trade (GATT) trade legislation.

— Public Citizen purchases a highly discounted building in Dupont Circle in Washington, D.C., from the Resolution Trust Corp. to serve as its headquarters and as a center for public interest group gatherings and press events.

1995

— Public Citizen's Global Trade Watch is launched to oppose trade deals such as the GATT and NAFTA that sacrifice American jobs, consumer protections and communities to benefit multinational corporations.

— Congressional gift ban and lobbying registration reform is passed after a major Public Citizen campaign.

— *Worst Pills, Best Pills News,* a newsletter based on Public Citizen's popular book, is introduced to provide consumers regular updates on dangerous and ineffective drugs.

— Public Citizen plays a key role in blocking pernicious regulatory rollback legislation, preserving health and safety protections for all Americans.

— Public Citizen documents the destructive effects of NAFTA on jobs, consumer protections and the environment with a major report, "NAFTA's Broken Promises."

— Public Citizen helps secure final Department of Transportation rules on anti-lock brakes on trucks and to prevent head injuries.

1996

— Public Citizen wins *Medtronic, Inc. v. Lohr*, a U.S. Supreme Court decision upholding the right of people injured by defective medical devices to sue for compensation.

— Public Citizen helps secure a veto of legislation that would have limited corporate liability for dangerous products.

— Public Citizen wins the release of 4,000 hours of Nixon White House tapes.

— Public Citizen helps bring the need for campaign finance reform to the top of the national agenda.

— Public Citizen successfully opposes legislation that would have mandated the transport to and permanent storage of the nation's nuclear waste at Yucca Mountain, Nevada, paid for by government, not nuclear power companies.

— Public Citizen leads a coalition to preserve a strong regulatory role for the FDA, blocking industry-led rollback efforts.

— Public Citizen publishes 13,012 *Questionable Doctors*, a nationwide listing of doctors disciplined for incompetence, substance abuse and other violations.

— Public Citizen helps win a Department of Transportation rule on truck rear-underride protection.

1997

— A Public Citizen report reveals significant differences in the safety records of various manufacturers' passenger-side air bags.

— Public Citizen exposes a series of unethical HIV experiments funded by the U.S. government and others in developing countries.

— A Public Citizen report reveals more than 500 U.S. physicians disciplined for sexual abuse or misconduct, with many still practicing.

— Public Citizen successfully spearheads opposition to a tobacco industry bailout in a lawsuit settlement.

— Public Citizen leads an effort to defeat damaging Fast Track trade legislation and publishes on its website secret details of the Multilateral Agreement of Investment trade treaty.

1998

— Public Citizen publishes 16,638 *Questionable Doctors*, a nationwide listing of doctors disciplined for incompetence, substance abuse and other violations.

— Public Citizen forces the Department of Transportation to rewrite its air bag safety standard and helps pass legislation to require advanced air bags that will not harm vehicle occupants.

— Public Citizen leads a push against the deregulation of the electricity industry, which is nonetheless approved and creates huge unregulated monopolies.

— Public Citizen launches a sustained lobbying effort to stop a national nuclear waste storage facility slated for Yucca Mountain, Nevada.

— Public Citizen is a major player in the call for reform of the Independent Counsel Act to avoid future Ken Starr-type fiascos.

— Public Citizen helps expose a special-interest deal to benefit a company in Mississippi, the home state of Senate Majority Leader Trent Lott, thereby killing a bill designed to limit the rights of consumers to hold corporations accountable in court for making dangerous products.

— Agreeing with Public Citizen, the U.S. Supreme Court in *Amchem Products, Inc. v. Windsor* affirms a Third Circuit decision saying that class actions cannot be used to deprive future victims of their right to sue.

1999

— Public Citizen stops "NAFTA for Africa" legislation intended to benefit corporations at the expense of local businesses in the developing world.

— Public Citizen publishes the third edition of *Worst Pills, Best Pills*, a popular consumer guide to avoiding drug-induced death or illness.

— Public Citizen wins the release of historic grand jury records relating to the 1948 indictment of alleged Soviet agent Alger Hiss.

— Public Citizen releases a report revealing strong links between Senate Majority Leader Trent Lott's Republican Party "soft money" fundraising from casino interests and his little-known legislative actions that protect the casino industry.

— Public Citizen publishes *Whose Trade Organization? Corporate Globalization and the Erosion of Democracy*, a book exposing the World Trade Organization's five-year record of weakening health, safety, environmental and labor standards.

— Public Citizen successfully pushes major truck safety legislation to create the Federal Motor Carrier Safety Administration under the Secretary of Transportation, replacing the ineffective Office of Motor Carriers and securing "safety is its highest priority" in the new law.

— Public Citizen leads a global coalition to organize massive landmark demonstrations in Seattle against the World Trade Organization's expansion plans.

— Public Citizen defends a California woman whose website is critical of a company, inaugurating the organization's involvement in Internet free speech cases.

— Public Citizen helps to establish a nationwide blood alcohol limit for drivers of .08.

2000

— A Public Citizen petition leads to a ban on the diabetes drug Rezulin after it causes 63 deaths from liver toxicity.

— Public Citizen publishes the sixth edition of *Questionable Doctors,* listing 20,125 physicians disciplined by state medical boards nationwide.

— Public Citizen, spearheading a coalition of auto safety advocates, wins new federal legislation called TREAD to strengthen safety in the wake of hundreds of deaths and injuries caused by rollover crashes involving Firestone tires and Ford Explorers. It establishes rules for tire inflation, child safety and consumer information on rollovers, and an early warning requirement that companies must notify NHTSA of possible safety defects.

— Public Citizen releases a report documenting the role of Big Tobacco in creating and financing a network of "lawsuit abuse" groups that advocate stripping legal rights from citizens.

2001

— Public Citizen wins passage of legislation to beef up inspections of trucks from Mexico entering the United States under NAFTA.

— Public Citizen documents corporate abuse of NAFTA investor protection provisions and NAFTA's negative impact on U.S. farmers.

— A Public Citizen report highlights 527 "questionable hospitals" that violated patient-dumping law.

— Public Citizen influences a new aviation security law after the September 11 terrorist attacks.

— Public Citizen issues a report linking political connections to regulatory actions by public officials to aid energy trader Enron Corp., which collapsed amid allegations of accounting fraud.

— In *Dendrite International v. Does 1 through 14,* a New Jersey appellate court largely adopts a standard recommended by Public Citizen for dealing with cases in which a company tries to discover the identities of anonymous Internet critics by going to court. The court rejected the company's attempt to unmask the identities of its critics, and the decision remains a leading precedent.

2002

— Congress passes the Bipartisan Campaign Reform Act of 2002 (also known as the McCain–Feingold Act), the first major campaign finance reform since the Watergate era, banning soft money and regulating phony issue ads, following a decade-long battle by Public Citizen and its allies.

— Public Citizen successfully sues the George W. Bush administration to win release of Reagan administration records under the Presidential Records Act.

— Public Citizen wins *Lee v. Kemna,* a U.S. Supreme Court decision in which a defendant was denied his rights to a fair trial and due process when a lower court refused to grant an overnight continuance to locate three missing alibi witnesses.

2003

— Public Citizen forces the Department of Transportation to issue new "hours of service" safety rules governing truck drivers.

— The FDA bans the dietary supplement ephedra two years after Public Citizen petitions for its removal and after 155 deaths.

— Public Citizen research and lobbying helps defeat legislation to unfairly restrict damages awarded to seriously injured victims of medical malpractice.

— The Consumer Product Safety Commission bans lead-wicked candles after a lengthy campaign by Public Citizen.

— Public Citizen launches WhiteHouseForSale.org to track special interest contributions to President George Bush's 2004 campaign.

— Public Citizen wins a federal appeals court ruling overturning an auto safety regulation allowing installation of ineffective tire-monitoring systems on vehicle dashboards, forcing the issuance of an effective rule.

— *Worst Pills, Best Pills News,* an online version of the popular newsletter, is introduced to provide consumers regular updates on dangerous and ineffective drugs.

2004

— Public Citizen exposes the failure of seat belts in automobile rollover crashes and campaigns for new auto safety legislation.

— Public Citizen exposes gaping holes in homeland security measures and links security failures to Bush administration policies favoring corporate campaign contributors.

— In a major win for highway safety, Public Citizen secures a federal appeals court victory striking down a Bush administration regulation that increased the number of consecutive and weekly hours truck drivers can drive without rest.

— The antidepressant Serzone, linked to liver failure, is withdrawn from the market after Public Citizen sues the FDA for failing to ban the drug.

2005

— After years of Public Citizen lobbying, Congress passes major auto safety improvements, including stability and roof-strength standards, in the 2005 highway bill.

— A Public Citizen petition and overwhelming statistical evidence force the FDA to remove the controversial pain prescription Bextra from the market.

— After intense Public Citizen lobbying, an amendment to extend the time truckers can spend on the road to 16 hours is withdrawn from the pending highway bill.

— Public Citizen, representing Advocates for Highway and Auto Safety, successfully challenges inadequate minimum training requirements for commercial motor vehicle operators.

2006

— Public Citizen's 2003 complaint against a Freddie Mac lobbyist's extravagant congressional fundraising results in a $3.8 million Federal Election Commission fine, the largest civil penalty it has ever issued.

— Following Public Citizen's unique report on the secret sponsorship by 18 superrich families of a proposed repeal of the estate tax, the Senate rejects permanent repeal of the tax.

2007

— Congress passes a landmark lobbying and ethics bill that was crafted with input from Public Citizen experts.
— Public Citizen is key to defeating the renewal of Fast Track trade legislation.
— Public Citizen successfully pushes to eliminate a cost-benefit loophole in the first congressionally mandated fuel economy standards in more than 30 years, which made 35 mpg by 2020 mandatory.
— Public Citizen again wins a federal appellate court case challenging inadequate truck driver "hours of service" rules.

2008

— After pressure from Public Citizen and its allies, Congress passes the Consumer Product Safety Improvement Act, which makes critical reforms to the Consumer Product Safety Commission.
— The FDA requires its most serious black box warning about the risk of tendinitis and tendon rupture on all packages of fluoroquinolone antibiotics, which include Cipro, Levaquin and Avelox, partly in response to a lawsuit filed by Public Citizen.
— Public Citizen helps a Georgia resident win a major victory for online free speech when a federal judge upholds the resident's right to criticize Wal-Mart using satire.
— Public Citizen's Global Trade Watch division publishes two books: *Federalism and Global Governance* and *The Rise and Fall of Fast Track Trade Authority.*
— Public Citizen files a friend-of-the-court brief and argues in support of New York City's health regulation requiring certain fast-food restaurant chains in the city to post calorie information on their menu boards; a federal judge later upholds the regulation.
— Public Citizen helps pass legislation to protect children with the use of rear-view technology in cars.

2009

— Public Citizen successfully sues the government to obtain documents about the safety of using a cell phone while driving. The records provide fodder for a *New York Times* story that sparks a national debate about cell phone usage in automobiles.
— A Public Citizen lawsuit, part of an ongoing battle on hours truckers may work, prompts the Department of Transportation and the Federal Motor Carrier Safety Administration to agree to rewrite a Bush administration regulation.
— Public Citizen and the Natural Resources Defense Council win a lawsuit stopping the Consumer Product Safety Commission from allowing the sale of phthalate-laden children's products that were made before a ban on them took effect.

— As a result of a Public Citizen lawsuit, the federal government launches a database that allows potential used car buyers to check the validity of a vehicle's title, mileage and history of theft or damage, as required by the 1992 Federal Anti-Car Theft Act.

— The FDA grants Public Citizen's 2008 petition and requires strong warnings to be issued to doctors and patients about the dangers associated with the use of botulinum toxin (Botox, Myobloc, Dysport).

— After pressure from Public Citizen and its allies, the Chrysler Group agrees to assume responsibility for product liability claims brought by people injured in post-Chrysler bankruptcy crashes that involve cars sold before the bankruptcy.

— Joan Claybrook resigns as president of Public Citizen after 27 years but remains on the Board of Directors. The organization's building at 20th and Q Streets NW is named in her honor.

— The Board of Directors selects Robert Weissman to succeed Joan Claybrook as president.

ACCOMPLISHMENTS OF PUBLIC CITIZEN'S
TEXAS OFFICE 1984–2009

Public Citizen opened an office in Austin, Texas, in 1984, to help consumers fight Southwestern Bell's proposed rate hikes. Public Citizen planned to be in Texas only for a few months, but after Southwestern Bell withdrew its proposed increase — a surprisingly quick victory — Public Citizen decided to stay. Through the years, primarily under the leadership of Tom "Smitty" Smith, it has been organizing, researching, educating and lobbying on a broad range of consumer issues. Here are some highlights of its work through 2009:

— Lobbied successfully for Texas to establish a state Ethics Commission and adopt a 13-point reform plan.

— Lobbied successfully for the Texas Legislature to adopt Public Citizen's 10-point insurance reform plan.

— Lobbied successfully for consumer protections, including protection of senior citizens applying for reverse mortgages, as part of legislation authorizing home equity lending in Texas.

— Won a power-plant cleanup program to reduce smog-forming nitrogen oxide emissions in the state by 50 to 88 percent.

— Was instrumental in creating the Texas Emissions Reduction Plan, which provides financial incentives to individuals, businesses and local governments to reduce emissions from the dirtiest diesel engines.

— Won passage of a law requiring utilities to generate 5,880 megawatts of electricity from renewable sources by 2015 and 10,000 megawatts by 2025. The target already has been met.

— Helped end the "grandfathered plant" loophole that allowed the oldest polluters to operate without emissions controls.

— Helped reform Texas "lemon law" with a stipulation that new car buyers must get their problems resolved within 45 days or they get a refund of the vehicle price.

— Helped establish the Texas medical patient complainants' bill of rights.

— Halted construction, through work with whistleblowers, at the South Texas and Comanche Peak nuclear power plants while safety improvements were made.

— Released a study showing that more than 80 percent of judicial campaign contributions were from attorneys who appeared before the judge raising the money, prompting the state to pass campaign finance limits for state judicial elections.

— Pushed successfully for rules to block the sealing of court records in important public health and safety cases.

— Released a report about children contaminated by pesticides, which helped prompt the state legislature to pass safeguards that require notice of pesticide applications at schools.

— Successfully lobbied for the Texas Legislature to strengthen environmental protections, becoming one of the first states to authorize regulation of greenhouse gases.

ACKNOWLEDGMENTS

THIS BOOK HAS BEEN a long time in the making. Many people have worked on it over the years — too many to name here. However, we'd like to give special thanks to Brian Dooley, the first Public Citizen communications director to take on this project; Booth Gunter, Brian Dooley's successor, who conducted more research, interviewed more people and wrote most of the text; Joan Claybrook, who reviewed and edited every version of the book and assisted with documentation; former *Public Citizen* magazine editor and author David Bollier, who edited an earlier version of the text; former *Washington Post* reporter Joanne Omang, who did a careful and comprehensive final edit and helped craft a final narrative; and Angela Bradbery, Public Citizen's communications director who faithfully double-checked hundreds of facts, inserted the final proofing edits and put all the pieces together into a final product. Special thanks go to Phil Donahue, who wrote the preface based on his many years of interviewing Ralph Nader and Public Citizen top staff, and hosting Public Citizen events. A big thank you to the following people, for their patience in reviewing material and answering questions: Ralph Nader, Alan Morrison, Sidney Wolfe, David Vladeck, Brian Wolfman, Tyson Slocum, Lori Wallach, Allison Zieve, Lisa Gilbert, David Arkush and Michael Carome. Thanks also to Jason Adkins, chair of Public Citizen Inc.'s Board of Directors, who ran the organization's Buyers Up program in the 1980s and provided detailed information about that home heating oil purchase program. We'd also like to thank communications department staffers and interns over the years who reviewed and proofed various versions of the book, with particular thanks to press officer Karilyn Gower, who spent hours combing through archives to verify accomplishments and helped proof the copy; and David Rosen, who also helped proof the copy. Finally, thanks to Public Citizen's Boards of Directors, as well as our members and supporters, who make all our work possible.

The book cover was designed by Seattle, Wash., graphic designer Jinna Hagerty, who also did the layout.